THE  TIMES

Guide to
the Middle East

THE CONTRIBUTORS

Peter Sluglett is Director of the Middle East Center, University of Utah.

Marion Farouk-Sluglett is Lecturer in Politics, University College of Wales, Swansea and Adjunct Associate Professor of Political Science, University of Utah.

The book also includes contributions from:

Martin Daly, University of Tennessee, Chattanooga

F. Gregory Gause III, College of Arts and Sciences, University of Vermont

William Hale, SOAS, University of London

George Joffé, SOAS, University of London; Exeter University; and Southampton University

Ibrahim A. Karawan, International Institute of Strategic Studies, London

Homa Katouzian, specialist and writer on Islam

Robert Mabro, St Anthony's College, Oxford

Richard Owen, *The Times*, London

Glenn Robinson, Naval Postgraduate School, Monterey, California; and University of California, Berkeley

Hootan Shambayati, Middle East Center, University of Utah

Charles Tripp, SOAS, University of London

Index compiled by Janet Smy

Spelling of Arabic names checked by Margaret Owen

THE TIMES

Guide to

the Middle East

the arab world and its neighbours

edited by
Peter Sluglett and Marion Farouk-Sluglett

TIMES BOOKS
London

Published in 1996 by Times Books
77-85 Fulham Palace Road
Hammersmith
London W6 8JB

First published in 1991 by Times Books
Second edition 1993
Third edition 1996

Copyright © HarperCollins*Publishers* 1991, 1993 and 1996

British Library Cataloguing in Publication Data
A catalogue record for this book is available from the British Library

ISBN 0-7230-0868-X

Typeset by Tradespools and Times Books

Printed and bound in Great Britain by Caledonian International Book
Manufacturing Ltd, Glasgow, G64

CONTENTS

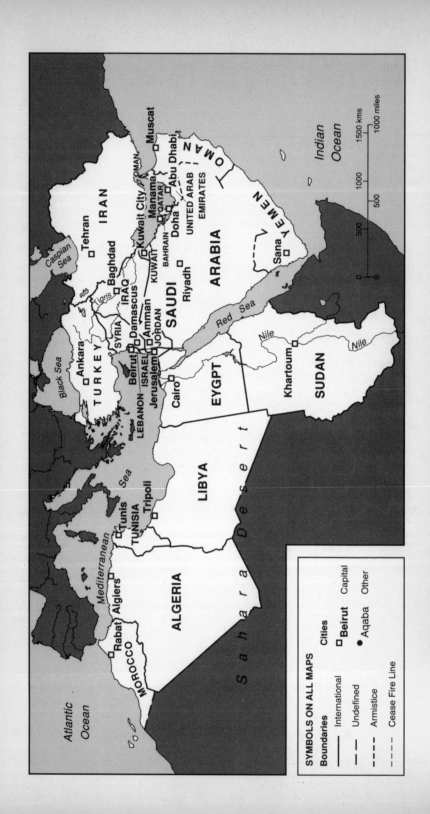

INTRODUCTION

AT THE BEGINNING of the 19th century, almost all the Middle East and North Africa was, at least nominally, part of the Ottoman empire. The Ottomans, with their capital at Istanbul, had conquered the area between what is now eastern Turkey and western Algeria in the 15th and 16th centuries; their rule extended over much of south-eastern Europe as well. In Iran, another dynasty, the Qajars, had ruled since 1779. By the time of the Treaty of Lausanne in 1923, which marked the end of most of the negotiations following the end of the First World War, the Ottoman Empire had disappeared – the last Qajar would be forced to abdicate in 1925 – and most of the area between Morocco and Iran, with the exception of Saudi Arabia, northern Yemen, the Turkish Republic (founded in 1923) and Iran itself, was ruled or controlled by Britain, France or Italy. Thus the 19th and early 20th centuries formed a period of great political and social change in the region, which was accompanied by far-reaching economic and demographic changes. In the process, 'traditional' society and social structure was shaken to its foundations, new ways of life and institutions came into being, and a new intellectual and moral climate created. The period was a time of very considerable ferment, although the extent to which this was taking place frequently went unnoticed by Europeans, whether politicians, or colonial officials, who cherished notions of an 'unchanging East' that had little foundation in fact.

THE COLLAPSE OF THE OTTOMAN EMPIRE
Between the middle of the 19th century and the end of the First World War, the Ottoman empire disintegrated, despite extensive efforts to reform its structure. Steady European commercial and colonial penetration undermined its economy, while growing demands for national independence among the subject peoples caused large areas to break away or to fall under foreign control.

The Napoleonic expedition to Egypt in 1798 was the first indication of a new kind of concern with the region on the part of the Great Powers. In spite of his defeat by Britain, Napoleon's invasion had a lasting impact, marking the beginning of an extensive period of acculturation between East and West. In Egypt itself, 1798 marked the end of direct control, however nominal, from Istanbul. Muhammad Ali, whom the Ottomans sent to restore order in 1802, founded a dynasty which lasted until the revolution of 1952. His son, Ibrahim Pasha, led expeditions to Najd to subdue the Wahhabis (*see* Saudi Arabia), adherents of a puritannical version of Islam who were challenging Ottoman authority in the Hijaz and in Iraq. Ibrahim Pasha also conquered the whole area between Egypt and what is now Turkey between 1831 and 1839, and only British and French pressure dissuaded him from attempting to overthrow the central authority of the empire itself. Egyptian pretensions were subsequently confined to Egypt itself and the northern Sudan.

Faced with this and other challenges to its authority the Ottomans initiated a series of major reforms – the *tanzimat* – in the armed forces, the law, education and administration. Two edicts, issued in 1839 and 1856, stressed the subjects' rights to security of life, honour and property, equitable taxation and limited military service, and emphasised that these rights applied equally to all Ottoman subjects, whether Muslim, Jewish or Christian. Here, as elsewhere, reality often fell short of ideals, and the reforms drew censure both from those who thought they should not be implemented at all, and from those who complained that their implementation was faulty or non-existent.

In addition, the stress on Muslim/Christian equality provided a ready excuse for the intervention of the European powers on the part of their Christian and other proteges: the Orthodox, the majority of Ottoman Christians, supported by Russia; the Maronites and other Catholics, protected by France; and the Druzes, under British protection. Foreign intervention contributed in particular to the Crimean War (1853-56) and the Lebanese crisis of 1860-61, while Russian and Austrian pressures were crucial in securing the independence of most of the Balkans by 1878: Bulgaria, Montenegro, Romania and Serbia.

Hence by the outbreak of the First World War the Ottoman empire had been reduced to a small corner of south-eastern Europe, Anatolia, and the Arab provinces in the Fertile Crescent and the Arabian Peninsula. Further west, North Africa was completely dominated by the Powers. The French had invaded Algeria in 1830, and by 1900 there were 400,000 French settlers installed there. Similar developments took place on a smaller scale in Tunisia after the French invasion of 1881; in Morocco – itself never part of the Ottoman empire – after 1912; and in Libya, invaded and colonised by Italy after 1911. In Egypt, the rise of nationalism and the dangers which this posed to some £100 million of foreign investment served as the excuse for the British occupation in 1882.

In the Arab provinces, there were stirrings of discontent, particularly during the long and oppressive reign of Abd al-Hamid II (1876-1909). Ideas of autonomy, encouraged by the revival of Arabic literature and moves to reform the Arabic language gradually gained wider currency. Abd al-Hamid had prorogued the Ottoman parliament, one of the major achievements of the second wave of Ottoman reforms, in 1878, and opposition to his rule culminated in the Young Turk Revolution of 1908-9, which was supported by members of most of the ethnic groups in what was left of the empire. After the revolution, however, the Turkish element in the government proceeded to 'Turkify' all administrative, legal and educational institutions, a step which succeeded in alienating many Arabs and contributed in considerable measure to the willingness of many to seek accommodation with Britain in the First World War.

As the progress of disintegration continued, new forms of trade and communication, largely funded by foreign capital, had begun to transform the empire. By 1914, Turkey and Egypt had substantial rail networks, with banks and mines and public utilities such as ports, tramways, water and electricity companies. North Africa and the Middle East became important markets for European goods, while Algeria began to export wine, Lebanon to produce silk, and, perhaps most spectacularly, Egypt to export cotton.

Parallel developments were taking place in Iran. The Qajars (1779-1924) had suffered constant Russian and British interference in their internal affairs, which culminated in the division of the country into British and Russian spheres of influence in 1907. The Tobacco Rebellion of 1891-92 and the Constitutional Revolution of 1905-11 served to arouse national consciousness and political awareness, and the Qajars were eventually to be overthrown by a military coup led by Reza Khan Pahlavi in 1924.

THE FIRST WORLD WAR AND THE PEACE SETTLEMENTS

In 1914 the Ottoman empire entered the war on the side of the Central Powers and thus emerged on the side of the vanquished, stripped of its Arab provinces and confined to Anatolia and eastern Thrace. However, the Turkish army was stung by further attempts on the part of the Allies to parcel out parts of Turkey proper, and its only undefeated general, Mustafa Kemal (Atatürk), rallied national feeling to his support, expelling French, Greek and Italian forces from the country by 1922. As first president of the Turkish Republic he signed the post-War territorial settlement (the Treaty of Lausanne) in 1923, and abolished the caliphate in 1924. After the foundation of the Turkish Republic. Turkey's fortunes became less closely involved with those of the rest of the Middle East.

During the war the Middle East became an important theatre of operations. Immediately after the declaration of war, Egypt, whose status had never been made formalised after some 32 years of British occupation, was made a protectorate of the British empire. Further east, in order to protect the oil installations at Abadan in southern Iran and to pre-empt a Turkish thrust towards the Gulf, British Indian troops invaded southern Iraq in the first weeks of the war, finally penetrating to Baghdad in March 1917. On the other side of the Fertile Crescent Turkish resistance lasted longer, with Syria and Palestine remaining in Turkish hands until the last months of the war.

Of equal importance, the Allies made a number of conflicting arrangements during the war – between themselves and various other groups – whose consequences are still with us today. In the first place, between March 1915 and May 1916, the British government conducted a protracted correspondence with the Ottoman-appointed governor of the Hijaz, Sharif Husayn of Mecca. The outcome of these negotiations known as the McMahon-Husayn correspondence (McMahon was British High Commissioner in Egypt) was that in return for collaboration with the Allies against the Ottomans, Sharif Husayn was promised 'Arab independence', albeit in somewhat vague terms:

> 'The two districts of Mersina and Alexandretta [both now in Turkey] and portions of Syria lying to the west of Damascus, Homs, Hama and Aleppo, cannot be said to purely Arab, and should be excluded from the limits demanded... As for those regions lying within those frontiers where Great Britain is free to act without detriment to the interests of her ally France... Great Britain is prepared to recognise and support the independence of the Arabs.'

In June 1916, Sharif Husayn and his sons launched the Arab Revolt, which was to culminate in the capture of Damascus by an Arab-Allied force in September 1918. Meanwhile, over much the same period Britain, France, Russia and Italy entered into a series of understandings, known collectively as the Sykes-Picot Agreement, under which in the event of an Allied victory the Arab part of the Ottoman empire would be divided into British and French spheres of influence; Palestine was to be under international control; while Russia was to receive Istanbul, the Straits, parts of Armenia and Kurdistan; and Italy parts of south-west Turkey and the Dodecanese Islands. With some important reservations, France was to have paramount influence in Syria and Lebanon and Britain in Iraq as well as control of the ports of Acre and Haifa. The precise form of government for these areas was not specified.

It is clear that the principles of the Sykes-Picot Agreement and the offer accepted by Sharif Husayn seem to conflict. The one apparently promises independence, the other some form of colonial rule. The episode has engendered heated, if largely inconclusive, scholarly controversy. In addition, whatever the intentions of the authors of the documents, the coexistence of the two sets of agreements is still a prime example of (particularly British) perfidy and dishonesty. It is also not clear how far Sharif Husayn was aware of the general principles of Sykes-Picot when he made his own agreement. The motives of those who composed the documents is of course less important than the fact that the arrangements which actually materialised approximated more closely to Sykes-Picot than to McMahon-Husayn – and that they fell far short of local aspirations. The matter was further complicated by yet another undertaking, the Balfour Declaration of 2 November 1917, under which Britain promised to facilitate 'the establishment in Palestine of a national home for the Jewish people'.

The war ended with Allied (almost entirely British) troops in occupation of most of the area. During and after it, in the course of the

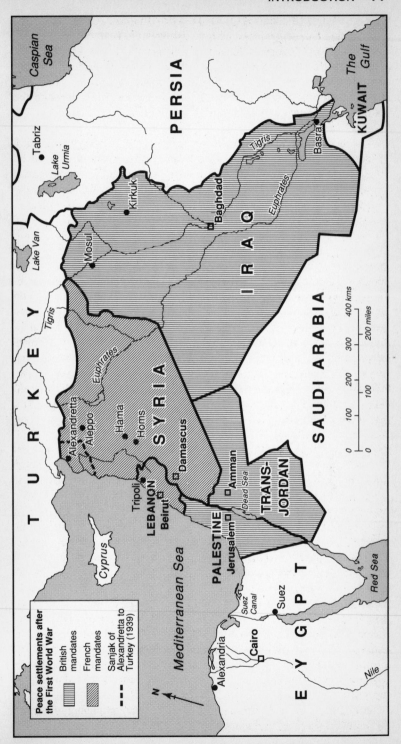

various peace conferences, the idea of direct colonial rule was discarded in favour of the mandate system, a form of international tutelage, which was to be supervised by the newly constituted League of Nations. The people of the region were not consulted as to the form of government they wished to have, and only very perfunctorily (and to no effect) as to which power they wished to run their affairs. Article 22 of the League of Nations Charter reads:

> Certain communities formerly belonging to the Turkish Empire have reached a stage of their development where their existence as independent nations can be provisionally recognised subject to the rendering of administrative advice and assistance by a mandatory, until such time as they are able to stand alone.

Naturally, any such 'advice' had to be taken. Britain took over Iraq, Palestine and Transjordan, France took over Syria and Lebanon. All the mandated states were virtually colonies, since the League's capacity to intervene in their affairs was extremely limited. In Palestine the problems were further exacerbated by the conflicts between Arabs and Jews which resulted from simultaneous attempts to implement both the Balfour Declaration and the mandate. All that was left of the 'independent Arab state' was the short-lived Kingdom of the Hijaz, which was absorbed into what is now Saudi Arabia in 1925.

THE INTER-WAR PERIOD

The new political order was widely contested in the Arab world. The mandate regimes were generally unpopular, especially in Syria and Palestine, though in Iraq, after having set up a compliant government, Britain felt able to make a formal withdrawal in 1932, although real independence was not obtained until 1958. In Palestine there was mounting tension between the Arab population and the Jewish settlers, who formed 11% of the population in 1922 and 29% by 1936. In 1939, Britain announced that Jewish immigration would be allowed to reach a certain ceiling and must then cease, a decision seen as criminally generous by the Arabs and criminally restrictive by the Zionists. In Syria and Lebanon the French were welcomed by the Maronites and the other Catholic Christians but by few others, since the new Lebanon had been carved out of Syria. In 1925-27 there was a major national rising in Syria which the French had considerable difficulty in controlling. Later, expectations were raised with the victory of the Popular Front government in 1936, although negotiations ceased when it fell, and independence was not granted until 1946.

Egypt escaped the mandate system, but had become a British protectorate. After the war a group of politicians wanted to send a delegation (wafd) to the Paris peace conference under the leadership of Sa'd Zaghlul. When permission was refused there was a widespread national rising in March 1919. Eventually Britain recognised a limited form of

Egyptian independence in 1922, though retained control over four 'reserved' points: the security of communications of the British empire; defence; protection of the interests of minorities and foreign powers; and matters relating to Sudan. The wafd won an overwhelming victory whenever there were free elections, but was never free to implement popular demands. Although an Anglo-Egyptian treaty enabling Egypt to enter the League of Nations as an independent state was signed in 1936, all but the third of the 'reserved points' remained, while Britain retained a large military presence even beyond the moment when Nasser seized power in 1952.

Inevitably, the politics of the region underwent a series of important changes in the inter-war period. The struggles for local autonomy from Istanbul of the prewar years gave way to a prolonged anti-colonial struggle, waged primarily against Britain and France but also against their local clients who were running the governments in many of the new states. A new form of Arab nationalism developed, with appeals to the glorious Arab past and to an Arab world now divided by British and French imperialism yet united by a common language and heritage. The anti-colonial struggle was temporarily halted by the Second World War, in which the Arab states generally supported the Allies, particularly after the Soviet Union joined them in 1941. In the decades after the war the influence of France and Britain in the region gradually declined, to be replaced by that of the US and the Soviet Union.

Although Iraq became nominally independent of Britain in 1932, Egypt in 1936 and Syria and Lebanon of France in 1946, strong economic and military ties bound the various states to their former European rulers. The constitutional arrangements made in Egypt and the mandated territories were based on European models, but it was well known that elections were rigged. Particularly after 1945 and the onset of the the Cold War, imprisonment without trial and torture of political offenders those suspected of 'communism' as well as members of Muslim fundamentalist groups, particularly in Egypt (where the Muslim Brethren were founded in 1929), were not uncommon. The creation of national armies and wider access to education in almost all the states of the Middle East had the effect of creating a new and highly influential social group, many of whose members were imbued with notions of social justice and national independence (and, in time, anti-Zionism), and who also came to believe that only a revolutionary break with colonialism would bring about genuine independence.

THE REVOLUTIONS OF THE 1950S

The first revolution came in 1952, in Egypt, masterminded, like so many of its successors in other Arab states, by disaffected elements in the armed forces. Like his Iraqi contemporary Abd al-Karim Qasim, Nasser was an army officer from a lower middle class background who had gained a commission in the new-style national army in the 1930s. Though Nasser's original intention seems to have been to force a radical change in the direction of Egyptian politics and then to return to the barracks, it gradually became clear, at least to him, that his continued presence at the helm was indispensable, and he remained in power until his death in 1970. His political philosophy was vague, pragmatic and somewhat naive. He believed that once liberated from imperialism Egypt would be able to pursue her own destiny independent of power blocs and alliances. His practical solutions for Egypt's immense problems were somewhat amateur, and the early reform programmes for agriculture and industry were hasty and inadequate. Nevertheless Nasser managed to win the hearts if not the minds of many Egyptians and of many other Arabs by his populist rhetoric and by his appeal for a united front against colonialism and Zionism. Even though recent studies have shown that the middle classes rather than the very poor were the main beneficiaries of Nasser's domestic policies, it is clear that the Nasser era marks a major turning point in modern Arab history. Syria, Iraq, Algeria and South Yemen went through comparable periods of change in the 1950s and 1960s.

Much of the early enthusiasm on which Nasser was able to capitalise across the Arab world derived from his constant emphasis on Arab unity, the premise that once the 'Arab nation' was free of colonialism and Zionism and (re)united in a single political entity, the Arabs would be able to resume their historic destiny. Though it largely ignores the considerable social, economic and political differences that exist within and between the various Arab states, this powerful notion lies at the heart of Ba'thism and Nasserism alike. Naturally, an internal social transformation would have required coming to terms with the inequalities and tensions within Egyptian society – as well as being far harder to achieve and much less immediately palatable than some lofty concept of a single Arab world.

After the death of Stalin, the Soviet Union began to adopt new attitudes towards what it now regarded as potentially friendly or neutral regimes. In the Middle East, this signified the beginning of a period of superpower tension and rivalry, but it also gave a certain amount of freedom of manoeuvre to various Arab leaders, who could now sometimes play the superpowers off against each other. Determined to get the best deal possible for Egypt, Nasser moved to take advantage of this new situation. In 1954 Britain and the US, with whom he was still on reasonably cordial terms, had offered Egypt a substantial development loan as well as the promise of further finance for the construction of the Aswan dam. The price, however, was Egyptian involvement in the collective security arrangement known as the Baghdad Pact. This Nasser was not prepared to entertain. After a particularly audacious raid on Egypt by Israeli forces early in 1955, Nasser entered arms negotiations with the Soviet Union via Czechoslovakia. In September the 'Czech arms deal' was concluded. The US and Britain promptly refused further aid and relations deteriorated, leading eventually to Nasser playing his own trump card, the nationalisation, and finally the closure, of the Suez canal in July 1956. This occasioned the tripartite invasion of Egypt by Britain, France and Israel in late October-early November, an extraordinary and, at least as far as Britain and France were concerned, ultimately humiliating venture, which was only halted by threats of a run on sterling by the US.

Along with the leaders of most of the 'revolutionary states' in their turn, Nasser eventually became almost completely dependent on the Soviet Union for arms supplies and other aid. Such arrangements had little effect on the internal affairs of these states in one important respect: communists were persecuted in Egypt at a time when relations with the Soviet Union were particularly cordial; the same was true for Iraq and, to a lesser extent, for Syria throughout the 1960s and 1970s. In addition, ties with the Soviet Union did not rule out substantial trading relations with the US and other Western countries.

PALESTINE, ISRAEL AND THE ARAB-ISRAELI CONFLICT

The existence of Israel has been probably the single most intractable problem of the Middle East in the 20th century. The notion of Israel, or of a Jewish state, dates from the late 19th century, a time of emergent nationalism in Europe generally which coincided with the increasing persecution of eastern European Jews. Migration to Palestine had begun in the late 19th century, and by 1914 the Jewish population of Palestine, both recent arrivals and Oriental Jews (i.e. those long resident in the country), was about 75,000 out of a population of 750,000 – 800,000. The Arab population consisted mostly of peasant farmers, with Jerusalem, Nablus, Hebron, Jaffa and Acre probably accounting for about a quarter of the total population.

Zionist lobbying in Britain, allied to the friendship between the head of the Zionist organisation, Chaim Weizmann, and the politician A.J. Balfour, were largely responsible for the Balfour Declaration in 1917. The Declaration was of course incompatible with the spirit of the promises made to the Arabs, and the smooth implementation of the Palestine mandate, which came into force in 1923, proved impossible. In the late 1920s there was some hope that the problem might disappear – in 1927 more Jews left Palestine than entered it – but Hitler's rise to power encouraged an enormous exodus of Jews from eastern and central Europe with nowhere else prepared to receive them. Between 1917 and 1948, when Britain finally left Palestine, there was little hope for a peaceful solution. The Arabs saw the Balfour Declaration as a monstrous imposition, fearing the effect of the incursion of hundreds of thousands of European colonists into their country, and also resented the land acquisitions of the Jewish Agency, although virtually all the land was purchased from absentee Arab landlords over the heads of the peasants. For their part the Jewish population of Palestine attempted to co-operate as far as possible with Britain while vigorously pressing for the right to unlimited immigration, while the Arabs refused any co-operation which might imply any legality either for the British or for the Zionist presence.

The climax came in 1947-48, when elements of the Jewish population, impatient at Britain's procrastination, attempted to force the issue by attacking British troops and Arab and British civilians. In November 1947 the UN resolved on the partition of Palestine into Arab and Jewish areas, and Britain announced that she would evacuate by 15 May 1948. Early in 1948 Jewish guerrilla forces began terrorist attacks on Arab communities, driving the Arab population from the area, a policy which, with the war which followed, resulted in 900,000 Palestinian refugees outside the state of Israel by 1949. As the evacuation date drew nearer, more serious fighting broke out, and on 14 May an Arab army of Egyptian, Iraq, Jordanian, and Syrian forces moved in to defend Palestine from the Zionist army. As well as being inferior in numbers, the Arab armies were badly equipped and poorly led. The war ended with half of Jerusalem in Israeli hands, and an Israeli state extending over two-thirds of the area of mandatory Palestine.

For much the same reasons as those which had prevented an amicable settlement before the end of the mandate, no comprehensive peace agrement has been reached since 1948, although at the time of writing (December 1995) it is likely that this will come in the near future. Apart from Egypt, which recognised Israel in 1979, no Arab state accepted Israel's right to exist until the Palestinian National Council's acceptance of UN Resolution 242 in November 1988. The Arab states always feared that one of their number would do what Egypt in fact did: split Arab ranks and make a separate peace. For its part Israel refused to discuss the problem of the refugees or to acknowledge the existence of the Palestinians as a political entity until Israel itself was recognised by its neighbours and belligerents.

Thus since 1948 three wars have taken place between Israel and the various Arab states: in 1956, 1967, and 1973. In 1956, Egypt refused passage through the Suez canal and the Gulf of Aqaba to ships bound for Israel, and when Nasser nationalised the canal Israel took part in the tripartite invasion. In the spring of 1967, with a particularly radical government in power in Syria, Nasser came under increasing pressure to demonstrate his leadership of the Arab world. He closed the Gulf of Aqaba again and asked for the withdrawal of the UN peace-keeping force in Sinai. On 5 June Israel launched a pre-emptive strike on Egypt, Syria and Jordan, destroying most of the Egyptian Air Force on the ground. Israel took possession of the Golan Heights, Sinai, the Gaza Strip and Jordanian territory west of the Jordan river, including Arab Jerusalem.

This crushing defeat had a devastating effect upon the Arab world. In particular, it gave new impetus to the Palestinians, many of whom saw it as a clear indication that their salvation lay in their own hands rather than in the hands of the leaders of the Arab states. In 1968 the Palestine Liberation Organisation (PLO), founded under Nasser's aegis in 1964, was taken over in 1967 by al-Fatah, the largest of its members,

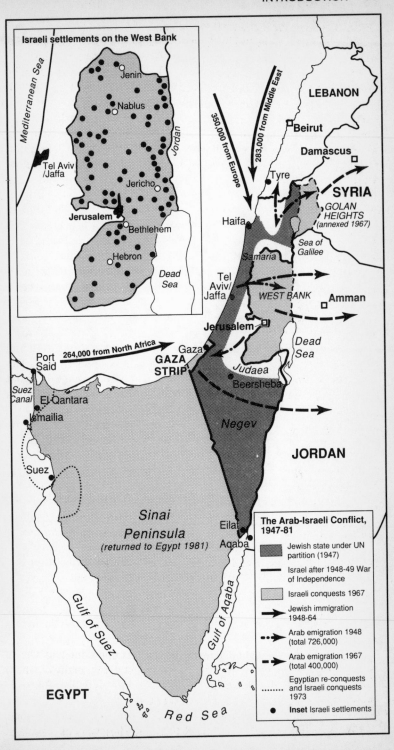

Israeli settlements on the West Bank

Mediterranean Sea

Jenin

Nablus

Tel Aviv/Jaffa

Jordan

Jericho

Jerusalem

Bethlehem

Hebron

Dead Sea

350,000 from Europe

283,000 from Middle East

LEBANON

Beirut

Damascus

Tyre

SYRIA

GOLAN HEIGHTS (annexed 1967)

Haifa

Samaria

Sea of Galilee

Tel Aviv/Jaffa

WEST BANK

Amman

Jerusalem

Dead Sea

264,000 from North Africa

Gaza

GAZA STRIP

Judaea

Beersheba

Port Said

Suez Canal

El-Qantara

Ismailia

Suez

Negev

JORDAN

Sinai Peninsula (returned to Egypt 1981)

Eilat

Aqaba

Gulf of Suez

Gulf of Aqaba

EGYPT

Red Sea

The Arab-Israeli Conflict, 1947-81

Jewish state under UN partition (1947)

Israel after 1948-49 War of Independence

Israeli conquests 1967

Jewish immigration 1948-64

Arab emigration 1948 (total 726,000)

Arab emigration 1967 (total 400,000)

Egyptian re-conquests and Israeli conquests 1973

● **Inset** Israeli settlements

under the leadership of Yasser Arafat. The PLO began to launch guerrilla raids on Israel from camps in Lebanon and Jordan, acting very
much as a state within a state, greatly alarming their host countries in
the process. One consequence was the expulsion of the PLO from
Jordan in 1970; another was that the Palestinian presence in Lebanon
was to be a major factor in the Lebanese civil war.

A further consequence of 1967 was the decision on the part of the
richer Arab countries to subsidise the 'front line' states, namely Jordan,
Egypt and Syria. At the Khartoum conference in September 1967 Saudi
Arabia and Kuwait agreed to pay £540 million annually to these states.
In November 1967 the Security Council passed Resolution 242, which
ended the conflict:

> The Security Council ... Emphasising the inadmissibility of the acquisition
> of territory by war and the need to work for a just and lasting peace in
> which every state in the area can live in security ... Affirms that the fulfill-
> ment of Charter principles requires the establishment of a just and lasting
> peace in the Middle East which should include the application of the fol-
> lowing principles:
> (1) Withdrawal of Isreali armed forces from territories occupied in the
> recent conflict
> (2) Termination of all claims or states of belligerency and respect for and
> acknowledgement of the sovereignty, territorial integrity and political inde-
> pendence of every state in the area and their right to live in peace within
> secure and recognised boundaries free from threats or acts of force ...

Israel did not merely greatly increase its territories after 1967, it
secured substantial military assistance from the US. At the same time,
it acquired an extra 1.5 million Arabs and began to build Jewish settlements on the West Bank, mostly on confiscated land, to the fury and
frustration of its inhabitants. However, 1967 was not followed by negotiations, nor by peace, and tensions continued.

On 6 October 1973, the myth of Israeli invincibility was challenged
when Egypt and Syria unexpectedly attacked Israel. But if the Arab
states were not victorious, their initial military success at least bolstered their morale, leading to increased aid to the front line states. At
the same time a new bargaining counter made its first appearance: the
threat to withdraw or decrease oil supplies. By 22 October the UN had
organised a ceasefire while Security Council Resolution 338 set up a
peace conference at which the belligerents and Jordan, the US and the
Soviet Union – but not the PLO – were to be represented. The conference met once, at Geneva on 21 December.

In the 1970s there were important but inconclusive developments in
the conflict. In October 1974, the PLO was recognised at Rabat as the
'sole legitimate representative of the Palestinian people', which gave
Yasser Arafat the right to negotiate on the Palestinians' behalf, a role
neither Israel nor any Western state recognised. After the 1973 war,

President Sadat of Egypt began negotiations with Israel through the medium of Henry Kissinger, the US secretary of state, who was virtually negotiating on Israel's behalf. As a result of Kissinger's efforts the Geneva Conference was adjourned indefinitely, and the Soviet Union excluded from the peace process. Although President Carter expressed willingness to include the Palestinians in any Middle East settlement, his efforts were stalled by the election of a hard-line right-wing Israeli government under Menachim Begin in May 1977 and, in November that year, when Sadat flew to Jerusalem to deal directly with Israel. This was followed by the Camp David Accords in 1978 and the Egyptian-Israeli peace treaty of March 1979, which removed Egypt from the Arab-Israeli conflict without securing any firm promises from Israel on the future status of the the West Bank, Gaza or East Jerusalem.

One major consequence of Egypt's withdrawal was that the unequal balance of forces between Israel and the Arabs was increased. In addition, a variety of other factors combined to initiate a civil war in Lebanon, where the PLO had made its headquarters after its expulsion from Jordan in 1970-71. Israel took the Syrian invasion and occupation of parts of Lebanon in the summer of 1976 as a pretext to extend its own influence in south Lebanon (from which the PLO had been launching raids and rocket attacks into Israel), and consolidated its position there with a proxy army in the south after a full-scale invasion of the area in March 1978. In the summer of 1982, Israel invaded Lebanon again, advancing as far as Beirut, in an attempt to destroy the PLO completely and to install a government which would do its bidding. These objectives were only partially realised, as the PLO was able to withdraw to new headquarters in Tunis, and Bashir Jumayyil, the Israelis' candidate for the Lebanese presidency, turned out to be far less pliable than anticipated. Jumayyil's assassination was followed by the massacre of thousands of unarmed Palestinians in the Sabra and Chatila refugee camps. Israel withdrew formally from Lebanon in September 1983, while maintaining its 'South Lebanese Army' under a former Lebanese army general.

By 1986, US aid to Israel was running at $3.7 billion annually while Egypt received $2 billion. In addition, in spite of various agreements between the Soviet Union and several Arab states since the mid-1950s, and however much the Soviet Union might rail against the US, it had been clear at least as early as 1973 that the Soviet Union would not assist the Arab states to defeat Israel or even encourage any state or combination of states to inflict very serious damage on Israel.

Throughout the 1980s peace plans were put forward, most of which were frustrated either by Israeli unwillingness to recognise or negotiate with the Palestinians, or the preoccupations of Arab leaders with maintaining themselves in power and the ramifications first of the Iranian revolution and then of the Iran/Iraq war. No sustained pressure could be put on Israel: Syria remained belligerent but ineffectual and a long-standing personal hostility between Asad and Arafat resulted in the departure of the PLO from the camps in Tripoli, its last stronghold in Lebanon, in 1984. By 1985 Jordan and the PLO appeared to be coming to a settlement of their long-standing differences and considering a joint approach to Israel that might isolate Syria further. The latter eventuality was averted by Syrian pressure, but Palestinian and Jordanian relations with Syria remained strained. In July 1988 Jordan announced that it would cut all legal and administrative ties with the West Bank, thus highlighting the PLO's independent status.

In December 1987 the movement known as the *Intifada* or uprising, began in Gaza and the West Bank. Broadly speaking, this took the form of a campaign of unarmed civil disobedience. It also involved violence, on the part of children and adolescents throwing stones at Israeli soldiers, and about 1,000 Palestinians have been killed by Israeli security forces since it began. It certainly galvanised and gave new momentum to the Palestinians in the Occupied Territories, but by the time of the invasion of Kuwait in the summer of 1990 it seemed to be running out of steam: not only had the the Israelis learned how to control it, they seemed largely impervious to the criticism their repressive tactics provoked.

ISLAMIC REVIVAL

The spread of literacy, increasingly wider access to education and the growth of modern communications networks had a swift and dynamic impact on Middle Eastern society in the first half of the 20th century. Traditional pathways to power were modified or blocked, and new ones came into being. In the inter-war and immediately post-1945 periods the Arab world and Iran experienced great ferment. New classes and political institutions came into existence, and there were growing pressures for an end to foreign rule and for wider and more meaningful political participation. Several political movements developed: leftist/communist; Arab nationalist; nationalist (in the sense of movements expressing 'Iraq for the Iraqis' or 'Egypt for the Egyptians'); quasi-fascist; and religious. In broad terms, apart from the Muslim Brethren most of the political movements were avowedly secular, and the Islamic ferment of today would have been unimaginable to most contemporaries at the time.

The 1950s in particular were years of great hope. The rise of Nasser and the triumph of his early years – his rejection of the West, his embrace of neutrality and the possibility of the revival of the fortunes of the Arabs in a strong united Arab world – seemed to herald a new era. Furthermore, the potential of 'socialism', or state-sponsored economic development, bolstered by the support of the Soviet Union and the possibilities held out by increasing oil revenues, gave new confidence. The reality, symbolised by the defeat of 1967, was infinitely less inspiring.

Between the early 1960s and the late 1970s Arab rulers tried a variety of expedients, ranging from the nationalisation of key sectors of the economy to the reintroduction of laissez-faire economics in order to

promote 'development'. Arab nationalism, Pan-Arabism, Arab socialism and even Islamic socialism were the labels for a host of piecemeal
solutions which had little effect on the region's most intractable social
problems – urban drift, rural decline, the Palestine problem, the
Lebanese civil war – all of which generated a general sense of bewil-
derment and uprootedness. This was accompanied by the rapid growth
of military establishments, with rich and poor states spending large
proportions of their GNP on armaments, and of unrepresentative governments propped up by increasingly ruthless and powerful security
agencies. Such democracy as there had been in the region had largely
disappeared by the end of the 1950s. Most Middle Eastern states were
ruled either by family oligarchies or forms of populist dictatorship. The
general consequence was a gradual alienation of the the populations
from their governments, the sense that government was quite beyond
the control or influence of ordinary individuals, above all that it was
often corrupt, arbitrary and oppressive. In addition, the absolute power
of the state, reinforced either by indigenous oil wealth or aid from oil-
rich neighbours, prevented the growth of authentic political movements. Politics and the political arena were appropriated by the state,
so that political activity was either opportunistic, in the service of the
state, or, if in opposition to it, extremely dangerous.

In this atmosphere of despair and resignation, Islam seemed to offer
another way. The failure of the ideologies imposed onto the Middle East
could be explained precisely because they had been imposed: they had
no local resonance, or, in the case of communisim, they were atheist or
propounded by atheists. One answer was to reject the seductions of the
West (or the communist East) and to return to 'true Islam', which was
familiar. In addition, many of those who embraced secular ideologies
retained their Islamic beliefs. The (Christian) founder of Ba'thism, for
example, Michel Aflaq, wrote that Arab nationalism and religion are
not incompatible since both 'spring from the heart and are issued by
the will of God'. Finally, for all that they claimed to be guided by secular values, none of the regimes in the region except Turkey is explicitly
secular. With the exception of Lebanon (which is also not a secular
state) all state constitutions, however otherwise disregarded, contain
clauses to the effect that Islam is the religion of the state and that the
president must be a Muslim. Hence, although the various Middle
Eastern regimes were both worried by and attempted to control manifestations of Islamic sentiment when 'political Islam' became a major
force in the 1970s, it was almost inconceivable that they would have
banned or otherwise restricted such activities as public worship in
mosques.

There are various explanations for the 'Islamic revival' of the 1970s.
The form and nature of the Iranian Revolution is so specific to Iran
and to Shi'ism that it cannot be discussed in the same terms as the phenomenon in Egypt and the other Arab states, although certain common
features do exist, and its success (in the sense of bringing an Islamic

Republic into being) probably gave impetus to other Islamic movements in the 1980s. 'Islamic revival' is probably best seen in terms of the sense of political impasse on major regional issues like the Arab-Israeli conflict; the slavishly pro-Western attitudes of many of the region's rulers; the perceived failure of the mass political movements; the increasing gap between rich and poor, both within and between states; the widespread misery and despair caused by war, inflation, unemployment and poverty; and the deeply undemocratic and unrepresentative regimes in almost all Middle Eastern states.

Given the immensity of the problems, it is hardly surprising that those who advocate an 'Islamic solution' do not themselves have ready answers to them. Here it is worth attempting to correct, or at least to highlight, some important misconceptions. In the first place, although Islam has rightly been characterised as being 'both religion and state', the 'state' in this context was the universal Islamic state rather than the national states of our own time, which the first Muslims neither knew nor could have anticipated. Secondly, within the traditional Islamic canon there is relatively little in the way of 'political theory'. Neither the Prophet nor his near contemporaries had very much to say about 'government' as such. The traditional role of the 'Islamic state', in the words of one authority, was the 'collective enforcement of public morals'. Islamic tradition is virtually silent on such matters as statecraft, diplomacy, the mutual obligations of ruler and ruled, lawful resistance to injustice and oppression and other ethical-political topics.

For this reason Islamic fundamentalist activists do not generally have a detailed blueprint for the kind of society that they would like to substitute for, say, contemporary Algerian or Egyptian society, however eloquent they may be in their condemnation of 'present ills'. Fundamentalist movements lay great stress on Islamic law, the Shari'a, an uncodified but exhaustive guide to life and conduct and the means through which man's relations with God and with men are regulated. Hence calls to adopt the Shari'a as the sole source of legislation can be heard from Islamic movements all over the Middle East. However, it goes without saying that like all sacred texts, the Qur'an is open to a variety of interpretations, and admonitions to embrace the Shari'a are rarely accompanied by detailed explanations of what this might mean in practice. This vagueness almost inevitably gives rise to fears that the replacement of military dictatorship by an Islamic or ideologically based state might amount simply to replacement of one form of authoritarianism by another.

IRAN AND THE IRANIAN REVOLUTION

Although the Iranian revolution can obviously be attributed to many of the causes mentioned above, certain features unique to Iran and Shi'ism make it unlikely that it will be the pattern for similar events elsewhere. In the first place, the 'clergy' in the Sunni Muslim world in modern times have generally acted both as the exponents of Islamic

orthodoxy and the mouthpiece of governments. Their power was greatly curtailed by the legal and educational reforms of the 19th century,
after which they ceased to monopolise the administration and interpretation of law and the teaching profession. In contrast, the Shi'i clergy,
never having been so trammelled, have tended to play a much more
independent and critical role.

In 1501 the Safavid dynasty, seeking to establish its own identity vis-
à-vis the Sunni Ottomans, declared Twelver Shi'ism the official religion
of the Iranian state. The Safavids were obliged to invite Shi'i clerics
from Iraq and south Lebanon to propagate Shi'ism within Iran and
were also dependent upon them for the recognition and validation of
their own legitimacy. Twelver Shi'i doctrine considers that the (12)
Imams, all descendants of the marriage of the Prophet Muhammad's
daughter Fatima and his cousin Ali, are infallible and all-knowing, the
source of law, and the interpreters of the Qur'an. On the death of the
eleventh Imam in 874, his son Muhammad was taken from his father's
house in secret and communicated with his followers through a series
of four intermediaries. The last of these intermediaries died in 941,
declaring on his death-bed that Imam Muhammad was entering into a
period of occultation, during which he would be in the world but make
no contact with his followers until his return as *mahdi* – redeemer, or
'expected one' – at the beginning of the golden age. The Twelvers continue to await his return; in his absence various levels of clergy known
as *mujtahid*, *ayatollah* or *marja' al-taqlid* (source of emulation) act as
interpreters of the law. Each believer may consult the interpreter of the
law of his own choice, to whom he pays a religious tax, which, together
with the revenue from religious endowments, provides the clergy's
income.

Three important points emerge from this brief summary. First, the
clergy are financially independent of the state. Secondly, at least in
theory, the state is no more than a convenient institution under which
order can be preserved and an Islamic society can function until the
return of the Twelfth or hidden Imam. Thirdly, the perceived legitimacy
of the state and its actions requires, to a greater or lesser extent, the
consent or validation of the clergy. By implication, the clergy's capacity
to confer legitimacy includes the right to withdraw it, and the right to
criticise what the state does.

In the late 19th and early 20th centuries, when the British and the
Russians were vying for influence over the Qajar shahs, the clergy were
in the forefront of the opposition to the state's cravenness in giving in to
the foreigners as well as in attempts to limit the Shah's absolutism.
Thus in 1891-92 the clergy organised a successful ban on the sale and
consumption of tobacco, in protest against a monopoly granted to an
Englishman. They were also prominent in the Constitutional Revolution
of 1905-6, which resulted in the granting of a parliamentary assembly
by the Shah.

In the chaos which followed the end of the First World War in Iran, Reza Shah, the leader of the Cossack brigade, the only organised military force in the country, managed to seize power. After crushing tribal opposition and deposing the last of the Qajars in 1925, he had himself proclaimed Shah. Reza Shah faced daunting obstacles, since Iran had not undergone a period of reforms comparable with those enacted in the Ottoman empire. Like his contemporary Ataturk, Reza Shah was a dictator; he too tried to impose secularism, but generally with less success. He was succeeded in 1941 by his son Muhammad Reza, then aged 21. The next decade saw an immense flowering of political activity in which leftists and nationalists allied with religious leaders against the monarchy and the national movement was only checked by the overthrow of the popular prime minister, Muhammad Mosaddeq, in a coup engineered by the CIA in 1953. For the next 26 years, Muhammad Reza Shah presided over a highly unstable dictatorship, enjoying close relations with Israel and the US. In the late 1950s and early 1960s the Shah introduced land reform and female suffrage, both of which outraged religious conservatives. The religious opposition was led by Ayatollah Khomeini (1902-1989), who was arrested in 1963 and deported the following year.

During the rest of his reign, particularly after the increase in oil prices after 1973, Muhammad Reza Shah attempted to modernise Iran at great speed. But although living standards rose, inflation soared while the infrastructure could not cope with the speed of change. Large numbers of Europeans, Americans and Japanese came to work on contracts in Iran, and the influx of Western habits and consumer goods in a country that had only recently been exposed to Western penetration on such a scale produced severe dislocations. In addition, the Shah's pivotal role as one of the US's principal allies in the Middle East made him highly unpopular. Once more, criticism of the government came from the clergy, including the exiled Khomeini, who spent the years between 1964 and October 1978 in the Iraqi shrine city of Najaf.

Matters came to a head in 1978, when demonstrators in Qum and other cities were fired on by armed police, and many thousands were killed. The opposition began to call for the overthrow of the Shah and the return of Khomeini, now living in France. On 16 January 1979 the Shah went into exile. On 1 February, Khomeini returned to Tehran. Over the next few months Khomeini and his supporters maintained the initiative they had seized in the last months of the Shah's reign, and succeeded in setting up the Islamic Republic of Iran by a referendum on 1 April 1979 in the face of opposition both from more moderate members of the religious establishment and from liberals and leftists. Although Khomeini did not take personal charge, he became *vali-i faqih,* or trustee of religious law. He considered that during the occultation of the Twelfth Imam, the clergy must establish a system for the implementation of Islamic law. This was a major innovation. No previous Islamic regime had insisted that the clergy themselves should rule the state. In Khomeini's view, according to one authority, 'a just and learned jurisconsult with administrative abilities has the same authority as the Prophet Muhammad in administering society.'

As the Islamic Republic began to establish itself, a campaign against those associated with the former regime was mounted. Figures vary, but the most conservative sources estimate that by 1985 at least 4,000 had been executed and 20,000 imprisoned. At the same time, many of the government's own supporters were killed by its internal opponents and there were struggles for power within the government, symbolised by the disagreements over the seizure of the US Embassy in Tehran on 4 November 1979. The (relatively) liberal cabinet was forced to give up its power to an Islamic Revolutionary Council. Over $10 billion of Iran's assets in the US were seized, economic sanctions declared and Iran's diplomatic standing severely damaged. The regime's apparent radicalism united Western (and most of world) public opinion against it and created an atmosphere in which few protests were made when Iraq invaded south-western Iran in September 1980. By then the Iranian Revolution had developed into a 'menace to the security of the region' and Iraq was initially regarded, by its Arab neighbours as much as by the US and the Soviet Union, as performing a valuable service by keeping it in check.

To an important extent, the eight-year war united the various factions within the country, although serious differences of principle continued. Khomeini's authority was challenged by the more moderate President Bani Sadr, who was supported by the Mojahedin-e Khalq, a Muslim guerrilla organisation founded to fight the Shah in the early 1960s. In 1981, many senior members of the Islamic Republican Party were killed in bomb attacks attributed to, if not always carried out by, the Mojahedin. However, by the mid-1980s the Islamic Republic was more securely established. If repression continued, it was on a diminished scale. In addition a measure of continuity has been preserved at the top in that three key figures, the president, Ayatollah Khamanei, the speaker of the *majlis,* (parliament), Hujjat al-Islam Rafsanjani, and the foreign minister, Ali Akbar Velayati, have held these or other senior offices from 1981 until the time of writing.

The war with Iraq continued until 18 July 1988, when Iran accepted UN Resolution 598, which had called for an immediate ceasefire. Khomeini himself died a year later. Well before his death, however, there were signs that the radicalism of the immediately post-revolutionary period had been modified in favour of a much less ideological approach. Apart from its influence among Lebanese Shi'is, fears that the revolution would find an echo in other Muslim states, particularly Iraq, had largely proved groundless, partly because of the Iran/Iraq war, partly because of the very specific quality of Iranian Shi'ism and its Iranian nationalist colouration.

In addition, the government of the Islamic Republic found it increasingly difficult to find 'Islamic solutions' to economic and social problems. Attempts to carry out land reform foundered on divisions between those who stressed a more egalitarian society and those who stressed the sanctity of property in Islam. Again, calls from Islamic radicals for Iran to side with Iraq against the coalition forces after Iraq's invasion of Kuwait in August 1990 fell largely on deaf ears. The Iranian regime understood that it was closely dependent on the good will and co-operation of the West to secure the economic recovery desperately needed after the upheavals of the previous decade.

THE WAR BETWEEN IRAN AND IRAQ

The war between Iran and Iraq from September 1980 to July 1988 was one of the most costly and futile conflicts of the 20th century. It is difficult to arrive at a reliable estimate of casualties, though perhaps as many as 400,000 were killed and 750,000 wounded. The war stemmed from two fundamental miscalculations on Saddam Hussein's part. In the first place, he evidently feared the influence of the Iranian Revolution on Iraq's Shi'i population. Secondly, it was widely believed that the Iranian armed forces had been reduced to such a state of disarray by the revolution that Iraq would have no difficulty in gaining an easy victory. It was also spurred by Hussein's overweening ambition to make himself leader of the Arab world, and, if less explicitly, the West's gendarme in the Gulf.

In the event, although Iran was eventually forced to concede defeat, Iraq's victory was largely technical and was in any case virtually nullified by the consequences of its invasion of Kuwait two years later. Iraq was only able to 'triumph' as a result of a combination of French weaponry, US naval and military assistance and the support from the Soviet Union, all of which became decisive from early 1986 (when Iraq appeared very likely to lose). Iran has more than three times the population of Iraq; the two countries share a common frontier some 1,300 kilometres long; and, apart from the oil fields, most major targets within Iran are a considerable distance from the frontier.

The war began in September 1980, when Saddam Hussein announced the abrogation of the Algiers Agreement, which he had signed with the Shah in 1975, thereby claiming full Iraqi sovereignty over the disputed Shatt al-'Arab waterway. Iraqi forces invaded Iran and remained on Iranian territory until they were forced out in the summer of 1982. The war then shifted to Iraqi territory where all action took place until August 1986. For the Iranians, the war was represented as the struggle of Islam against unbelief, the Great Satan in Baghdad; for Iraq, its troops were fighting the Iranian threat to the Arab nation, the Arabian Gulf, the Arabian Peninsula, and, somewhat more incongruously, Zionism and its Iranian collaborators.

As well as the toll in human lives, the war caused immense damage to the infrastructure of both countries. It is difficult to gauge the extent of domestic opposition to it, particularly in Iraq, where the personality cult around Saddam Hussein and the repressive tactics of the regime both greatly increased. By August 1983 Iraq's foreign exchange reserves had almost disappeared and it became dependent on handouts from Saudi Arabia, Kuwait and other Gulf States. Although there were efforts at external mediation, one somewhat Machiavellian factor should not be overlooked: in a world where oil prices were falling dramatically, it was scarcely a matter of great urgency either to the other oil exporters or to the major companies that production in two of the region's main producing states should be restored to pre-1980 levels.

Although the war ended officially in July 1988, no permanent settlement had been reached by August 1990. A few days after the invasion of Kuwait, Saddam Hussein offered Iran a full settlement based on the implementation of Resolution 598 and the restoration of the Algiers Agreement of March 1975, which Iran accepted, although, apart from exchanges of prisoners, there has been little in the way of concrete progress since. On the other hand, the removal of the military threat had the effect of calming Iranian apprehensions. In addition, Iran has shown no signs of being in a hurry to return the Iraqi military aircraft flown to Iranian air bases at the beginning of the Gulf War.

Once the threat of 'exporting Islamic revolution' had begun to recede, the war between Iran and Iraq generally ceased to engage the active attention of most of the other states in the region. Indeed, many neighbouring states, while deploring the conflict, either (in the case of the oil states) regarded bankrolling Iraq as a price they would grudgingly be prepared to pay or (in the case of many of the others) were evidently not averse to profiting from it. Thus Turkey's agricultural exports to both sides increased considerably while the Jordanian economy was boosted by sales of agricultural produce as well as by transit dues from the port of Aqaba. There was also substantial road construction to facilitate the transport of Iraqi goods. Egypt, still ostracised in the Arab world because of Camp David, edged its way back to respectability under Mubarak, exporting several hundred thousand workers to Iraq to take the place of the men at the front, and providing Iraq with much-needed spare parts for its Soviet-made weaponry.

Among the Arab states Syria alone maintained a passive alliance with Iran (in the sense of siding with Iran without taking an active part against Iraq), played host to various factions of the Iraqi opposition and generally consolidated its own position in Lebanon. However, a major and damaging consequence of the Iran/Iraq war as far as the Palestinians and Lebanon was concerned was its effect in distracting attention from the Arab/Israeli conflict. Although other factors were at work, this preoccupation partly explains the lack of response from the Arab states to the Israeli invasion of Beirut in 1982 and the relegation of the Palestinian question for much of the 1980s.

THE INVASION OF KUWAIT AND ITS AFTERMATH

If the invasion of Kuwait can be seen as emanating from the folly and the ambition of Saddam Hussein, it also both highlighted and reflected the principal change in world politics and international relations that had been taking place since the mid-1980s: the decline of the Soviet Union as a world power and serious contender for influence alongside the US. It is a measure of Hussein's isolation and lack of judgment that he did not immediately realise either that such excesses as the annexation of an oil state would not be tolerated by the major consumers of oil or that his neighbours would not willingly condone such an infringement of territorial sovereignty. It may be that he was sufficiently out of touch with reality to believe that his military might was sufficient to ward off any possible challenge. In any case no government threw itself wholeheartedly behind Iraq, although some Arab states, notably Jordan and Yemen, did not join in the chorus of condemnation. Some of Iraq's neighbours actually sent forces to join those of the US-led coalition ranged against it.

The result of the fighting was a foregone conclusion, although it must be underlined that there was no sense in which the war itself was inevitable. Hussein could have withdrawn from Kuwait at any time. However cynical some of the real intentions of the West may have been, a stream of high-level politicians from all over the world paid visits to Baghdad in an attempt to avert what they saw as certain catastrophe. The invasion was not a popular cause in Iraq, its population exhausted after eight years of fighting Iran. However, the aftermath of the Gulf War demonstrated either the gullibility, the indecision or the irresponsibility of the coalition, whose troops were not prepared nor permitted to come to the aid of those popular uprisings in Kurdistan and the south of Iraq which were savagely put down by Hussein's Popular Army.

THE FUTURE

In much of the Arab world, the hesitant and unco-ordinated response of most regimes to the invasion of Kuwait aroused displays of frustration and anger among their populations. The knee-jerk reaction of some of the 'Arab masses' had been to demonstrate broad support for the Iraqi invasion, less perhaps out of conviction of the justice of the cause than as an expression of frustration at the moral and political bankruptcy of their own governments and with the unequal distribution of wealth and political power in the Arab world as whole. For the more reflective, the need for the introduction of more responsible and accountable governments throughout the region became even more acute.

The invasion of Kuwait had other important consequences for the Middle East. In the first place, although the legitimacy of the regimes in Kuwait, Saudi Arabia and the Gulf was called into question, and will continue to be so long as the ruling oligarchies there retain all power in their own hands, Saudi Arabia's position within the region and as a

US ally was greatly strengthened. It doubled its oil production and exports in response to the stoppage of exports from Iraq and Kuwait, thus averting an energy crisis by keeping oil prices down and at the same time ensuring its control over OPEC, at least in the short run. Secondly, the US became more firmly embedded in the Arab world than ever before, with orders for arms worth over $19 billion (mostly for Saudi Arabia) taken within a mere 17 months of the Iraqi invasion of Kuwait.

Furthermore, although there is no direct causal relationship, the crisis served to highlight the region's most deep-seated problems, which cannot be excluded from any discussion of its future. Perhaps the most immediate of these is the steep decline in living standards and employment since the early 1980s, partly as a result of the falling or stagnant price of oil, accompanied by soaring inflation. This has brought about a profound sense that there is 'no future' for much of the population of the region, a high percentage of which is under 15.

A major consequence has been the extraordinary impetus given to 'political Islam' in the first half of the 1990s. This phenomenon has been fairly general throughout the Arab world, but most marked in Algeria, Tunisia, Egypt, Palestine, Sudan, many of the Gulf States, Yemen and even Saudi Arabia, as well as in Iran. In general, anger and frustration are directed less against the West than against what are regarde as corrupt and illegitimate domestic regimes. Tragically, violence has not been confined to the struggle against tyranny and injustice, but has been directed against advocates of toleration and democracy, especially in Algeria and Egypt. Most governments in the Middle East and North Africa have responded with varying degrees of heavy-handed repression, both against Islamists and those urging respect for human rights. The first round of the Egyptian elections of early December 1995 made more than a mockery of the democratic process: all those elected, without exception, were members of the government-sponsored National Democratic Party.

None the less, there has been some progress towards the defusing of tensions in the region since the invasion of Kuwait. The conflict in Lebanon appears to have come to an end, although it is doubtful whether the underlying tensions have genuinely been resolved. Similarly, the Arab-Israeli conflict as it existed since 1948 is effectively over: a number of Arab states now have more or less correct and formal relations with Israel, and those who have not taken such steps will follow suit in due course. There have also been significant changes in the relations between Israel and the Palestinians, although the framework adopted in September 1993 puts the Palestinians at such a grave disadvantage that it is questionable whether this will continue to represent the breakthrough so eagerly hailed at the time. The question of Palestinian sovereignty has been skirted, as have the problems arising from the Israeli settlements on the West Bank and the future of Jerusalem. In addition, the mounting political polarisation and violence within Israel, culminating in the assassination of Yitzhak Rabin in November 1995, is an indication of the uncertainties on the road ahead, especially if the right wing makes significant headway in the 1996 elections.

On a more sombre note, the Iraqi regime remains in power – and seems likely to remain so in spite of the continuing boycott by the international community. Reports from Iraq tell of the enormous sufferings of the population, severe malnutrition and high child mortality. While it is probably true that smuggling and other informal arrangements temper some of the severity of the boycott, Saddam Hussein's tenacious grip on power is a vivid illustration of the extremes to which Middle Eastern regimes can resort in order to protect themselves.

Tragically, to many people in the region Hussein does not seem particularly exceptional so much as emblematic, albeit in extreme form, of regional realities. Furthermore, the widespread belief that ultimately it is the the West, above all the all-powerful US, which underpins the survival of regimes such as Hussein's because the alternatives are even less appealing to them, only reinforces anti-Western prejudices. The resulting combination of cynicism and disillusionment leads in turn and seemingly inevitably to the atavistic conclusion that 'Islam' is the only 'solution'.

Marion Farouk-Sluglett and Peter Sluglett

1
EGYPT

DURING THE 19TH CENTURY Egypt was virtually an autonomous state, ruled by the Muhammad Ali dynasty, although in strict legal terms Muhammad Ali and his successors were merely viceroys of the Ottoman Sultan in Istanbul. The British military occupation of Egypt in 1882 placed Great Britain in de facto control of the country, but did not alter Egypt's legal status. Only in 1914, after the outbreak of war, did Great Britain declare Egypt to be a British protectorate, thereby ending four centuries of Ottoman sovereignty. After the end of the war in 1918, Egyptian nationalists pressed Great Britain to grant Egypt its independence and formed a delegation (*wafd* in Arabic) to present their case at the Paris peace conference. The scale and force of the Wafd's agitation throughout Egypt during the following years eventually obliged Great Britain in 1922 to grant Egypt its formal independence as a sovereign state under King Fuad of the Muhammad Ali dynasty. There were, however, severe limitations on this sovereignty. Among other things, the British reserved for themselves alone the right to organise the defence of Egypt and to ensure the security of 'imperial communications'. This meant the continuation of British military occupation.

Consequently, one of the major preoccupations of Egyptian politicians during the following decades was the negotiation of a complete British military withdrawal from the country. At the same time, the royal palace was locked in competition with the Wafd, as the former tried to assert the royal prerogative and the latter tried to realise the principle of popular sovereignty laid down in the Constitution of 1923. Both factions resented the continued British presence, but both sought to enlist British support in their struggles. The Treaty of 1936 signalled a formal end to the British military occupation, Great Britain agreed to withdraw its forces to the Canal Zone and Egypt became a fully independent member of the League of Nations. In reality, British influence remained predominant and was reinforced by the outbreak of war in 1939, when Egypt became central to British strategy. Only after the end of the Second World War did Great Britain begin to disengage from the shaping of Egyptian politics.

By that stage, however, new forces were emerging in Egypt, impatient with the record of the dominant political and economic order. Both the King and the Wafd were accused of having failed to win complete independence for Egypt and for having collaborated with the British. The formal existence of a parliamentary system of government derived from the Constitution of 1923 had not prevented the frequent suspension of parliament, rule by decree and rigged elections. Nor had it allowed much progress on social or economic issues, since the parliament throughout the period was dominated by large landowners and other economically powerful figures who regularly placed their own interests above those of the national community. The indictment of the regime was not confined merely to one part of the political spectrum. The nationalists of the Young Egypt party, the socialists and the communists, the Islamic activists of the Muslim Brotherhood – all were vocal in their denunciation of the established order and were listened to by an increasing number of Egyptians.

In the midst of this period of disorder and protest came the military disaster of the 1948 Palestine war in which the Egyptian armed forces were defeated by the forces of the newly established state of Israel. The general political discontent and the specific humiliation of the defeat found a focus in the Egyptian officer corps. A group calling itself the Free Officers was formed by Gamal Abdel Nasser and his associates. They may have differed in their ideological sympathies, but all were united by their belief that something radical needed to be done to change the status quo in Egypt – as well as by their conviction that, as officers of the Egyptian army, they had both the right and the means to bring about that change. In July 1952 they acted and carried out a coup d'état which inaugurated the Egyptian revolution. King Farouk was forced to abdicate in favour of his infant son, a land reform law was brought in which eliminated the economic power of the great landowners, the constitution of 1923 was annulled and the political parties associated with the old regime were banned. In June 1953 the Republic of Egypt was proclaimed.

EGYPT UNDER NASSER AND SADAT

Nasser rapidly emerged as the dominant figure among the Free Officers and formalised this position by becoming President of the Republic in 1954. His personal authority, but also his skilful use of the administrative and coercive apparatus of the state, made his position one of virtually unassailable power. In addition, his ability to appeal to the aspirations of large numbers of Egyptians by using themes of social equality and national independence, gave him an authority and a mass following on a remarkable scale. However, it rapidly became clear that he could neither tolerate opposition, nor bear to be beholden, ideologically or otherwise, to any other group or faction in Egyptian politics.

Concentration of power in his own hands allowed him to chart his own course and to become the eponymous originator of Nasserism. This mixture of ideas was to have considerable appeal throughout the Middle East, especially after the defiant stance adopted by Nasser during the Suez war of 1956. Nasserism came to symbolise anti-imperialism, non-alignment, pan-Arabism, republicanism, social justice and, increasingly, state socialism. It was an exciting mixture for the times and seemed to hold out the promise of a radically reshaped Arab world, united in purpose, and offering the possibility of a better life for its inhabitants. The reality was rather different. Nasserism created enemies as well as enthusiasts, not least because many saw it as a vehicle for Egyptian domination. The ill-fated

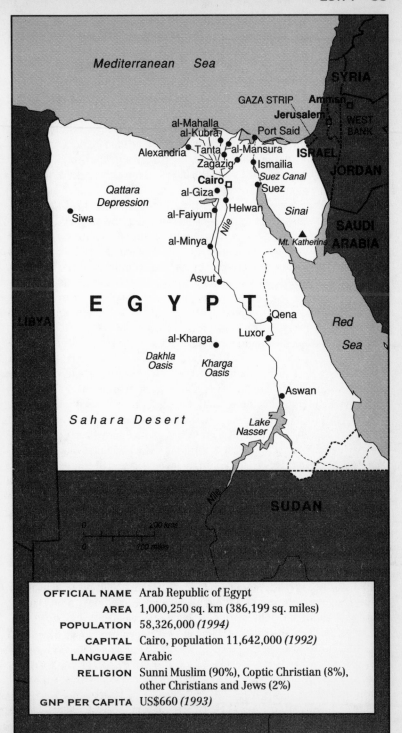

OFFICIAL NAME	Arab Republic of Egypt
AREA	1,000,250 sq. km (386,199 sq. miles)
POPULATION	58,326,000 *(1994)*
CAPITAL	Cairo, population 11,642,000 *(1992)*
LANGUAGE	Arabic
RELIGION	Sunni Muslim (90%), Coptic Christian (8%), other Christians and Jews (2%)
GNP PER CAPITA	US$660 *(1993)*

union between Egypt and Syria in the United Arab Republic (1958-61) seemed to confirm this impression. Even within Egypt itself it was difficult for many to see any consistency in the Nasserist project as Nasser's ideological eclecticism became more pronounced during the 1960s.

The decade began with a spate of nationalisation and all the principal sectors of the Egyptian economy were taken under state control. At the same time, even more stringent land-reform measures were taken, seeming to herald a far-reaching change in social and economic relations in the Egyptian countryside. However, within a few years, Nasser was having second thoughts: nationalisation was not producing the surplus required to fund the provisions of the welfare state; and the expectations of radical change in the countryside threatened his own vision of political order. The only consistent feature was Nasser's determination to retain absolute control of the process through the subservient sole political party, the Arab Socialist Union (ASU), through state control of the media and industry, and through the use of the intelligence services to suppress dissent.

In 1967 the scale and speed of Egypt's military defeat by Israel shook Nasser's rule to its foundations. He continued in office, but his authority and his system of power were now openly questioned. Increasingly, calls were heard for the accountability of government, for an end to the police state and for greater freedom in political and economic life. Nasser, however, was preoccupied with rebuilding Egypt's shattered military strength, with the economic consequences of a failing state socialist experiment, and with the attempt to deal with the effects of the loss of Sinai and the closure of the Suez Canal. Nasser died in 1970, having solved none of these questions, and leaving them, in consequence, as the legacy with which his successor was obliged to cope.

Anwar Sadat, Nasser's Vice-President and a fellow Free Officer, succeeded to the Presidency on Nasser's death. He immediately began to consolidate his own position. Initially, this involved moving against those on the left within the ASU, as well as their allies in the military and the bureaucracy. In their place, Sadat encouraged the advocates of greater economic liberalisation and the adherents of the Muslim Brotherhood, whom he released from the prisons where they had been incarcerated for much of Nasser's rule. At the same time, he took the decision in 1972 to expel the 15,000 Soviet military advisers stationed in Egypt. This not only secured the support of the Egyptian military, but also greatly enhanced Sadat's authority in the country at large and in much of the political apparatus. Egyptians saw in him the hope of change and above all of escape from the economic, political and diplomatic burdens of Nasser's legacy.

In this atmosphere Sadat launched the October War against Israel in 1973. The initial successes of the operation, regardless of the military reversals which followed, restored the confidence of the Egyptians in themselves and boosted Sadat's authority. He had intended the war not simply to efface the shame of the 1967 defeat, but also to break the diplomatic deadlock with Israel. This, in turn, he believed would allow him to open the country up to much needed capital investment from abroad.

However, the disengagement talks with Israel during 1974-75, the policies of the Infitah or 'economic opening' and the marked alignment with the West and the United States in particular produced more limited results than Sadat had expected. The military debt to the USSR remained large, foreign investors were wary of placing funds in Egypt, the expected aid from the oil-rich Arab states was not forthcoming and the massive subsidies on basic food and consumer items needed to be maintained. The widespread, violent riots of January 1977 demonstrated the political risks which the Egyptian government ran in trying to cut back on this aspect of the welfare state. Faced with this impasse and the threats of disorder produced by underlying frustration, Sadat made another of the dramatic moves for which his Presidency became famous. In November 1977 he flew to Jerusalem to address the Israeli Knesset.

This was the first in a series of moves which led to the American brokered negotiations between Israel and Egypt and to the signing of a formal peace treaty in March 1979. Under its terms, Israel agreed to withdraw from Sinai within three years, Egypt agreed to let Israeli ships pass through the Suez Canal and full diplomatic and trade relations were established between the two states. The United States was the guarantor of the treaty, supervising the Israeli withdrawal from Sinai and its subsequent demilitarisation, whilst simultaneously pledging equal amounts of substantial military and economic aid to both Egypt and Israel. The issue of Palestinian autonomy was left until the moves to establish bilateral relations and trust had been completed.

These developments provoked consternation among most of the other Arab states and in 1979 Egypt was expelled from the Arab League. Within Egypt itself, opposition to the treaty with Israel came chiefly from the remnants of the Nasserist left and from the growing Islamic trend. They were disconcerted by moves so much at odds with the course charted in the Arab world by Egypt during the previous 40 years. Nevertheless, Sadat was able to rely on the support of a political class which shared his views of Egypt's national interests. In addition, a mixture of Egyptian nationalism and a belief that these moves heralded a new and more prosperous future for Egypt created considerable initial popular enthusiasm.

Once again, however, the almost instantaneous prosperity which Sadat had promised his countrymen failed to materialise for the majority of Egyptians. Unrealistic as this may have been, it was noticed that some sectors of Egyptian society began to reap considerable profits from the economic opportunities offered by the encouragement of private sector activity. Inequalities of wealth, never absent from Egyptian society, became more marked as new forms of consumption became available to the rich. Inevitably, criticism of these developments arose, not only on the left of the political spectrum, but also from the Islamic wing. When linked to the condemnation from these same groups of increasing Egyptian reliance on the United States and of the apparently bilateral peace process with Israel, these became the foundation for a wide-ranging critique of the regime, a critique to which Sadat was extremely sensitive.

Mistrustful of the Nasserist tendencies of the ASU and aware of the need to allow greater freedom of expression, Sadat began to establish a more varied party system. Cautiously at first, and then with increased speed in 1977, the ASU was broken up into three separate parties which Sadat believed would provide him with a platform of support and a semblance of opposition. Genuine opposition was harder for him to tolerate. The short-lived revival of the New Wafd in 1978 and the increasing difficulties faced by the Nasserist/Marxist National Progressive Unionist Party (NPUP) showed there were limits to Sadat's liberalisation. Although he had encouraged the re-emergence of more open political debate and a relaxation of the tight grip of government, Sadat found it difficult to accept the consequences when it led to criticism of his own policies. Nor did he believe that he should be answerable to those over whom he ruled – he was convinced that he knew better than they where their true interests lay.

Like his predecessor Nasser, Sadat relied increasingly on his control of the state administration and the security services to enforce conformity with his views. Those who dissented, he regarded at best as guilty of folly and at worst as subversive of the whole political and social order. In the late summer of 1981 he demonstrated his thesis by arresting virtually every prominent critic of his regime, regardless of their political affiliations. However, whilst much of his attention was focused on his public critics, there were more dangerous enemies in the shadows.

During the 1970s small groups of Islamic radicals had protested publicly and often violently against what they saw as an impious and unjust social order. Clashes with the security forces and between Copts and Muslims marked the emergence of these groups. Possibly disillusioned with the relative quietism of the legally sanctioned Muslim Brotherhood, these groups advocated violence as the only means of destroying the existing corrupt state. Their vision was of an Islamic order governed by the *shari'a* (Islamic law) arising out of the ruins of the old order. In 1981 the mass arrests seem to have galvanised one of these groups, al-Jihad, into action. Its members became convinced that the death of the President was a duty incumbent upon them as devout Muslims and might bring closer the moment when a truly Islamic order could be established in Egypt. In October 1981, at the military parade commemorating the war of 1973, they assassinated President Sadat.

EGYPT UNDER MUBARAK

Although the President was killed and there was some associated violence in Asyut, there was no attempt to overthrow the government of Egypt. Political order remained intact, since the state establishment and the armed forces rallied round the surviving leadership, headed by Husni Mubarak, the Vice President, who succeeded Sadat as President of the Republic. Whatever misgivings some may have had about Sadat's increasingly autocratic course, there was little disagreement within the political elite over the priorities which he had set for the country. President Mubarak was able, therefore, to capitalise upon the support of the political establishment as well as that of the public opposition. However, the nature of this support was ambiguous. On the one hand, some saw Mubarak as a guarantor of stability and order, and thus a figure of continuity with the previous regime. On the other hand, there were many who believed that the change of president in such a highly centralised system of power held out great hopes for progress in the fields of political and economic liberalisation. Seeking to appeal to both constituencies simultaneously has been the mark of Mubarak's presidency.

The resulting contradictions have been noticeable features of the past 15 years. Mubarak himself seems to have a largely authoritarian vision of political power. He is a former air force general and the inheritor of a political order which founds its claim to legitimacy on a revolution carried out by the officer corps of the armed forces. Consequently, Mubarak is sympathetic to the arguments which suggest that the armed forces are not simply the defenders of the country's borders, but are also the ultimate guarantors of order against possible social and political chaos. This seemed to be borne out graphically for him by the decisive part played by the armed forces in suppressing the violent Central Security Forces mutinies in early 1986. It has been further reinforced by the use he has made of Military Courts to try those – mainly Islamists – accused of terrorism since the draconian anti-terrorist laws introduced in 1992.

Nevertheless, his summary dismissal in 1989 of the long-serving Minister of Defence, Field Marshal Abu Ghazala, proved that Mubarak did not want to become beholden to any one military officer, however powerful. His replacement, General Abu Talib, was replaced in May 1991, when the President appointed General Tantawi as Minister of Defence. These moves stem partly from particular considerations appropriate to the times they were made, but they are also due to the President's determination to assert his own control of the armed forces. The latter form an important element in the dominant structure of order, just as their senior officers are generally influential in the political elite. However, the clear message is that the armed forces should be at the disposal of the President and his political establishment, rather than vice versa.

As far as the realm of civil politics is concerned, Mubarak's vision of acceptable political behaviour allows for criticism and organised opposition, but only to a certain level and only in certain spheres of policy. The condition of its existence seems to be that it should neither disrupt nor challenge his own political and economic preoccupations as President. Nevertheless, a gradual opening up of political life has taken place: new parties have been allowed to form; they have been allowed a greater, although scarcely threatening, degree of representation in the People's Assembly; freedom of the press has been enhanced, with a greater variety of opinions represented than at any time since the revolution of 1952.

Welcome as these developments have been for those who wish to see the greater liberalisation of Egyptian politics, there has been an uneasy feeling that all these manifestations of political freedom exist only on government sufferance. There exists the fear that behind the apparent willingness to encourage the emergence of a plural political order, an unreconstructed apparatus and set of authoritarian prejudices endure. This has been evident in the security services of the Ministry of Interior, in the prominence accorded to the armed forces in national life and in the convention that the President himself is somehow 'above politics' – and thus above criticism – when, in fact, he is supremely powerful. The most recent example of this authoritarian impulse was the government's attempt to introduce a highly restrictive Press Law in 1995. Stung by criticism not simply of government policies, but also by the allegations of corruption levelled at senior members of the administration and, indeed, against his own son by the opposition press, the President reacted sharply. In May 1995 he rushed through Parliament a bill imposing heavy fines and gaol sentences on those responsible for publishing information deemed to be false or which 'holds government officials or public institutions up to ridicule'. Not only the editors and journalists of the papers concerned were to be held accountable, but also the leaders of the political parties which backed the publications in question. This was met by outrage, not simply on the part of the opposition parties and press, but also by journalists on the government papers. Sit-ins, protests and threatened strike action made the President realise the widespread nature of the opposition and compelled him to suspend the Press Law whilst referring it to the Constitutional Court. Mubarak's presidency has, therefore, been characterised by a series of gradual, incremental and occasionally reluctantly-taken steps towards greater freedom of political expression and activity. The fact that some of these steps have been forced upon the government by an increasingly active and independently-minded judiciary, has been one of the more noteworthy aspects of this process.

The judiciary's activity can be seen as a determination on the part of many in the legal profession never to allow the arbitrariness of Nasser's dictatorship to re-emerge. They have thus taken the President seriously when he proclaims himself committed to the 'rule of law' and the 'state of institutions'. A series of court decisions in 1983 and 1984 obliged the government to accept the legal existence of the New Wafd party and allowed the surviving pre-revolutionary leaders of the party to play an active role in public life once more. In 1995, the Constitutional Court ruled that the controversial Press Law was unconstitutional in some of its aspects and effectively compelled the President to establish a broad-based commission to re-draft it. Another series of court rulings in 1986 and 1987 found the electoral law of 1983 unconstitutional. This forced the government both to amend the law and to call for new elections, since the legality of the existing People's Assembly had been called into question. There were some who were still dissatisfied with the amended electoral law and, in May 1990, the litigation arising from this dissatisfaction came to fruition. Once again, the Supreme Constitutional Court ruled that the electoral law, as amended in 1986, was unconstitutional and that the People's Assembly elections of 1987 were invalid. This obliged the President once again to dissolve the assembly and to call for new elections in November 1990.

THE 1990 AND 1995 ELECTIONS

The circumstances surrounding the 1990 general election demonstrate some of the limits to the gradual dismantling of the authoritarian political order in Egypt. In the elections of 1984 and 1987, some opposition parties had succeeded in winning representation in the People's Assembly. However, the overwhelming majority of the President's National Democratic Party (NDP) was never in question (in 1984 it had won 390 of the 448 seats; in 1987 it won 346). Quite apart from the proven problems of the electoral law, the opposition parties had alleged in both years – with considerable justification – that the elections could not be regarded as free. The NDP, through the President and the government, had an overwhelming advantage in the form of state patronage and control of broadcasting. More seriously, the opposition asserted that it was difficult to conduct free elections under the State of Emergency legislation which had been in force since the assassination of President Sadat in 1981. There were charges against local security forces for intimidating opposition candidates and for preventing opposition supporters from accessing polling booths. The Ministry of the Interior was accused of ensuring that, by whatever means necessary, the majority returned for the NDP was sufficiently overwhelming not simply to give the government a free hand in the People's Assembly, but also to reinforce the impression of near-unanimous acquiescence in President Mubarak's authority.

As a result of these complaints, the main opposition parties (the Wafd, the Liberals, the Socialist Labour Party (SLP) and the Muslim Brotherhood – the latter is not strictly or legally a party, but it is certainly a contestant) declared that they would boycott the 1990 elections unless the State of Emergency was lifted and the conduct of the elections was transferred from the Ministry of the Interior to the Judiciary. The government refused these demands and the elections went ahead, contested by the ruling NDP, the NPUP, a large number of Independents and some smaller parties. In all, 3,000 candidates contested the 444 seats (two seats for each of the 222 constituencies). The result was, of course, an overwhelming majority for the NDP which won 348 seats, whilst 83 went to Independents and six to the NPUP. The People's Assembly which was elected in 1990 ran its five-year course and new elections were held in November/December 1995. A record number of political parties participated, but there were widespread allegations of government interference. The result was a new Assembly in which the ruling NDP enjoyed an even greater majority than before: 416 seats, as against a mere 28 for the opposition (15 Independents; 6 Wafd Party; 5 NPUP; 1 Nasserist Party; 1 Liberal Party).

GOVERNMENT AND OPPOSITION

The system of government in Egypt remains centred on the presidency. Consequently, the parliamentary elections have little to do with the actual or possible transfer of power. Rather, they provide an acquiescent Assembly which then lends legitimacy to the laws which the President wishes to see enacted and the initiatives that he decides to pursue. The

Assembly also nominates the presidential candidates whose names must be submitted to popular referendum every six years. In July 1993, only 15 members of the 454 member Assembly refused to back Mubarak's nomination and, consequently, as on the previous two occasions, his was the only name to be put to the popular vote in October 1993. Needless to say, he 'won' the referendum with ease and began his third term as Egypt's President, apparently endorsed by the overwhelming approval of both the parliament and the populace.

The elections are also important for gauging the willingness of the President to give dissent a voice. Mubarak evidently sees some utility in this exercise, although he is unwilling to tolerate opposition that establishes itself independently of the state's control. This has been demonstrated most clearly by the conflict between the government and the professional syndicates. The latter bring together members of the appropriate professions, such as doctors, engineers, lawyers and journalists. Their members have often been critical of aspects of government policies. More importantly, during recent years, there has been a concerted attempt by the Muslim Brotherhood to gain control of the syndicates by winning the elections for their executive committees. This is in part due to the Brotherhood's desire to use them as a platform for its ideas, but is also due to their determination to act more effectively in defence of their members who run foul of the state authorities. The combination of opposition, especially Islamist opposition, and an electoral mandate was more than the President could bear. In 1993, Parliament rushed through a law which stipulates that, for syndicate elections to be valid, at least 50 per cent of the membership must vote in the first ballot and that at least 33 per cent must vote in the second or third ballots. Anything less, and the government would appoint the syndicate's president and executive committee. Since the turnout in these elections is notoriously low, amounting often to 25 per cent or so of their members, this was clearly aimed at invalidating the Muslim Brothers' mandate. This rested essentially on the committed and organised minority which could be relied upon to vote for their candidates. In 1995, the government introduced a law intended to strengthen the role of the judiciary in supervising syndicate elections. Many in the secular opposition and within the syndicates themselves knew that the Muslim Brotherhood candidates were far from representative of the profession as a whole. Nevertheless, the government's action provoked ironic and hostile comment since the turnout in national elections, whether for Parliament or for the President, has always been notoriously low, despite official claims to the contrary.

At the same time, there are those within the state administration who have a more restrictive view of politics and find it difficult to distinguish dissent from treason or subversion. President Mubarak has consistently appointed such people and charged them with maintaining public order. This is as crucial for the maintenance of his authority among the elite as are any pretensions to liberalisation. Between 1986 and 1990, this tendency was personified by the notorious Minister of the

Interior, Zaki Badr, who represented the unreconstructed and repressive side of the regime. When this became too obvious and an embarrassment to the President both in Egypt and abroad, Badr was dismissed. His successors, General Abd al-Halim Musa (1990-93) and General Hasan Muhammad al-Alfi (1993-), have come up by the familiar route of police service and governorship of troublesome provinces. They have been less outspoken than their predecessor in their attitudes to the legal opposition. However, the forces under their command have been no less ruthless when dealing with disruptive expressions of opposition, such as street demonstrations, factory sit-ins, or the activities of underground organisations.

ISLAMIST CHALLENGES

During the past ten years, such organisations have carried out sporadic acts of violence. Chief among these have been the groups called loosely al-Jama'at al-Islamiyya (the Islamic groups) or the organisation al-Jihad. These espouse a radical Islamic ideology of protest, but others have also occasionally appeared, such as the Nasserist-nationalists of the group 'Egypt's Revolution' in the late 1980s. The activities of al-Jama'at have taken a number of forms. There have been attacks on figures of authority, ranging from the President himself and his Ministers down to local police officers. In 1993, they attempted to assassinate the Prime Minister, as well as the Ministers of the Interior and of Information. In 1994 they succeeded in killing the Deputy Chief of state security. In June 1995, there was an attempt on the life of President Mubarak in the Ethiopian capital, Addis Ababa. Al-Jama'at have also organised attacks on people believed to symbolise some aspect of Egyptian government policy of which the perpetrators disapprove – such as Israelis, Americans or foreign tourists. Some of the more extreme Islamic protest groups have attacked fellow Muslims whom they regard as having deviated from the strict interpretation of Islamic dress or behaviour which they wish to impose. Others have attacked Copts, Coptic property and churches, especially in Upper Egypt, in the towns of Asyut and Minya.

Although this violence has not yet been sufficiently sustained to threaten the political order seriously, it is difficult to view it with complacency. Between 1992 and 1995 an estimated 650 people died as a result of the Islamists' attacks and the government's shoot-to-kill tactics. Furthermore, the activities of the Islamic groups have been used by the government to justify the slow pace of liberalisation and as the rationale behind the renewal of the State of Emergency, in force since 1981, for a further three years in April 1994. Under its terms, the security forces have detained thousands of people on suspicion of association with al-Jama'at in periodic sweeps of the parts of Cairo and of Upper Egypt where they are thought to have most support. The authorities have also used such tactics as collective punishment, the taking of suspects' families hostage, as well as torture. All of these measures have brought increasing criticism of the Egyptian government by human rights organisations in Egypt and abroad.

In 1992, the power of the security services was augmented by the antiterrorism law. This places those accused of terrorist acts, of belonging to, or even associating with terrorist organisations, under the jurisdiction of the Military Courts. The more limited rights of defence and appeal, the despatch with which they operate and the death sentence which they have the power to impose on those found guilty have made these courts a marked feature of public life in Egypt. Since 1992 they have sentenced over 60 people to death, of whom over 40 had been executed by the end of 1995. Paradoxically, it is against this background that Egyptian political life has become more open and free than at any time since the 1952 revolution. Nevertheless, the apparent reluctance of the government to abandon the emergency laws is a disturbing indicator of the degree to which authoritarian ideas of governance persist among the ruling elite.

The activities of the Islamic protest groups alone cannot be held to justify the retention of this legislation. Appealing in the main to relatively small numbers of urban and provincial educated young people and junior officials, the seriously conspiratorial groups do not constitute major threats to the political order. Although they have caught public and press attention through some of their activities, the chief representative of those who want to see a more identifiably Islamic order instituted in Egypt is still the Muslim Brotherhood. Led by Hamid Abu'l-Nasr since 1986, the Muslim Brotherhood has explicitly renounced violence and has worked within the existing laws of the state, seeing its task chiefly as one of education, propaganda and the advancement of the *shari'a* as the sole foundation for public life in Egypt. Although it has been denied legal recognition as a political party, it is allowed to organise, to publish its journals and to put up candidates in parliamentary elections, as long as they are sponsored by one of the legal political parties. This led to an alliance with the Wafd in 1984 and with the SLP and the Liberals in 1987. In the 1990 elections a substantial number of Muslim Brotherhood sympathisers were elected as Independents. However, it could not remain unaffected by the battle raging between the government and the radical Islamists. In 1994, the security authorities began a campaign of sustained harassment against the Muslim Brotherhood, summoning its leader, arresting some of its members and raiding its premises. As President Mubarak made plain in 1995, he was convinced that there was no difference between the Muslim Brotherhood and the terrorists of the radical al-Jama'at. Consequently, the campaign against the organisation intensified. Fifty or so of its leading members were detained across the country, a number of whom were subsequently indicted for links with 'terrorist organisations' and were therefore obliged to appear before the Military Courts.

The centre of gravity of the Egyptian political system remains the presidency and, consequently, much of Egyptian political life is spent speculating on the next moves of the President, interpreting his words and deeds, as well as manoeuvring to catch his eye. It is an institution which has demonstrated its resilience, in the sense that the unexpected deaths of the two previous incumbents did not destabilise the system as a whole. However, the assassination attempt against President Mubarak in 1995 sent a shudder through the Egyptian political world because, unlike his predecessors, he has consistently refused to appoint a Vice-President. In the event of his sudden death, therefore, the succession might not be so smooth. There is no doubt that the personality and the vision of the President is important in shaping not only the direction of government policy, but also the dimensions of national political debate. Neither as conspiratorial, nor as insecure as his two predecessors, President Mubarak has shown himself able to tolerate a degree of transparency and of criticism which has allowed political life to revive. Nevertheless, his determination to oversee the whole process remains strong. Mubarak's vision of Egypt's future may not be as grandiose as those of Nasser or Sadat, but from his perspective even the more modest goals of economic solvency and public order require a close and controlling presidential hand.

ECONOMIC PROBLEMS

In January 1996 Dr Kamal Al-Ganzoury was appointed Prime Minister. The fact that he is, like his long-serving predecessor Dr Atif Sidqi, a trained economist, underlines the nature of the task with which the President has entrusted him. On the one hand, he is responsible for the conduct of negotiations with Egypt's external creditors, both bilaterally and through the International Monetary Fund (IMF). On the other, he is in charge of the gradual diminution of state control of the economy, in both the industrial and service sectors. The scale of the task facing him in all these areas is formidable. However, some remarkable successes have been achieved since the introduction of the IMF reform package in 1991.

By 1995 the country's total external, non-military debt had fallen to $32 billion (from $50 billion in 1990). The budget deficit had fallen to about 2.5 per cent of Gross Domestic Product (GDP) (compared to 22 per cent of GDP in 1990). Although the trade balance is still in the red, the gap has been closing and in 1995 Egypt looked set to achieve record exports of $4 billion. Agricultural imports to feed Egypt's relentlessly growing population (an estimated increase of one million every ten months) account for nearly half of the current deficit, but present growth rates of about four per cent per annum and an inflation rate that has now fallen below ten per cent give some grounds for optimism. To meet its import requirements, Egypt has four chief earners of foreign currency – oil, tourism, Suez Canal dues and the remittances of the estimated 3.5 million Egyptians working abroad. During 1994-95 these brought in roughly $11 billion in foreign exchange and Egypt now enjoys foreign currency reserves in the region of $16 billion. However, since 1990 all of Egypt's major sources of revenue have been shown to be vulnerable to developments over which the Egyptian government has no control. Prior to the Gulf crisis, the oil revenues suffered from the collapse in the oil price. Thereafter, the uncertainties of the Gulf crisis and war led to a sharp drop in tourism, the return of many Egyptian workers from the region and a fall in the volume of shipping using the

Suez Canal. Tourism revenues have also been affected by the Islamists' tactic of aiming their violence at tourists and tourist sites.

Domestically, the government is seeking to privatise some of the many economic sectors brought under state control during the Nasser era. The public sector still accounts for roughly 70 per cent of GDP and includes all the major industrial and service sectors of the economy. However, during the past few years there have been cautious experiments in privatisation in certain governorates. Some small-scale industrial concerns have been sold off and the management structure of a number of state enterprises overhauled. The relative success of these efforts has led to more ambitious plans to sell off state tourist company hotels, public sector interests in joint venture enterprises and state-run factories producing consumer goods and foodstuffs. Nevertheless, the principal industries, such as textiles, iron and steel and consumer durables are likely to remain state-run concerns for the foreseeable future.

EGYPT'S MILITARY STRUCTURES

Another economic sphere in which the state is dominant is that of military production. During the 1980s there was considerable investment in and development of the arms industry, partly in conjunction with foreign military suppliers and partly as an indigenous development. It was due to the Egyptian government's determination to become self-sufficient in the production of ammunition, spare parts and basic items of military equipment. Not only was this thought necessary for national security, it was also seen as a means of reducing the growth of the military debt, estimated in 1989 to stand at around $10 billion. At the same time, closer relations with Iraq during the war with Iran led to an increasingly lucrative export market for Egyptian manufactured arms. During the last three years of that war, from 1985-88, it was estimated that Iraq was importing between $800 and $1 billion worth of Egyptian military supplies each year. Precise figures on the growth of this sector are understandably impossible to obtain. However, it is clear that considerable resources have been dedicated to the military industries and, further, that the organisation of this state-run sector of the economy has been one of the more successful examples of industrial enterprise. It is perhaps not surprising that this should be the case, given the importance attached to the objective of re-armament and the place in the political hierarchy enjoyed by the military in Egypt.

Nevertheless, the great bulk of Egypt's armament comes from abroad, obliging the Egyptian government to incur considerable foreign military debts. In 1987 the government succeeded in coming to an agreement with the USSR on Egypt's military debt of $3 billion. Generous rescheduling terms were granted by the USSR, largely because the latter was anxious to improve the state of its rather cool relations with Egypt. Unable to raise the capital required to repay those loans, Egypt was instead trading on its importance as a key Middle Eastern state for outside powers.

This asset was particularly in evidence during the Gulf crisis. The Arab creditors of Egypt (chiefly Saudi Arabia and Kuwait) cancelled the $6.5 billion owed to them by Egypt and made an outright grant to Egypt of $2 billion. The US cancelled the whole of Egypt's military debt of $7 billion. During the preceding ten years the question of the military debt burden had been an irritant in US-Egyptian relations. Not only did the Egyptian government take exception to the way in which the loan had been structured, but it also clearly resented the fact that it was being forced to accept terms far less generous than those offered to Israel. The military debt to the US thus became both an addition to the overall economic burden of the government, as well as a symbolic issue on which the opposition could focus its criticism of the meagre rewards of the alliance with the US. The cancellation of the debt was, therefore, a highly effective way for the US to reward the Egyptian government for the active part it played in the coalition formed in 1990 to eject Iraq from Kuwait.

DEBT, REFORM AND SUBSIDIES

As far as the Egyptian government is concerned, the political significance of its overall debt burden is twofold. Firstly, there is the restriction which it places on Egypt's independence of action. Not only does it restrict the options open to the government, it also places the Egyptian government in the rather humiliating positon of a petitioner, constantly having to plead its case before such organisations as the Club of Rome, the Paris Club, the IMF and the World Bank. There is a perennial concern that this humiliating posture undermines the authority of the government and provides ammunition to those critics who claim that the government is incompetent in its protection of Egypt's interests. Secondly, as the series of negotiations with the IMF and others have demonstrated, the Egyptian government fears the domestic political consequences of some of the more stringent reform measures demanded by its creditors as a condition of rescheduling Egypt's debt.

In particular, these proposals invariably include demands that the government remove or reduce the very extensive subsidy system operating in Egypt which makes a range of items available to the population at well below their true economic cost. These include not simply subsidised seed, fertiliser and energy for the agricultural and industrial sectors, but also a large range of basic foodstuffs for the population as a whole. For Egypt's creditors the reduction and eventual removal of these subsidies is thought to be imperative if the Egyptian economy – and thus its ability to generate the surplus required to repay the debts incurred – is to be established on a sound footing. However, the Egyptian government is clearly anxious about the possible impact of the removal of subsidies on the mass of the urban poor who depend upon these in fundamental ways. The protests and disorder which are thought likely to follow any dramatic move on this front have been a strong deterrent to action.

Nevertheless, the government has recognised the economic arguments for reform and is equally aware that the subsidy system has been greatly abused. Under the present Prime Minister, some reforms have been attempted and there have also been cautious, phased moves aimed at reducing the overall cost of the subsidies to the government. This received added impetus in 1991 when the leading industrial states of the Paris Club offered to wipe out roughly one-third of Egypt's debt (between $5 billion and $10 billion) on condition that Egypt accept the reform package proposed by the IMF. This included the usual package of exchange rate reform, effective devaluation of the Egyptian pound, the freeing of interest rates, the reduction of state subsidies, especially on energy and basic foodstuffs, and the imposition of a sales tax. In April 1991 the Egyptian government reached an agreement on these terms with the IMF, having already set up a social fund, financed largely by the World Bank, which was intended to protect the poor from the worst effects of the inevitable price rises. In return, one-third of Egypt's debt was cancelled and the remainder was rescheduled, making debt repayment far less onerous.

The issue of subsidies, however, is not only affected by fears of public reaction and possible disorder in the streets. It is also intimately bound up with the structure and impulses of elite politics in Egypt. In the final analysis, it goes back to the basic question of the interests which the government is intended to serve. As in the case of political liberalisation, so with the attempted economic deregulation, the Egyptian government finds itself subject to conflicting pressures from different sectors of the elite. On the one hand, there are those who are entrenched in the massive structures of the state bureaucracy. They argue that without the protection afforded by state control of industrial and economic interests, free competition, operating through private enterprise and foreign capital, will lead to the running down of Egyptian industry and a loss of independence. Given the social and corporate structure of the elite, these people are in a position to make their voices heard. Their appeal to the principles of economic nationalism strikes a sympathetic and popular chord with many in Egypt. It is a theme which President Mubarak has often taken up in his occasional denunciations of 'cowardly capital' and in his often expressed frustration that private enterprise does not always act in the public interest.

On the other hand, there are many who believe that this bureaucracy stifles initiative and who hold it responsible, therefore, for the poor performance of the Egyptian economy, with all the loss of independence which that implies. After all, they argue, a $32 billion external debt and periodic debt rescheduling agreements are not ideal conditions in which to assert economic independence. This faction has advocated a much faster pace of privatisation which they believe will afford them greater economic opportunities and, in the process, strengthen the competitiveness of Egyptian agriculture and industry. They see the negative social consequences of this as either necessary or temporary or both. Confusingly for outside observers, the groups of people who hold these conflicting views do not constitute identifiably separate elites. On the contrary, they are generally closely linked to each other by ties of marriage, kinship, education and background. Equally, their contrasting views are represented in the government and are stressed by the President at different times, depending upon which audience he happens to be addressing.

As in the case of political liberalisation, Mubarak seems to have forged, if not a consensus then an agreement on fundamentals which allows members of the same administration to hold rather different views on how those fundamentals might best be protected. The appearance of consensus may also be, in part, a symptom of inertia. Considerable interests have built up over the years in the structure and maintenance of the state-run economy. Ideologies and rationales to justify these interests are also widely held both among the elite and in Egyptian society in general. Radical reform will clearly have social costs, as the comfortable, if inefficient and costly apparatus of state subsidies is dismantled. Nor is there any guarantee that the reforms will work as intended. Consequently, the desire to avoid fundamental conflict prevails and the search focuses on the pursuit of some 'middle way' which may not hold out much hope of dramatic economic improvement, but at least prevents serious dissent among the elite. In such an environment, the priority is clearly the preservation of the political order as presently constituted and the achievement of as great a degree of national independence as possible.

FOREIGN POLICY

A similar kind of minimal consensus exists in the field of foreign policy. There may be differences over the interpretation of the exact ingredients of Egyptian national interests, as well as over the best ways of securing them. However, there is general agreement that the independence, security and prosperity of the national community of Egyptians should take precedence over all else. This relative unanimity about national identity and interests makes Egypt noteworthy among the Arab states of the Middle East. It has also given its leaders considerable latitude in formulating foreign policy, as well as a secure base from which to take foreign policy initiatives. This helps to explain not only why Sadat was able to sign a peace treaty with Israel in 1979, but also why Mubarak has been able to abide by the terms of that treaty over the past ten years. During his presidency Egypt has maintained correct, if not necessarily cordial relations with successive Israeli governments. The same feature also explains the confidence with which the Egyptian government was able to oppose the Iraqi annexation of Kuwait, to successfully rally the Arab members of the international coalition against Iraq and to participate actively by sending 35,000 troops to join the coalition forces.

In the aftermath of the assassination of President Sadat, it was one of the priorities of the Egyptian government to reassure Israel that Egypt would continue to abide by the treaty. This reassurance was successful and the final phase of the Israeli withdrawal from Sinai was completed in April 1982. The Israeli invasion of Lebanon which came soon after led to a 'freezing' of the relationship, but did not cause any fundamental breach. It did, however, frustrate any idea the Egyptian government might have entertained to press for the implementation of the second part of the Camp David accords which had referred to the central question of the future of the Palestinians and the occupied territories. Nevertheless, it was evident by the mid-1980s that Egypt had succeeded in repairing its relations with the Palestine Liberation Organisation (PLO) and that, increasingly, the latter saw Egypt as a possible advocate of its cause in any attempt to arrange negotiations between Israel and the Palestinians. During 1989-90 the Egyptian government became deeply involved in helping to put into effect the so-called Baker Plan which had precisely such an end in view. Egypt, therefore, encouraged the resulting Madrid peace process. When the PLO and Israel signed the Declaration of Principles in 1993, the Egyptian leadership could only welcome the mutual recognition of Palestinians and Israelis which this represented, although they might have reflected wryly upon the fact that this did not constitute as good a deal for the Palestinians as that which had been offered to them when Egypt was negotiating with Israel in 1978-79. Nevertheless, for Egypt the satisfaction lay in the fact that during 1993 and 1994 much of the Arab world was coming round to the position which Egypt had long held.

On the purely bilateral level of Egyptian-Israeli relations, once these had thawed sufficiently in the aftermath of the Lebanon episode, the issue of the Taba enclave in Sinai came to the fore. This dispute concerned a small area of the coast which both sides claimed and from which Israel had refused to withdraw in April 1982. It was a considerable achievement of Mubarak's government to persuade Israel to submit the case to international arbitration. In 1989 the Egyptian handling of the issue was vindicated when the arbitration commission ruled in Egypt's favour and Israel agreed to withdraw from Taba. The reassuring aspect of this case, as far as Egyptian foreign policy was concerned, lay not simply in the fact that Egypt had won its argument, but also that the issue itself – border demarcation between two sovereign states – and the method of its resolution – peaceful arbitration – symbolised the very normality of the relationship between Egypt and Israel which had developed since 1979. The peace treaty may not have lived up to the utopian expectations of some in Israel and Egypt, but it had introduced an element of stability and non-contentious normality in the relationship between the two states.

This was particularly necessary at a time when passions among many in Egypt were running high as a result of the continuing Palestinian Intifada and Israeli efforts to suppress it. In fact, such passions had been evident at a number of times during the years since the signing of the treaty. They had occasionally erupted into isolated acts of violence against individual Israelis by Egyptians who found it difficult to reconcile themselves to the implications of peaceful co-existence. More generally, however, they were evident in the repeated charge by most of the opposition parties that the Egyptian government was being too passive in its response to Israeli behaviour in the Occupied Territories and too cautious in advancing the cause of the Palestinians.

The fact that the opposition press could voice openly what many felt, even among the supporters of the government, made the government sensitive to such criticism. Yet beyond the formal steps of diplomatic displeasure, which might in any case have been considered counterproductive at a time when Egypt was trying to promote negotiations between Israel and the Palestinians, there was not a great deal that Egypt could do. A complete rupture in relations and the abrogation of the treaty would have had immediate and severe consequences for Egypt's national security. Nor did the Egyptian government ever consider it. Interestingly, only those on the extreme fringes of the opposition ever advocated such a dramatic reversal of Egyptian foreign policy. The rest of the opposition seemed prepared to accept it as a pillar of Egyptian security, or, at the very least, as a fact of life. The pressures which this had generated have, to some degree, been eased by the signing of the Israeli-Palestinian accords and the Israeli withdrawals from the Occupied Territories.

A growing trend accepting the need to come to terms with Israel emerged among the Arab states which had initially ostracised Egypt for signing a peace treaty with Israel. This was encouraged by the Egyptian government as it sought to repair its relations with the rest of the Arab world. Mubarak made plain at the outset, however, that this reconciliation would take place on Egypt's terms. That is, Egypt's treaty with Israel would remain in place and the other Arab states would have to accept it. The very confusion and the dilemmas afflicting much of the rest of the Arab world during the 1980s considerably strengthened the Egyptian argument that the isolation of the most populous and significant of the Arab states made little sense and could only harm Arab interests.

By the late 1980s, therefore, as a result of the growing involvement of Egypt in the search for a settlement of the Palestine question, relations with the PLO and with Jordan were restored. At the same time, a close relationship, founded mainly on military sales and advice, was built up between Egypt and Iraq. These improvements in Egypt's relations with the Arab states were finalised with the re-admission of Egypt to the Arab League in May 1989 and the restoration of formal diplomatic relations even with those Arab states, such as Syria, which had been the fiercest critics of the Egyptian-Israeli treaty.

Ironically, the restoration of Egyptian relations with the Arab states occurred not long before the Arab League was faced with its gravest challenge. The Egyptian government had been concerned for some time by the prospect of Iraq's ambitions and the dangers of its leader's frustrations in the wake of the ending of the war with Iran in 1988. As part of a strategy of reassurance and as a means of moderating the thrust of Iraqi ambition, Egypt had helped to found the Arab Co-operation

Council (ACC) in February 1989. This had brought together Egypt, Iraq, Jordan and Yemen into an arrangement of formal co-operation, ostensibly dedicated to economic goals, but in reality aimed at establishing a form of consultation whereby Egypt might act as a moderating influence on Iraq. Set against the insecurities and ruthlessness of Saddam Hussein, this had little chance of success. When Iraq invaded and annexed Kuwait in August 1990, the ACC virtually ceased to exist, the Arab League was split and Egypt aligned itself with the Gulf states and Syria in vehement condemnation of Iraq's action. Subsequently, Egypt became an active member of the coalition of states which sent forces to Saudi Arabia, first to protect the kingdom and then to drive Iraq from Kuwait by military means, under the terms of the United Nations Security Council resolutions.

Although many in Egypt were disconcerted by a chain of events which led to Arab being pitted in battle against Arab, and which saw the armed forces of Egypt, Syria and Saudi Arabia co-operating with the United States and other Western powers to inflict military defeat on another Arab state, there was little public reaction in Egypt against the policy pursued by the government. On the contrary, the return to Egypt of nearly one million Egyptians who had been working in Iraq added to public resentment of that country's regime, largely because of the stories of the humiliating and brutal treatment which they had received. Equally, the claims made by Saddam Hussein that he was acting in the name of Arabism and of Islam fell largely on deaf ears in Egypt. Few were willing to concede that the actions of his armed forces furthered the cause of Arab nationalism. As far as the Islamic groups in Egypt were concerned, the followers of the Muslim Brotherhood were split between their dislike for Saddam Hussein, their links with Saudi Arabia and their unease at the rapid and massive Western military build-up in the region. The only protest demonstrations in Egypt took place after the war had begun in January 1991. Even then, they were limited either to small opposition parties or to the campuses of universities. The violence which erupted during these demonstrations appears to have been due as much to the over-reaction of the security forces as to the vehemence shown by the demonstrators.

In the aftermath of the liberation of Kuwait, the centrality of Egypt in the Arab world was publicly acknowledged once again. The headquarters of the Arab League returned to Cairo and Egypt's former Minister of Foreign Affairs, Ismat Abd al-Magid, was elected Secretary-General of the organisation. However, this does not signify a reassertion of Egyptian ascendancy in the manner of the 1950s or 1960s. Neither Egypt nor the Arab world itself are in the same situation as they were then and, if anything, state sovereignty is even more jealously guarded by Arab governments than it has ever been. The bold declaration in Damascus in March 1991 that Egypt, together with Syria, would constitute one of the pillars of a future regional security order in the Gulf has since foundered on the realities of inter-Arab politics: the Gulf states did not really want large numbers of soldiers from Egypt and Syria permanently based on their territories. The states involved (Saudi Arabia and its five allies in the Gulf Co-operation Council, as well as Egypt and Syria) still pay lip service to the 'principles' of the Damascus Declaration, but it is now essentially a dead letter.

EGYPT'S FUTURE

The maintenance of national elite and popular consensus, on both domestic and external issues, is one of the major preoccupations of the Egyptian government. The concern of the President is that there are forces at work which may exert sufficient pressure to cause it to fly apart and fragment. This would not only make his position and that of the dominant order less secure, but would also reduce his capacity to formulate policy and exercise leadership. Some of these pressures are visible in the effects of the perennial economic crises or in the activities of those who hold out a radically different, but seductive alternative by using the slogan 'Islam is the solution'. Less visible are the pressures at work within the structures of the state itself. There are conflicts of economic interest between the state administrators and the would-be economic liberalisers when it comes to crucial questions of the distribution of economic power. Similarly, the demand for more open forms of political expression and activity is a challenge to the imagination, as well as to the interests of those who cling to the short-term reassurances of an authoritarian state.

Clearly, President Mubarak and his government are an integral part of this system. The question which arises, therefore, concerns their abilities to deal with the more insidious forms of resistance to a more open political order. The President has succeeded in maintaining the impression that he is no less desirous than some of his principal critics for the establishment of a plural political system. Within limits, this is probably the case. The crucial question, however, is whether the limits on representation, openness and answerability envisaged by the President respond sufficiently to the aspirations of those within the political class who are asking for more. Equally, the effect of economic insecurity on the government's confidence in handling the issue of political liberalisation is of central importance. Much will depend, therefore, on its capacity to extricate the Egyptian economy from its perennial crisis. These are not easy tasks. However, the fact that President Mubarak has managed to foster a measure of consensus within quite flexible limits gives grounds for optimism that a political system is being created which can handle debate, dissent and controversy without throwing its own existence into question.

Charles Tripp

2
THE GULF STATES

LTHOUGH EACH OF THE FIVE Gulf states has its own history and identity, their evolution in the 19th and 20th centuries has been shaped by a number of common political and socio-economic features: their close ties with Britain until the 1960s or 1970s; their relations with Saudi Arabia; the presence of substantial oil deposits within their territories; the fact that (with the exceptions of Bahrain and Oman) the indigenous populations are greatly outnumbered by foreign migrants who form the bulk of the labour force; and that all are dynastic monarchies or principalities – in the case of the United Arab Emirates (UAE) a federation of principalities – in which political power lies within a single family dynasty.

The British connection began in the 19th century and was due principally to Britain's concern 'to keep the route to India safe and open'. In 1820 Britain concluded a treaty of maritime peace with the tribal leaders of Bahrain and the area now roughly corresponding to the UAE. In 1853 the sheikhs signed a Perpetual Maritime Truce and in 1892, largely to counter possible French intrusion, Bahrain and the lower Gulf emirates signed further agreements with Britain under which they agreed to conduct their foreign affairs through the British government.

Kuwait and Qatar, who had not been parties to the earlier treaties, signed similar exclusive agreements with Britain in 1899 and 1916 respectively, largely because of their desire to escape Ottoman and Saudi tutelage. It is important to emphasise that the pre-eminence of what are now the ruling families was only firmly established by their recognition as such by Britain and the authorities in British India.

Between 1892 and the Second World War the British connection kept the Gulf states in semi-isolation from the outside world. After 1945, signs of chafing at British control began to show, especially in Bahrain and Kuwait. In the lower Gulf, the British had created a defence force, the Trucial Oman Levies (later the Trucial Oman Scouts) in 1951; in the 1940s and 1950s Qatar and various members of what are now the UAE were involved in constant frontier disputes, most notoriously with Saudi Arabia over the Buraymi oasis following the discovery of oil in eastern Arabia, and the rulers' desire to maximise territorial claims.

All the Gulf states, except Bahrain, have been involved in disputes with Saudi Arabia, particularly during the Saudi state's expansion after the capture of Riyadh by Abd al-Aziz ibn Saud in 1902. By the end of the 1920s Ibn Saud was in control of Najd, Jabal Shammar and the Hijaz. He had generally been abetted by the British, especially under the Uqayr protocol of 1922, which settled the borders of Kuwait, Iraq and Saudi Arabia much to the disadvantage of Kuwait. In 1929, some of the more zealous members of the *Ikhwan* (*see* page 246) began to see no reason why they should remain confined to the Arabian peninsula. They attacked Transjordan and Iraq (both under Hashemite rule) from Kuwait, whose ruler Sheikh Ahmad al-Sabah was sympathetic because of Ibn Saud's recent territorial aggrandisement and because of the blockade on trade between Kuwait and Najd, imposed by Ibn Saud in 1920. For reasons of British prestige Ibn Saud could not be allowed to invade Kuwait to defeat the rebels. The British worked out a face-saving formula and Kuwait handed over the *Ikhwan* rebel leaders to Ibn Saud after the latter had promised to spare their lives. Thereafter, Ahmad (who ruled from 1921 to 1950) benefited from Saudi support, particularly in his confrontation with the opposition movement of the 1930s.

Saudi interference was also a potent factor in Qatar. The claim to legitimacy of the ruler, Sheikh Abdullah al-Thani (1913-48), was contested by several of his male relatives, who regularly appealed to Ibn Saud. After the alliance with Britain in 1916 Abdullah's position was more secure, but he still paid Ibn Saud a substantial annual sum to guarantee his non-interference. Saudi influence was also apparent in the coup which brought Sheikh Hamad to power in 1972, and in the various territorial disputes between Qatar and Bahrain between the 1950s and the 1980s.

The Trucial States – Abu Dhabi, Ajman, Dubai, Fujaira, Ras al-Khayma, Sharja and Umm al-Qaywayn – had also long been objects of Saudi interest, particularly since Saudi borders with these states were not fixed. Ibn Saud threatened both the Trucial States and Muscat in the late 1920s, succeeding in making some of the region's tribes pay tribute to him, effectively detaching them from their various overlords on the coasts. Much of this activity had to do with oil concessions and struggles between British and US oil companies. After 1945, however, Ibn Saud felt less constrained, especially given Britain's reduced status in the world. In 1949 he claimed some 50,000 square miles of eastern Arabia, much of which was at least theoretically under the control of Abu Dhabi, Oman and Qatar. The Buraymi dispute, as it is known, lasted 25 years, and was over oil. In 1955, Saudi forces were ejected from the Buraymi oasis by British and Trucial States troops and the conflict was eventually resolved in favour of Oman in 1972 and of Abu Dhabi in July 1974. Even since the formation of the Gulf Cooperation Council (GCC) in May 1981 by the five Gulf states and Saudi Arabia, suspicion of Saudi intentions and fear of Saudi domination remains a potent factor in inter-state relations.

The earliest discoveries of oil were made in Bahrain and Kuwait before the Second World War, while Oman only began production in 1967. The oil revenues have resulted in a series of economic booms since the 1950s which, in certain years, produced some of the highest average per capita incomes in the world. Since all the states are what Robert Mabro has termed 'desert-oil' economies (*see* Chapter 17) their opportunities for economic diversification are extremely limited, and much of the 'surplus'

OFFICIAL NAME	The State of Bahrain
AREA	691 sq. km (267 sq. miles)
POPULATION	549,000 *(1994)*
CAPITAL	Manama, population 120,937 *(1991)*
LANGUAGE	Arabic
RELIGION	Sunni Muslim (50%), Shi'i Muslim (50%),
GNP PER CAPITA	US$8,030 *(1993)*

OFFICIAL NAME	The State of Kuwait
AREA	17,818 sq. km (6,880 sq. miles)
POPULATION	1,620,000 *(1994)*
CAPITAL	Kuwait City, population 237,892 *(1993)*
LANGUAGE	Arabic
RELIGION	Sunni Muslim (80%), Shi'i Muslim (20%),
GNP PER CAPITA	US$19,360 *(1993)*

OFFICIAL NAME	The Sultanate of Oman
AREA	271,950 sq. km (105,000 sq. miles)
POPULATION	2,077,000 *(1994)*
CAPITAL	Muscat, population 380,000 *(1990)*
LANGUAGE	Arabic
RELIGION	Ibadi Muslim (75%), Sunni Muslim (25%),
GNP PER CAPITA	US$4,850 *(1993)*

OFFICIAL NAME	The State of Qatar
AREA	11,437 sq. km (4,416 sq. miles)
POPULATION	540,000 *(1994)*
CAPITAL	Doha, population 293,000 *(1990)*
LANGUAGE	Arabic
RELIGION	Sunni Muslim (80%), Shi'i Muslim (20%),
GNP PER CAPITA	US$16,240 *(1992)*

OFFICIAL NAME	The United Arab Emirates
AREA	77,700 sq. km (30,000 sq. miles)
POPULATION	1,861,000 *(1994)*
CAPITAL	Abu Dhabi, population 363,432 *(1989)*
LANGUAGE	Arabic
RELIGION	Sunni Muslim (93%), Shi'i Muslim (7%),
GNP PER CAPITA	US$21,430 *(1993)*

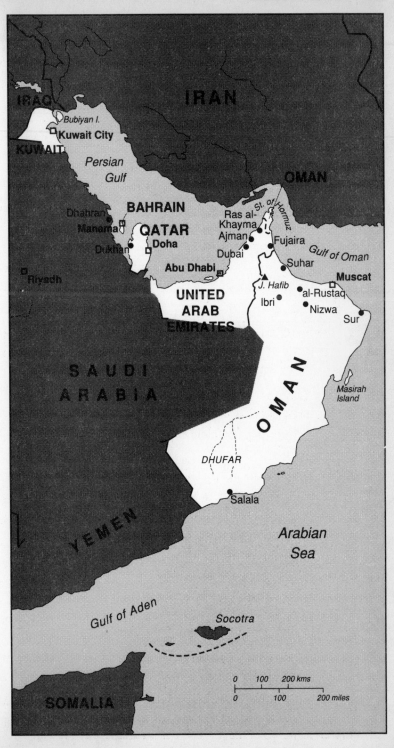

income from oil has been invested abroad. In 1986, for example, Kuwait's overseas investments generated more income than the country's oil revenues. With an eye on the steady fall in oil prices, some states are making efforts to industrialise, mostly in manufacturing petrochemicals and fertilisers. However, the relatively small populations of the states is a permanent difficulty in sustaining balanced economic development.

Labour in most of the states, at all levels, generally comes from abroad. The indigenous populations, many of whom are now highly educated, work as professionals, bureaucrats and supervisors. With few exceptions these expatriate populations have no residence rights and there has been an increasing tendency to employ non-Arabs, generally Indians, Pakistanis, Bangladeshis and Koreans on short-term contracts.

Finally, all the Gulf states, including the UAE, are ruled by extended families in what is assumed to be a 'traditional' fashion. In fact, in the same way that the pre-eminence of the present ruling families derives largely from their recognition by Britain, the form of government in the Gulf today is also a recent invention. Hereditary absolute rule was never a part of Arab tribal tradition, since there were constant challenges to the leader's authority.

By the late 1960s all the Gulf states were producing greater or lesser quantities of oil. Kuwait had become independent of Britain in 1961, but the other states still had their British advisers. In January 1968, as part of a general run-down of its overseas commitments, Britain announced its intention to leave the Gulf by the end of 1971. This caused consternation to the rulers, who felt vulnerable both to the rhetoric of Arab nationalism and anti-imperialism and to some form of takeover by one or other of their powerful neighbours (Iran, Iraq or Saudi Arabia). Some rulers even offered to pay Britain to continue to defend them, but eventually the Trucial States, and, initially, Bahrain and Qatar, formed a federation around Abu Dhabi and Dubai. However, when Iran finally dropped its claim to Bahrain in May 1970, Bahrain lost interest in a wider federation, and Qatar, which had strong ties to Dubai but a history of animosity towards Abu Dhabi, also decided not to join. The two became independent entities in 1971. The UAE came into being in December 1971. It consisted initially of six of the former Trucial States, and was joined by Ras al-Khayma in February 1972. After a long period of isolation from the world under Sheikh Said, Oman began to assume something like its present form in 1970, after a coup facilitated (though not carried out) by British officials, in which the sultan was replaced by his son Qabus. Oman joined the Arab league and the United Nations in 1971.

After Britain left the Gulf in the 1970s, the US attempted to build Saudi Arabia and Iran into strong, well-armed client states able to resist the perceived threat of Soviet influence and, perhaps more realistically, the threat from supposedly radical Arab regimes. This policy was abruptly terminated in 1978-79 with the events leading to the overthrow of the Shah of Iran, after which the US was obliged to rely on Saudi Arabia, and, increasingly, Iraq. Saddam Hussein's desire to replace Iran as the US's gendarme in the

Gulf was certainly sincere, but his ill-judged invasion of Iran in 1980 effectively thwarted his ambitions.

In May 1981, in response to pressures brought about by the Iran-Iraq war, the five Gulf States and Saudi Arabia formed the GCC. However, the GCC has made little progress towards economic, political or military co-operation. There is no coherent plan for arms procurement and no planned compatibility between the defence systems of members. The member states evidently put more faith in the US than in themselves or each other for defence against external aggression, while their political and administrative organisation is too autocratic to permit much in the way of co-operation. However, in spite of their superficial similarities, political, social and economic, the states exhibit a number of distinctive, differentiating features.

BAHRAIN

Bahrain, like Kuwait, is socially and economically advanced. Neither was isolated in the way that Abu Dhabi was under Shakhbut (1928-66) or Oman under Said (1932-70). Both began to export oil earlier than their neighbours and invested the proceeds in social and educational services. In Bahrain, the al-Khalifa family, members of the Utub tribe originally based in the Qatar peninsula, expelled their Iranian rulers at the end of the 18th century. They signed treaties with Britain in 1820 and 1862 in return for British protection, mainly against Iran's claims. The present ruler, Sheikh Issa, succeeded his father in 1961.

Although the ruling family is wary of any form of power-sharing, there have been various constitutional experiments. A national assembly was introduced in 1973, but dissolved in 1975 when labour unrest provoked widespread anti-government demonstrations. In January 1983 a 30-member appointed consultative council came into being; trade unions and political parties have been banned since 1985. Bahrain has been connected to Saudi Arabia by a 25 km (15.5 mile) causeway since 1986 and its relaxed atmosphere attracts many tourists from neighbouring states.

By 1991 Bahrain's oil and gas resources had begun to diminish considerably. Efforts have been made to diversify: the world's largest aluminium smelter went into production in 1972; a major dry dock was constructed in 1977; and Bahrain also produces iron pellets, paints and pharmaceuticals. It has a stock exchange and functions as an off-shore banking centre, although this has been adversely affected by the general centralisation of world banking since the mid-1980s and by the Gulf War.

Recent years have seen a general down-turn in the economy and relatively high levels of unemployment among the indigenous population. In late-1994 there was serious rioting in the capital, Manama, and the Saudis sent 4,000 National Guard to restore order. These disturbances, officially alleged to be of Iranian instigation, continued in the spring of 1995, with calls for the restoration of parliament and the removal of the unpopular British security chief.

KUWAIT

In 1899 Sheikh Mubarak al-Sabah (1896–1915) signed an exclusive agreement with Britain, prefering British protection to increasingly vigorous Ottoman control. The al-Sabah family had come to power in the mid-18th century, tracing its origins to the Bani Utub, the tribe which also provided the rulers of Bahrain. Kuwait was a moderately prosperous trading centre before the discovery of oil, with an economy based on pearling, ship building and entrepôt trade. At this time the power of the al-Sabahs was by no means absolute, since their income (from taxes on commerce) was dependent on the merchants, who could and did migrate to other parts of the Gulf if the rulers leaned too heavily upon them. The give and take of authority which this encouraged ended with the discovery of oil. In addition, there was a degree of rivalry within the ruling family: Mubarak had two sons, Jabir, who succeeded him between 1915-17 and Salim, who ruled from 1917 until his death in 1921. The succession was then contested between Ahmad, son of Jabir, and Abdullah, son of Salim. Ahmad succeeded, ruling until his death in 1950, when Abdullah took over until 1965. This rivalry produced a degree of factionalism which the opposition, anxious to curb the power of the Sabah family, could exploit. A group of leading merchants organised an opposition movement in 1938, and set up an assembly that lasted six months before being dissolved by Ahmad al-Sabah with the tacit encouragement of Britain.

During the 1940s and 1950s the al-Sabah gradually consolidated their hold on the state, acquiring huge tracts of land on the then outskirts of Kuwait city. Oil revenues rose dramatically, from less than $1 million in 1946 to $16 million in 1950. In the 1950s opposition to Kuwait's close ties with Britain grew. The connection was formally terminated in 1961, followed, almost immediately, by one of Iraq's periodic claims on Kuwait. British forces briefly returned, but were soon replaced by those of the Arab League. A national assembly was elected in January 1963.

In the 1960s and 1970s Kuwait's wealth soared, and by 1980 its GNP per head was third in the world, surpassed only by Qatar and the UAE. Much of the proceeds were invested abroad as well as being used to fund aid programmes in Egypt, Jordan and Syria after the Six Day War, and various Palestinian organisations. Kuwait further increased its credibility among Arab radicals by leading a movement to reduce oil output after the war of 1973. In 1977, shortly after the accession of the present ruler, Jabir, the state took over the national oil company; in 1982 the company expanded its operations in Europe, taking over hundreds of Q8 petrol stations.

Inevitably, the Iranian Revolution had repercussions in Kuwait. An estimated 30 per cent of the population are Shi'is; there were ten Shi'is in the 50-member national assembly of 1975. Events in Iran set off a wave of religious opposition, both Sunni and Shi'i, to the corruption and ostentation of the Kuwaiti regime. In December 1983 a series of car bombs, traced to al-Da'wa, an Iraqi religious opposition group based in Tehran, caused several deaths and serious injuries. In May 1985 there was a failed attempt to assassinate Jabir.

Such incidents encouraged the ruling family to construct a powerful security apparatus. In July 1986 the national assembly was dissolved, after its increasing criticism of the government and individuals involved in the 1982 stock market crash. Early in 1987, when oil tankers in the Gulf were threatened by mines and bombs, Kuwait approached the US, the Soviet Union, and the USA again – which then responded with greater alacrity – for protection, which took the form of reflagging Kuwait tankers with US flags. This aroused much public opposition in Kuwait.

The cease-fire in August 1988 brought a respite, and it seemed that relations with Iran and Iraq would improve. In June 1990 slightly over half the electorate voted for a 50-member national council; in July OPEC met at Geneva and apparently settled disputes about over-production for which Kuwait and other Gulf states had been blamed. On 2 August Iraq invaded Kuwait, taking the state completely by surprise. The Iraqi occupation, which lasted eight months, was clearly a massive miscalculation on Saddam Hussein's part, particularly that those opposed to the al-Sabah family would welcome the invaders. By October 1990, 60 per cent of the population (Kuwaiti and expatriate), about 1.3 million people, had left the country, and most of the ruling family had fled to Saudi Arabia.

The Iraqis left Kuwait in February 1991. Substantial amounts of money were revealed to have been 'lost' immediately before and during the war, and a member of the ruling family was accused of embezzlement, fanning the flames of a pro-democracy movement. Those who had sat out the war in Kuwait resented the fact that the rulers had fled. In October 1992 a 50-man national assembly was elected (by slightly over half an electorate of 81,400 males), in which 35 members could be identified with the opposition. However, the government's human rights record since 1991 has not been impressive, and it is evidently apprehensive about permitting the expression of dissent. The Iraqi threat is regularly held up as a rallying cry for national solidarity, but calls for greater accountability and criticisms of government mismanagement continue to be heard.

OMAN

Oman, the largest Gulf state, has the longest history as a political entity. Its history is distinctive, largely because of the introduction of Ibadism (a form of Islam) in the latter part of the 7th century. Ibadism is tolerant towards other forms of Islam, but its survival in Oman has been reinforced by its confinement to the interior of the country, surrounded by Sunni and Shi'i settlements on the coasts. The present dynasty, the Al Bu Said, acquired the Ibadi imamate by election in the late 1740s; the dynasty's founder had expelled Persian invaders from Suhar and Muscat in 1744.

Early in the 19th century two major political developments took place. Firstly, the Ibadi imamate was divided between the imamate and the sultanate, the former controlling the interior of the country based either at al-Rustaq or Nizwa, the latter acting as temporal ruler from headquarters at Muscat on the coast. Secondly, the rulers of Oman increasingly turned their attention to East Africa, especially Zanzibar, where the dynasty was based in the mid-19th century. British arbitration divided Oman's African and Arabian dominions, although various claimants fought each other for control of what is now Oman for much of the rest of the century. Britain consolidated its influence by an exclusive treaty signed in 1891.

In 1913 the election of a new and vigorous imam brought new conflict between imamate and sultanate (the latter supported by the British). In January 1915 the imamate troops unsuccessfully attacked Muscat. A de facto division of the country was formalised under the British-brokered Treaty of Sib in 1920, which essentially recognised the autonomy of the interior. Britain also obliged the sultanate to accept a financial adviser and a regular military force in 1921. Taymur ibn Faysal was sultan between 1913–1932, when he abdicated in favour of his son Said.

At first Said seemed a dynamic and capable ruler, tightening his influence over the areas controlled by the sultanate and attempting, in the mid-1940s, to exert control over the area controlled by the imamate. However, he was unable to move decisively until the death of Imam Muhammad ibn Abdullah al-Khalili in 1954, when Said sent his forces into the interior and routed those of the new imam. With the beginnings of oil exploration the conflict was now between a set of strange bedfellows: Britain, Petroleum Development Oman and the sultanate on the one hand, and the imamate, Saudi Arabia and the Arab nationalists on the other. In 1955 the (British-officered) Trucial Oman Scouts expelled the Saudis from Buraymi. The forces of the imamate were eventually defeated in 1959, and the opposition took refuge in Saudi Arabia.

In 1958 Said had left Muscat for the greater freedom of Salala, the port of the southern province of Dhufar, where he remained until overthrown in July 1970. However, in 1962 much of Dhufar joined in an armed uprising against him, which was only put down by his son Qabus in 1975. It is curious that this rebellion, which took place in one of the most remote and least developed parts of the Arab world, should have adopted a Marxist-Leninist ideology, a Guevarist strategy and have attracted support from the Soviet Union, China and Iraq.

The most important aspect of the rebellion was its threat to the development of Omani oil. Said's obstinacy and his unwillingness to delegate led to his deposition in 1970 in favour of Qabus, under whom power has been centralised to an extreme degree, even by local standards. The sultan is prime minister and minister of defence, foreign affairs and finance. For a brief period (August 1970-December 1971) Qabus' uncle, Tariq ibn Taymur, served as prime minister, but the two could not work together and Tariq resigned. Although Qabus is clearly more dynamic and outward-looking than his father, he has retained much of his father's autocratic style. There is a consultative council, but its powers are even less significant than those of similar bodies in other Gulf states. One distinctive aspect of the political situation is that Qabus has no children, has divorced and not re-married, and has not named an heir.

The oil sector, on which much of state revenues are based, is fairly buoyant, although Oman is a small producer and has modest reserves. A series of development plans have allocated substantial sums to education, health and subsidised housing. Oman is on reasonable terms with its immediate neighbours, although difficulties have frequently arisen because the country's borders are not clearly demarcated. There have been disputes with Ras al-Khayma (Oman has an enclave on the Musandam peninsula) and more serious tensions with Yemen both before and after Yemeni unification in 1992 and during the Yemeni civil war in 1993-94. Soon after his accession Qabus made peace with the Saudis, following uneasy relations through most of his father's reign. Although a founder member of the GCC, Qabus has always been lukewarm about suggestions of joint defence, and, with Kuwait, was not party to the Gulf Security pact signed by other GCC members in November 1994.

Opposition to Qabus' close ties with his British and US advisers, the extreme centralisation of power and blatant corruption and nepotism may have been one of the reasons for a wave of Islamist activity in 1994 and 1995, compounded by a downturn in the economy resulting from falling oil prices. The fact that Qabus' father and the British effectively ended the Ibadi imamate in 1959 means that Qabus' own legitimacy can always be questioned, especially in a society where tribal loyalties still exercise considerable influence. As in many other states in the region, regime continuity is not necessarily synonymous with stability.

QATAR

Qatar was a dependency of Bahrain until the mid-19th century, becoming independent after an series of battles in 1867 and 1868. In 1868 the British signed a treaty with the ruler, Muhammad al-Thani, similar to those with the other sheikhdoms. His successor Qasim (1876-1913) wavered between Britain and the Ottomans, who had occupied Hasa (roughly the area between Kuwait and Qatar) in 1871. In 1913, Hasa was taken by the Saudis, and in 1916 Qasim's son and successor Abdullah (1913-49) signed a more binding treaty with Britain.

Before the discovery of oil Qatar was extremely poor; its population lived mainly from the proceeds of pearling. Qatar was particularly vulnerable to Saudi designs and there were many within the ruling family who were quick to appeal to Ibn Saud. The oil concession with Anglo-Persian was signed in 1935, but operations stopped between 1942 and 1949 and there were no significant revenues until the mid-1950s. In 1949 in-fighting over the sharing of oil revenues among the ruling family forced Abdullah to abdicate in favour of his son Ali. Britain oversaw these arrangements and obliged Ali to accept a British Political Officer.

Succession troubles continued. Ali (1949-60) was forced to abdicate, as was his successor Ahmad (1960-72), and Ahmad's successor, Khalifa, in June 1995. There is much conflict among the numerous ruling family (especially at a time of shrinking oil revenues), all of whom consider themselves entitled to stipends. Another factor in Ahmad's deposition was his advocacy of Qatari membership of the UAE. In fact, by the mid-1960s Ahmad had effectively handed over the day-to-day running of the country to his cousin Khalifa. Khalifa regularised the budget and spent considerable amounts on social services and education. By the early 1990s, in the aftermath of the invasion of Kuwait, Khalifa seemed content to let his son Hamad (nominated Crown Prince in 1977) take increasing control until Khalifa himself was eventually ousted by Hamad in 1995.

Qatar's foreign policy has earned it something of a maverick reputation. It enjoys reasonably good relations with Iran and reopened its embassy in Baghdad at the end of 1993. Qatar became the first Middle Eastern oil state to sign an agreement, in the autumn of 1995, to supply natural gas to Israel and was also quick to re-establish relations with the PLO, recognising Palestinian authority in Gaza and Jericho. This independent line is probably a result of Qatar's desire to gain allies in its border conflicts with Saudi Arabia and Bahrain.

UNITED ARAB EMIRATES

In 1971, at the time of Britain's departure from the Gulf, the former Trucial States of Abu Dhabi, Ajman, Dubai, Fujaira, Ras al-Khayma, Sharja and Umm al-Qaywayn combined to form the UAE. Abu Dhabi dominates, accounting for 86 per cent of the surface area, 41 per cent of the population and 70 per cent of oil production. Dubai is the site of the federation's main commercial port and has 38 per cent of the population and produces 29 per cent of UAE oil, the remaining one per cent coming from Sharja; small deposits have also been found in other emirates. The UAE also produces large quantities of natural gas.

Branches of the Qawasim (al-Qasim) family rule Sharja and Ras al-Khayma, and two clans of the Bani Yas rule Dubai and Abu Dhabi. Relations between and among the families have never been particularly harmonious, but since the foundation of the UAE outstanding border disputes have been resolved and a modus vivendi achieved. Nevertheless, six rulers continue to exercise independent control over parts of an area slightly smaller than Portugal – mostly uninhabited – and meaningful political integration has some distance to go.

From the 1970s to the mid-1980s, the emirates entered an era of unparalleled affluence. In 1980 oil income amounted to $19 billion; in 1985, $11 billion; in 1988, $7 billion and in 1991, $14 billion. The fluctuations of the 1980s and 1990s inculcated a sense of realism and pragmatism, although the emirates' oil reserves are extensive and there is no question of the oil running out in the foreseeable future. The UAE contributed generously to the PLO and the 'front line states' in the 1970s and 1980s, and to Iraq in the Iran-Iraq war, although contributions were reduced after falling oil prices in 1984. The UAE was a founder member of the GCC in 1981, and seems to favour keeping it as loose an association as possible. The UAE is involved in a long-standing dispute with Iran over sovereignty of Abu Musa and the two Tunb islands in the Gulf, but has generally acquiesced in de facto Iranian occupation since 1970.

After the invasion of Kuwait, in line with its neighbours, the UAE continues to be dependent on the US for external security; in 1993 the US association of electronic industries estimated that the Gulf States and Saudi Arabia would spend $93 billion on armaments over the next five years.

In terms of domestic politics, the federation has a council of rulers and a council of ministers, as well as a 40-member national assembly. Internal dissent, quite lively during the 1980s, has been more cautious since the invasion of Kuwait. The extent to which any loosening of autocracy will be demanded or allowed will be determined by developments in Saudi Arabia, and perhaps – although economic interests will almost certainly maintain the upper hand – by pressure for change from the US and the West. The fact that a considerable sharing of oil wealth has been necessary to secure domestic peace has made calls for greater democracy more muted in the UAE than in some neighbouring states.

Peter Sluglett and Marion Farouk-Sluglett

3
IRAN

IRAN (FORMERLY PERSIA) is an ancient country that has formed several empires in the past two-and-a-half millennia. In the 7th century AD the Muslim Conquest broke up the Sassanian Empire and brought Islam to Iran. Later, the loosening of the caliphate in Baghdad led to the creation of a number of autonomous kingdoms, followed by the formation of various Turkic and Mongol empires by invaders from central and east Asia. In the 16th century the country was once again reunited through the creation of the Safavid Empire, which established Shi'i Islam as Iran's official religion. The fall of the Safavid Empire early in the 18th century led to turmoil and disintegration which – except for a brief period under the Zand dynasty – continued until the end of the century when the Qajar state was established. In the 19th century, the rise of industry and empire in Europe exposed Iran's weaknesses vis-à-vis the European powers. It led to loss of territory to Russia and the growing domination of the country by European powers in general, Russia and Britain in particular. Attempts at partial reforms within the traditional framework having failed, attention was increasingly drawn to the possibility of drastic action for political and economic development. This led to the Constitutional Revolution at the beginning of the 20th century.

THE CONSTITUTIONAL REVOLUTION
The Constitutional Revolution of 1905-11 was a product of many factors. The rise of industry and empire in 19th-century Europe had provided a mirror against which Iranian political and economic backwardness could be critically examined. At the same time, it had supplied a model for political modernisation and economic progress. The revolution had had a successful prelude in the Tobacco Rebellion of 1891-92 when, for the first time in Iranian history, an organised popular campaign forced an arbitrary monarch to retract an important state decision.

The central aim and objective of the revolutionary movement was the abolition of arbitrary rule (*estabdad*), and the establishment of the rule of law. Inevitably, however, this led to further demands for the granting of a written constitution to limit the powers of the monarch and lead to a form of parliamentary government. Almost all urban social classes were represented in the revolution, including merchants, religious leaders and preachers, urban-dwelling absentee landlords, notables of the bureaucracy, and intellectuals, with landlords and notables emerging as the main beneficiaries of its successful outcome. Nationalist, modernist and liberal ideas were represented by the intellectuals, but these remained

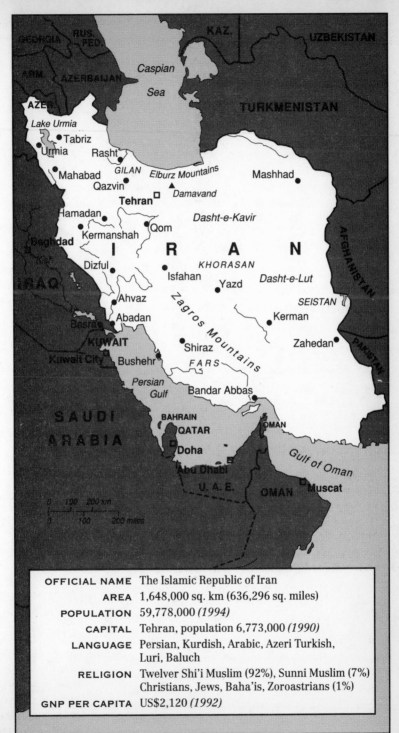

OFFICIAL NAME	The Islamic Republic of Iran
AREA	1,648,000 sq. km (636,296 sq. miles)
POPULATION	59,778,000 *(1994)*
CAPITAL	Tehran, population 6,773,000 *(1990)*
LANGUAGE	Persian, Kurdish, Arabic, Azeri Turkish, Luri, Baluch
RELIGION	Twelver Shi'i Muslim (92%), Sunni Muslim (7%) Christians, Jews, Baha'is, Zoroastrians (1%)
GNP PER CAPITA	US$2,120 *(1992)*

strictly on the sidelines, until later developments led to their emergence and domination of Iranian politics for decades to come. The constitution (together with its supplementary articles) was an essentially secular document modelled mainly on the Belgian constitution, although it declared Shi'i Islam the state religion and provided a mechanism for the vetting of parliamentary legislation by the religious authorities.

THE FIRST WORLD WAR

The revolution ended traditional arbitrary rule, strengthening private property in land and merchant capital; but it achieved little else. Iraq was still poor and backward, its politicians far from united, and foreign imperial influence was still strong. In 1911, a Russian ultimatum forced the government to dissolve parliament, which was resisting a Russian demand for the dismissal of the American financial adviser, Morgan Shuster.

The First World War brought greater chaos and political disintegration. While the central government remained neutral, some of the more radical democratic and nationalist politicians were in favour of siding with the Central Powers. This eventually led to the formation of Nezam al-Saltaneh's provisional government in Kermanshah, which existed side by side with the central government in Tehran, but declared war on the Allies. Meanwhile, various northern, western and southern provinces were occupied by Russian, Turkish and British forces, and German agents intensified their activities especially among the central and southern nomadic tribes. At the same time, a group of younger constitutionalists, led by Kuchik Khan, began a guerrilla campaign in the Caspian province of Gilan with the aim of achieving full independence and democratic government for the whole of Iran.

AFTER THE WAR

The Russian Revolution and the end of the First World War introduced new factors to an already complex socio-political situation. The Bolsheviks renounced Tsarist concessions and ambitions in Iran, but at the same time encouraged dissent among Iranian socialists and nationalists, especially in the northern provinces. Britain emerged as the sole foreign power in Iran, appearing to democrats and nationalists as a domineering imperialist power, to conservatives as the country's potential saviour from domestic chaos and the threat of Bolshevism. There were British (or British-led) forces in the provinces of Fars, Khorasan and Gilan. The forces in Khorasan and Gilan were initially intended to contain possible German and Turkish drives southwards, but those in Gilan later brushed with the Bolsheviks and were then concentrated in Qazvin as a deterrent against a thrust by Kuchik Khan who had reluctantly entered an alliance with (Russian-backed) Iranian Bolsheviks in the Soviet Socialist Republic of Gilan. The situation demanded a strong government and, in 1918, Vusuq al-Dowleh became prime minister.

In August 1919, Vusuq's cabinet entered an agreement with Britain. This provided for the reform and reorganisation of the Iranian army, administration and finance under the supervision of British advisers – employed and paid by the Iranian government – against a British loan of £2 million, to be repaid over 20 years at a seven per cent annual rate of interest. The agreement (the brain-child of Lord Curzon, the British foreign secretary) was given an almost completely hostile reception by the Iranian political public. It was viewed as no less than an attempt by Britain to turn Iran into its protectorate, a sentiment that was intensified when it became known that the ministers who had negotiated it had received a certain sum from Britain for which no public account was available. It was decided to submit the agreement to parliament for ratification after the general election. But Vusuq's cabinet fell in July 1920, and the agreement was already a dead letter when it was abrogated by Sayyed Zia's government early in 1921.

THE 1921 COUP

On 21 February 1921 the Iran Cossack force stationed near Qazvin occupied Tehran, arrested a number of politicians of all colours and persuasions, and declared martial law. The coup was jointly led by Sayyed Zia al-Din Tabataba'i and Brigadier Reza Khan. Sayyed Zia, who became prime minister, was an ambitious journalist with well-known ties with the British legation in Tehran. Reza Khan, now commander of the Cossack Division, was an officer from humble origins who had risen from the ranks. The British Foreign Office had no knowledge of the coup before the event, though some British military and diplomatic officers in Iran had a hand in encouraging and/or organising it. This was the beginning of a new era in Iranian politics, for all that it took a few years for the full implications of the event to be assimilated.

Sayyed Zia's government proved impermanent, though Reza Khan played an increasingly important role, first as minister of war and then as prime minister. He managed to divide the opposition of old-school politicians, attract sufficient support from nationalists and modernists, and suggest himself to both Britain and the Soviet Union as Iran's only effective leader. The military forces were expanded, reorganised and turned into a uniform body. Regional political, ethnic and nomadic unrest was largely subdued. Sheikh Khazal's semi-autonomous role in Khuzistan was ended. Meanwhile, press freedom began to be curbed, the military tended to dominate political life, especially in the provinces, and the parliamentary majority swung behind Reza Khan for both genuine and opportunistic reasons. The parliamentary opposition was led by Sayyed Hasan Modarres, supported by a number of independent deputies, the most significant among whom was Muhammad Mosaddeq.

Having become prime minister as well as commander-in-chief of the armed forces, Reza Khan decided to depose the ruling Qajar dynasty and place himself permanently at the helm. At first, his military and civilian supporters led a campaign for the declaration of a republic. The attempt failed: many feared the rise of a dictatorship while the religious establishment was anxious that Reza Khan was planning a wholly secular state. Having allayed the fears of the religious authorities, Reza Khan and his supporters then moved to bring down the Qajars and establish the Pahlavi dynasty. This was done by a vote in parliament in October 1925 and ratified by a special constituent assembly early in 1926.

IRAN UNDER REZA SHAH

The outlook and objectives of Reza Shah (formerly Reza Khan) and his lieutenants was to centralise and modernise Iran along Western European models. Legal and administrative reforms were effected, roads and railways constructed, cities modernised, education expanded and industrial plants purchased and installed. However, three fundamental issues were ignored in the process: the need to reconcile modern values with Iranian culture and civilisation; the necessity of land reform to avoid the creation of an increasingly dualistic society; and the importance of political development for social and economic progress. Indeed, in the realms of politics there was retrogression, with the Shah increasingly assuming dictatorial and, later, arbitrary powers, ridding himself of his advisers and creating an over-centralised state which tended to suppress regional and ethnic differences. The compulsory wearing of European hats by men, for example, and the ban on veils for women – which led to revolt and bloodshed in the holy city of Mashad – were twin instances of Reza Shah's dictatorial embrace of Western values. While imposing himself in this idiosyncratically modernising manner, Reza Shah, whatever his insistence on absolute probity in public life, neglected few opportunities to raid the public purse or to appropriate private property, in the process amassing a huge fortune and alienating his unfortunate people still further.

Oil exports from Iran began in earnest during the First World War and rapidly became an important factor in politics. From the 1920s there were disagreements with the Anglo-Persian (later Anglo-Iranian) Oil Company over the terms of the 1901 D'Arcy oil concession. Protracted negotiations failed to resolve the problem until 1932, when the Shah ordered the unilateral abrogation of the concession. The British government, which owned 51 per cent of the company's shares, took the dispute to the League of Nations, but the conflict was later resolved with the conclusion of the ill-fated 1933 Oil Agreement, which extended the concessionary period by a further 30 years. This led to charges of 'treason' in the 1940s when the agreement's ex-officio signatory, Sayyed Hasan Taqizadeh, publicly declared that he had signed it under duress.

With the rise of Nazi Germany, Reza Shah began to develop and extend Iran's economic and political relations with that country. Germany was viewed as an important countervailing power to both Britain and the Soviet Union. Further, Nazi propaganda about the superiority of the Aryan race found an enthusiastic audience in (Aryan) Iran. Germany enjoyed the additional advantage of having never attempted to impose itself imperially in Iran, unlike both Britain and the Soviet Union. In consequence, though Iran remained neutral in the Second World War, its sympathy for Germany was clear.

WAR AND AFTER

In August 1941, the Anglo-Soviet allies invaded Iran from the north and west. For some time they had been warning Iran against the activities of 'German agents' in the country. But the invasion is more likely to have been due to a fear of a possible German drive through the Caucasus, the need to protect Britain's oil supplies and the importance of the trans-Iranian railways in sending supplies to the Soviet Union. The Shah first ordered military resistance to the invasion, but called it off quickly and agreed to co-operate with the Allies. However, it soon became apparent that there could be no settlement so long as he remained on the throne. Reza Shah abdicated in favour of his son, Muhammad Reza, and was taken to Mauritius. He later went to Johannesburg where he died in 1944.

The Allies did not take over the administration of the country and agreed to withdraw their troops when the war ended, although it was clear that their needs were not open to negotiation with the new Iranian government. The devaluation of the rial, coupled with administrative ineptitude and Allied demands for Iranian goods and services, led to high inflation, shortage of basic goods and the threat of famine. Meanwhile, parliamentary government was restored, press censorship was lifted and organised political activity once again became possible. The Tudeh party was formed by a combination of Marxists and (old as well as new) democrats and socialists, although its leadership and activists were dominated by Marxist elements. Its original programme was the promotion of parliamentary government, social reform and redistribution of income. By 1950, however (after the split in its ranks of 1948 and its official banning in 1949), it had become a fully fledged communist party.

The decade 1941 to 1951 was marked by instability and disorder. Cabinets were short-lived; nomadic power had been largely restored; centrifugal ethnic and regional forces were rekindled. The parliament tended to enjoy excessive powers relative to the executive. It was dominated by landlords and provincial magistrates, but it lacked a mechanism (such as large and lasting parliamentary parties) that would result in durable parliamentary alliances, and hence durable governments. Press freedom was at times excessive, resulting in licentious behaviour. It was the product of lack of political development at a time when the authority of an all-powerful state had been lifted.

In September 1944, while Soviet troops were still in Iran, the Soviet Union formally demanded a concession for the exploration and exploitation of northern Iran's oil. Neither the government of Muhammad Sa'ed nor the conservative parliamentary majority were in favour of granting such a concession, though they were concerned about the consequences of its outright rejection. Yet though the Tudeh party and its parliamentary deputies were caught in a dilemma they eventually threw their weight behind the Soviet demand. Muhammad Mosaddeq seized the opportunity, and as a popular and non-partisan deputy with a firm reputation for opposing dictatorship as well as foreign dependence, he launched a campaign against the granting of the proposed concession. He put forward his policy of 'passive balance', which proposed both that Iran should not give new concessions to foreign powers and that it should attempt to remove existing ones. This was to become the theoretical basis for the nationalisation of Iran's oil six years later. Mosaddeq further managed to pass a parliamentary bill that laid down that the government could not give any concession to foreigners without the approval of parliament. This act enabled the following parliament to reject Ahmad Qavan's oil concession to the Soviet Union, granted as a part of his policy to resolve the Azerbaijan crisis.

Late in 1945 the Democratic party of Azerbaijan, led by Sayyed Ja'far Pishevari – an old-style communist – seized power in that province and declared autonomy. The people of Azerbaijan had many grievances against the central government's attitude and policy towards them under Reza Shah, whose abdication made it possible for them to be aired. But the movement quickly fell into the hands of the Democratic party of Azerbaijan, itself being manipulated by the Soviet authorities whose ultimate aim was the integration of the Iranian province into the Azerbaijan Soviet Republic. The province was still under Soviet occupation, and the successive governments of Mohsen Sadr and Ebrahim Hakimi were unable to cope with the situation.

In January 1946 Ahmad Qavan became prime minister, with Soviet backing, in the hope of resolving the crisis. He brought the Tudeh party (who backed the Azerbaijan movement) into his cabinet for a short but crucial period, visited Moscow where he negotiated with the Soviet government, and tried to enlist the United Nations (UN) to persuade Russia to withdraw its troops from Iran. Whether or not the American government delivered a secret ultimatum to the Soviet Union is a matter for historical disagreement, but Qavan's negotiations with the Soviet ambassador in Tehran finally led to an agreement which effectively exchanged the Soviet withdrawal from Azerbaijan for the promise of north Iran's oil concession to the Soviet Union, a promise later rejected by parliament. The Iranian army was then sent to Azerbaijan. The Democrats were defeated, and the Kurdish republic of Mahabad, which had meanwhile been set up in the neighbouring province of Kurdistan, was also overthrown.

OIL NATIONALISATION

With successive waves of labour unrest in the southern Iranian oil fields, growing public attention was drawn to Iranian grievances against the Anglo-Iranian Oil Company (AIOC), and the 1933 Oil Agreement. Early in 1949, negotiations between the Iranian government and the AIOC management led to the Gass-Golsha'iyan (Supplemental) Agreement, which proposed a number of amendments to the existing (1933) agreement. This was regarded as inadequate, and was met with a small but vociferous opposition in parliament, led by Mozaffar Baqa'i and Hosain Makki, who began to attract widespread popular support outside the Assembly. This was towards the end of the parliamentary session, and the campaign for the next general election began soon afterwards.

Mosaddeq emerged as leader of the popular movement and stood as a candidate for Tehran. In the following months the National Front (NF), a coalition of democratic and nationalist parties and personalities, was formed, and sent eight deputies to parliament. Mosaddeq became leader of the opposition and the NF demanded the nationalisation of Iranian oil. The government of General Ali Razmara – a gifted and ambitious soldier politician – wished to pass the Gass-Golsha'iyan Agreement through parliament, but parliament set up an oil committee, chaired by Mosaddeq, to report on the proposed agreement. In March 1951 Razmara was assassinated by a member of the Feda'iyan'e Islam, although there is a strong belief that the royal court was also implicated. This event was quickly followed by the parliamentary approval of Mosaddeq's oil nationalisation bill, and in April 1951 (following a short-term caretaker government), Mosaddeq was elected prime minister.

It is now clear why agreement between Mosaddeq and AIOC would have been impossible as long as both parties remained committed to their basic aims, as they in fact did. Mosaddeq was prepared to compensate the AIOC, but he was determined not to grant a new concession to it or any other foreign company. The AIOC, on the other hand, would not consider any compensation short of a new agreement that would once again enable it to produce and market Iran's oil. That is why from the very beginning Britain's effort was directed towards the removal of Mosaddeq's government. At first, Mosaddeq enjoyed a certain sympathy from President Truman's government. But later, under Eisenhower, British and American attitudes began to converge, and this eventually led to the coup d'état of August 1953. Early in 1952, Mosaddeq made the mistake of turning down the World Bank's offer of mediation in the oil dispute, primarily for fear of appearing to substantiate Tudeh party accusations that he was an American puppet.

The export and sale of Iran's oil having been boycotted by the world's major oil companies, Mosaddeq faced a difficult economic problem. He obtained delegated powers from parliament that enabled him to enact important laws to run for six months before being submitted to parliament. Later, the period was extended by a further year, although not without some vocal opposition. Britain took the oil dispute first to the UN Security Council, then to the International Court at The Hague. On both occasions Iran's argument that the matter was in the jurisdiction of Iranian courts carried the day.

At first the Tudeh party labelled Mosaddeq as an American agent who wished to replace the AIOC with American oil companies. This attitude was somewhat modified later, but the party remained in opposition throughout Mosaddeq's government. Both the Shah and the conservative opposition were unhappy about Mosaddeq's oil policy as well as his attitude to domestic political relations. The Shah was especially offended by Mosaddeq's slogan that 'in a democracy, the Shah must reign, not rule'. In July 1952, Mosaddeq suggested to the Shah that the latter should not appoint the minister of defence but should let the ministry be 'supervised' by Mosaddeq himself. The Shah disagreed, and Mosaddeq resigned. Ahmad Qavan became prime minister, but his threats against political unrest in a radio broadcast angered the public. There was a general strike, which led to bloodshed. Qavan resigned and Mosaddeq returned to office.

Further developments led to a split in the leadership of the Popular Movement (PM). The disagreements – led by Ayatollah Kashani and Mozaffar Baqa'i – were the result more of personality problems than policy differences. They were nevertheless damaging to Mosaddeq both at home and abroad. Meanwhile, Mosaddeq's policy of cuts in defence expenditure, and his retirement of some top army officers on charges of corruption or disloyalty, alienated an organised minority within the army. The stability of Mosaddeq's government was severely tested by riots on 28 February 1953, and the kidnap and murder of the police chief the following April. In July, fearing a vote of no confidence in parliament, Mosaddeq held a referendum to dissolve the chamber and hold new elections. On 16 August, an attempted coup was aborted, and the Shah, who had dismissed Mosaddeq and named General Fazlollah Zahedi as the new prime minister, suddenly left the country. This led to anti-Shah demonstrations, followed by another successful coup on 19 August. The plot to overthrow Mosaddeq had been planned and financed by American and British intelligence, but it enjoyed the support and co-operation of some leading politicians, some leading ayatollahs as well as sections of the army in Iran itself.

AFTER THE COUP

Bolu Zahedi's government and the parliament elected during his premiership reflected the coalition of domestic forces which had supported the coup against Mosaddeq. The elections were not free, but the deputies were not simply hand-picked by the Shah and his entourage, as became the practice later in the 1960s and 1970s. Mosaddeq and other NF leaders and activists were interned and put on trial. The NF and other PM forces, though not formally suppressed, were effectively banned from political activity. The campaign against the Tudeh party was savage and effective. Many of the party's leaders had already left Iran for Eastern Europe before the coup. A few more managed to do likewise. Most of the remaining activists and many ordinary members were arrested and jailed, with or without trial. The party's extensive military network was uncovered and destroyed. Within a couple of years, little of the party's considerable apparatus was left intact.

Zahedi's government restored diplomatic relations within Britain and, in 1954, concluded the (Amini-Page) Consortium Oil Agreement, with 40 per cent of the shares going to British Petroleum, another 40 per cent to American oil companies, 14 per cent to Royal Dutch Shell, and six per cent to the French Oil Company. Iran's royalties were to be 50 per cent of the net proceeds, and the concessionary period was to run for 25 years. Meanwhile, the American government provided financial aid, enabling Zahedi to deal with pressing economic problems while oil royalties were still, temporarily, at a low ebb. In addition, the Soviet Union entered an agreement with Zahedi to repay its war debts in Iran, although the actual payment was made to his successor.

Zahedi's government was replaced by that of Hosain Ala in 1955, which itself gave way to the government of Dr Eqbal the following year. This rapid turnabout marked a tendency for the Shah to begin concentrating power in his own hands, and reduce the influence of independent, though loyal, politicians in his administration. In 1955, Iran joined the Baghdad Pact which included Turkey, Iraq and Pakistan as well as Britain and the USA, and was changed into the Central Treaty Organisation (CENTO) after 1958, in the wake of Iraq's departure from it. Soviet-Iranian relations began to warm despite these developments, and, in 1959, the two countries were about to enter a non-aggression pact when Iran made a mutual defence pact with the USA instead. This event greatly soured relations between Iran and the Soviet Union until a rapprochement in 1963.

In 1949, an ad hoc planning body had been set up to draft a statement of state investment projects, the Seven-Year plan (1949-56). The plan allocated a quarter of its proposed expenditures to agriculture, 32 per cent to social and public services, and 24 per cent to industrial and mining projects. However, since much of the funds required were expected to come from oil revenues and World Bank loans, the Anglo-Iranian oil dispute meant that only a small proportion of planned investments could be carried out. In 1955, the planning organisation was turned into a permanent and extensive body with special powers, and was charged with the preparation and execution of the Second Plan (1955-62).

The funds earmarked for the Second Plan were much larger than for the first, comprising 75 per cent of the annual oil revenues. In practice, only 54 per cent of the revenues were spent, the rest being diverted to the military and civilian budget. This, together with related problems, gave rise to growing frictions between the planning organisation's strong managing-director, Abolhasan Ebtahaj, on the one hand, and the Shah and the prime minister on the other. In 1959, Ebtahaj resigned, and the organisation lost the autonomy which it had briefly enjoyed. Meanwhile, over 70 billion rials were spent on a variety of projects for the development of the infrastructure, agriculture, industries and mines.

Late in 1957 an attempted coup by General Vali Qarani, head of the army intelligence, was foiled. This was a sign of growing alienation of a wider public from the Shah and the government. It was followed by the dismissal of Ali Amini, Iran's ambassador to the USA, who was fast emerging as the leader of the regime's reformist wing. Meanwhile, the government policy of creating a middle-class consumer boom, together with a liberal importing policy, led to rising inflation and a balance of payments deficit that was to become acute towards the end of the 1950s.

THE CRISIS OF 1960-63

The parliamentary session having ended in 1960, new elections provided an opportunity for the expression of public dissent. The economic crisis added to domestic unrest and foreign criticism led to the dismissal of Dr Eqbal and his replacement by Ja'far Sharif-Emami. At the same time, a second National Front was formed by Mosaddeq's former associates, and Ali Amini declared his programme for a land reform. The new parliament met early in 1961, but the wave of unrest continued unabated, and a teachers' strike for higher pay resulted in street clashes with the police.

In April 1961 the Shah reluctantly appointed Ali Amini premier. Amini asked him to dissolve the landlord-dominated parliament so that he could implement his land-reform policy. The Shah had already begun to distribute his own agricultural lands against payment by the government, but these were the lands that had been appropriated by Reza Shah, and the proceeds of the sales were diverted to the Pahlavi Foundation, whose operations involved much financial irregularity. Amini's Land Reform Law of 1962, subsequently known as the First Stage, eventually affected about 20 per cent of the peasantry. Although it was later modified to temper the opposition of the landlords, it was still more progressive than the following three stages of land reform, which were carried out under the Shah's direct leadership.

Amini's government fell in June 1962 following his disagreement with the Shah over the size of the military budget. His downfall was inevitable because the Shah, the landlords, as well as the NF were opposed to his government, and hence there was little logic for the American support he had initially enjoyed. He was replaced by Asadollah Alam, a close friend of the Shah. The Shah decided to take over the land reform and turn it into his own 'White Revolution'. The programme of the White Revolution initially contained six points of principle: distribution of arable land; nationalisation of woods and forests; electoral reform, including the right for women to vote and be elected to parliament; denationalisation of some state monopolies to finance the land reform; company profit-sharing for industrial workers; and the creation of a 'literacy corps' to campaign against illiteracy in rural areas. This was put to a referendum in January 1963, and was predictably endorsed by a large vote.

Yet opposition to the Shah was growing daily. The landlords were opposed to land reform and the consequent loss of political power. Religious leaders were becoming restless for a variety of reasons, including the land reform, women's suffrage and the Shah's assumption of dictatorial powers. The NF still demanded free elections and constitutional government. The movement reached its climax during a three-day uprising in June 1963, which was crushed by the army. It was led by landlords and religious leaders, but it included the bazaar, university students and the urban crowd. It was a dress-rehearsal for the revolution of 1977-79.

OIL AND THE STATE: 1963-72

The general elections that followed led to a 'classless' parliament, because the government now had the total power to decide who would enter parliament, a pattern which persisted until the revolution. A new cabinet, consisting mainly of young technocrats, and headed by Hasan Ali Mansur, was installed. However, Mansur was soon to be assassinated after he had granted judicial immunity to American advisers in Iran, a decision vehemently denounced by Ayatollah Khomeini, leader of the uprising of June 1963. The Ayatollah was banished to Turkey, whence he went to Iraq until his return, via Paris, early in 1979. Meanwhile Amir Abbas Hovaida was made prime minister, and was to remain in office until August 1978, when increasing political unrest compelled the Shah to replace him.

These political developments coupled with steadily rising oil revenues greatly strengthened the state, and made possible a strategy of high growth and economic modernisation, although this was not pursued in a realistic manner, especially (though not exclusively) after the quadrupling of the oil prices late in 1973. Economic development was based on an import substitution strategy, yet it resulted in fast-growing imports which were paid for by the oil revenues. Manufacturing expanded, but the highest growth was experienced by public and private services as well as construction. Modern education also expanded rapidly at primary, secondary and tertiary levels. The third stage of land reform, the creation of farm corporations each comprising a number of villages, led to disenchantment among small farmers, and tended to concentrate ownership in the villages affected. The fourth stage went much further and turned huge tracts of agricultural land into bureaucratic agro-business industries. Agriculture grew at a much slower rate than other economic sectors, the gap between the urban and rural sectors increased rapidly, and there was massive rural-urban migration. The high rate of population growth added force to these tendencies in creating urban unemployment, housing shortages and pressures on public services. While the general standard of living was rising fast, the distribution of income and wealth was becoming increasingly uneven. Widespread public and private corruption fuelled social discontent.

With the power of the state increasing and the demise of the old social classes, it became almost impossible to air any opinion, however moderately, criticising the Shah and the state. Parliament was reduced to no more than a legislative instrument, which passed government bills with little debate or disagreement. Later, it even became difficult for ministers and high officials to disagree with the Shah on routine matters of social and economic policy. SAVAK, the civilian secret service, was founded in 1957, expanded rapidly in the 1960s and 1970s, and extended its operations to every sphere of political, social and economic life. It tried to stifle any expression of dissent by means of arrest, imprisonment and torture. Open public opposition became impossible, with the inevitable result that dissenters were forced underground and became progressively more willing to embrace guerrilla warfare.

The quadrupling of the oil prices late in 1973 led to an intensification of all existing political and economic problems, and paved the way for the revolution. The unprecedented increase in the oil revenues led to an immediate doubling of planned public expenditures. But the economic and social capacity could not absorb such a sudden influx of cash into the economy. Ports, roads and other infrastructural facilities were congested, there was labour shortage in such sectors as education and construction, the supply of some goods and services fell short of the demand for them, and inflation became rampant. The sense of insecurity which the politico-economic situation created led to a rapid flight of capital out of the country; by 1976-77 Iran had a deficit on its capital account.

In 1974, the Shah launched his one-party state by creating the National Resurgence party (NRP). The existing official political parties – Iran'-e Novin and Mardom – were dissolved, and it became all but compulsory for members of the public to join the new party. Meanwhile, political discontent was spreading fast, and the Feda'iyan-e Khalq (Marxist-Leninist), and Mojahedin-e Khalq (Islamic-Marxist) groups were continuing their guerrilla campaigns in towns and cities. The Islamic parties had also been secretly active since the early 1960s, although they did not resort to guerrilla tactics.

THE REVOLUTION

Early in 1977 a combination of increasing economic and social dissociation at home, and pressures for human rights reforms from abroad, led to a loosening of the tight political grip that had been hitherto maintained on public criticism. Some political prisoners were released, the use of torture was officially banned, and limited freedom of expression was tolerated. This resulted in a growing expression of political dissent that spread rapidly. In August 1977, Hovaida resigned and was replaced by Jamshid Amuzegar, the interior minister and former oil spokesman.

In January 1978, a personal attack on Ayatollah Khomeini, published in a leading daily on instructions from the court, resulted in riots and bloodshed in the holy city of Qom. The demonstrations soon spread to Tabriz, Tehran and other towns and cities. Late in August 1978, the burning of a cinema in Abadan resulted in 400 deaths, and was widely believed to have been the work of the SAVAK. This, together with the spread of public disorder, led to the resignation of Amuzegar's cabinet and its replacement by Ja'far Sharif-Emami's. The latter adopted a liberal stance and promised rapid political and economic reforms, but the revolutionary movement continued unabated.

On 8 September, following a declaration of martial law, soldiers fired on a large crowd of unarmed demonstrators in central Tehran. Huge numbers were killed, though precise figures have never been established. In the meantime Ayatollah Khomeini had been calling for the overthrow of the Pahlavi regime from his exile in Iraq. Iran's pressure on the Iraqi government to restrict the Ayatollah's activities forced him to leave Iraq. Kuwait being unwilling to play host, the Ayatollah flew to Paris, and continued his campaign amid a glare of Western publicity. The revolutionary movement was thus united behind the leadership of the Ayatollah and his call for the downfall of the Shah's regime.

The Shah turned to Gholamhosain Sadiqi, a highly respected former associate of Mosaddeq. Sadiqi agreed to act on the condition that the Shah gave up all executive power and moved to the Iranian island of Kish in the Gulf. The Shah refused and turned to Shahpur Bakhtiyar, the NF's effective deputy leader. Bakhtiyar accepted on condition that the Shah left Iran for an unspecified period, which he agreed to do. Taking advantage of a state visit to Egypt, the Shah departed with at least a semblance of dignity rather than face the humiliation of formal abdication. Bakhtiyar introduced further measures of political liberalisation and declared his opposition to Islamic government. But his government failed to stem the tide of the revolution, and he himself was expelled from the NF. On 11 February 1979, following armed clashes between revolutionaries and the royal guards, the army declared itself neutral and withdrew the troops to their barracks. Bakhtiyar's government fell. The revolution succeeded. Ayatollah Khomeini, who had returned to Tehran ten days earlier to a tumultuous welcome, named Mehdi Bazargan – a devout Muslim and former associate of Mosaddeq – prime minister.

THE ISLAMIC REPUBLIC

Shortly after the revolution a referendum was held which abolished monarchy and established an Islamic government. But Bazargan's Provisional Government was short lived. It had to face the combined opposition of leftist and Islamist parties, which enjoyed large popular support and which demanded more drastic action at home and in foreign relations than the Provisional Government was prepared to take. A constituent assembly was elected, and it drafted a constitution with which the government disagreed. The main bone of contention was the provision of the office of *velayat-e faqih* (the Guardianship of Jurisconsult) as the ultimate arbiter of state decisions. The constitution also provided for a National (later renamed Islamic) Assembly, an elected president, and an executive cabinet led by a prime minister. Constitutional reform later in the 1980s abolished the office of prime minister, and placed the president at the head of the cabinet. The constitution also created a Council of Guardians, made up of senior Islamic jurists, to vet parliamentary legislation on the basis of Islamic law and the principles of the constitution. Two further bodies later came into being: an Assembly of Experts, for the interpretation of the constitution; and a Council of Determining the Expediency of the Islamic Republic, charged with approval of legislative and executive decisions.

In November 1979, the Provisional Government resigned in the wake of the hostage-taking of American diplomats in Tehran. This was an important turning-point in the post-revolutionary period and resulted in a radical shift in domestic policy as well as international relations. Meanwhile, elections were held both for the National Assembly and for the presidency, and Abolhasan Banisadr, a committed Muslim and former Mosaddeq supporter, was elected president. However, the power struggles were to intensify until the opposition, led by Ayatollah Beheshti (president of the Supreme Court), won the day. Banisadr was impeached by the National Assembly, and left Iran for Paris in August 1981. This provoked an uprising by the Mojahedin and other leftist parties, which was comprehensively crushed. For a few years afterwards terror and counter-terror was to continue until the country achieved a relative measure of stability.

THE IRAN-IRAQ WAR

In September 1980, Iraq attacked Iran. The Iraqis had hoped for a quick victory in the face of Iran's revolutionary turmoil, which had weakened army morale and greatly diminished its effectiveness. In fact, the war was to continue for almost eight years at great human and material cost. The Iraqis received military supplies from the Soviet Union, France, and a number of other Western countries. But in view of its international isolation, Iran had to resort to costly informal markets for military equipment. This was compensated for by a mobilisation of large numbers of young volunteers (*Basij*) who were used in massive infantry attacks. In turn, the Iraqis resorted to the use of chemical weapons.

Apart from its human and social costs, the Iran-Iraq War had a devastating effect on the Iranian economy. With declining oil prices and diminishing world demand for crude oil, much of the oil revenue had to be diverted to the war effort, starving industry of funds for investment and curtailing non-military imports. The restriction on consumer goods imports, coupled with the expansion of military-related domestic goods and services, led to a shortage of many basic goods. The government introduced rationing, which is still partially in operation. Its effect was, at least partly, to encourage a thriving black market.

Homa Katouzian

THE ECONOMY

The end of the Iran-Iraq war in 1988 and the election of the more pragmatic Ali Akbar Hashemi Rafsanjani as president in 1989 raised hopes for improvements in the economic situation. These hopes were strengthened by the parliamentary elections of May 1992, when Rafsanjani's supporters emerged as the dominant group. Despite some early successes, however, the health of the economy remains Iran's main domestic problem today.

These problems have deep roots, some of which date back to the period before the Islamic Revolution of 1978-79. Iran's oil-driven economy has always encouraged a pattern of consumption which relies heavily on imports at the expense of local production. This trend was strengthened in the post-revolutionary period as the political and economic uncertainties of the revolution and the war with Iraq discouraged investment in domestic production and pushed investors towards imports. At the same time, importers were allowed to buy hard currency at the artificially low government-subsidised rate and sell the imported items at the much higher rate prevalent on the free market. Thus, investors were allowed to collect high rents on imports.

The economy's heavy reliance on imports combined with the high cost of post-war reconstruction and falling oil revenues have made it vulnerable to fluctuations on the hard currency markets and have prevented the government from establishing effective control over the economy. Although multiple exchange rates were formally abolished in 1993, the 'gray market' in hard currency continued to operate alongside government controlled banks. The situation reached a crisis point in spring 1995 when President Clinton announced a total embargo against Iran. This action caused the devaluation of the Iranian currency from 2,500 rials to the dollar in early May to 7,000 rials to the dollar by the end of the month. In order to stop the run on the currency the Iranian government fixed the value of the dollar at 3,000 rials and banned all trading in hard currency at prices above the official rate. The new restrictions were accompanied by public attacks on foreign currency dealers who were labeled 'economic saboteurs' and 'foreign agents', and many of them were arrested. Another source of pressure on the economy is foreign debt which at present stands at US$33 billion. The government has succeeded in rescheduling part of its foreign debt; nevertheless, repayments still consume half of Iran's total oil revenues.

Measures taken to deal with the country's economic problems have generally been successful in the short term. Still, with an official annual inflation rate of 40 per cent Iran's economic outlook continues to be bleak. Furthermore, measures taken to control the economy also have the potential of undermining the social base of the regime. Attempts at privatisation, for example, have been slow and have resulted in charges of favoritism as those with close ties to the leading personalities of the regime have emerged as its main beneficiaries. Similarly, the attack on money lenders, many of whom have close ties with the bazaars, is likely to have a negative effect on the regime's relations with the merchant community. The bazaar community has also been blamed for the high rates of inflation. Government efforts to eliminate the bazaari middlemen through a chain of government controlled stores has been met with guarded but negative reaction from the bazaaris. Finally, corruption remains rampant. In the spring of 1995, in a high profile case, eight individuals close to the regime were accused of defrauding the state-run Saderat Bank of US$400 million.

Since the fall of the Soviet Union, Iran has tried to take advantage of its strategic location as a gateway to markets in central Asia. Numerous agreements have been negotiated with the various central Asian republics. However, success will depend on Iran's willingness and ability to improve its position on an international front.

THE POLITICAL SCENE

Political divisions among the leadership are among the main obstacles to reform in Iran. Despite the leading role played by the state in the economy, the government lacks a coherent economic policy. Economic policy making has often been piecemeal and has tended to be a reaction to immediate economic problems instead of being based on long-term planning. Consequently, policies advocated by the state have sometimes had contradictory objectives and have failed to restore confidence in the economy.

Divisions within the leadership partly reflect divisions within the economic elite itself, as various groups in the bazaar and the general business community have allied themselves with political leaders sympathetic to their cause. A more fundamental problem, however, is the difference in approach among political and religious leaders, particularly President Rafsanjani and Ayatollah Ali Khamenei, the Supreme Leader (*rahbar*) of the Islamic Republic. In recent years the differences between the two have developed into a public rift as both leaders have openly jockeyed for position.

These differences are also reflected at the lower levels of the government. In a surprise move in May 1995, while the president was on a state visit to India, Ayatollah Khamenei promoted the head of the irregular *Basij* forces to the rank of Major General, thus outranking the heads of both the regular army and the Revolutionary Guards. The move is widely believed to have been both an affront to President Rafsanjani and a response to the regular army's refusal to take action against anti-government demonstrators in the city of Qazvin.

In recent years, the number of anti-government demonstrations has increased as economic hardships have alienated some of the early supporters of the regime including the urban poor. However, it would be a mistake to conclude that the regime is in any danger of collapse. The main armed opposition group is the Mojahedin, an Islamic-Marxist group. Popular support for the Mojahedin, however, has been seriously undermined by the group's alliance with Iraq, which has provided it with bases on its territory.

President Rafsanjani, who is barred from seeking a third term by the constitution, will end his term in 1997. A new president may be able to overcome some of the divisions within the regime. The root of these divisions, however, is inherent in the constitution itself under which the Supreme Leader functions as an extra-parliamentary overseer of the presidency. In the absence of a charismatic and popular leader like the late Ayatollah Khomeini, the present system is always likely to produce major divisions between the presidency and the office of the Supreme Leader, regardless of the individuals in office.

Hootan Shambayati

4
IRAQ

THE MODERN STATE OF IRAQ was created in 1920, as part of the peace settlement after the First World War. The victorious Allies divided the Arab provinces of the former Ottoman Empire between them, and Britain, which had been in occupation of the provinces of Basra and Baghdad for most of the war, and Mosul by the end of the war, was appointed mandatory power under the new system of international trusteeship established by the League of Nations.

Although parts of the country had been united under a single government at various times in the past, the entity which emerged in 1920 had had no previous independent existence as a nation state. Britain imported a king, Faysal, the son of Sharif Husayn of Mecca, and endowed Iraq with a constitution and a bicameral legislature. The mandate, a form of indirect rule where Arab ministers and officials were closely supervised by British advisers whose advice had to be taken, came to an end in 1932, when Iraq was admitted to the League of Nations as an independent state. By this time Britain had secured Iraq's present northern boundary, had made sure that the concession for oil exploration and exploitation was given to the Iraq Petroleum Company, a conglomerate of British, Dutch, French and United States oil interests, and had created a social base for the monarchy by confirming 'suitable' tribal leaders in full possession of what had previously been the customary holdings of 'their' tribes. In addition, Britain retained military bases in Iraq and generally continued to exercise strong political and economic influence.

In 1941, a group of Iraqi officers led a short-lived resistance movement against Britain which resulted in a second British occupation until the end of the war. Between 1945 and 1958 the country was governed by a succession of 24 cabinets, most of which contained combinations of the same handful of individuals, often headed by the veteran pro-British politician Nuri al-Sa'id. Genuine opposition parties were banned for most of this period, which meant that there was little room for the development of a democratic tradition. Many Iraqis believed that the country's most urgent need was national independence, which would be followed by economic development and social reforms, both of which were being blocked or denied by the monarchy and its British sponsors. At the same time the state was almost universally seen as the 'natural' vehicle to carry out these reforms and to implement the development so urgently needed. This kind of thinking – usually but not always associated with 'socialism' – had wide currency elsewhere in the Middle East in the post-war period and was by no means unique to Iraq.

During and after the Second World War, members of the rising middle classes were expanding their investments in manufacture, commerce and real estate, a process which accelerated in the 1950s when oil began to make a major impact on the economy. Although oil revenues were still modest, they were sufficient to finance the expansion of the bureaucracy, the educational system and other services, and this increase in government expenditure had a generally stimulating effect on the economy.

Private capital was mostly concentrated in the hands of some 25 families, many of whom had controlling interests in several different kinds of business. Between them these families controlled more than half of all private corporate commercial and industrial wealth. Far below them in status and wealth were medium to small property-owners, religious dignitaries and local notables, wholesale and retail merchants, manufacturers, owners of workshops and repair shops, petty traders and so on, as well as the newly emerging intelligentsia of professionals, lawyers, army officers and civil servants. This latter group together with large sections of the urban poor felt acutely aware of the exclusive nature of the political system and came to form the core of the independence movement in the 1940s and 1950s. The beginnings of a working class were also emerging, particularly in the large foreign-owned enterprises such as the railways, Basra port and the Iraq Petroleum Company. Because of its close links with the independence movement, organised labour developed into an effective political force in the years preceding the revolution.

ETHNIC AND SECTARIAN DIVISIONS

On another level, in spite of the far-reaching effects of these changes, Iraqi society contained, and continues to contain, elements which, as we have already mentioned, had never previously been combined in an independent and separate polity. Then as now, the population was divided into a variety of overlapping categories, including social and ethnic origin, religious sect, occupation and regional and tribal background. Apart from the Christian (3.6 per cent), Sabaean and Yazidi (1.4 per cent) communities, some 95 per cent of Iraqis are Muslims. About a quarter of the Muslims are Kurds, who are mostly Sunni Muslims, the remainder Arabs. The Arab Muslims are divided into Sunnis and Twelver Shi'is, the latter forming the largest single religious community in the country as a whole.

Iraqi censuses do not provide details of sectarian affiliation, but as the two sects live in distinct parts of the country (apart from Baghdad and Basra, which are mixed) it is possible to make some broad generalisations. The Shi'is form some 52 per cent of the total Muslim population, and perhaps more significantly, some 70 per cent of the Arab Muslim population. Southern Iraq is predominantly Shi'i, while the centre, west and north of the country are mainly Sunni. The main shrines of Twelver Shi'ism (the 'state religion' of Iraq's neighbour Iran) are located in Iraq, at Najaf, Karbala, Samarra, and Khadimayn, a district of Baghdad. These shrines are major centres of religious learning as

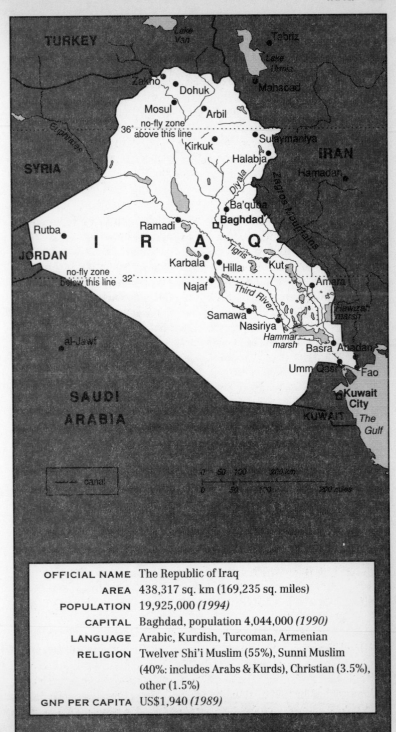

OFFICIAL NAME	The Republic of Iraq
AREA	438,317 sq. km (169,235 sq. miles)
POPULATION	19,925,000 *(1994)*
CAPITAL	Baghdad, population 4,044,000 *(1990)*
LANGUAGE	Arabic, Kurdish, Turcoman, Armenian
RELIGION	Twelver Shi'i Muslim (55%), Sunni Muslim (40%: includes Arabs & Kurds), Christian (3.5%), other (1.5%)
GNP PER CAPITA	US$1,940 *(1989)*

well as the traditional residences of the spiritual leaders of the world-wide Twelver Shi'i community.

As the Ottoman Empire was a Sunni institution, what state educational facilities existed in Iraq before 1914 were mainly for Sunnis; in addition Shi'is were both disinclined to enter, and not recruited into, government service. Furthermore, before the First World War most Shi'is were concentrated either in the countryside far away from the centres of government or in the shrine towns, which had a fairly independent existence. Hence, when the new state was created in 1920, very few Shi'is entered government service, a situation which only changed with the very rapid expansion of (secular) education in the 1940s, 1950s and 1960s. In consequence the Shi'is 'started off' by being under-represented politically. This general tendency has continued and been compounded by other factors such as an increasingly repressive state, which reinforces communal identity, the exclusive nature of the regime since 1968 and the generally hostile nature of Iraq's relations with Iran. In the latter context, however, it should be said that although Iraqi and Iranian Shi'is are members of the same sect, Iraqi Shi'is feel themselves to be Arab Iraqis and Iranian Shi'is feel themselves to be Iranians. While there is a certain affinity between Shi'is, relations have not always been cordial, and there is also a degree of rivalry between the religious establishments at Qum and Mashhad and those at Karbala and Najaf.

The population is also divided along ethnic lines. About 75 per cent are Arabs, 18 per cent are Kurds – there are also Kurdish communities in Iran, Syria and Turkey – while the remaining seven per cent consist of Turcomans, Assyrians, Armenians and other smaller ethnic groups. The Kurds, who are mostly Sunni Muslims, form a compact majority of the population in the north and northeast of the country. Most Kurds were originally members of semi-nomadic tribes, but constraints on cross-frontier transhumance and other economic factors have encouraged sedentarisation, and wider educational provision, rural to urban migration and various political developments have tended to reduce tribal ties. In general, both the sectarian and ethnic divisions mentioned above were becoming less important in the decades preceding the 1958 revolution, as the national independence movement acted as a unifying factor and helped to transcend them.

THE ROLE OF POLITICAL PARTIES BEFORE THE REVOLUTION

For a variety of reasons, no liberal democratic party was able to muster anything like mass support or to build up an effective machinery under the mandate and monarchy (1920–58). Such parties as existed tended to be loose organisations centred around prominent personalities. After the mid-1920s most of the leading Iraqi participants in the Arab Revolt (*see* Introduction), in company with King Faysal himself, made their peace with the mandatory power (unlike their Syrian counterparts; *see*

Chapter 14, Syria) and had become dependent on Britain for the maintenance of the status quo and their own positions within it. As long as they
remained in control it was virtually impossible for an effective pluralistic
democratic system to emerge, and no genuine opposition party could
gain power through the ballot box. As a result, constitutional democracy
had become widely discredited by the end of the 1950s and the military
came to be regarded as an acceptable vehicle for initiating change.

It is a peculiarity of Iraqi politics that the independence movement
functioned almost exclusively underground, and that many of its members
came under the influence of the Communist Party (founded in 1932),
which organised almost all the massive demonstrations and strikes of the
1940s and early 1950s. After Nasser's rise to power in Egypt in 1952, the
Pan-Arab nationalists and the Ba'thists also began to gain influence, especially among the Sunni population. Before Nasser, partly because of Iraq's
ethnic and communal heterogeneity, pan-Arabism had made little headway – Iraqi nationalism had a far wider appeal. Even in the late 1950s
there was no Nasserist party as such, and the Ba'th, founded in Syria and
brought to Iraq by Syrian schoolteachers in the early 1950s, had only 300
members in 1955, the year when Saddam Hussein joined.

THE IRAQI REPUBLIC

On 14 July 1958 a group of military officers seized power, overthrew the
monarchy and abolished the old political order. The new government was
headed by self-styled Free Officers, under Brigadier Abd al-Karim Qasim,
and cabinets consisted of a combination of military and civilian members.
The feebleness of the parliamentary tradition and the limited commitment
to parliamentary democracy became particularly obvious when the Free
Officers began to make overtures to 'moderate' civilian politicians to
whom they might hand over after a period of consolidation. Although
some of them, notably Muhammad Hadid, Kamil Chadirchi and Mahdi
Kubba were well-known and respected, none of them had a properly
functioning political party at his disposal, nor any government experience.

In addition, there seems to have been some kind of unspoken agreement among these politicians and the Free Officers that it was important to block communist participation in government. Probably
overestimating the proportion of the electorate which would vote for
the communists, Qasim preferred to stall the democratic process. An
ironic consequence was that the main pressure to hold elections came
from the communists, who organised massive demonstrations (1959
and 1960) in favour of free elections and the legalisation of the
Communist Party. Since no elections were ever held the extent of communist support can only be conjectured. Nevertheless, as elsewhere in
the Middle East the spectre of communism continued to dominate the
political scene, which became polarised between the Pan-Arab
nationalists and their supporters and the communists and theirs.

In the autumn of 1958 the immediate point of contention became
the question of whether Iraq should join the United Arab Republic

(UAR) of Egypt and Syria, which had been formed the previous February (*see* chapter 14, Syria). The nationalists and Ba'thists wanted to join the UAR, partly out of conviction and partly as a means of controlling the communists, since Nasser had made political parties illegal. The communists opposed it, again partly out of conviction and partly because they understood its implications for their own future. For his part, Qasim had no desire to defer to Nasser and thus quite fortuitously found himself on the same side as the communists, whose political views he did not share. In an attempt to distance himself from the communists, Qasim began to clamp down on the left and to dismiss individuals suspect of communist sympathies from the army and other key positions. In doing so he undermined his own political base (since he had irretrievably alienated himself from the Pan-Arabists in the early 1960s) and thus fell easy prey to a coup engineered by nationalist and Ba'thist officers in February 1963.

At the time, the atrocities of February 1963 marked the most savage repression yet perpetrated by any Middle Eastern government against its population. Qasim was killed and the Ba'thist-Arab nationalist junta which seized power under the leadership of Abd al-Salam Arif established a reign of terror against their communist adversaries. The most notorious of those involved in this bloodshed, particularly Ali Salih al-Sa'di, were Ba'thists. Some nine months later the Ba'thists fell out with the Nasserists and with Arif, who sent most of their leaders into exile in Spain, and the intensity of political persecution diminished. Arif's presidency was mainly taken up with fighting a fruitless and expensive war in Kurdistan and with keeping himself in power. After his death in a helicopter accident in 1966 his brother Abd al-Rahman Arif took over as president, but was ousted by another Ba'th coup in July 1968.

THE PRINCIPAL POLITICAL GROUPS IN POST-REVOLUTIONARY IRAQ

The main groupings in Iraqi politics after 1958 were the communists, the Kurds and the pan-Arab nationalists, both Nasserist and Ba'thist. With their roots in the shanty-towns, the emerging labour movement and the professional middle classes, the communists were probably the leading political force in the country in the years immediately after the revolution, but their position was ambivalent. They supported President Qasim, partly because of his welfare state measures and his attempts to negotiate with the Iraq Petroleum Company – his Law 80 of 1961 was the first major restriction on the activities of foreign oil companies in any Arab country – and partly because the communist leadership did not support the idea of a military takeover by the party. Although this issue remained highly contentious within party circles for many years, the possibility of such a coup had definitely passed by 1961, since most of the party's supporters in the army had been dismissed.

The second political force, the Kurdish national movement, was divided into a number of factions, the most important of which was the

Kurdistan Democratic Party (KDP) and its leader Mulla Mustafa Barzani. Most Iraqi Kurdish politicians and parties have sought some form of regional or local autonomy within the Iraqi state, but Kurdish organisations and political groupings have been in armed conflict with the authorities in Baghdad for much of the period since the inauguration of the state in 1920, largely because of the authorities' refusal to countenance such aspirations.

The party which has achieved the greatest long-term success in post-revolutionary Iraq is the Ba'th, which is still in power at the time of writing. The basic tenets of Ba'thism, 'one Arab Nation with an Eternal Mission' expressed in the slogan Unity, Freedom and Socialism, were first developed in Syria by Michel Aflaq and Salah al-Din al-Bitar in the 1940s and early 1950s. Unity is the unity of the Arab nation, Freedom is freedom from imperialism and Zionism, and Socialism expresses a general aspiration towards state-directed economic development supported by a mixed economy. Ba'thism is a variety of pan-Arab nationalism, based on the general premise that there is a single Arab nation, which has been divided artificially, first by the Ottomans, and subsequently by European and American imperialism and Zionism. Once the Arabs are liberated and united, it is believed, social conflicts within particular states (or 'regions of the Arab nation') will subside.

Ba'thism first came to Iraq in 1951 but was slow to take root, partly because pan-Arab nationalism was not particularly attractive to Shi'is or Kurds and partly because the political scene was dominated by the communists. Nevertheless, the Iraqi Ba'th Party, which had some 300 members in 1955, joined a National Front with the communists and other parties in 1957, and welcomed the Revolution of 1958. Although the Ba'thists never attracted mass support they eventually succeeded in taking and maintaining power by a combination of skilful organisation, ruthlessness and an alliance with key military officers.

THE SECOND BA'TH COUP

On 17 July 1968 a group of Ba'th officers led by Ahmad Hasan al-Bakr (who had been prime minister in 1963–64) organised another Ba'th coup, taking over the government in a second coup two weeks later. Both al-Bakr, who became President, and his deputy and successor Saddam Hussein, came from Takrit, a small town about one hundred miles north of Baghdad. The Ba'th had very few roots in Iraq and was primarily remembered for its reign of terror in 1963. At various times over the next few years it attempted to convince the communists and the Kurdish Democratic Party to join in a national government, in which the Ba'th would play the 'leading role', while simultaneously attacking and sometimes killing members of both the other parties. At the same time, it attempted to increase its popularity by advocating wide-ranging social and economic reforms and pursuing apparently progressive and anti-imperialist foreign policies, stridently attacking Zionism and imperialism and supporting the left in the rest of the Arab world.

In this general spirit Iraq signed a 15-year treaty with the Soviet Union in 1972 and thus fortified, went on to nationalise the Iraqi Petroleum Company in the same year, a popular move. Largely because of their espousal of such policies, the Ba'thists finally convinced the communists to join them in a National Progressive Front, although the KDP refused to participate. The regime's confidence and economic power was boosted even further by the massive rise in oil prices which followed the Arab-Israeli war of October 1973: between 1972 and 1974, oil revenues increased tenfold, from $575 million to $5700 million.

THE BA'TH AND THE KURDS

Although the KDP refused to join the National Progressive Front, other overtures on the part of the Ba'th appeared to be bearing fruit. In March 1970 an agreement was reached between the government and Mulla Mustafa Barzani which envisaged the inauguration of an autonomous Kurdish area four years later. However, it soon became clear that the March Manifesto was nothing but a ruse on the part of the Ba'th, which wanted to gain time until it was in a position to recast its Kurdish policy to its own advantage. One of most crucial stumbling blocks in the subsequent negotiations – which continued until 1974 – was whether Kirkuk, where one third of Iraq's oil is produced, should be included in the autonomous area. The KDP insisted that Kirkuk had a Kurdish majority population and was therefore part of Kurdistan. The Iraqi government denied this but also refused to carry out the census which the Kurdish side requested.

When it became clear that the Ba'th's promises on Kurdish autonomy were not going to be fulfilled, a major conflict between the armed forces and the Kurds broke out in the spring of 1974. The Kurds were supported by the Shah of Iran, who took the Ba'th's radical and leftist rhetoric seriously and was worried about Soviet influence in the region. Barzani's access to sophisticated weapons made the KDP into a formidable foe, to such an extent that it was impossible for the Iraqi government to defeat it. The Ba'th made capital out of the Shah's support for the Kurds, and presented itself as the victim of an imperialist conspiracy masterminded by the West and its agents: in this campaign the Ba'th was supported by the communists.

By the end of 1974 the stalemate familiar from previous confrontations between the Kurds and the government had set in. In addition, the Ba'th leadership was preoccupied with internal intrigues and power struggles and was keen to 'solve' the Kurdish problem. In October 1974 King Husayn of Jordan arranged preliminary meetings between representatives of Iraq and Iran, which paved the way for the Algiers Agreement between the two countries in March 1975. Within hours of the agreement Iran withdrew its heavy artillery and closed the border so that the Kurds could not regroup or attack from Iran. The Kurdish resistance collapsed; Barzani himself went into exile, dying in the USA in 1979. Relations between Iraq and Iran now became extremely cordial and continued to be so until the Iranian revolution of 1979. In the autumn of 1978, after a request from the Shah, Baghdad obligingly expelled Ayatollah Khomeini from Najaf, where he had been in exile for the previous 15 years.

The Algiers Agreement meant the settlement of the Kurdish question on the Ba'th's terms as well as the resolution of the frontier dispute which had bedevilled relations between Iran and Iraq since the 1930s. Briefly, the Algiers Agreement restored the boundary between the two countries along the Shatt al-Arab waterway along the *thalweg*, the lowest point in the riverbed. This arrangement effectively divided the waterway equally between the two countries while the previous arrangement imposed by the Iraqis had insisted that Iraqi territory extended to the high watermark on the eastern (Iranian) side of the Shatt, thus making Iranian use of the waterway dependent on Iraqi good will. The Agreement had been masterminded by Saddam Hussein, the real power behind the al-Bakr regime, and was to mark the beginning of an important U-turn in the Ba'th's internal and regional policies.

The Ba'th took the most ruthless measures to prevent any revival of the Kurdish resistance. The strip of territory parallel to the borders with Iran and Turkey was turned into a *cordon sanitaire*. The villages in the area were destroyed and their inhabitants rounded up in trucks and taken to southern Iraq or resettled in specially constructed villages surrounded by barbed wire and fortified posts. Although now more divided internally with the creation of the Patriotic Union of Kurdistan under Jalal Talabani in 1975 (roughly speaking, the KDP's membership is from northern, and the PUK's from southern, Kurdistan), the Kurds had regrouped sufficiently by the beginning of 1977 to mount guerrilla operations in the area. Other opposition forces, including the communists, began to join in these activities in 1979.

THE EMERGENCE OF SADDAM HUSSEIN

By the late 1970s the dividing lines between the Party leadership and the state and its institutions had almost disappeared. At the same time, the spectacular rise in oil revenues during the 1970s meant a parallel increase in the economic muscle of the leadership. In addition, having 'solved' the Kurdish question, the Ba'th were no longer in need of the communists, and turned against them once more. In May 1976, twelve communists were executed, allegedly for carrying out political activities in the army, and in July 1978 the Ba'th enacted a blanket decree making any non-Ba'thist political activity illegal and membership of any other political party punishable by death for all members and former members of the armed forces. In the context of universal conscription, the decree applied to all adult males. The National Progressive Front gradually lost all significance and although never officially dissolved was no longer meeting by 1979. Over the next few years, hundreds of thousands of individuals opposed to the Ba'th, of whatever persuasion, were imprisoned, murdered or forced into exile.

Between 1975 and 1979 Iraq gradually returned into the general orbit of the West on a global level and towards the moderate Arab states on a regional level. Within the Party itself, real power moved away from the Ba'th Party and the RCC and became concentrated almost exclusively in the hands of Saddam Hussein and a few particularly trusted subordinates. The Party itself was transformed into an instrument of the state and gradually assumed the characteristics of a national rally, in which adulation of the party and its leaders came to take the place of whatever political discourse may have existed formerly. By 1979 it was clear that it was only a matter of time before Saddam Hussein would take over full control of the state. President Ahmad Hasan al-Bakr, whose contacts with senior army officers had been crucial in the first few years, had handed over the Ministry of Defence to his son-in-law (and Saddam Hussein's brother-in-law) Adnan Khayrullah Tulfa in October 1977. In addition, a number of rival security services, all reporting directly to Saddam Hussein, had been assiduously built up and it came as no surprise when al-Bakr appeared on television on 16 July 1979 and announced his resignation and the succession of Saddam Hussein.

Potential internal Ba'th opposition to these developments was preempted 12 days later after the 'discovery' of a plot, allegedly masterminded by Syria, to overthrow the regime. A special Party court was set up under Na'im Haddad and five RCC members and 17 other Party members were sentenced to death. These 'democratic executions', as Na'im Haddad called them, were carried out personally by Saddam Hussein and the remaining members of the Ba'th leadership. The victims included Abd al-Khaliq al-Samarrai, a prominent Ba'th figure who had been in prison since July 1973, Adnan Hamdani, one of Saddam Hussein's most intimate friends, and other key members of the leadership. The fact that even those who had been closest to the leader could fall so suddenly and fatally from favour showed that no opposition whatever, whether inside or outside the party, would be tolerated.

THE IMPACT OF OIL WEALTH

The spectacular rise in oil prices during the 1970s meant an equally spectacular rise in the country's revenues and expenditures. Huge sums were spent on welfare and infrastructural projects, and higher wages and salaries which, together with the new employment opportunities generated by an expanding economy, helped to bring about substantial improvements in living standards. In addition, as the Ba'th leadership had full control over these revenues – and was not accountable as to how they were spent – increases in receipts from oil automatically increased the independence of the state from society.

The combination of the new oil money and the successful elimination or subordination of most of the opposition gave Saddam Hussein a major boost of confidence. He promoted a spectacular personality cult around himself, with massive portraits and statues of the benevolent leader visible everywhere. Towns, suburbs, public buildings and streets were renamed in his honour. He also expanded his own personal presidential force, the Republican Guard, an elite corps originally founded in November 1963. The Guard was gradually transformed into Saddam Hussein's personal instrument, officered and manned exclusively by Takritis, and given the most up to date weaponry. It was further expanded and its military capacities enhanced during the war with Iran.

The country's oil wealth also permitted Saddam Hussein to equip the various parallel security services with the most up-to-date means of surveillance and control. Together with a greatly expanded communication system, these security services made the state machinery more efficient than ever before. During the 1980s security was further refined with the construction of huge underground complexes, mostly designed and built by British firms, to serve as emergency headquarters in the event of attacks upon the regime. These were to be put to use with considerable effect when Iraq was attacked by the coalition forces early in 1991. In this way the regime became both more distanced from the population and more apparently invulnerable.

THE SHI'I OPPOSITION

The existence of a Shi'i political movement in Iraq dates back to the late 1950s. Disconcerted by the extent of support for the communists among the Shi'i community, a number of religious leaders (*ulama*) in Najaf, led by Ayatullah Muhammad Baqr al-Sadr, formed a political organisation, the Association of Najafi *ulama*, in the autumn of 1958. Its aim was to raise the consciousness of the Muslim community as a whole and to arrest the spread of communism and atheism. In their publications the *ulama* tried to refute Marxism and also criticised Western economic and social thought and philosophy.

By the late 1960s, the *ulama's* main concern was no longer communism but the Ba'th Party itself, and the Association of Najafi *ulama* formed itself into a political party called al-Da'wa *al-Islamiyya* (The Islamic Call). The foundation of al-Da'wa, as it became known, was partly a reaction against the secularism of the Ba'thist state, but more particularly against the state's new-found determination to interfere directly in the affairs of the Shi'i clerical hierarchy, a highly sensitive area from which all previous Iraqi governments (including the Ottomans) had tended to keep their distance. The Ba'th responded to al-Da'wa's activities in familiar fashion: in 1974 five *ulama* were executed without trial; in February 1977 numerous arrests were made in the Holy Cities during the Muharram ceremonies, after which eight members of the clergy were executed and 15 sentenced to life imprisonment. In 1979, encouraged by the Iranian Revolution, al-Da'wa began to engage the government in open conflict, attacking Ba'th Party offices and police posts and openly declaring its support for the new government in Iran.

The Ba'th responded by intensifying its campaign against al-Da'wa, making membership of the party punishable by death. In April 1980 Ayatullah Muhammad Baqr al-Sadr and his sister Bint Huda were executed. A few months after this Iraq invaded Iran. This had the effect of shifting Shi'i opposition to the regime to a different plane, in the sense that it could be represented as an attack on Iraq and Arabism and thus tantamount to treason. It is difficult to gauge how strong the appeal of al-Da'wa was, but although the majority of Iraqi conscripts (like the majority of Iraqis) were Shi'is there was no mass desertion or any other manifestation of widespread feelings of common cause between Iraqi and Iranian Shi'is. Nevertheless, the fact that the Shi'i community was the principal target of the Iraqi government's domestic repression throughout the war had the effect of heightening its sense of identity. Hence, although repression effectively pre-empted the revival of al-Da'wa, it made many Shi'is more aware of their Shi'ism than ever before.

THE IRANIAN REVOLUTION AND THE WAR BETWEEN IRAQ AND IRAN

The Iranian Revolution of 1978–79 had momentous significance for Iraq, because it meant the end of the friendly relations between the two countries that had existed since 1975. In particular, the fall of the Shah meant the de facto abrogation of the Algiers Agreement and the resurrection of the Kurdish question. In addition, the establishment of a populist Shi'i government in Iran was a matter of grave concern for the rulers of Iraq, where, as elsewhere in the Arab world, populist Islam was beginning to fill the void created by the ideological bankruptcy of Arab nationalism and Arab socialism (*see* Introduction). Underestimating the enthusiasm engendered by the Revolution, misjudging the nature of its impact on the morale and efficiency of the Iranian armed forces and overestimating his own economic and military strength, Saddam Hussein resurrected the old disagreements over the boundary between the two countries in the Shatt al-Arab and the status of the southwest Iranian province of Khuzistan /Arabistan, and took the frequent cross-border incidents as a pretext for going to war with Iran on 22 September 1980. In Saddam Hussein's calculations, a quick defeat of the new Islamic Republican regime in Iran would have made him into the undisputed master of the Gulf and Iraq into a major regional power. These ambitions were given a considerable boost by Western and Saudi fears of the spread of a militantly anti-Western form of Islam and the possible consequences for the region as a whole.

However, although the Iraqi attack met with initial success, Iranian forces were more resilient than expected. An impasse developed which lasted until the spring of 1982, when Iran began to advance and expelled Iraqi troops from its territory. A further long period of stalemate developed until Iran took Fao in 1986 and advanced to within 40 miles of Basra. In the meantime KDP forces under Barzani's son Mas'ud had reformed and managed to gain control over much of the Kurdish mountains. By the middle of 1986, the tremendous losses sustained by both Iran and Iraq had resulted in a stalemate where both contenders were bogged down in entrenched positions with no end in sight. In addition, the burden of having to support Iraq financially was beginning to cause strains on the economies of Kuwait and Saudi Arabia. As the Organisation of Petroleum Exporting Countries (OPEC) Conference in October 1985 had failed to reach a satisfactory agreement on export quotas, Saudi Arabia decided to increase its own oil exports and thereby to drive the price of oil down in an attempt to cripple the Iranian economy. Saudi exports increased from an average of two million barrels per day to an average of 4.5 million barrels per day, and the price of oil dropped from $27 per barrel in 1985 to $15 per barrel in early 1986.

By 1987 the cumulative effect of these developments had led to a major shift in the war. Iran and Iraq began to make serious attempts to destroy each other's oil export facilities, and Iraq made sustained if generally unsuccessful attacks on tankers carrying Iranian oil in the spring and summer of 1987. Ironically, worried about the wider repercussions in the region of an Iraqi collapse, Iraq's Arab neighbours now committed themselves unequivocally to its support, especially after the Iranian offensive against Basra in January and February 1987, and the 'War of the Cities' which accompanied it. In this way Saddam Hussein achieved his objective of regionalising the war and of drawing Saudi Arabia, Kuwait and their Western allies more seriously into it.

Kuwait's attitude to the war had been affected by Iran's successful Fao offensive in 1986, which Kuwait had felt to be too close to home for comfort. It put its forces on full alert and began to take a more publicly pro-Iraqi stance. In return, following Iraqi raids on Iranian oil terminals in August 1986, Iran began to step up its attacks on Kuwaiti tankers. As a result Kuwait approached both the Soviet Union and the USA with requests for naval protection. Although the Soviet Union's involvement remained marginal (it leased a few tankers to Kuwait), even the hint of Soviet participation in such an endeavour in what were still the early days of *perestroika* was sufficient to enable the Reagan administration to obtain full support from Congress to mobilise a suitable American response. The general effect of this was to align the USA firmly on the Iraqi side, a tendency which was to gather momentum and to become a decisive factor in Iran's eventually losing the war. As well as marking a major and permanent shift towards Iraq on the part of the USA, 1987 also saw the Soviet Union coming firmly down on the Iraqi side: Soviet-Iraqi trade increased to $1200 million, an increase of 46 per cent over 1986.

On 20 July 1987, after considerable international pressure, the United Nations (UN) Security Council passed Resolution 598, which called for an end to the war and promised the establishment of a commission of enquiry to determine which of the parties was the aggressor. Iraq accepted the resolution; Iran did not. However, although evidently greatly weakened, Iran still retained the capacity both to inflict serious damage on Iraq and to occupy Iraqi territory. In the spring of 1988 Iran launched an offensive in northern Iraq with the assistance of the two most prominent Iraqi Kurdish organisations, the PUK and the KDP, capturing the city of Halabja on 15th of March (*see* Chapter 7, The Kurds). The next day the Iraqi Air Force bombed Halabja with poison gas, causing over 6,000 deaths among the civilian population. In April and June Iraqi forces again used chemical weapons to recapture Fao and Mehran.

By this time Iranian resistance was clearly crumbling. The government in Tehran was further demoralised by the shooting down of an Iranian airliner by an American cruiser at the beginning of July. A series of military reverses resulted in Iran losing almost all the Iraqi territory it had captured by the middle of July, and on 18 July Khomeini announced that the Iranian government would now accept Resolution 598 without conditions. During the rest of July the Iraqis proceeded to drive Iranian forces out of central and southern Iraq and by 20 August a cease-fire had come into effect.

THE COSTS OF THE IRAN-IRAQ WAR

The human and economic costs of the war were staggering. According to Western sources there were nearly 400,000 dead, roughly a quarter Iraqi and three-quarters Iranian, and perhaps 750,000 wounded. One commentator has estimated that the total costs of the war were some $452.6 billion for Iraq and $644.3 billion for Iran, based on a combination of damage to the infrastructure, estimated oil revenue losses and estimated gross national product (GNP) losses. To put this in perspective, the total figure exceeds by $678.5 billion the entire oil revenue received by Iran and Iraq since they started to sell their oil on the world market in 1919 and 1931 respectively.

After the cease-fire of August 1988 Iraq dragged its feet in the peace negotiations, largely because of Saddam Hussein's desire to be seen to have gained a meaningful victory, and partly because the implementation of Clause 6 of Resolution 598 ('inquiring into the responsibility for the conflict') would have indicated that Iraq had started the war. Iraq rejected a Soviet offer to chair (and thus presumably to speed up) face-to-face negotiations early in 1989, and this generally inconclusive state of affairs continued until the invasion of Kuwait. In a dramatic volte-face a few days after the invasion of Kuwait in August 1990, Saddam Hussein offered Iran a settlement based on the full implementation of Resolution 598 and the restoration of the Algiers Agreement of March 1975 (which he had ceremoniously torn up on Iraqi television ten years earlier): a public admission that the whole war, with all its human and material costs, had been utterly meaningless.

THE ECONOMIC IMPACT OF THE WAR ON IRAQ

Apart from the terrible devastation it had caused in terms of human loss and suffering, the war had greatly distorted the Iraqi economy. In additional to infrastructural damage, Iraq had amassed foreign debts estimated at between $60 and $80 billion. In the early years, the Ba'th had tried to insulate Iraqi society from the war as much as possible, continuing its lavish development programmes and putting no restrictions on imports. In consequence, Iraq's foreign reserves of some $35 billion declined rapidly, while the effects of Iranian attacks on the southern oilfields and on Basra, and Syria's closure of the pipeline to Baniyas in 1982, caused oil revenue to fall dramatically, from $29 billion in 1980 to $9 billion in 1982 and to $7 billion in 1983.

Iraq's greatest debts were to Saudi Arabia and Kuwait, which sold 'war relief crude' worth some $18-20 billion on its behalf. If these counterpart sales are included, Kuwait and Saudi Arabia alone provided Iraq with about $50-60 billion. At the end of 1987 Iraq owed $24 billion to member states of the Organisation for Economic Co-operation and Development. Given Saddam Hussein's constantly reiterated claim that he had fought the war on behalf of 'the Arab nation', and since his Arab creditors had no effective means of enforcing repayment even if they had wished or intended to do so, Iraq's 'real' debts were those it owed to the West: the repayment of its debts to the Soviet Union, estimated at $10 billion, does not seem to have been considered a top priority. This very considerable indebtedness complicated the transition from a war to a peace economy. Apart from the debt, Iraq's annual food bill amounted to at least $3 billion (half from the USA and half from Turkey), and inflation was running at 40 to 50 per cent.

THE POLITICAL AND ECONOMIC SITUATION AFTER THE IRAN-IRAQ WAR

Although severely damaged, Iraq emerged from the war a far more substantial military power than it had been in 1980. In 1979–80 the Iraqi Army numbered some 190,000 men: by 1987–88 it had more than quintupled, to around one million, and there were comparable increases in military hardware. In addition, there was now an important armaments industry whose products included a surface-to-surface missile based on the Soviet Scud, developed with Egyptian and Argentinian assistance. A new Ministry of Industry and Military Industrialisation was created to oversee these activities in July 1988, headed by Husayn Kamil Majid, Saddam Hussein's son-in-law. By 1989–90 the scale of military production was beginning to give rise to serious international concern as it became widely known that Iraq was manufacturing chemical weapons and sophisticated missiles and was not far from acquiring the means to produce nuclear weapons, the essential components of which were being provided by firms in Western Europe and the USA.

Although he had frequently appeared in field-marshal's uniform before the outbreak of the war, Saddam Hussein had no military training and in fact only honorific military rank. As the war progressed and no immediate end appeared in sight, the officer corps became more important, and there was always the possibility that a rival or challenger to the President might appear from within its ranks. In order to guard against this Saddam Hussein exerted as much control as possible over the army and its commanders, which seriously hampered the conduct of the war. Not only was it difficult for commanders to make independent decisions, but they were also constantly aware that they were likely to be punished if they made mistakes or were defeated. Several officers were reportedly executed after the rout at Fao in the spring of 1986. A similar fate awaited anyone suspected of 'disloyalty'. Conversely, successful commanders were sometimes removed or transferred if it was felt that their exploits might turn them into heroes.

The immense military build-up served ultimately to ensure Saddam Hussein's consolidation in power. After the war he made use of his 'victory' over Iran to make explicit claims to the leadership of the Arab world, which he and the 'noble people of Iraq' had so assiduously defended for eight years. Nevertheless, his power base within the country consisted almost entirely either of members of his own extended family, or of those who had in some sense been incorporated into it by marriage or by long association with him. Thus his son Udayy was married to the daughter of the Vice-President, Izzat al-Duri; Husayn Kamil Majid, the Minister for Industry and Military Industrialisation, himself a distant cousin of Saddam Hussein, was married to Saddam Hussein's daughter Raghad; and his brother, Saddam Kamil, a colonel in the missile brigade, to another daughter, Rima'. Until his untimely (and somewhat unseasonable) death in a helicopter accident in a sandstorm near Basra in April 1989, Adnan Khayrullah Tulfa, a maternal cousin of Saddam Hussein and the brother of his wife Sajida, was Minister of Defence; Adnan's wife was the daughter of the former President, Ahmad Hasan al-Bakr; and Adnan and Sajida's father, Khayrullah Tulfa, a former primary school teacher, was for some years Mayor of Baghdad, during which he became a wealthy businessman. Qusayy, Saddam Hussein's youngest son, was married to the daughter of General Mahir Abd al-Rashid, but apparently separated from her when her father fell out of favour in the autumn of 1988. Saddam Hussein's two other closest colleagues, Tariq Aziz, a Christian from Mosul and Taha Yasin Ramadhan, from the Jazira (north-western Iraq), were not relatives by blood or marriage, but were already closely associated with him before the Ba'th takeover in 1968.

INFITAH

The Ba'th's increased development expenditures had not only stimulated the economy but had also made the state – with its substantial oil revenues – into the principal generator of opportunities for private business. Although most major capital-intensive schemes were carried out by international companies or corporations, local firms also profited enormously, especially in areas such as urban real estate, construction, transport, communications, services and agriculture. In addition, many local businessmen acted as contractors or middlemen for foreign firms, a particularly lucrative activity. Nevertheless, although Ba'th rule provided fantastic opportunities for making money, the economic might of the state remained dominant, as reflected in the country's continuing dependence on oil, which accounted for over 90 per cent of foreign exchange. Hence, Iraq's capacity to muddle through after the end of the war with Iran depended crucially on its OPEC quota and its ability to defer or reschedule its debts to its international creditors.

In the early years of the war the regime had attempted to encourage private capital to diversify away from real estate, contracting, commerce and services towards light and medium manufacturing, and had enacted a number of regulations to encourage this. Some measures of privatisation were introduced, particularly in agriculture, in an attempt to reduce food imports, to promote better quality and more regular supplies, and to broaden support for the regime among the burgeoning entrepreneurial middle classes. However, as the war progressed the economic situation steadily deteriorated and a more drastic economic reappraisal became necessary. Claiming to have been a longtime closet supporter of the market economy, Saddam Hussein took the opportunity to come out in favour of giving private enterprise a more prominent role. He made a series of declarations and policy statements, known collectively as the 'administrative revolution' whose intention was to reduce the powers of the bureaucracy. This also implied a reduction in the influence of the Ba'th Party, as party officials controlled the key positions in the civil service.

This combination of deregulation and relaxation of bureaucratic controls in the state economic sector and the declining emphasis on Ba'th ideology was symptomatic of the regime's efforts to build up new constituencies among the middle classes and the military establishment. The President and his circle continued to base their powers almost exclusively on the various instruments of coercion (the police and the various internal intelligence services) and on the military, whose political significance had grown substantially as a result of the general militarisation of politics and the military investments mentioned above. All this was accompanied by an intensification of the already relentless cult of personality and the erection of a plethora of 'victory' monuments. According to Iraqi exiles, all key positions in these services and the military are occupied by some 700 Takritis who constitute the core of the elite and have a vested interest in the maintenance of the regime; they would not only lose their privileges but would also be the first to suffer if the regime was to be brought down.

The much vaunted economic initiatives, heralding a return to or an advance towards greater liberalisation, were also accompanied by declarations of intent to move towards greater political liberty. Elections to the National Assembly, a parliamentary body provided for in the provisional constitution, were first held in 1980, but a second election was announced for 1 April 1989, against a background of further promises of privatisation and somewhat vaguer assurances that opposition political parties would be licensed at some time in the future. None of these measures had any long-term effect on relieving the economic crisis in which Iraq was floundering in 1989 and 1990. This was largely because the kind of economic reform which Saddam Hussein thought would set

Iraq on the road to reconstruction could not be achieved without a radical transformation of the political system and the establishment of the rule of law. He thus found himself trapped by the incompatibility between his desire to maintain and expand his personal dictatorship and the basic requirements of a market economy.

THE BACKGROUND TO THE INVASION OF KUWAIT

Although Iraq's economic situation after the war was precarious, it could not be described as desperate, given the country's very substantial oil reserves. Prudent housekeeping, tight control of imports and checks on government spending would have brought about gradual economic recovery, provided that there was no disastrous collapse in the price of oil. However, such policies were not adopted. While the rebuilding of the cities, the infrastructure and industry was certainly an important target, $5 billion per year between 1988 and 1992 was allocated to rearmament and $2.5 billion to reconstruction, which included such projects as 'victory' monuments and a new presidential palace, a clear expression of Saddam Hussein's priorities.

At the same time, the various efforts to restructure the economy that have been mentioned led to high inflation and steep rises in prices and in the cost of living. As might have been expected, private capital had responded to the privatisation measures by speculative or 'quick' rather than sustained investment, which meant that the rich got richer and the middle and lower classes got poorer. Also, the 'cuts' imposed on the bureaucracy since 1987 had led to high unemployment, which meant that rapid demobilisation was politically undesirable. In addition, after eight years of war and suffering there were widespread hopes that peace would bring greater prosperity and security.

Two interconnected points should be made here. In the first place, in spite of the fact that Iraq had and has one of the most, if not the most, vicious and tyrannical regimes in the Middle East, Saddam Hussein had always attracted a certain following both within Iraq and in the rest of the Arab world. Some of this was opportunistic, in the sense that the support was bought. But, where it was not bought directly, his strident anti-imperialist, and particularly anti-Israeli, rhetoric found an echo on the streets and in the refugee camps, especially in Jordan, the West Bank and Gaza. There was also the sense that, however wicked and ruthless Saddam Hussein might be, he 'got things done', somewhat in the spirit of an Italian predecessor who 'at least' made the trains run on time. Again, although he would have lost the war with Iran had it not been for the arms and the support which the West gave him, the folk memory in the region was sufficiently selective or short term for it to be widely believed that, unlike most of the other rulers in the area, he was not afraid to stand up to the West. In this respect Saddam Hussein always had his finger on the pulse of certain sentiments in the Arab world, and knew well how to exploit them.

The second point is connected with the changes in the Soviet Union and Eastern Europe. It had long been clear, well before Gorbachev's assumption of power in 1985, that the Soviet Union was too concerned about its relationship with the USA to throw its weight decisively behind any Arab policy or manoeuvres which might threaten Israel. Nevertheless, since no Arab state or combination of Arab states had seriously entertained such ideas since 1973, this consideration had gradually become less important. Soviet support was essential in a variety of other ways: it was not until 1986, for example, that the USA and the West felt it prudent to make the high technology weaponry available to Iraq which was to enable it to defeat Iran in 1988 and to invade Kuwait and threaten Israel and Saudi Arabia in 1990–91. Almost all Iraq's basic weaponry came from the Soviet Union and, as long as superpower considerations determined Soviet policies, Iraq could count on Soviet support if it was ever to fall out seriously with the West. The pragmatism worked both ways. The fact that Saddam Hussein was utterly ruthless in his persecution of communists did not affect Iraq's standing as a major customer of the Soviet arms industry. Between 1985 and 1989 Iraq spent nearly $12 billion on arms, of which nearly $7 billion went to the Soviet Union; France, Iraq's second major supplier, received just over $2 billion over the same period.

However welcome they were elsewhere, *glasnost* and *perestroika* were highly unsettling to rulers like Saddam Hussein. The events of 1989 must have seemed particularly chilling: the fall of Honecker; the destruction of the Berlin Wall; the takeover of Czechoslovakia and Poland by democratic movements; and perhaps most frightening of all, the overthrow and execution of Ceaucescu, were all the results of popular revolts against more or less severe forms of dictatorship. A familiar world seemed to be in complete disarray and none of the former certainties seemed to count any longer. As far as the people in the streets and in the camps were concerned, the fall of the Eastern European dictators may have given them some comfort by reminding them of the mortality of their own rulers, but it was also frightening to the extent that they began to realise that they were now entirely at the mercy of the USA and Israel. The limited protection they might have had in the past from the Soviet Union and Eastern Europe would no longer be forthcoming.

Hence, when the report of the US-based Human Rights Watch on Iraq was the subject of questions in Congress in February 1990, Saddam Hussein understood this and other portents as indications that the West was going to turn against him and that the close relationship forged over the previous four years was coming to an end – in an international context in which his Soviet friends could no longer be relied upon. Taking the view that the best form of defence is attack, Saddam Hussein made use of the widespread unease in the Arab world at the Soviet Union's apparent inability to act as a counterweight to American ambitions, (*see* Introduction) to launch a virulent campaign against the USA whom he accused of preparing to establish its hegemony in the region.

These sentiments were summarised in a speech which he gave to the members of the Gulf Co-operation Council assembled in Amman on

24 February 1990. He laid out the possible consequences for the Arab world of the decline of the Soviet Union as a world power and the affirmation of American superiority which this implied: the Gulf would become an American lake, and the USA would use its naval power to control the price of oil. To pre-empt the permanent establishment of American hegemony, the Arabs should agree on a definite plan of action to build themselves into a regional power capable of setting the agenda on a more equal basis. This was clearly an attempt to present himself as the Bismarck around whom lesser leaders should rally.

Over the next few months the discourse continued and became more strident. Several more incidents enabled Saddam Hussein to present himself as 'embattled', the victim of conspiracies forged by Zionism, imperialism and the agents of imperialism in the region. A few weeks after the Human Rights Watch report came the 'trial' and execution of the 32 year-old British journalist Farzad Bazoft, which occasioned widespread verbal condemnation of Iraq in the Western media. In April a scandal erupted over the so-called Iraq supergun and over the discovery of essential parts for nuclear weapons in the baggage of Iraqi travellers passing through Heathrow. These incidents were represented as evidence of machinations against Iraq and the 'Arab nation', and the virulently anti-American campaign which followed had a considerable echo around the Arab world.

Iraq's neighbours were also accused of betraying Iraq and/or the interests of the Arab nation. There were major differences of opinion on oil pricing policy within OPEC. Kuwait and the UAE were apparently flouting their oil export quotas while Iraq, which was producing well within its capacity, was keen to press for a price increase. Early in 1990 Iraqi officials lobbied the Gulf rulers to lower their production and to push the price up from $18 to $20 per barrel, which they were unwilling to do. At the same time Saddam Hussein became determined to provide Iraq with access to a deep water anchorage on the Gulf, probably to accommodate the new fleet of frigates and corvettes which he had ordered from Italy. Iraq was confined to the port of Umm Qasr and the shallow narrows at the head of the Gulf and Saddam Hussein was casting his eyes on the Kuwaiti islands of Bubyan and Warba, which would provide an ideal alternative anchorage. In the spring of 1990 he raised the stakes further, demanding access to the islands and resuscitating Iraq's claim to that part of the Rumayla oilfield which ran from Iraq into northern Kuwait. He also castigated Kuwait for allegedly having had the temerity to demand repayment of some of Iraq's debts. In July 1990 part of the Iraqi army was sent to the border, and on 2 August, when Kuwait refused to give in to Saddam Hussein's demands, Iraq invaded, and subsequently annexed, Kuwait.

THE INVASION OF KUWAIT AND THE GULF WAR
Reaction to the invasion was swift. In broad terms, no state supported Iraq, but some Arab states, notably Jordan, hesitated to condemn the action outright, seeking to maintain a position from which they might

mediate. On a broader international level, the UN Security Council quickly passed a number of resolutions condemning Iraq. Resolution 660 of 2 August called for the immediate withdrawal of Iraqi troops. Britain, France and the USA froze all Iraqi assets the same day, with Germany and Japan following suit a day later. On 3 August Iraq moved troops to the Iraqi/Saudi border. On 4 August the American Secretary of State and the Soviet Foreign Minister issued a joint declaration suspending arms deliveries to Iraq. UN Resolution 661 of 6 August declared a commercial, financial and military boycott of Iraq. On 7 August President Bush ordered an immediate airlift of American troops to Saudi Arabia. On 8 August Iraq proclaimed that Kuwait was an integral part of Iraq (it was to become Iraq's 19th province on 28 August). Resolution 662 of 9 August declared the annexation of Kuwait illegal. The Iraqi pipelines across Turkey and Saudi Arabia were closed. Arab and Asian workers began to pour out of Kuwait across Iraq towards the Jordanian border, where they were crossing at the rate of 10–15,000 a day during August and September. Within a few days it became clear that Western contract workers and visitors to Iraq were not going to be allowed to leave; Saddam Hussein announced this explicitly on 18 August. Western embassies in Kuwait were closed and their staffs sent to Baghdad.

Over the next weeks and months Iraqi troops killed large numbers of Kuwaitis indiscriminately and rounded up all Iraqis in Kuwait, taking them into custody. Several thousand Kuwaitis were arrested and many have not been seen since. Hospitals and other public buildings were stripped of their equipment and looting of property and attacks on civilians became commonplace. The price of oil rose steadily, from about $20 per barrel before the crisis began to above $40 by mid-September. Neither Iraq nor Kuwait was exporting oil. Various attempts at mediation were made. On 12 August Saddam Hussein first began to talk in terms of 'linkage' with the Palestinian issue, that he would withdraw from Kuwait if Israel withdrew from the Occupied Territories. More joint US/Soviet declarations were made condemning Iraq's actions, although the Soviet Union made it clear that it would not join in any military campaign against Iraq. On 15 August Iraq accepted Iran's peace terms unconditionally, restoring the status quo ante in the Shatt al-Arab to what it had been under the Algiers Agreement of March 1975.

In some parts of the Arab world, especially Jordan, the Occupied Territories and the towns of North Africa, there was great popular ferment, and widespread support for Saddam Hussein. In general, there was little love lost between the Palestinians and the Arab Gulf states. Anti-American and anti-Western feeling rose to new heights and, ever alert to currents which he might turn to his advantage, Saddam Hussein called for a *jihad* or holy war against the enemies of Islam. The aged Ayatullah Abd al-Qasim al-Khu'i issued a *fatwa* on 17 August, condemning any alliance of Muslims, i.e. Saudis, with unbelievers against other Muslims. Saddam Hussein continued to appeal to Islamic sentiment over the next few months, rather quaintly condemning the stationing of non-Muslim troops on the sacred soil of Arabia: since the non-Muslim troops were several hundred miles from Mecca and Medina, he was giving rather a broad interpretation to the notion of 'sacred soil'. However ill the notion of Saddam Hussein fighting a sacred 'war of Islam against unbelief' suited the facts, his defiance of the USA certainly gained him some support in the Arab and Muslim world.

One of the great unanswered questions of this whole terrible episode must be why Saddam Hussein persisted in a course of action which he could not conceivably have carried through. Nasser's seizure of the Suez Canal was often mentioned, but Nasser was taking over a waterway which ran through his own country and his cause was widely regarded as just. In contrast, Saddam Hussein had not only invaded the territory of a small and defenceless neighbour which had spent much of the previous decade paying his debts, but his forces also killed and imprisoned many of its inhabitants, laid the country waste and took its portable assets off to Baghdad. All this aside, there was no sense in which Kuwait was engraved on every Iraqi's heart. While the invasion may have been a great morale booster for the Palestinians, most Iraqis were heartily sick of military adventures and had little enthusiasm for fighting after eight years of war with Iran.

In the five months between the invasion of Kuwait and the start of the Gulf War in January 1991, an impressive array of forces from Saudi Arabia, Egypt, Syria, Morocco, Britain, France, Pakistan and Bangladesh, spearheaded by some 500,000 troops from the USA, mustered in Saudi Arabia, backed by the moral support of the EC countries, Japan, and the states of the then Warsaw Pact. No state gave military assistance to Iraq. Most Arab states, even those relatively well disposed to Iraq, were unequivocal in their condemnation of the invasion. Algeria, Jordan, Libya, Sudan, Tunisia, Yemen and the Palestine Liberation Organisation gave varying degrees of moral support to Iraq when the extent of the USA's determination to force it to withdraw from Kuwait became clear.

At the end of November the UN, under great pressure from the USA, issued Resolution 678, the most crucial so far. This authorised member states to use all means necessary to force Iraq to withdraw from Kuwait if it had not done so by 15 January 1991. Over the next few weeks various mediation efforts were made, but Saddam Hussein remained adamant – the only progress made was in the freeing of the Western hostages, all of whom were released and repatriated by 17 December. On 17 January 1991, the USA and its allies began to bomb various 'strategic' targets, causing countless civilian deaths and considerable damage to the country's infrastructure. Iraq retaliated by launching Scud missiles at targets in Israel and Saudi Arabia and about fifteen Israelis died in Tel Aviv from causes attributable to the missile attacks, against which Israel did not retaliate. After some five weeks of bombing, a ground offensive was launched on 23 February, which ended with the rout and destruction of much of the regular Iraqi Army on 27 February, when a cease-fire was declared.

THE AFTERMATH OF THE GULF WAR

According to one observer, the invasion and the war (i.e. the period between 2 August 1990 and 27 February 1991) resulted in at least 100,000 deaths among both the military and civilian population and some 300,000 wounded. As many as 2.5 million people were displaced (in the sense of being forced to leave, or leaving, their homes and places of work). Over $170 billion in property and infrastructural damage was caused in Iraq, perhaps $60 billion worth in Kuwait, excluding the environmental effects of the firing of Kuwaiti oil wells. Two hundred thousand Palestinians and 150,000 Egyptians were forced to leave Kuwait, together with 600,000 Asians. A further 350,000 Egyptians left Iraq when Egypt joined the coalition.

The effect on the economies of the Middle East and South Asia was catastrophic. Jordan lost about $400 million per annum in remittances and Egypt about $500 million. Bangladeshis in Kuwait lost some $1.4 billion worth of deposits and assets. In addition, Jordan lost its transit fees for Iraqi goods, its cheap oil from Iraq, about $500 million in grants from Kuwait and Saudi Arabia and its export market in Saudi Arabia, because of its support for Iraq. Similarly, some 700,000 Yemenis were expelled from Saudi Arabia between September and December 1990. Extended curfews in the West Bank and Gaza (especially after the Temple Mount killings on 8 October) meant that most of the workers who commuted daily to Israel were unable to get to their jobs, thus losing income estimated at around $2 million daily.

A few days after the war ended, popular insurrections broke out in southern Iraq and in Kurdistan. By 4 March Kurdish forces had taken Sulaimaniyya and by 24 March were in control of most of Kurdistan, including the towns of Arbil and Kirkuk. Although the 'rebels' gained control of large areas between the end of February and the beginning of March, units of the Republican Guard responded with exceptional brutality and were able to gain the upper hand fairly quickly in Basra, Najaf and Karbala. In the southern cities, the insurgents, venting their hatred of the regime, had captured and killed local Ba'thist officials, members of the security services and their families. When the Republican Guard regained control of the southern cities they carried out indiscriminate mass executions of the population. Many tanks were painted with the slogan 'No Shi'is [will survive] after today' and there was widespread destruction of Shi'i shrines and other mosques in the Holy Cities. The devastation of the south was almost entirely the work of the regime itself after the end of February.

In the last week in March, Iraqi helicopters and troops launched raids on Kirkuk and other Kurdish cities. Kirkuk was recaptured after a massive bombardment on 28 March, and Sulaimaniyya on 3 April. A mass exodus of Kurds to the Iraqi/Turkish and Iraqi/Iranian borders began. By the end of April there were about 2.5 million refugees, comprising both Kurds and southerners. The Kurds fled largely because they feared a repetition of the regime's bombing of Halabja with chemical weapons, which had killed more than 5000 people. Figures for casualties in these uprisings are difficult to estimate, and several thousands more died of exhaustion and exposure on the borders of Iran and Turkey. In April 1991 safe havens, essentially a military exclusion zone north of latitude 36°N, were set up in the Kurdish areas, enforced by Britain and the US. In time, although the area was subjected to a fairly rigorous economic blockade from the south, this arrangement permitted the emergence of a de facto Iraqi Kurdish state with its own government and national assembly.

Western policy towards Iraq in the aftermath of the Gulf war was vacillating and confused. The Kurdish and Shi'i risings had certainly been encouraged by the US and its allies, but no effective external assistance was forthcoming. At the same time Saudi Arabia and Turkey expressed unease over any covert or overt American support which might strengthen the Shi'is (and behind them, Iran) or the Kurds. But these apprehensions seemed to diminish during 1992 and 1993. Early in 1992 the Saudis invited a delegation from the Iraqi Shi'i opposition to Riyadh and in the autumn there was evident co-operation between Iraqi Kurdish forces and the Turkish army against units of the PKK (*see* page 145) who had fled into northern Iraq from their bases in Syria.

The view of the US administration in the period since the war seems to have been that, reprehensible as Saddam Hussein's government might be, it was probably 'safer' to accept its continuing existence than to throw itself wholeheartedly behind any one or more of the various opposition groups. However, as the Iraqi regime's capacity to flout the various directives and resolutions of the UN seemed almost infinite – especially in the matter of the disclosure to UN inspectors of the whereabouts of Iraq's weapons of mass destruction, and their safe disposal – a number of active measures were taken. Thus in December 1992 the US decided unilaterally to enforce a second air exclusion zone over southern Iraq (south of latitude 32°N) in a generally unsuccessful attempt to halt the forcible evacuation of the marshlands (which provided good natural cover for opponents of the regime). There were air attacks against targets in Iraq in January 1993 and, some six months' later, US bombers destroyed Iraqi intelligence headquarters in Baghdad.

During 1994 and 1995 there were a number of attempts by the Iraqi government and some of its friends and neighbours (notably Turkey, France and the Commonwealth of Independent States) to persuade the UN Security Council to lift sanctions, but faced with the threat of a US veto, and also by fairly compelling evidence of Iraqi non-compliance on matters related to chemical and bacteriological weapons, they remain in place at the time of writing (October 1995). It is certain that Jordan and Turkey are particularly hard hit by the effects of sanctions, to the extent of some $3-4 billion annually in the case of Turkey alone. It was estimated early in 1995 that about 250,000 barrels per day of oil (some eight per cent of 'normal' production) was leaving the country every year through black market channels into Iran, Jordan and Turkey. The black market value of the dollar has soared from ID300 in April 1994 to ID650 in January 1995 and to ID2000 on the foreign exchange market in Amman.

Within Iraq, the situation has remained grim with hyperinflation a daily reality. A US medical report in September 1992 stated that mortality among children aged under five had tripled since the end of the war. In January 1994 the Iraqi Ministry of Health claimed that 400,000 individuals, one-third of them small children, had died of malnutrition as a result of sanctions. The UN made several offers to set up mechanisms to enable Iraq to sell oil into a special account which would be used specifically to purchase medicines and foodstuffs, but these were always rejected (most recently in August 1995) by the Iraqi government on the grounds that they constituted an unacceptable infringement of national sovereignty.

A presidential referendum in October 1995 gave Saddam Hussein a not entirely unexpected 100 per cent of the vote, but it is extremely difficult to obtain a clear picture of the realities of the internal situation. A report of the UN Human Rights Commission in February 1992 declared that public executions and hangings were taking place daily. Coup attempts, each generally followed by massive reprisals, were reported in January, February and June 1992, and other attempts to overthrow the regime were made by senior military officers in September and November 1993, July 1994 and March, May and June 1995. There were reports of mutinies in the Republican Guard, especially in units composed of the Jubburi and Dulaymi tribe, in the spring and summer of 1995, as well as a number of high level defections. Wafiq al-Samarrai, the former head of military intelligence, joined the Iraqi National Council in December 1994 and, perhaps most spectacularly, two of Saddam Hussein's daughters defected to Jordan with their husbands in July 1995. One of the sons-in-law, General Husayn Kamil Majid (a distant cousin of Saddam Hussein), was formerly Minister of Defence and thus able to give an accurate picture of the regime's military capacity. One consequence of this has been the rise in importance and responsibility of Udayy, Saddam Hussein's eldest son, whose reputation is almost as unsavoury as his father's.

Nevertheless, although such high level defections indicate Saddam Hussein's increasing isolation, there is no hard evidence that the regime is crumbling. It remains the case that the sophisticated technology so eagerly supplied to Iraq by western countries in the 1980s has allowed Saddam Hussein to dig himself in to the extent that he is almost impregnable. For these and other reasons, no opposition can organise within Iraq and the effectiveness of the Iraqi National Council has been greatly reduced by the longstanding divisions and mistrust within Kurdish ranks, as well as by expressions of unease on the part of some of Iraq's neighbours at the possibility of the country's disintegration. While a change of regime would be almost universally welcomed within Iraq, it is difficult to imagine how this might be brought about by conventional means. Thus, some five terrible years after Iraq's defeat in the Gulf war, there are still no obvious grounds for envisaging any speedy resolution of its people's sufferings.

Marion Farouk-Sluglett and Peter Sluglett

5
ISRAEL

ISRAEL IS A STATE BORN IN WAR, a standing challenge to the Arab states, which long refused to accept its very existence. Some would argue that the question of Israel lies at the heart of the seemingly endemic instability of the Middle East. It's a view not all share. It cannot be denied, however, that conflict has been, and continues to be, at the core of Israel's story. Israel has been embroiled in war six times in its brief history, sometimes in its own defence, sometimes as the aggressor: in 1948-49 (the War of Independence); in 1956 (the Sinai Campaign); in 1967 (the Six Day War); in 1973 (the Yom Kippur, or October War); in 1982 (in Lebanon, 'Operation Peace for Galilee'); and in 1991, albeit only indirectly (the Gulf War).

The War of Independence brought to a head the struggle between the Jewish and Arab populations of mandatory Palestine, which had raged throughout the years of the British occupation and mandate (1917-48). It pitted a largely unpoliticised Palestinian Arab population of one million, supported by generally ineffective military detachments from Egypt, Iraq, Lebanon, Syria and Transjordan (the CIA estimated 46,800 Arab troops in July 1948) against 650,000 Jews intent on forming a Jewish state. The Jewish forces consisted of the Haganah and Palmach (the regular forces) with 75,000 well-trained volunteers, as well as irregulars and guerrilla groups such as the Irgun (12,000) and the Stern gang (700). These irregulars, whose methods were frequently extreme, were forcibly incorporated into the regular forces by David Ben Gurion, Israel's wartime commander and first prime minister.

Arab attacks began the moment the state of Israel was declared by Ben Gurion in May 1948. After bitter fighting and two UN-imposed truces, armistices were signed in 1949. Under their terms Israel gained control of the coastal plain, the Negev and Galilee. Jordan, whose British-officered Arab Legion was by far the best of the Arab armies, took over the West Bank of the River Jordan, annexing it formally in April 1950. Jerusalem was divided between Israel and Jordan. The war turned several hundred thousand Palestinian Arabs into refugees.

The Zionist victory set in train a groundswell of popular opposition against what were regarded as 'imperialist puppet regimes' in the Arab world, leading to the assassination of King Abdullah of Jordan in July 1951, accused of 'collusion' with Israel, and the overthrow of the Egyptian monarchy in 1952. In late 1955, President Nasser of Egypt announced that he would block Israeli navigation in the Straits of Tiran on the Red Sea and formed a joint command with Syria. The

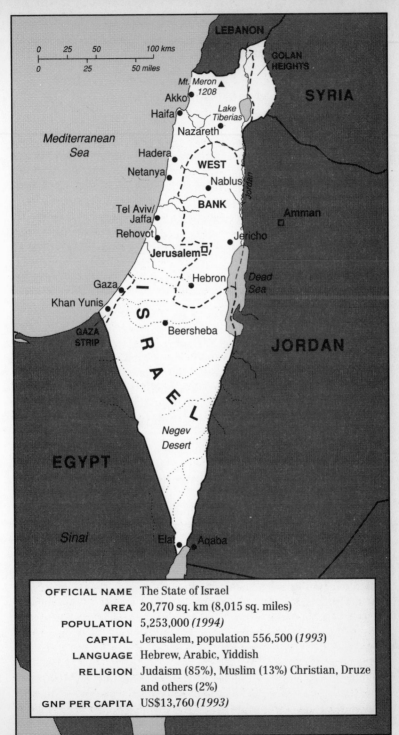

OFFICIAL NAME	The State of Israel
AREA	20,770 sq. km (8,015 sq. miles)
POPULATION	5,253,000 *(1994)*
CAPITAL	Jerusalem, population 556,500 *(1993)*
LANGUAGE	Hebrew, Arabic, Yiddish
RELIGION	Judaism (85%), Muslim (13%) Christian, Druze and others (2%)
GNP PER CAPITA	US$13,760 *(1993)*

following year, Nasser nationalised the Suez Canal, a private company in which British and French interests were the majority shareholders. There followed the 1956 Anglo-French-Israeli war against Egypt, which ended with humiliating reversals for France and Britain and considerable military successes for Israel. The fighting was ended by a UN cease fire in November 1956 with Israel obliged to withdraw from the lands it had occupied during the fighting, including Gaza and Sinai.

After 1956 the Israeli-Egyptian border stayed quiet. But there were increased attacks on Israel from Syria, which shelled Israeli settlements from the Golan Heights, and from Jordan, including raids by the Palestine Liberation Organisation (PLO), founded in 1964. In 1967 the Egyptians demanded the removal of UN observers from Sinai, and Nasser sent two divisions there. For his part Yitzhak Rabin, then Israeli chief of staff, warned Damascus and Cairo that Israel would not tolerate further 'provocations'. King Hussein of Jordan also cast in his lot with Egypt and Syria on 30 May. Faced by 250,000 Arab troops, 2,000 tanks and 700 fighters, and urged on by Moshe Dayan, Israel's defence minister, Israel launched a pre-emptive strike. On 5 June 1967, Israel destroyed the Egyptian air force on the ground; those of Jordan and Syria were similarly devastated. As well as taking possession of the whole of the West Bank including Jerusalem, Israel also captured the Golan Heights, Gaza and the Sinai peninsula. For the Arabs the defeat was in many ways more traumatic than in 1948, since it revealed the yawning gap between the bombast of Arab nationalist rhetoric and the reality of Arab military ineptitude.

The Israelis had thrown off the image of the European ghetto Jew and had stunned the world with their military prowess. Perhaps in partial consequence, Israel was lulled into a false sense of security. On 6 October 1973 – Yom Kippur, the Jewish Day of Atonement, when Israel was at prayer – Syria and Egypt struck again. Caught unawares, Israel initially suffered serious reverses as Egypt launched a remarkable crossing of the Suez Canal. Once installed in Sinai, however, the Egyptian forces did not consolidate their gains, and Israel was able to retake the Suez Canal. Eventually, President Sadat was forced to appeal to his Soviet backers for a cease-fire.

Though the victory was Israel's, the Arabs none the less felt they had regained their honour. Ironically it was partly this new pride which enabled President Sadat of Egypt to go to Jerusalem to seek peace with Israel in 1977. There followed the Camp David Agreement, negotiated by Sadat, the Israeli prime minister, Menachem Begin, and the American president, Jimmy Carter, and the Israeli-Egyptian peace treaty of 1979. Until 1994, Egypt was the only Arab country to have made formal peace with Israel.

If the October War dented Israel's image as the military superpower of the Middle East, the 1982 Lebanon campaign went far towards undermining its moral reputation. The campaign, launched in June 1982 with an invasion across the Litani River, pitted Israeli forces against both Syria and the PLO in an all-out drive to force the PLO from Lebanon. Israel's 'hidden agenda' was the installation of a pro-Israeli Christian Phalangist regime in Beirut. These hopes suffered a substantial setback when Bashir Jumayyil, Israel's preferred presidential candidate, was murdered in September. A further blow came when Phalangists entered Palestinian refugee camps at Sabra and Chatila, with the evident blessing of the Israeli forces, and massacred the residents. Combined with the Israeli shelling of West Beirut, it was an event that sharply polarised world, and Israeli, public opinion. In 1985, Israel withdrew from Lebanon, retaining a 'security zone' in south Lebanon, which it still patrols with the Israeli-financed South Lebanese Army, led by the former Lebanese army officer, General Antoine Lahd.

In 1987 Israeli attention turned to the Intifada, the 'internal war' waged against Israel by the Palestinians 'of the inside' – those resident in the territories occupied by Israel since 1967. After 20 years of occupation, ordinary Palestinians of all ages and classes rose up in an attempt to force Israeli troops to leave the West Bank (*intifada* means 'shaking off' or 'eruption' in Arabic). The image of Israel took a further blow as television audiences worldwide saw Israeli soldiers shooting and beating Palestinians armed only with stones.

By 1990-91, with the Intifada losing momentum, Israel found itself indirectly drawn into the Gulf War when Iraq launched Scud missiles at Israeli cities. In a transparent ruse to gain support for the invasion of Kuwait, Iraq claimed that the invasion itself had been carried out in the name of the 'Arab nation' as part of the struggle against imperialism and Zionism. This tactic generally failed to gain support, however, except in Jordan with its substantial Palestinian population, and in the states of North Africa. The Arab world suffered a serious split, and the creation of the American-led coalition, under UN auspices, gave rise to an extraordinary situation in which Israel found itself effectively on the same side as several of the states with which it was still technically at war.

The announcement in August 1991 that Israel was prepared to join the peace talks tenaciously pursued by the American secretary of state, James Baker, almost certainly marked the beginning of the end of more than 40 years of conflict. In spite of the progress that has been made, a number of outstanding points of dispute remain, including the status of Jerusalem, claimed by Jews and Palestinians alike as their 'eternal' capital, the Israeli settlements on the West Bank and the status of the Palestinian refugees world wide.

THE SEARCH FOR PEACE

However permanent Israel's presence in the Occupied Territories may be in practice, in theory at least the West Bank and Gaza, unlike Jerusalem and the Golan Heights, have never been annexed by Israel. Instead, in Israeli terminology, they have been 'administered', on the assumption that their final status is subject to negotiation. UN Resolution 242 of November 1967 requires the withdrawal of Israeli forces 'from territories of recent conflict' and the guaranteed peaceful existence of 'every state in the area ... within secure and recognised boundaries'.

The Palestinians long sought to persuade the international community to make Israel 'give back' the West Bank and Gaza. For its part, Israel refused (at least publicly) to deal with 'extremist' Palestinian leaders whose real aim, in Israel's view, was not compromise but the destruction of the Israeli state. While some Palestinians would not settle for anything but a return to a pre-1948 bi-national Palestine, with Arab and Jewish communities, most have shown themselves prepared to settle for a reduced homeland. However, an ominous recent development has been the split within Israel between those Israelis who believe that the only way to achieve peace and security is to follow the broad outlines of the policy of the present Labour government, and those who are opposed to any compromise with the PLO (or Arab states such as Syria) which will diminish Israeli control over strategically or religiously significant parts of the West Bank or the Golan Heights. The murder of Yitzhak Rabin on 4 November 1995 has been an obvious reflection of what is undoubtedly a deep rift in Israeli society. It is important to understand that although its more recent manifestations hint at the presence of an entirely new kind of radical right within Israel, the question of whether to make some form of accommodation with the Arabs or to confront them head on has been one of the most intractable of the differences within the Zionist movement since its members first came to Palestine at the end of the 19th century.

ISRAELI SOCIETY TODAY

The shift to the right in Israel and the rise of extremist ultra-Orthodox groups underline the fact that in many ways the prevailing image of Israel in the West is outdated. Europeans and Americans still tend to think in terms of pioneering mandatory Palestine and immediately post-1948 Israel, with Zionist volunteers working on kibbutzim (cooperative farms) 'making the desert bloom'. It is also widely believed that Israeli political culture is still dominated by the European-born left-wingers who formed the backbone of Mapai, the Labour party, which ruled until 1977.

This rugged ideal of Israel was further reinforced by the Six Day War, but profound changes have taken place since then. In the first place, agriculture and the kibbutzim, though still of symbolic importance, have little economic weight. In 1991 agriculture accounted for 6% of domestic production, and about 130,000 people (3% of the population) lived on kibbutzim. Secondly, Israel has increasingly had to take account of the Sephardic Jews, mostly of North African and Middle Eastern origin who migrated in the 1950s and early 1960s, who have tended to rally to the populist anti-Arab rhetoric of Likud, in contrast to the Ashkenazi (European) Jews, who shaped the state and led it in its early years. It must be stressed, however, that the principal figures within the Likud party, which formed the government between 1977 and 1992 – Shamir, Arens and Sharon, for example – are of European origin, as are many Likud supporters. Furthermore, spiralling political violence, as exemplified by the assassination of Yitzhak Rabin, the downturn in the economy, suspicion of US and European intentions, and the gradual deterioration of Arab-Jewish relations have also encouraged the rise of an extra-parliamentary radical right, egged on to some extent by Likud's dogged opposition to the peace process.

The rise of the religious right-wing has helped create an impression of religious intolerance in Israel not dissimilar to the spread of Islamic fundamentalism in the Arab world and Iran, although in reality the great majority of the population is secular in outlook. Israel remains committed to the democratic values of its founders, and is still, with Turkey, the only functioning democracy in the region. To a degree, democracy was also inherited from the laws and institutions of the British mandate (as were the various undemocratic emergency regulations, which remain the basis of Israeli actions in the Occupied Territories). Israel's democracy is vividly expressed in the parliament, the Knesset, with its multitude of parties, noisy debates and complex procedures. The chaotic parliamentary scenes, and the disproportionate influence wielded by the ultra-Orthodox, have led to demands for electoral reform (see below).

Israel is also the only Middle Eastern country to enjoy a virtually free press (subject to censorship on security matters), an independent judiciary and freedom of assembly, although the Israeli Arabs (those living within the frontiers of pre-1948 Israel) both feel and are treated as second-class citizens. Israelis love to argue and do so fully and freely, with endless debates in homes, in cafés and on television. The spiritual and ideological roots of the country lie firmly in Judaism, with even secular Jews observing rituals such as circumcision and bar mitzvah. Israel remains an outdoor society, with a strong emphasis on healthy living, hiking, and hard work. Drug abuse, although on the rise, is rare by outside standards. Finally – and this is perhaps the very basis of society – older Israelis of European origin are bound together by the memory of the Holocaust, and by the belief that Israel must serve as a refuge for Jews and as a vigilant guardian against future occurrences of anti-Semitism.

Support for Labour declined in the mid-1970s, partly but not entirely because of its failure to address the social and economic problems of the Jews of Middle Eastern and North African origin, who turned increasingly to Likud. The 1977 elections, which brought Likud under Menachim Begin to office, marked the end of a 30-year period in which the Israeli establishment was synonymous with Labour, led by such dominant figures as David Ben Gurion and Golda Meir. Rabin and

Peres, despite participation in the Likud-Labour coalition government of 1988-90, were unable to maintain Labour's grip. This period effectively came to an end with the elections of June 1992, whose results seemed to indicate that a substantial number of Israelis had come to accept that some form of normalisation of relations with their Arab neighbours and the Palestinians was both necessary and desirable.

'KIBBUTZ LEFT' VERSUS 'SETTLER RIGHT'

The crisis in the kibbutz movement is clearly related to the problems of the left. Kibbutzim still thrive, and will remain a feature of Israeli life, with their stress on thrift and the communal life. But many are deeply in debt, and although admired for their role in the creation of Israel, they no longer automatically produce the country's political and military elite. A new middle class has grown up in areas like Tel Aviv, with *nouveaux riches* – Israelis addicted to consumer goods, yachts and expensive cars. The ideal of an egalitarian society, which motivated the pioneers fleeing from ghettoes and persecution, no longer has the same appeal.

Right-wingers, by contrast, some of them recent immigrants from the United States, have gained ground. In its most militant form the right embraces such groups as Kach and its offshoot Kahane Chai (both proscribed by the Israeli government in March 1994), which follow the overtly racist precepts of Rabbi Meir Kahane, murdered in New York in November 1990, and advocating a form of 'ethnic cleansing' against Arabs, and Eyal, the movement with which Yitzhak Rabin's assassin was associated. Such militants trace their modern origin to the Jewish Underground, formed from radical Jewish settlers on the West Bank who committed acts of violence against Palestinian leaders in the early 1980s, including attempting to assassinate several West Bank Arab mayors. Although the Jewish Underground was broken up by Israeli police and its ringleaders arrested, its spirit lives on, not least among members of the settler movement Gush Emunim (Bloc of the Faithful) led by the extremist Rabbi Moshe Levinger.

ASHKENAZI, SEPHARDIC, ORTHODOX AND SECULAR

The swing to the right in Israel can be explained partly in terms of the revival of an important historical trend in Zionist thinking, and partly along the lines of the balance between the Ashkenazi and Sephardic communities. To some extent the two have intermingled: 20 per cent of Israeli marriages are 'mixed'. But the Jews who arrived en masse from North Africa, Yemen and Iraq in the 1950s and early 1960s still have a separate identity, and have progressed from being a poor and backward minority, an Israeli underclass, to being a force to be reckoned with. A poll by the Smith Institute published in *Davar* in December 1990 showed that 63 per cent of Sephardic Jews supported Likud and its right-wing allies, while only 19 per cent voted for Labour and the left. This was mirrored by the Ashkenazi side: only 28 per cent of

Israelis of European origin voted for Likud, while 50 per cent supported Labour. This is a marked change from the 1960s and 1970s when half the Sephardic community were Labour voters.

The same poll showed that support for Labour was still drawn largely from Israel's secular population. The influential ultra-Orthodox Jews of Israel, a familiar part of the scene in their black hats and ringlets, support either Likud or religious parties such as the National Religious Party (NRP), Degel, Ha-Torah and the Sephardic SHAS, although the latter is an uneasy member of the present Labour-led coalition. Because of Israel's proportional representation system and the proliferation of parties, the small religious groups have tended to hold the balance of power in the Knesset and have received generous state funding for religious seminaries (*yeshivas*). This has exacerbated tensions between secular Israelis, who observe Sabbath rituals lightly if at all and want Israel to be a haven for Jews of all kinds, and the ultra-Orthodox, who want stricter religious laws and a life devoted to study of the Torah.

Not entirely paradoxically, many Orthodox or *haredim* (meaning 'God-fearing') Jews regard the creation of the state of Israel as premature, since, strictly speaking, such a state should be created by God rather than by man. and could only come into existence after the Messiah makes himself known on earth. As has already been mentioned, this has not prevented the religious parties from taking part in politics, and indeed manipulating coalitions to great effect. The Orthodox parties are pressing for stricter criteria for the Law of Return, which allows Jews to settle in Israel. In the wake of the assassination of Yitzhak Rabin in November 1995, there has been talk of revising the Law of Return in a different way: to prevent right wing extremists, mostly from the United States, from entering the country.

Secular, left-wing Israelis fear the growth of religious influence, and are increasingly vocal in their demands for electoral reforms which would ensure that the religious parties are reduced to their 'proper status'. Israelis on both left and right have joined the movement for electoral reform, with voters of all shades of opinion finding the process of coalition-haggling which follows any election distasteful and demeaning. Reformers opposed to unstable coalitions and the excessive power of the Orthodox groups have been able to mobilise tens of thousands of supporters on the streets of Jerusalem and Tel Aviv, with direct elections for the post of prime minister as one of their aims. There have been hunger strikes and petitions to the Knesset, with the then president, Chaim Herzog, joining the ranks of the reformers and describing the present system as a 'mockery of democracy'. However, the vested interests involved are so entrenched that neither Labour nor Likud appears willing to risk upheaval by forcing the necessary changes through the Knesset.

The absurdity of the process was well illustrated in the election in June 1992. Labour won 44 out of the 120 Knesset seats, Likud 32 seats. In order to form a government, the Labour leader, Yitzhak Rabin, needed to gain the support of other parties. One, Meretz, with 12 seats (to which the controversial Shulamit Aloni belongs), is reasonably close to Labour ideologically, but Mr Rabin's other partner was the religious party SHAS, with six seats, whose Hebrew acronym translates as 'Torah Observing Sephardim'. Under such circumstances 'policy-making' is fraught with complications.

THE ISRAELI ECONOMY

In the early years of the Jewish state, economic progress was remarkable. Substantial foreign investment, new irrigation techniques and sheer hard work did, indeed, make the 'desert bloom'. In industry, growth rates averaged nine per cent in real terms between 1960 and 1973, with inflation kept down to single figures. Trees were planted, swamps drained, roads built, and an advanced defence industry took shape to give Israel military self-sufficiency. A modern banking system developed. The burden of high defence spending was (and is) largely borne by loans and aid from the United States.

The underlying strains in the economy came to the fore after the 1973 Yom Kippur War and the impact of the OPEC (Organisation of Petroleum Exporting Countries) oil embargo the same year. If Israel clearly suffered from the Arab economic boycott, it still suffers from an antiquated state-dominated economic structure in which a huge concern like Koor, owned by the Histadrut, the trade union organisation, can control a large proportion of Israeli manufacturing and retailing. This tradition of state interventionism, coupled with a bureaucracy which is one of the world's most complex and Byzantine, creates severe obstacles to initiative and growth. Israel launched a privatisation programme, with one eye on the competitive trade conditions which were an inherent part of the completion of the Single European Market in 1992. But entrenched attitudes are proving hard to shift, and foreign investors are often alienated by Israeli statism.

The tradition of state intervention and control has its origins in the pioneering days of the state and the socialist ethic which Israel's European-born elite brought with it as part of its vision of Zionism. By 1985, the faults in Israel's economy had become obvious, with inflation running at around 400 per cent and foreign reserves dangerously low. Under Shimon Peres, then Labour prime minister, and with American help, the Israeli leadership succeeded in imposing an austerity programme and brought inflation down to below 20 per cent. Some state subsidies, for example in transport, were phased out, and expensive projects such as the Lavi fighter aircraft were cancelled. Budget deficits dropped from 15 per cent of GNP to under two per cent.

None the less the essential problem of turning a bureaucratised, monopolistic system into a Western-orientated free-market system remained. Foreign debt and defence expenditure together account for a staggering 60 per cent of the Israeli budget. Twenty years ago, according to the Israeli Centre for Social and Economic Progress, one in five Israelis were employed by the government: today the figure is one in three. Nearly a third of all business activity, according to Israeli economists, is controlled by cartels and monopolies, and competition in agricultural products such as fruit and vegetables is strictly regulated by a state marketing board. Protectionism abounds in all commercial sectors. The building industry is also inhibited by the scarcity and high cost of land – nearly all land is leased by the Israel Land Authority and by a complex and stifling system of planning permission and licensing. In 1990 workers at moshavim co-operative farms which combine agriculture with light industry in the north of Israel staged Intifada-style strikes. The annual trade deficit fluctuated from $3-5 billion between 1990 and 1992.

Some economists propose, as a drastic measure, that annual American economic aid to Israel – currently $3 billion – should be reduced or even eliminated, forcing Israel to face harsh economic realities and introduce market reforms faster. Others put their faith in the privatisation programme, under which a number of state-owned companies, such as the Israel Electrical Corporation and Maman Cargo Handling, have been sold off. The state airline, El Al, now emerging from receivership after becoming bankrupt, is to be offered to private investors. However, investors often find that privatisation contracts are hedged about with conditions which allow for a degree of continued state control, especially if the company concerned has some strategic value or is considered crucial to the national interest.

SOVIET-JEWISH IMMIGRATION

Strains in the already overburdened Israeli economy were increased by the massive influx of Soviet Jews into Israel, which began in late 1989 and gathered momentum in 1990, partly because of the freedoms opened up by Gorbachev and partly because of rising anti-Semitism, itself a product of the political loosening-up in Russia. But Israeli leaders, and for that matter ordinary Israelis, welcomed Soviet Jewish immigration on a huge scale as a 'miracle', a fresh infusion of blood into the Jewish state which could only strengthen Israel and give it new vigour and economic growth.

According to the Jewish Agency, which together with the Ministry of Absorption and Immigration deals with immigration matters, 200,000 Soviet Jews arrived in Israel in the course of 1990, and 170,000 in 1991, rather less than had been anticipated. Of the 200,000 who arrived in 1990, a quarter came from the Ukraine, some 40,000 from European Russia and 25,000 from Central Asia. About half had received higher education and professional qualifications: 20,000 were classed as 'engineers', and there were some 5,000 physicians among the new immigrants. A major difficulty has been finding jobs for Soviet immigrants in a country which has an unemployment rate of between ten and twelve per cent. Soviet doctors, for example, have gone to development towns like Beersheba, which boasts an excellent hospital and medical school, only to find that there is a surfeit of medically qualified personnel and that the only way to make a living – at least for the time being – is to undertake manual work or even (in some documented cases) sweep the streets.

Despite the efforts of settler groups, such as Gush Emunim, to attract Soviet olim, less than one per cent have in fact chosen to go to the West Bank or Gaza. Ariel, near Nablus, the most successful settlement in attracting Russians, has some 1,200 Soviet immigrants living in suburban-style conditions. But few Russians find the idea of living a pioneer life on a rural settlement surrounded by hostile Arabs an attractive proposition, and most tend naturally to settle in areas such as Tel Aviv and Haifa, where friends and relatives from earlier waves of Soviet immigration already live. Some ten per cent of the Soviet arrivals have chosen to live in the newly built Jewish suburbs of East Jerusalem, which has been annexed by Israel as part of its 'united and eternal capital', but which the international community regards as occupied land whose final status has yet to be negotiated.

The issue of demography and settlement remains an explosive one, and has been the cause of strains in relations between Israel and the United States. Many of the Soviet Jews arriving in Israel would almost certainly have preferred to emigrate to the United States. The Israelis, for their part, have turned to the US, and above all to American Jewish groups, for financial aid in raising the $2 billion needed for the absorption of immigrants.

Meanwhile, ten per cent of the new arrivals live temporarily in rundown, often squalid 'absorption centres' while they try to find their feet in Israeli society. Some experts, such as Julia Mirsky, a Hebrew University psychologist who helps newcomers to adjust, complain that many of the new arrivals are not committed Zionists in the manner of earlier refusenik immigrants such as Natan Sharansky, but rather refugees from the privations and pressures of post-USSR Russia. After the killing of 18 Arabs on Temple Mount in October 1990 and the revenge stabbings of Jews by Arabs which followed, some Israeli employers began laying off Arab labourers and hiring Soviet immigrants instead. But as Sharansky, who runs the Soviet Jewish Zionist Forum in Jerusalem, has observed, 'many of the immigrants are physicians, engineers, musicians and other professionals. They are not looking for jobs on building sites'.

US-ISRAELI RELATIONS

It is widely assumed in the Arab world that Israel is a 'client state' of the US, and that US policy in turn is influenced if not shaped by the American Jewish lobby. The US is indeed Israel's most loyal supporter in the international community, and its main financial benefactor; the influence of the Jewish lobby in Washington is also not to be underestimated. On the other hand, stresses have grown in relations between the US and Israel, with the American Jewish lobby often expressing concern over Israel's policies in the Occupied Territories, particularly its refusal to halt the construction of new settlements there. Such strains reflected a new degree of alienation between the US and Israel. In the late 1980s and early 1990s this took the form of the US support for resolutions in the UN Security Council critical of Israel, and temporary US refusal in February 1992 to underwrite further Israeli loans unless settlement activity ceased (although this threat was lifted in spite of the fact that settlement activity was not halted). Hence in spite of the closeness of the link and the considerable leverage the US exerts upon Israel, it is difficult to imagine that substantial progress towards a peace settlement could have been made if, for example, the Israeli electorate had voted Shamir and the Likud back into office in June 1992.

However, Israel's self-restraint when subjected to Iraqi missile attacks in the Gulf War ensured it a great deal of future credit. In formal terms, and apart from ties based on the American-Jewish connection, the US-Israeli relationship is based on a strategic co-operation agreement. In financial terms, relations revolve around US aid to Israel of $3 billion a year, an annually renewable gift, of which $1.75 billion is earmarked as military aid to help Israel defend itself. The rest is economic aid to support Israel's troubled economy. In addition the US government further supports Israel through loan guarantees and tax credits on charitable donations.

The refusal of the Shamir government to accede to the Baker proposals for Israeli-Palestinian talks in 1990 caused a strained atmosphere between Washington and Jerusalem, and in personal terms, between Bush and Shamir. US disapproval of Likud policies toward the Occupied Territories, and in particular the continued expansion of Jewish West Bank settlements, led the Bush administration to withhold aid programmes and even military equipment. The failure of the US to supply Israel with the advanced Patriot anti-missile system in time to prevent Iraq's Scud missile attacks on Tel Aviv in January 1991 caused particular bitterness in Israel.

Such tensions came against the background of growing US public dismay over Israel's handling of the Intifada from December 1987 onwards. Even some American Jewish groups and supporters of Israel in the US Congress voiced concern over television images of Israeli troops behaving with brutality toward Arab protesters and the alarming number of killings of young people. Israel's heavy-handed actions did much to undermine the instinctive American sympathy for Israel which had been part of the mental climate of US foreign policy since the foundation of the state.

The Bush administration, moreover, was perceived as far less sympathetic toward Israel than the Reagan administration had been. One flashpoint came after the Temple Mount killings on 8 October 1990, when Shamir resisted US efforts to persuade Israel to co-operate with a proposed UN investigation into the incident. 'So long as the Palestinian problem is unsolved, so long as Shamir believes time is on his side, Israel will be at odds with the US,' wrote *Hadashot* in November 1990. The ending of the Cold War and the Soviet-American rapprochement of 1990 also had an important effect on the Israeli-US relationship. While still providing Israel's underpinning, the United States no longer needs Israel to the same extent as 'a low cost land-based aircraft carrier' to represent Western interests in a regional East-West confrontation. The Gulf War also illustrated this, with the US forging a new alliance with Saudi Arabia, Egypt and Syria to wage war on Saddam Hussein.

While rejecting the 'linkage' Saddam Hussein had created between Kuwait and Palestine, the US was clearly obliged by its new coalition with anti-Iraq Arab states to engage in harsher criticism of Israel at the UN and to demonstrate a firm commitment to a resolution of the Palestinian question. At the same time, the US distanced itself from the PLO by breaking off the US PLO dialogue following Arafat's failure to condemn Palestinian terrorist acts in sufficiently clear and precise terms.

Equally, US financial support for Israel shows no sign of diminishing, despite calls from some American politicians for a five per cent reduction. In November 1990 Congress voted to cancel Egypt's $6.7 billion military debt to the US without cancelling Israel's, while the Senate overwhelmingly approved the annual $3 billion aid package for Israel and added $700 million worth of military equipment. A further major intelligence and military assistance package was negotiated at the end of 1992.

Israel's agreement to refrain from retaliation against Iraqi Scud attacks in the early stages of the Gulf War was swiftly rewarded with the supply of US-made Patriot anti-missile systems, with American crews. This helped to forge a new understanding between Washington and Jerusalem, but it did not end the Bush administration's insistence that Israel should be more flexible over the Palestinian issue, nor did it reduce the US' support for the idea of an international peace conference, a proposal Israel vehemently opposed. In April 1991 Israel agreed to a Baker proposal for a 'regional' peace conference leading to bilateral Arab-Israeli talks, but the Arab states accused Israel of using a device to avoid a fully fledged international conference with UN involvement. US irritation on the issue had already surfaced in mid-1990 when Baker told the Israeli government publicly: 'Our telephone number is 456-1414. When you're serious about peace, call us.'

THE QUESTION OF JERUSALEM

Since 1967 all Jerusalem has been in the hands of Israel which claims the city as its capital. Nonetheless, Palestinians still regard Jerusalem as their capital. This struggle for a city at once holy to Muslims, Jews and Christians is one of the most intractable of Arab-Israeli issues.

While the 1947 UN partition plan envisaged a Jerusalem under international control (as a corpus separatum), Israel now sees this solution as irrelevant. The 140,000 Palestinians living in East Jerusalem carry Israeli papers as residents of an annexed area. Faysal Husayni, the leading Palestinian in Jerusalem and a descendant of the city's former mufti, proposed unsuccessfully to Teddy Kollek, the veteran former mayor, in January 1991, that there should be 'one city but two municipalities, one Arab and one Jewish'. Kollek repeatedly invited Palestinian residents to take part in municipal elections, but this was resisted on the grounds that to do so would be to acquiesce in the annexation.

For Arabs and Jews alike, the emotive focus is the Old City, where the Muslim shrines of al-Aqsa and the Dome of the Rock stand on the site of the Jewish Temple. In theory Israel allows Muslims free access to the site, but Muslim worshippers have been banned at times of tension. The most serious such incident occurred on 8 October 1990 when 18 Arabs were killed by Israeli border police. Israel accused Arabs of starting the riot by throwing large stones down on Jewish worshippers at the Wailing Wall below as part of a PLO conspiracy to foment unrest and help the cause of Iraq in the Gulf crisis. The Arabs said the deaths were due to unprovoked Israeli police brutality, and that the large Arab presence on the Mount was to prevent an attempt by a small group of Jewish zealots (the Temple Mount Faithful) from trying to lay the foundation stone of a new Temple. An Israeli inquiry referred to 'indiscriminate shooting' by security police but blamed the Palestinians for the riots. As will be discussed below, the present US administration appears to be rather less robust on the question of Jerusalem than its predecessors.

THE PEACE PROCESS

In the spring and summer of 1991, US secretary of state James Baker made several tours of the region, remarking that the 'window of opportunity' had opened, but that it would not remain open for ever. By July, Syria and Jordan had agreed to take part in negotiations. In August, Yitzhak Shamir also agreed to take part, on the condition that neither the PLO nor the Palestinians from East Jerusalem form part of the Palestinian delegation; instead, a number of Palestinians were attached to the Jordanian delegation. In a wry fashion, Israel's rejection of the PLO backfired to its disadvantage, since it resulted in the Palestinian case being presented in the US by individuals of the calibre of Faysal Husayni, Dr Haydar Abd al-Shafi' and Dr Hanan Ashrawi rather than the discredited Yasser Arafat who had warmly embraced Saddam Hussein.

Little significant progress was possible while the Likud government continued in office, although there was no immediate breakthough in June 1992 when Labour won the elections. This was partly due to the small size of Labour's majority, but also because of the rise of a vocal rejectionist opposition to the concept of 'land for peace' which was to increase in stridency as the negotiations proceeded and the first small steps were taken. As has been mentioned, this phenomenon, while representative of a clearly recognisable tendency within Zionist politics, emerged with renewed vigour in the first half of the 1990s. In broad terms the opposition believes that the West Bank (Judaea and Samaria) is an integral part of Eretz Israel and that to allow Palestinian Arab sovereignty over it is tantamount to treason; in its more extreme manifestations it believes that there is no place at all for Arabs in a Jewish state. Even among moderates, there is a sense of great unease at the prospect of transferring power to the PLO, given that organisation's past record.

The sense of anti-climax and frustration which followed the stalled opening rounds in the peace talks lasted until and perhaps beyond September 1993, when Israel and the PLO signed the 'declaration of principles'. During this time, settlement activity continued apace, and the PLO, already partially eclipsed in the Occupied Territories by the indigenous leadership of the Intifada, was further marginalised by the increasing visibility of Hamas. Hamas, an Islamist extremist group, had originally been encouraged by Israeli intelligence as a counterweight to the PLO but had long assumed an independent role. In 1991 and 1992 there were serious clashes between Fatah and Hamas activists on the West Bank, and Hamas members claimed responsibility for a number of assassinations of Israeli soldiers and civilians. Early in 1992 the situation in South Lebanon deteriorated after an apparently unprovoked incident in which the leader of Hizbullah was killed in an Israeli helicopter attack. At this stage, all the Israelis were prepared to offer the Palestinians in the various rounds of bilateral talks was the prospect of municipal elections.

In August 1992 Rabin, now prime minister, travelled to Washington where the Bush administration, presumably concerned to further its re-election chances, granted the loan guarantees it had withheld from Shamir without obliging Rabin to agree to a freeze on further settlement activity. In November, Bill Clinton won the US presidential elections; both Clinton and his vice-president, Al Gore, had made statements to the general effect that Jerusalem should be the unified capital of Israel which greatly increased Palestinian forebodings on the likely future direction of US policy.

In December 1992 Israel arrested some 400 Islamist activists and summarily expelled them to Lebanon, whose government refused to accept them. A Security Council resolution demanded their immediate return, but US intervention effectively neutralised efforts to impose sanctions on Israel. At this stage it had become extremely difficult to convince the Palestinians and the other Arab participants in the peace process that the talks were leading anywhere, and further attempts to bring the parties together foundered with the return of the deportees. In April 1993, Rabin ordered the closure of the Occupied Territories 'indefinitely', and many thousands of Palestinians working in Israel lost their livelihoods as a result. In July the US rejected Palestinian demands that peace talks should include discussion of a independent Palestinian state with its capital in East Jerusalem. At this stage several senior figures in the Palestinian negotiating team threatened to resign.

The breakthrough, if it can be accurately so described, came at the end of August, when Israel and the PLO announced their joint 'declaration of principles', the result of highly secret negotiations which both parties had been conducting in Norway on an entirely separate track from those taking place in Washington. The declaration, sometimes known as 'Gaza-Jericho first', involved *inter alia* formal Israeli recognition of the PLO, the handing over of responsibility for education, culture, health, social welfare and direct taxation to 'authorised Palestinians' in the West Bank and Gaza within a month; and the initiation of talks on the withdrawal of Israeli forces from an (undefined) area round Jericho and from Gaza. It also stipulated that elections to a Palestinian Council would be held in the course of 1994 and that the permanent status of the area would be decided and a permanent settlement reached by December 1998. The declaration, which by then had the tacit if not enthusiastic approval of President Asad of Syria and King Husayn of Jordan, was signed on the White House lawn on 13 September 1993.

While the declaration can certainly be called a milestone, it was scarcely a panacea. In the first place, the long time-frame meant that much could go wrong before anything very substantial or 'irreversible' could be implemented. Secondly, it said nothing about Israeli settlements beyond a statement to the effect that Israeli armed forces would continue to be responsible for the settlers' security. To put this in perspective, there were 300,000 Israelis living in settlements on the West Bank (including the 'suburbs of East Jerusalem') in February 1995, and a further 7,000 in 18 settlements in Gaza. Thirdly, the declaration did not mention Jerusalem. Fourthly, it effectively handed over the administration, first of Gaza-Jericho and then of whatever extension the mini-state might subsequently have, to Yasser Arafat and the PLO, and bypassed the grass-roots leadership that had been nurtured by the Intifada.

A few days later Jordanian-Israeli negotiations on mutual recognition began. These ended with the signature of a comprehensive peace treaty a year later, in October 1994. Negotiations for a similar treaty with Syria have foundered over the timing of Israeli withdrawal from the Golan Heights, and have not been concluded at the time of writing (November 1995); in January 1994, Rabin announced that there would be a national referendum on any comprehensive settlement with Syria. In Israel SHAS resigned from the coalition; several hundred Palestinian prisoners were released from Israeli jails. Throughout the rest of 1993 and 1994 there were outbursts of violence in the Occupied Territories; killings of settlers by Palestinians; of Palestinians by settlers; of Fatah members by Hamas; of Hamas members by Fatah. On 13 December Israeli forces were due to be withdrawn from Gaza; this eventually took place on 25 May 1994.

On the surface, there has been considerable progress since September 1993, but the limitations inherent in the agreement have made themselves felt. One early problem was financial: the Palestinian Authority had no money, and donors hesitated to entrust funds to a body entirely made up of Arafat's personal appointees whose account-ability was at best ambiguous. This was eventually solved, but the highly undemocratic nature of the Authority (and indeed the accusa-tions of human rights abuses that have been made against it) continues to be a matter of major concern.

In late February 1994 an armed Israeli settler killed 30 Muslim worshippers at the mosque in Hebron. All contacts between Israel and the PLO ceased for a few weeks, until Israel agreed that a lightly armed Scandinavian observer force could be deployed there tem-porarily. However, in spite of opposition within the Israeli cabinet, it was decided that the 400 settlers living in the middle of Hebron (sur-rounded by a population of over 100,000 Palestinians) should remain there, guarded, inevitably, by Israeli armed forces. In July 1994 Arafat arrived in Gaza to take possession of his fiefdom, controlled by Palestinian policemen since the Israeli police withdrawal in May. Violence in Israel and the Territories continued, revealing the pro-found opposition to the 'peace process' on both the Palestinian and Israeli sides. Hamas suicide bombers planted bombs in bus stations and conducted other acts of terrorism both against Israelis and PLO sympathisers in the months that followed.

One necessary precondition for the future stability of the Palestine Administration, first in Gaza-Jericho and then in those parts of the West Bank which Israel permits it to administer, is that it should be economically viable, perhaps not on its own but through some form of integration with the economies of Israel and Jordan. Apart from the fact that rather little of the promised international aid package has materialised so far, Israel's sporadic sealing off of the West Bank and Gaza since April 1993 meant that the number of Palestinians working in Israel declined sharply, from about 70,000 to about 30,000 (10,000 from Gaza and 20,000 from the West Bank). In April 1994 Israel issued 17,000 six-month work permits for foreign (non-Arab) workers to enter the country – an indication, perhaps, that its ultimate intention was to do away entirely with its dependence on Palestinian unskilled and semi-skilled labour. Unemployment in the West Bank and Gaza stood at about 40 per cent in April 1994, and UNRWA continued to play its key role in providing the population of the refugee camps with food and other basic necessities. A further problem stemming from this is that a low level of income generation means that the Palestine Authority's taxation base, and thus its capacity to fund itself, is corre-spondingly small.

Again, the status of Jerusalem remains a major unknown. Israeli building and settlement activity has been so directed that Arab East Jerusalem is now virtually surrounded by Israeli 'suburbs', with the result that the Jewish population of East Jerusalem has recently overtaken the Palestinian population. These 'suburbs', like all the settlements deeper inside the West Bank, have of course been built on confiscated Arab land. It is possible to envisage a future scenario under which the more isolated settlements might be dismantled, but, given the sheer density of what has been constructed around Jerusalem, it is hard to imagine how it would be possible to return to any status quo ante.

THE ASSASSINATION OF YITZHAK RABIN

Yitzhak Rabin, several times Labour prime minister and commander in chief of Israeli forces in the war of 1967, was shot as he was leaving a large peace demonstration in Tel Aviv on the evening of 4 November 1995. This was the culmination, or perhaps merely a symptom, of a deep and almost unbridgeable rift within Israel, one fundamental to the existence and nature of the Israeli state in its present form. Peace with the Palestinians means concessions to the Palestinians; to Rabin's enemies and opponents, even the limited concessions which have been made represented a betrayal of the principles of Zionism. Over the past two or three years there have been increasingly bitter attacks on Arabs by Jewish settlers – in response, or parallel, to attacks on Jews by Arabs. But there has also been a notable increase in Hebrew graffiti with messages amounting to 'Death to the Palestinians'. In addition, some extremist rabbis had branded Rabin a traitor, and intimated that he should be put to death.

There will be elections in Israel in 1996. Meanwhile, Shimon Peres has succeeded Rabin as prime minister, and has pledged to continue the peace process. A wave of horror at Rabin's death has swept through Israel, and it may be that this will ensure that the next Israeli government will be able to continue the process that Rabin initiated. However, still more needs to be done to ensure peace. It is to be hoped that Peres and his successors will be given the mandate they require and that they will be able to take the bold and imaginative steps that are so sorely needed.

Richard Owen and Peter Sluglett

6
JORDAN

MORE, PERHAPS, THAN ANY OTHER Middle Eastern state outside the Arabian peninsula, the Kingdom of Jordan has revolved around the fortunes of a single family – those of the Hashemites. It is scarcely an exaggeration to say that Jordan owes its establishment in 1921 to the fortuitous coincidence of Britain's interest in establishing some sort of political authority under its own aegis on the east bank of the Jordan with Abdullah ibn Husayn's presence in the area at the time, and that modern Jordan is almost entirely the creation and creature of his grandson Husayn.

Under the Treaty of San Remo in April 1920, Britain had been given the mandate for Palestine and Iraq, and France the mandate for Syria. A month earlier, a gathering of Arab nationalists and notables, the General Syrian Congress, had elected Faysal, son of Sharif Husayn of Mecca, king of Syria, and his older brother Abdullah king of Iraq. Faysal had already been king of Syria since October 1918. However, the French had other plans for Syria in which the Hashemites, thought to be too close to Britain for France's comfort, did not feature. Forced out of Syria in July 1920, Faysal was invited by the British to become king of Iraq in December 1920, and was crowned in Baghdad in August 1921.

Although less dashing, Abdullah was no less ambitious than his brother Faysal. While Faysal's dreams had long been fixed on 'Syria' (in the sense of the area to the north and northwest of the Hijaz), Abdullah's gaze had been directed south and east, towards Yemen and central Arabia. While Faysal was heading north to lead the Arab revolt in June 1916, Abdullah remained in the Hijaz and, after the surrender of the Turkish garrisons of Mecca, Jidda and Ta'if by the autumn of that year, embarked upon the siege of Medina, whose garrison held out until February 1919. A few months later, on 21 May 1919, Abdullah's ambitions to dominate the peninsula were brought to an abrupt and violent conclusion. His forces were routed at Turaba, some 80 miles east of Mecca, by the man rapidly emerging as the principal power in Arabia, Ibn Sa'ud.

For a while Sharif Husayn clung to what he had in the Hijaz, but as Ibn Sa'ud's star waxed in Arabia the Hashemites' own waned. The Sharif himself was eventually deposed by Ibn Sa'ud in 1925 and the Hijaz was absorbed into what is now Saudi Arabia. For his part Abdullah stayed in the Hijaz for over a year after Turaba, his suspicions of Faysal at first allayed after the latter's defeat at Maysalun, but revived when he saw Britain preparing him for the throne of Iraq. At the end of September 1920 he headed north out of the Hijaz and settled with a considerable

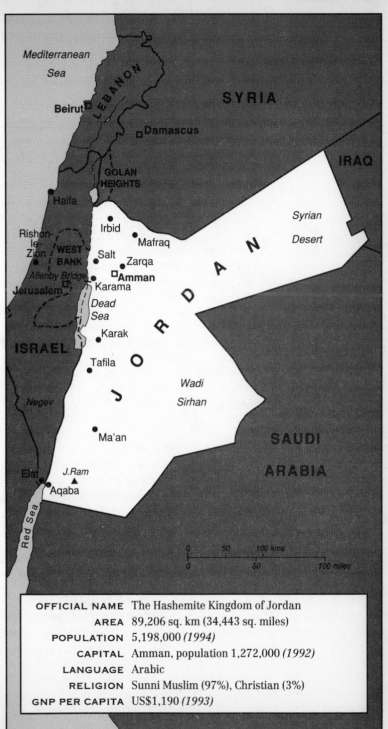

OFFICIAL NAME	The Hashemite Kingdom of Jordan
AREA	89,206 sq. km (34,443 sq. miles)
POPULATION	5,198,000 *(1994)*
CAPITAL	Amman, population 1,272,000 *(1992)*
LANGUAGE	Arabic
RELIGION	Sunni Muslim (97%), Christian (3%)
GNP PER CAPITA	US$1,190 *(1993)*

entourage at Ma'an, in the south of what is now Jordan. Ostensibly, he was on his way to wrest Syria from the French and restore it to the Arabs.

At this stage in 1920, the status of Transjordan, or the East Bank, had not yet been decided – or, to put it another way, it had not occurred either to the British or the French at San Remo to delimit the southern boundary of 'Syria'. Ottoman administrative maps of the period are imprecise as far as the Syrian interior is concerned; the province of 'Syria' simply peters out in the vicinity of Aqaba – a degree of vagueness that would prove a fruitful source of irritation between Ibn Sa'ud and Abdullah in the future when the borders between the two old rivals in Transjordan and Saudi Arabia needed to be drawn up. In 1920–21, however, Britain, as mandatory for Palestine, was concerned to keep the French as far from the Suez Canal as possible. With this in mind it was decided in London in August 1920 that Transjordan should have some loose form of administrative attachment to Palestine. A few British political officers, but no British troops, were despatched from Palestine a couple of months before Abdullah arrived with his followers at Ma'an.

During the autumn of 1920, while his brother was being offered the throne of Iraq in London, Abdullah held court in southern Transjordan, surrounded by Arab nationalist 'refugees' from Syria. By February 1921 it had been decided in London that Transjordan should be administered separately from Palestine and that the clauses in the Palestine mandate referring to Zionist settlement should not apply to the area, which would have an Arab ruler, Abdullah. In March 1921 Winston Churchill invited Abdullah to Jerusalem for talks, at the end of which Abdullah agreed to govern Transjordan for an initial period of six months. Thus, the Emirate of Transjordan, subsequently the Kingdom of Jordan, came into being.

JORDAN UNDER ABDULLAH, 1921–51

Both the emirate and its emir were British creations, and the relationship with, and dependence upon, Britain, remained central to Transjordanian politics up to, and well beyond, Abdullah's assassination in 1951. The transparency and the closeness of the connection were to prove awkward for Abdullah, who felt cramped within the borders of his small state – 'a falcon trapped in a canary's cage', as one historian has put it. The mainspring of almost all his actions seems to have been his ambition to play a wider regional role, for which he needed a more substantial political base. He succeeded in consolidating his position in Transjordan in the course of the 1920s and 1930s, checking tribal raids from the east and south, and having the boundaries of the state (with Syria and Saudi Arabia) recognised internationally, but he seems to have regarded Transjordan as a stepping stone to greater things. For most of his life he directed his attention either towards obtaining the throne of Syria, or latterly towards the creation of a greater Jordan which would include the Arab parts of Palestine.

Almost as remarkable as Abdullah's persistence in these two objectives was the extent to which he was prepared to ignore his isolation in pursuit of them; no more than a handful of Palestinians or Syrians ever supported him in either endeavour, but this did not deter him. In addition, he does not seem to have taken any particular pains to conceal his double dealing – his negotiations with the Zionists, and the subsidies he received from them for most of the 1930s, were common knowledge. He and other Transjordanian landlords sold options on leases of their land to the Jewish Agency in 1932, and these were renewed annually in the face of routine denials from the royal palace. His support of schemes for the partition of Palestine between Arabs and Zionists both before and after the Second World War, which greatly assisted the Zionists, was so blatant as to form the principal motive for his assassination.

The area which Abdullah took over in 1921 had a population of about 225,000, about half of whom were nomadic tribesmen. Amman, the present capital, had a mere 2,400 inhabitants in 1921. By 1946, when the Emirate gained its formal independence from Britain and became the Hashemite Kingdom, just before the creation of the state of Israel, the population had risen to around 435,000, about 100,000 of whom were nomads. After the creation of Israel in 1948, the population doubled with the influx of some 450,000 Palestinian refugees. In April 1950, Jordan proceeded to annex the West Bank (against the wishes of most of its population), which it had held under military occupation since May 1948, thus bringing a total of some 1.5 million people under Hashemite rule, two-thirds of whom were Palestinians and many of whom regarded Abdullah as being at least partially responsible for their current plight.

Left to their own devices few Palestinians would have chosen Abdullah, but economic and political realities after 1948 left them with little choice. Some no doubt consoled themselves, in April 1950, with the belief, or perhaps the hope, that the unification of the West Bank and Transjordan was merely a temporary expedient pending a full settlement of the dispute between Israel and the Arabs. It is a wry tribute to Abdullah's geopolitical prescience, if not to his sense of self-preservation, that his creation has so long survived his death.

HUSAYN: THE EARLY YEARS

Abdullah was assassinated on 20 July 1951 while on his way to pray at the al-Aqsa mosque in Jerusalem, most probably by supporters of the Mufti of Jerusalem, Hajj Amin al-Husayni, the unofficial leader of the Palestinians. He was succeeded by his eldest son Talal, who had a history of mental instability and was removed a year later in favour of Abdullah's grandson, Husayn, who attained his majority and became King of Jordan in May 1953.

Husayn had been educated at Harrow and Sandhurst and at first continued his grandfather's policy of maintaining close relations with Britain. His reputation as a survivor is well-deserved, given the extraordinary tensions both within and around Jordan since the early 1950s. The most obvious of these has been the divisions between, and the different political aims of, the original (Trans)Jordanians and the

Palestinians, although it should not be thought that either group's aims are entirely monolithic or axiomatically opposed to the other. The immense upheavals of the late 1940s and 1950s brought entirely new population strata into Jordan, changing its character almost as much as the loss of the West Bank would do in 1967. Although for most part sharing a common Arab/Islamic culture (some 97 per cent of the population is Sunni Muslim) many of the incomers had otherwise little in common with their new compatriots; they were generally better educated and more dynamic than the East Bankers and considered themselves superior to them. Of course, not all Palestinians were able to better themselves in Jordan. In 1987, 840,000 Palestinians were registered as refugees in Jordan by UNRWA, mainly in refugee camps, with a further 370,000 on the West Bank and 440,000 in Gaza.

Understandably, many of the Palestinians yearned to return to their homes, and could not easily identify with the pro-Western or at least generally conciliatory policies of the Jordanian government. Their alienation from it gradually increased, first with Nasser's championing of pan-Arabism in the 1950s and 1960s and subsequently with the rise of the Palestine Liberation Organisation (PLO) in the 1960s and 1970s. On the other hand it must be said that forces for cohesion, including frequent intermarriage and business and other partnerships, have meant that the divisions between Jordanians and Palestinians have tended to become less rigid with the passage of time.

With all its obvious limitations (its general failure to stress democratic accountability and the extreme vagueness of goals) Pan-Arabism was extremely attractive to the Palestinians and to the dispossessed of the Arab Middle East in general. The revolutionary states (Egypt, Iraq, Syria and later Algeria and South Yemen) were to raise the banner of Pan-Arabism in the crusade against Zionism, imperialism and the local 'lackeys of imperialism'. In the eyes of his opponents, King Husayn was one of the most prominent of these lackeys. For a while in 1955 it seemed that he was prepared to bow to British pressure to join the pro-Western and anti-Soviet Baghdad Pact, and until March 1956, when the King dismissed him, the Jordanian army was commanded by an Englishman, Glubb Pasha.

In October 1956 parliamentary elections were called in an atmosphere of rising tension. President Nasser had nationalised the Suez Canal a few weeks before and anti-Western feeling was running high. The results reflected the situation, as the nationalist, leftist and Islamic parties between them gained a majority of the seats, and the leader of the largest party, Sulayman Nabulsi of the National Socialists, became Prime Minister. Anti-Western feeling naturally increased after the tripartite invasion of Egypt in October-November. In March 1957 Nabulsi negotiated the termination of the Anglo-Jordanian treaty and with it the annual subsidy which Jordan received from Britain. To make good the shortfall, Husayn appealed to the United States, thus initiating a close relationship which, though not without its vicissitudes, has endured to the present day.

This turn of events was not at all to the government's liking and Nabulsi tried to organise a coup, assisted by the commander of the army. Decisive action on Husayn's part ensured that the coup was repulsed and the king secured complete control of the army. Political parties and trade unions were banned, and until 1989 all parliamentary elections were tightly controlled. There were further upheavals in 1958, first after Husayn's adhesion in February to a 'Fertile Crescent Union' between Jordan and Iraq – to counter the Arab nationalist-inspired United Arab Republic of Egypt and Syria – and then after the overthrow of the Iraqi monarchy in mid-July. In the same month the USA sent marines to Lebanon, and Britain sent troops to Jordan.

In spite of apparent differences in political alignment between Jordan and most of her neighbours, opposition to Husayn became less strident as time passed, and a modus vivendi with the other Arab states began to be found. This came about for a number of reasons. First, as we have seen, a certain stability developed from the maintenance of the relationship with the United States. Secondly, Husayn moved closer towards his family's former foes, the Saudis, largely because of a shared hostility to Arab nationalism and communism, at a time when the Saudis were increasingly able to assist him financially. Thirdly, albeit reluctantly, Husayn gave his approval to the creation of a separate political organisation to represent the Palestinians, the PLO, founded under Nasser's aegis in 1964. In addition, he greatly increased his authority within the state by his control of all crucial appointments in an army which expanded from 6,000 in 1948 to some 55,000 in 1967.

THE SIX-DAY WAR AND THE PLO

Husayn further increased his credibility, both domestically and externally – although at tremendous cost – by casting his lot with Egypt and Syria on 30 May 1967, when it was clear that war with Israel was about to break out. By 10 June, Israel was in occupation of the Sinai peninsula, the Golan Heights, East Jerusalem and the West Bank of the Jordan. The effects on all three countries were devastating, but especially for Jordan, which lost a third of its population and its prime agricultural land, and control of the Islamic and Christian sites in Jerusalem. Of some eventual benefit to Jordan was that Israel's obduracy in the face of United Nations (UN) Resolution 242 (which called for withdrawal from the occupied territories) was sufficiently irritating to the USA to encourage it to give Husayn a considerable part of the wherewithal to rebuild his armed forces. In addition, Jordan began to receive substantial financial aid from other Arab states after the Khartoum summit in September 1967. A considerable part of this went to the West Bank, where Jordan continued to pay the salaries of public employees and maintained schools and other public institutions until it gave up its claim to the area in July 1988.

The enormity of the defeat brought about a sea change in the attitude of the Palestinians, large numbers of whom now became convinced that the Arab regimes were either unable or unwilling (or perhaps both) to liberate Palestine. The PLO's new tactics began to pose a severe threat to the continuation of the Jordanian monarchy. Palestinian guerrillas, based in Jordan, began to make raids into Israel, occasioning severe Israeli reprisals. As the PLO's confidence increased, its presence became increasingly disruptive and its relations with the Jordanian authorities increasingly strained. In mid-June 1970 the Jordanian army entered Amman to assert its authority over the guerrillas, and a conflict began which lasted over a year, in the course of which some 3,000 Palestinians, civil and military, were killed, and some of the refugee camps in Jordan virtually razed to the ground by Jordanian artillery. Driven out of Jordan, Yasser Arafat and the remaining armed guerrillas moved to Lebanon where history was to repeat itself, after a fashion, over the next decade and a half.

Over the next few years the Jordanian government gradually reasserted its authority over the country, and a highly efficient security service and surveillance system was developed to check and deter dissidents. There was no elected parliament, a state of affairs which continued until 1984. Jordan did not participate in the war of October 1973, though the dividend from this circumspection was less than King Husayn expected, and certainly less than he thought he deserved. *Faute de mieux*, Husayn, along with his fellow Arab leaders, was obliged to recognise the PLO as the 'sole legitimate representative of the Palestinian people' at the Rabat Arab summit in October 1974, which inevitably diminished both his authority, and much of what was left of his appeal, on the West Bank.

Presumably in attempt to regain some of his standing as an interlocutor for the Palestinians, Husayn held secret negotiations with Israel in 1975 and 1976, but the Allon Plan, Israel's offer, was unacceptable because it would have entailed Israel retaining some 30 per cent of the West Bank. In the late 1970s a new dimension was added to Arab/Israeli relations with the sequence of events beginning with President Sadat's visit to Jerusalem in November 1977 and ending with the Camp David accords in September 1978; Jordan was neither consulted nor asked to participate. In addition to his misgivings about the negotiations in general, Husayn naturally resented the fact that Camp David provided for autonomy for the West Bank rather than its eventual re-absorption into Jordan. In addition, the terms and general tenor of the agreements were such that Husayn could not have accepted them without gravely weakening his position both domestically and in the Arab world.

In consequence, Jordanian/PLO relationships improved, at least on a superficial level, and Arafat and Husayn were soon formally reconciled (they had had no official contact since 1971) in Amman. Throughout the early 1980s amity between the two prevailed, much to the alarm of Syria. The United States put forward the Reagan plan involving a confederation between the West Bank and Jordan, and in the course of 1982 and 1983 Husayn almost succeeded in persuading Arafat to allow him to negotiate with Israel jointly on behalf of both Jordan and the Palestinians. In November 1984 Husayn told the 17th Palestine National

Council, which he had invited to Amman, that Jordan and the PLO should make a settlement together with Israel on the basis of 'land for peace'. In February 1985 an accord between Husayn and Arafat appeared to give Husayn a mandate to open peace negotiations with Israel under UN auspices. Fearing complete isolation in the region, Syria eventually forced Husayn to abandon this particular tactic, partly by a series of assassinations of Jordanian diplomats abroad and partly by arranging a joint command between Abu Nidal's terrorist organisation and Abu Musa, Arafat's main rival, to attack the accord. At the end of 1985 President Asad of Syria and Husayn issued a joint statement rejecting any direct negotiations with Israel and the two rulers exchanged visits to each other's capitals, in Asad's case the first for nine years.

Israel's response, at least while Peres took his turn as prime minister between September 1984 and September 1986, was to strike hard at the PLO, Asad and Qadhafi (in such incidents as the bombing of PLO headquarters in Tunis in October 1985) who were labelled 'terrorists' in an attempt to draw Husayn away from the more militant Arab leaders and into direct talks. By February 1987 this had succeeded to the extent that Peres had convinced Husayn to enter into bilateral negotiations, although this was eventually blocked by Shamir. Together with his party Likud, with its ideological commitment to the West Bank as part of Eretz Israel, Shamir had never shown great enthusiasm for negotiations with Husayn, and the Reagan administration was neither prepared to put pressure on him nor to give Husayn satisfactory pledges of support if Husayn were indeed to 'go it alone'. The peace process was stalled, and was to remain so until the major initiatives of 1991.

On a regional level, Jordan enjoyed fairly cordial relations with most of its neighbours in the late 1980s after the reconciliation with Damascus in 1985. Jordan re-established relations with Egypt in 1983, and King Husayn used his good offices generally on Egypt's behalf. At the Amman summit in November 1987 most of those Arab states who had not so far done so were persuaded to restore diplomatic relations with Egypt. Relations with Saudi Arabia, cordial for much of King Husayn's reign, remained close until their near rupture as a result of Husayn's equivocation over Iraq's invasion of Kuwait in August 1990.

However, although their outward political orientations might seem to have precluded such an alignment, Amman's closest political and economic ties for most of the 1970s and 1980s were with Baghdad. Before the invasion of Kuwait, given Iraq's perennially poor relations with Syria, it was important that Iraq's relations with Jordan should be, if not always cordial, at least always correct, which is more or less what they had been since the Iraqi Ba'th came to power in the summer of 1968. It is only a slight exaggeration to say that King Husayn owes his throne to the fact that neither Iraqi nor Syrian troops intervened in support of the PLO guerrillas in the fighting in Jordan in September 1970.

A mixture of noisy radicalism and quiet realism or opportunism characterised Iraq's policy towards Jordan for most of the 1970s. King

Husayn's policies towards the West and the Palestinians were regularly attacked as reactionary and pro-imperialist in the Iraqi media, while economic exchanges between the two states were increasing, and Iraq was financing improvements at the port of Aqaba and the development of the Jordanian road system, which were soon to stand it in good stead.

More cordial official relations were inaugurated after the Baghdad summit of November 1978, at which Jordan was given promises of $1.25 billion annually for not participating in Camp David. Jordan's support for Iraq in the war with Iran was unswerving and, at least initially, the Jordanian economy benefited greatly as Aqaba became the main port of entry for goods bound for Iraq. By 1988, however, following Iraq's deregulation of foreign trade after the end of the war, its outstanding debt to Jordan had so far exceeded the quota agreed between the two countries that the Jordanian Central Bank suspended export financing, thus causing a major flight from the Jordanian dinar. Iraq's enthusiasm for postwar reconstruction tended to exceed its financial capacity or immediate willingness to pay for what it wanted, and of all Iraq's creditors the Jordanians found the strain particularly difficult to bear.

In the latter part of the 1980s King Husayn made a number of attempts to reconcile Hafiz al-Asad and Saddam Hussein, but without success, although the two apparently met secretly on Jordanian territory in April 1987. As we have seen, relations between Syria and Jordan were erratic in the late 1970s and early 1980s partly because of Syria's fears that Jordan would do a separate deal with Israel and partly because Damascus believed, not without some justification, that Jordan was financing or otherwise assisting the Muslim Brotherhood in its campaign against it. Again, Asad was not pleased at King Husayn's immediate pledge of support for Saddam Hussein when Iraq invaded Iran in September 1980. However, by 1985, relations had begun to improve. The two governments continued to disagree over Jordan's relations with Iraq and with Egypt, but were united by their distrust and dislike of the PLO. It was largely at King Husayn's initiative that Syria was persuaded to take part in the Amman summit in November 1987, at which the Arab states signed a joint statement condemning Iran for occupying Iraqi territory and for failing to implement UN Security Council Resolution 598. At the same summit, the English text of the resolutions adopted pointedly omitted the standard reference to the PLO as the 'sole legitimate representative of the Palestinian people'.

JORDAN AND THE INTIFADA
In the course of the 1970s and 1980s the PLO consolidated its influence on the West Bank and especially among Palestinians outside Jordan. In spite of all attempts to reinforce it, Jordanian influence on the West Bank gradually diminished as the idea of a Palestinian state began to take more significant shape. Whatever support Jordan retained on the West Bank was further marginalised by the Intifada, beginning at the end of 1987, which did not even pay lipservice to Jordanian sovereignty ·

and, at least in the beginning, greatly enhanced the role of the PLO. At the same time, the government was seriously concerned that unrest, or at least demonstrations of solidarity, would break out in Jordan itself. After eight months of the Intifada Husayn took the momentous decision to cut his ties with the West Bank for good. On 31 July 1988 he announced formal Jordanian disengagement from the Occupied Territories. This step had important economic as well as political implications, since Jordan would no longer fund the social, educational, health and other services in the Territories.

A few months later on 15 November 1988, the PLO took the equally historic step at the Palestine National Council in Algiers of announcing the inauguration of a Palestinian state in the Occupied Territories with its capital at Jerusalem. At the same time, the PLO voted to accept UN resolutions 242 and 338, thus, by implication, recognising the state of Israel within its pre-1967 frontiers. After further negotiations in the Stockholm Declaration of 7 December, the PLO specifically recognised the existence of two states in Palestine, one Jewish, one Arab. This opened the way to informal US/Palestinian discussions in Tunis in the first months of 1989.

These events naturally had serious repercussions in Jordan. The ending of the link with the West Bank caused the value of the dinar to fall sharply, and money-changing activities were severely restricted in 1988 and 1989. Austerity measures, including sharp rises in import taxes and rises in charges for work permits and exit visas, were announced in November. In April 1989 there were increases in the prices of fuel, alcohol and cigarettes and a new austerity programme, as the result of negotiations with the World Bank to reschedule Jordan's $6.6 billion external debt. In the middle of May there were mass demonstrations in the towns of Ma'an and Karak, areas traditionally steadfast in their support for the regime, in which eight people were killed and 83 injured; ten of the country's 11 professional and trade union associations called for the resignation of the government and the formation of a government of national unity. King Husayn cut short a visit to Britain to return to Jordan to take personal charge of the situation, dismissing the Prime Minister, Zayd Rifa'i (who had been in office since April 1985) replacing him with his own cousin General Zayd ibn Shakir. Large numbers were arrested, but most were released during May and June. On 29 May the governor of the Central Bank announced that Jordan had lost a third of its gold reserves over the previous six months.

In July 1989 it was announced that parliamentary elections would be held in the autumn. These were the first general elections since 1957, and a new electoral law was promulgated, dividing the country into 80 constituencies. This time there were, of course, to be no representatives from the Occupied Territories. Political parties, banned since 1957, were to be permitted, though not immediately. Jordan's foreign debts were further rescheduled by its major creditors. In August the six Gulf Co-operation Council states deposited some $400 million in the Central Bank in an attempt to relieve Jordan's most pressing financial difficulties. Only 52 per cent of those eligible voted in the elections, held in November; abstention was particularly high among Jordanians of Palestinian origin. The results cannot have been particularly welcome to Husayn. Thirty-four out of the 80 seats went to 'Islamic' candidates and 18 to 'leftists'. Further steps in the direction of measures of democratisation, including the release of prisoners of conscience and the recruitment of a number of former teachers dismissed for political reasons, were taken early in 1990.

THE CRISIS OF 1990

In spite of these and other concessions, it was becoming apparent in the period immediately before the Iraqi invasion of Kuwait that the political system was under immense strain, and that the stability and even the integrity of the country were under grave threat. There were a number of reasons, some economic, some political. On the economic front, it was estimated in April 1990 that the dinar had lost two-thirds of its value in less than two years, and that 20 per cent of the economically active population was officially unemployed. Every few months the King and other prominent personalities were obliged to tour Arab capitals with begging bowls simply to keep the country from imminent bankruptcy, and no end to this bleak prospect seemed in sight.

In addition, the peace process had reached that depressingly familiar point in its cycle where progress seemed as far away as ever. In the spring of 1990, several prominent right-wingers had gained portfolios in a particularly intransigent Israeli cabinet. Ever more settlements were being constructed on the West Bank, partly as a consequence of the huge influx of Jews from the Soviet Union, perhaps the largest single wave of immigrants since the early 1950s. The Intifada was not making any tangible impact. In the disturbances following the killing of seven Palestinians by an apparently mentally deranged young Israeli at Rishon-le-Zion on 20 May, a further eight Palestinians were killed and 65 wounded in the Occupied Territories, now under almost permanent curfew. Finally, President Bush officially terminated the Palestinian/US dialogue on 30 May, after Arafat refused to dismiss Abu'l-Abbas (the Palestine Liberation Front) from the executive committee of the PLO following a raid on the Israeli coast carried out by the Front.

On 14 May 20,000 people marched towards the Allenby Bridge, threatening to cross it to return to the Occupied Territories. At a press conference on 10 June Husayn delivered his sombre judgment that Jordan was going through the most difficult period in its history and made an impassioned, if all too familiar, appeal for Arab aid. On 15 July, the Muslim Brethren demanded that the government should arm the citizens to protect them against Israel. In such circumstances Husayn's room for manoeuvre seemed to be shrinking by the minute. His former interlocutors in Israel were by and large out of power, he had no money, and his inaction was seen as proof of his deference to Israel and the USA.

Although the Kuwait crisis added enormously to his difficulties, the fact that the new problems were of a different nature, and that they replaced more directly threatening concerns, combined with Husayn's adroitness in handling them, provided an unexpected and, as events were to show, highly opportune breathing space. Politically, Husayn emerged from the crisis with his position substantially enhanced. He managed to be sufficiently equivocal to alienate neither his domestic constituency nor his friends in the West, although his estrangement from his natural allies in the Gulf and the Arabian Peninsula took rather longer to repair. Hence, however serious the strains on the Jordanian economy, the sword of Damocles no longer hung over the Jordanian polity as menacingly as it did in the summer of 1990.

Thus Jordan joined enthusiastically in the peace process when it was launched at Madrid in October 1991. At Israeli insistence, the PLO was not officially a party to the talks, but PLO 'sympathisers' were attached to the Jordanian delegation, a marriage of convenience which became more or less redundant when Labour won the Israeli elections in June 1992. The apparent stagnation in the peace process after its inception caused some dismay in Jordan, but although King Husayn had not apparently been given prior notice that a secret Israeli-PLO accord was being hammered out in Norway in the spring and summer of 1993, he accepted it philosophically enough, as he was to accept the further agreement concluded in September 1995. By that time Husayn had signed an agreement ending the state of war with Israel in July 1994, followed by a full peace agreement in October, and ambassadors had been exchanged between the two countries. The parliamentary elections of November 1993 further strengthened Husayn. The Islamists, who had gained 32 seats in the previous elections in 1989, only managed to retain 18 of them. In the course of 1993 and 1994 attempts were made to mend fences with Jordan's former allies in the Gulf, although King Fahd refused to receive Husayn officially when he visited Saudi Arabia in March 1994. It will be of some interest to see how Jordan's relations develop with the Palestine National Authority as Israel gradually leaves the West Bank – the Jordanian/Israeli Agreement recognises King Husayn as the custodian of the Holy Places in Jerusalem and, in the economic field, several branches of Jordanian banks have already been opened in the West Bank.

As expected, Jordan's financial difficulties were substantially eased as a by-product of the peace process. By the autumn of 1991, $21 million worth of US military aid was unfrozen, and in March 1992 about 20 per cent of Jordan's foreign debt was rescheduled by the Club de Paris. In July 1994, the USA announced the annulment of $680 million worth of Jordanian debt, and negotiations for a major reduction in Jordan's debt to Japan ($1.8 billion) were taking place in the summer and autumn of 1995. As for many other countries in the region, the major remaining uncertainty for Jordan (given reasonably smooth future progress of outstanding issues in Palestine) is the continuing pariah status of Iraq, formerly Jordan's principal trading partner.

One crucial further question in Jordanian politics has been the state of the King's health. In August 1992 one of his kidneys was removed in the course of an operation for cancer in the USA. He returned to hospital there in January 1993, when doctors announced that the cancerous cells had not spread, and a further visit a year later confirmed this diagnosis. Neverthless, this illness and the fact that Husayn is now nearly 60 has inevitably aroused speculation about the succession.

THE JORDANIAN ECONOMY

An important, though as it was to turn out short-lived, positive development for Jordan in the 1970s and early 1980s, was an annual growth rate of some 10 per cent. This was made possible by a combination of foreign aid and labour remittances. These were the years of the oil boom in the Gulf, and during them some 350,000 Jordanians (including Palestinians) were working abroad. Two other factors assisted Jordan's prosperity during these years: the devastation wrought upon Beirut caused many of its financial and other services to be transferred to Amman; while the Iran/Iraq war and the closure of the Shatt al-Arab transformed Aqaba, and the transit route across Jordan, into a vital supply line for Iraq.

However, although the country undoubtedly enjoyed a considerable increase in prosperity, this did not rest upon solid foundations. Apart from a small but lively agricultural sector, and some phosphates, Jordan has little in the way of natural resources. Thus in 1988, agriculture, mining and manufacture *together* contributed only 22.5 per cent to gross domestic product (compared with 27.4 per cent for Syrian agriculture alone), which means that the economy is dominated by services and thus extremely vulnerable to events entirely outside its own control. Remittances, which far outstripped export earnings between 1975 and 1985, began to fall drastically when oil prices halved in 1985–86, and many Jordanians (along with other expatriates) were obliged to leave the oil-rich states.

Economically, the invasion of Kuwait was an utter catastrophe for Jordan, as almost all its aid, as well as its transit earnings as an entrepôt for Iraq, together with most of its agricultural and manufacturing export earnings (also largely from Iraq) were suddenly cut off. For this reason, and because of other factors operating well before the Gulf crisis – the Jordanian dinar, worth around $2.7 in 1988, was worth only $1.6 at the end of 1990, partly because of the severing of ties with the West Bank and partly because of the crisis – Jordan's long and short term economic prospects are not particularly bright. Again, although peace with Israel has certainly eased Jordan's immediate financial difficulties, there must be serious doubts about the country's capacity to compete with Israel in the long-term, especially in agriculture and industry.

Peter Sluglett and Marion Farouk-Sluglett

7
THE KURDS

KURDISTAN IS THE NAME given to a geographical area on the borders of Iran, Iraq, Syria and Turkey, the homeland of the Kurds, a pastoral nomadic people of Indo-European origin. In the words of one authority, the Kurdish people have the 'unfortunate distinction of being probably the only community of over 15 million persons which has not achieved some form of national statehood, despite a struggle extending back over several decades.' Kurdish is an Indo-European language, so that of the other languages in the area it is most closely related to Persian. There is no structural relationship between Arabic and Kurdish or between Turkish and Kurdish. Partly because of the isolation of the mountain regions in which they live and partly because of the wide geographical distribution of the Kurdish community, there is no 'standard Kurdish'. There are several different dialects in addition to the three main divisions, Sorani (or Kurdi), spoken in Iran and northeast Iraq (around Sulaymaniyya), which is recognised officially and taught in schools in Iraq, Kurmanji, spoken in northwest Iraq and much of eastern Turkey, and Zaza, spoken in parts of central Turkey. These dialects are not mutually intelligible (although an individual might know more than one dialect). Thus Zaza speakers might well only be able to communicate with Sorani speakers through the medium of another language.

The majority of Kurds are Sunni Muslims and many belong to the Qadiriyya and Naqshbandiyya religious brotherhoods, manifestations of 'popular' Islam which gained adherents in the area in the mid-19th century. Many Kurds in southern Iranian Kurdistan and in the south and southeast of Iraqi Kurdistan are Shi'is, although most of the latter, the Fa'ilis, were expelled to Iran in the 1970s. There are also three other heterodox religious groups to which some Kurds adhere: Alevi Shi'ism, Ahl-i Haqq and Yazidism, as well as the Assyrian and Syrian Orthodox Christian sects and a very few Jews. This variety of sects reflects both the plurality, and generally, unless incited otherwise by governments or other external forces, the tolerance, of the peoples of the area.

In broad terms, most Kurds probably no longer aspire to a Grand Kurdistan extending over eastern Turkey, western Iran and northern and north-eastern Iraq. Rather, they aspire more realistically to some form of self-government or local autonomy within the borders of the state in which they live. To some extent, although the structures are still extremely fragile, this has been achieved in northern Iraq since the end of the Gulf War in 1991. For most of the period since 1918, the Kurds' main problem has been to attempt to persuade the governments of the newly created national states in which they have found themselves that a grant of local autonomy would not imply the derogation of sovereignty which the states themselves profess to fear.

Estimating the Kurdish population is fraught with difficulty, largely because ethnic affiliation is not usually recorded in the censuses of the countries concerned. In 1980, the Minority Rights Group estimated that Kurds formed 19 per cent of the population of Turkey, 23 per cent of Iraq, 10 per cent of Iraq and 8 per cent of Syria, with smaller communities in Lebanon and the Soviet Union. If this is applied to the latest census figures for each country, it would produce a total Kurdish population of between 24 and 25 million. Most Kurds can trace their origins to particular tribes, although increasing rural to urban migration (and, in the case of the Turkish Kurds, migration to western Europe) has tended to weaken tribal bonds. Furthermore, the passage of time and political constraints on cross-frontier transhumance have combined to increase sedentarisation. An additional focus of loyalty, and often of political power, has been provided by the leaders of the various religious orders; thus, in Iraq, Sheikh Mahmud of Sulaymaniyya, Mulla Mustafa Barzani and Jalal Talabani have derived at least part of their authority from their sheikhly backgrounds. In Turkey, according to one authority, 'Even since 1970, when leftist movements ... started to make real inroads into Kurdish society, the unpoliticised have still voted for candidates who are [tribal] chiefs or [religious] sheikhs, or possess these connections. Loyalty will persist even in an exploitative situation for a long time.'

HISTORY

Until the end of the First World War, the Kurdish populations as a whole were generally subject, at least nominally, to the jurisdiction either of the Shah of Iran or the Ottoman sultan, with a few small communities in the Russian Caucasus. The boundary between Iran and the Ottoman Empire was not finally charted until 1913, which meant that attempts on the part of both governments to assert their authority in the Kurdish areas could be kept in check by reinforcement from the 'other side'. In general terms, the Ottomans' efforts to consolidate their authority over the Kurds caused major risings in 1837–52 and 1880–81, but by the end of the century they had managed to recruit many Kurdish tribesmen into the Hamidiyya cavalry, named after Sultan Abd al-Hamid (1876–1909), which was used to put down Armenian risings in Eastern Anatolia in the 1890s. In general it is clear that 'government authority' had not been universally accepted in either the Iranian or Ottoman Kurdish areas by the First World War.

In common with the other non-Turkish peoples of the Ottoman Empire, the Kurds were affected by the currents of nationalism in Europe and Asia in the second part of the 19th century. Kurdish intellectuals began to form

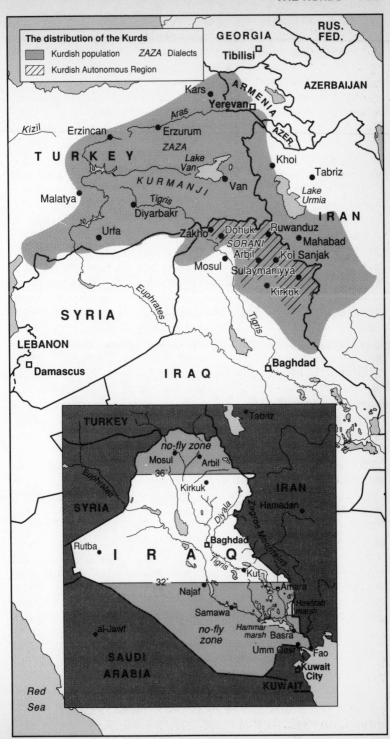

The distribution of the Kurds
Kurdish population   *ZAZA* Dialects
Kurdish Autonomous Region

secret societies aiming either at some form of decentralised administration of the Kurdish provinces, or (more rarely) complete independence from the Ottoman government. In an essentially rural and tribal society, however, such activities were to have little effect unless they were accompanied by the support of powerful tribes and their leaders, who could produce the weapons and the men necessary to effect political change.

During the First World War, the Turks and the Russians were on opposite sides, while Iran remained neutral. However, Russian troops had been stationed in Iran since 1909 (when they had intervened on the Shah's side in the Constitutional Revolution), and Turkish troops actually captured Tabriz from the Russians for 10 days early in 1915. After the Treaty of Brest-Litovsk in December 1917, when Russia withdrew from the war, there was a power vacuum in eastern Turkey until well into 1919, and also in western Iran until Reza Khan's seizure of power in 1921. In general, the absence of any centralised authority in the area permitted widespread disorder and the massacre or expulsion of most of the Assyrian and some of the Armenian populations, who, as Christians, had tended to take the Russian side. Farther south, Mosul town was occupied a little after the Treaty of Mudros (30 October 1918), and the area of British occupation was soon afterwards held to extend over the whole of Mosul province. Kurdish nationalists in exile outside Turkey, and local tribal leaders in ex-Ottoman Kurdistan, saw the defeat of the Ottomans and the occupation of Mosul as a golden opportunity for pressing their claims. In this they were encouraged by President Woodrow Wilson's Fourteen Points (8 January 1918), the twelfth of which states that 'the nationalities now under Turkish rule should (in the event of an Allied victory) be assured an undoubted security of life and an absolutely unmolested opportunity of autonomous development.'

At this time the two southern Iraqi provinces were under direct British administration, but because of the circumstance of the occupation of Mosul province, and because of its mountainous terrain, it could not be occupied in the same way. In fact, the whole question of the future of Mosul, and whether it was to be returned to Turkey, or be part of the new state of Iraq, was not to be settled until 1925. In mid-November 1918, it was British policy to encourage the appointment of suitable local figures to administer the area with British political advisors. The most prominent of these notables was Sheikh Mahmud Barzinji, who was installed as governor of Sulaymaniyya.

A variety of factors combined to ensure that this was not to be the prelude to the creation of an independent or quasi-independent Kurdish state. In the first place, the British government gradually became committed to the establishment of an Arab state in Iraq under British auspices, and to the inclusion of the oil-bearing province of Mosul within that state. Secondly, the defeat of the Ottomans was followed by the rise of a national resistance movement in Anatolia in the spring of 1919, the prelude to the war of independence, which ended with Atatürk and his forces victorious, compelling the British and Greek occupying armies to withdraw from Anatolia by October 1922. In these changing circumstances the Kurds both north and south of the present Turco-Iraqi frontier naturally hesitated over whether to throw in their lot with Britain or with Turkey, since Britain's *locus standi* in the area was by no means clear. Finally, and very significantly for the future, the whole concept of an 'independent Kurdistan' or 'self-determination for the Kurds' required some consensus on the part of the Kurds themselves over suitable representatives. At this stage, the desire for Kurdish autonomy did not, because of traditional clan and tribal rivalries, produce any coherent movement towards Kurdish unity; Sheikh Mahmud was removed by the British in May 1919 largely because his support base was so inadequate that he could not control areas less than 20 miles from Sulaymaniyya.

Throughout 1919 and for most of 1920, there were constant risings in northern Iraq. Some were attempts to drive British forces out of the Mosul area, but some were the normal Kurdish expression of distaste at the imposition of outside authority. In the summer of 1920, a few months after the award of the mandates for Palestine and Iraq to Britain and Syria and Lebanon to France, the Istanbul government accepted the Treaty of Sèvres, against the wish of the Grand National Assembly convened by Atatürk and his supporters in Ankara. The Treaty amounted to the dismemberment of what was left of Turkey and its partition between Italy and Greece, with 'independent states' in Armenia and Kurdistan. Although the rise of Atatürk ensured that Sèvres was never ratified, it marked an important turning point in the history of the evolution of the Kurdish movement, as the first formal declaration of intent to set up a separate, specifically Kurdish, political entity.

TURKEY AND IRAN IN THE INTER-WAR PERIOD

By the early 1920s, therefore, the political geography of the Kurdish areas had begun to assume much of the shape that it does today, with the Kurds divided between Turkey, Iraq, Iran and Syria. In general terms, Turkish governments, particularly under Atatürk but also under his successors, have pursued consistently repressive policies towards the Kurdish population, amounting to a virtual denial of its separate ethnic and linguistic identity. Drastic reprisals, involving executions, massacres and mass deportations were taken against any attempts to assert Kurdish nationalism or independence. The risings led by Sheikh Sa'id (1925), the Khoybun revolt (1929–30) and the Dersim rebellion (1937) were all put down with great ferocity.

In Iran, the early 1920s were filled with uncertainty. The Iranian Kurds were told firmly by the British to respect the rule of the Iranian government, and to expect no assistance from Britain in setting up a Kurdish political entity. However, the Russian revolution had removed the Iranian monarchy's main support, which meant that there was anarchy throughout most of the country. In the Kurdish area, Simko

Agha, the chief of the Shakkak tribe, seized power shortly after the end of the war. Although checked by the Cossack brigade, he managed to gain the support of several Kurdish tribes in the Mahabad region, and began to talk of creating a Kurdish state, taking the towns of Mahabad and Khoi in the autumn of 1921. By July 1922, however, the Iranian Army had been reorganised sufficiently to defeat Simko and his allies, and he was forced to flee across the border into Iraq. Throughout the inter-war period Reza Shah extended his centralising policies to the Kurdish areas, confiscating the land of recalcitrants and often moving tribes to other parts of the country.

IRAQI KURDISH POLITICS, 1920–1946

In Iraq, the situation of the Kurds was more complex. In 1922 the British mandatory authorities had promised the Kurds a form of autonomy in northern Iraq, but by this time Sheikh Mahmud Barzinji, whom the British had reinstated, *faute de mieux*, in Sulaymaniyya, seems to have decided against accepting any form of Iraqi suzerainty. Eventually his attempts at rebellion were crushed, at least temporarily, and Rowanduz, Koi Sanjak and Sulaymaniyya were occupied by British troops in 1924. By this time, the League of Nations had decided to send a special Commission to decide whether the Mosul *wilaya* should be part of Iraq or part of Turkey. After several months' deliberation, the Commissioners decided that Mosul should be part of Iraq, a recommendation which, by and large, found favour in the region. Early in 1926, the Prime Minister of Iraq declared that civil servants in the Kurdish area should be Kurds, that Kurdish and Arabic should be the official languages of the area, and that Kurdish children should be educated in Kurdish. Although these provisions were only halfheartedly carried out, it is fair to say that the Kurds' separate ethnic identity has generally been recognised to a greater or lesser extent by subsequent Iraqi governments, and token Kurds served as ministers in virtually all the governments under the monarchy.

However, much of the Kurds' enthusiasm for the state of Iraq derived from their belief that their status would in some sense be underwritten by the British presence. Hence Britain's announcement in 1930 that she would support Iraq's application for independence in 1932 caused serious misgivings, especially when it became known that the treaty contained no minority guarantees. After serious rioting in Sulaymaniyya in September 1930, Sheikh Mahmud indicated that he was once more prepared to go on the offensive and fighting broke out in the spring of 1931. The revolt was decisively defeated, but almost simultaneously, a new and generally more effective nucleus of Kurdish opposition was developing, in the Barzani tribal lands in the subdistrict of Baradost. Mulla Mustafa Barzani, the younger brother of the Barzani religious and tribal leader Sheikh Ahmad, emerged in the early 1930s as the principal figure in Iraqi Kurdish politics, a position he was to retain until his death in exile in 1979.

After organising a series of revolts against the Iraq government in the Barzan area, the Barzani brothers were finally forced to surrender and to live under a loose form of house arrest in Sulaymaniyya in 1936. Here Barzani came into contact with Kurdish political writers and thinkers, some of whom joined together to form the clandestine *Hewa* (Hope) Party in 1939 which included individuals from both the left and the right. On the one hand, there were those who believed that social reforms were an essential prerequisite for the Kurds to achieve their national rights, and on the other, those who felt that the key to obtaining Kurdish rights lay in Britain's hands, and that some form of alliance with Britain was necessary. Barzani himself was inclined to favour some sort of accommodation with Britain.

After the reoccupation of Iraq by a British military force in April 1941, the Iraqi government was preoccupied with events in the south and left the north more or less to its own devices. In 1943 Barzani escaped from Sulaymaniyya and proceeded to make overtures to the British authorities in an attempt to gain British support for a formal recognition of Kurdish autonomy, although this eventually came to nothing. By the summer of 1945 the Iraqi government evidently felt sufficiently confident to launch a campaign to restore its authority in the north. Fourteen thousand troops were dispatched, and this army succeeded in chasing Barzani out of Iraq and into Iran in October 1945.

THE REPUBLIC OF MAHABAD

In June 1941, Nazi Germany invaded the Soviet Union, which immediately joined the Allied side. In order to supply the Soviet Union, the Allies needed to use the land routes across Iran, and when Reza Shah attempted to resist this he was deposed and exiled. With the collapse of the Iranian army the Kurdish tribes were once more virtually autonomous in their own areas, a situation reminiscent of the hiatus between the end of the First World War and the assumption of power by Reza Khan in 1921. By May 1943 the authority of the Iranian government in northwest Iran had collapsed altogether and Soviet officials from across the border had begun to make approaches to influential Kurdish figures in the area. The political centre of the region west of Azerbaijan was the small town of Mahabad, south of Lake Urmia which had a population of some 16,000 inhabitants in 1945. In 1942 a Kurdish nationalist association, the *Komala*, had been formed in the region and had developed links with *Hewa* in Iraq. In October 1944 the leading citizen and judge of Mahabad, Qadi Muhammad, was asked to become a member of the *Komala*.

At the same time, Soviet officials were encouraging a separatist movement in the northern Iranian province of Azerbaijan. The Kurds and the Azeris regarded the Soviets as natural partners, since they were encouraging the autonomous movements in both areas. In the autumn of 1945, after a meeting with Soviet officials in Nakhichevan, just across the frontier, Qadi Muhammad and a number of other prominent citizens of Mahabad founded the Kurdistan Democratic Party, at almost exactly the same time as Mulla Mustafa Barzani and his supporters were preparing to enter Iran from Iraq.

The arrival of Barzani meant the addition of some 3,000 fighting men pledged to the Kurdish cause. Accordingly, the Iranian Kurds proclaimed an autonomous Republic of Mahabad, which was inaugurated by Qadi Muhammad on 22 January 1946. However, with the beginning of the cold war in 1946, and with the knowledge that the Soviet Union was anxious to obtain an oil concession in northwest Iran, the British and American governments began to press for the withdrawal of all foreign troops. The implication was the eventual restoration of the authority of the Iranian government over all parts of the country. The effects of this took some time to be felt in Mahabad, where the republic was building up a defence force composed largely of Barzani's tribal irregulars. The Soviet government provided military equipment, but also promised the Iranian government that it would withdraw its own troops some time in May 1946.

Like many other Kurdish politicians after him, Qadi Muhammad did not want total independence, but, in his case, some kind of federal association with the government in Tehran which would not involve the entry of Iranian troops into the territory of the republic. He wanted education to be conducted in Kurdish, a locally based administration and a locally controlled military force. Although the presence of Soviet troops in the neighbouring area had been essential for the republic's initial foundation, Mahabad itself had never been occupied by the Red Army, but it had enjoyed a degree of de facto independence for some five years. None of its citizens' aspirations were to be achieved. On 16 December 1946 the Iranian army entered Mahabad, and on 31 March 1947 Qadi Muhammad and two of his close relatives and political allies were hanged in public in the main square.

For his part Barzani now sought to come to some kind of accommodation with the Iranian government through the good offices of the British Embassy in Tehran, but in vain. He was eventually forced out of Iran into Iraq, and in mid-May 1947 he and 600 of his followers undertook a daring journey to the Soviet Union across Turkey and Iran, crossing the Aras river between 15 and 18 June, covering 220 miles over very mountainous country in about a fortnight. They stayed in the Soviet Union until 1958.

THE KURDS IN TURKEY 1920–C.1980

As has already been described, the policies of most modern Turkish governments towards the Kurds since the 1920s have been harsh, generally concerned to repress and deny the existence of a separate Kurdish ethnic and linguistic identity. Although most Kurds had fought first for the Ottoman Empire and then for Atatürk, they did not support Atatürk's 'Turkism' or his secular policies. When the caliphate was abolished in 1924, all Kurdish associations, schools and publications were closed or banned. This provoked revolts against the central government in the Kurdish areas, often led by religious leaders, who were represented as obscurantist enemies of progress by the new government in Ankara. The 'pacification' of the area was brutal. Perhaps a quarter of a million Kurds were killed and over a million deported from their homes to other parts of Turkey. Simultaneously, large numbers of Turks were moved into the area from outside. Much of Turkish Kurdistan remained under martial law for several decades.

The situation eased somewhat in 1950, when a non-Kemalist party was elected to power. Although they could not identify themselves as such, Kurds became members of parliament and ministers and efforts were made to develop the Kurdish areas economically. Especially after the Iraqi revolution of 1958, Turkish Kurds became aware of the activities of Kurdish political organisations in Iraq. In addition, the hundreds of thousands of displaced Kurds in the cities of western Turkey became increasingly conscious of their national status, and a separatist Turkish Kurdish Democratic Party (KDP) was founded in 1965. The paradox of Turkish political life in the 1950s, 1960s and 1970s was that although most of the members of parliament for eastern Turkey were Kurds, they could not organise as such; as late as 1979 a prominent ex-minister was sentenced to two years' imprisonment for a speech in which he stated that there were both Kurds and Turks in Turkey.

In the late 1960s various left-wing parties and organisations were founded in the area, and there were mass anti-government demonstrations in Sivas and Diyarbakr in 1967. The 1970s saw great instability throughout Turkey generally, with Kurdish urban and rural guerrilla groups being especially active. A radical organisation, the Workers' Party of Kurdistan (PKK) emerged in the late 1970s under the leadership of Abdullah Öcalan, proclaiming armed struggle against the government in the Kurdish area, denouncing and sometimes killing local leaders and members of opposing political organisations as 'collaborators'.

A major difficulty for the forging of a unified Kurdish movement in Turkey (as elsewhere) has been the basic cleavage between (generally pro-Barzani) strictly nationalist groups on the one hand, and leftists, attached either to mainstream left-wing Turkish parties or to groups like the PKK, on the other. Both sides have often been as vehemently opposed to each other as to the Turkish government. Since the military coup in 1980 about half the Turkish army has been permanently stationed in southeast Turkey, and has carried out a series of campaigns against the opposition forces there.

IRAQI KURDISH POLITICS AFTER 1947

With the fall of Mahabad and the departure of Barzani, Kurdish politics remained virtually in limbo until the overthrow of the Iraqi monarchy. In Iran the KDP was proscribed. It reappeared briefly in support of the government of Muhammad Mosaddeq in 1951–53, but suffered in the reprisals against the left that followed Mosaddeq's fall. In 1956, still underground, it published a draft programme calling for Kurdish autonomy. Broadly speaking, the principal events in the history of the Kurdish movement since 1947 relate to its activities in Iraq. This is because, in spite of the unwillingness of successive Iraqi governments to render more than lip service to the principle, the Iraqi Kurds enjoyed certain basic freedoms denied to their fellows in Iran and Turkey. Most significantly, this has been the recognition – tacit and grudging though it may often have been – of their separate ethnic status. In Turkey, and to a lesser extent in Iran, Kurds were persecuted as Kurds. In Iraq, provided that they did not actually engage in activities directed against the central government the Kurds were generally no more – and no less – deprived of civil liberties than their Arab fellow citizens. This attitude only changed significantly with the bombing of Halabja with chemical weapons in 1988 and the persecutions and massacres which followed.

Perhaps the most important development in Kurdish politics between Mahabad and 1958 was the foundation and rise to maturity of the Iraqi Kurdish Democratic Party (KDP). At first an Iraqi branch of the Iranian KDP had been founded in Mahabad in 1946 by Barzani and his close associate Hamza Abdullah, who was charged with organising the party in Iraq, but his mission ended in the creation of a separate Iraqi KDP. This had the effect of formalising a permanent administrative separation in terms of Kurdish politics between Iraqi and Iranian Kurdistan. Thus in August 1946 the Iraqi KDP was formally inaugurated, with Abdullah as secretary general and Mulla Mustafa, then still in Mahabad, as president. At the same time there was a branch of the Iranian KDP in Iraqi Kurdistan, based at Sulaymaniyya, under the leadership of Ibrahim Ahmad (a long standing rival of Barzani), who denounced the new Iraqi KDP as a potentially dangerous derogation of the authority of Qadi Muhammad and the Mahabad Republic. After the fall of Mahabad, Ahmad reluctantly joined the Iraqi KDP, becoming its secretary-general in 1951, taking advantage of Barzani's absence in the Soviet Union to push the party to the left. The KDP now worked mainly among students and intellectuals and had little support in the countryside, which continued to be dominated by tribal leaders and landlords.

When the Free Officers seized power in 1958, Ibrahim Ahmad, then under house arrest in Kirkuk, immediately telegraphed a message of congratulation. For the time being at least, the auguries seemed favourable. The new constitution stated that 'Arabs and Kurds are partners in the Iraqi homeland, and their national rights are recognised within the Iraqi state.' On 6 October 1958 Barzani returned from 12 years of exile to a rapturous welcome from his Kurdish supporters and what seemed to be expressions of genuine cordiality from the new leader, Abd al-Karim Qasim. A new era in Arab-Kurdish relations appeared to have begun.

The Free Officers had no special commitment to the Kurdish question – none of them was Kurdish – but their general attitude towards the Kurds was positive. A distinguished Kurdish civil servant and former army officer, Khalid al-Naqshabandi, was made a member of the three-man ceremonial 'sovereignty council'. In the conflict that ensued in 1958–59 (*see* Chapter 4, Iraq) over whether Iraq should join the United Arab Republic, the Kurds' attitude was generally negative, since the pan-Arab-inspired UAR was a most unlikely vehicle for the furthering of their aspirations, however defined. As Qasim himself was also opposed to unity with Egypt, relations between the central government and the KDP, which had now been taken over by Mulla Mustafa Barzani, continued to be amicable. However, the prospect of the extension of the new land reform to Kurdistan caused alarm among Barzani and his circle, especially as such policies would have widespread popularity. This was a further manifestation of the contradiction between 'social reform' and 'national aspirations' which has acted as such a major brake on the effectiveness of the Kurdish movement in recent times.

In January 1960 the KDP was legalised. In the course of the same year Ibrahim Ahmad and his son-in-law Jalal Talabani managed to find their way back into Barzani's favour so that by October 1960 Ahmad had been 're-elected' secretary general of the party. Gradually, however, it became clear that many of the more conservative Free Officers were opposed to any real concessions to the Kurds, and also that Qasim's own commitment was limited. For his part, Barzani's basic instincts and sentiments were those of a tribal leader. Although he was also interested in gaining the support of Kurdish intellectuals and urban dwellers, his real power base lay in his own tribe, and his force of some 2,000 fighting men. Hence such arcane matters as the wording of the party programme was not as important to him as to the 'politicals', who saw the Party as a means of political and ideological mobilisation. For their part the 'politicals' were often obliged, against their better judgment, to defer to Barzani, precisely because he was the only Kurdish figure with sufficient magnetism, tribal following and military experience to be able to carry the day in Kurdistan.

Eventually it became clear that Qasim was not willing to grant real autonomy to the Kurds and by the beginning of 1961 he began to turn against Barzani. He favoured the leaders of tribes opposed to Barzani (especially the Herki and Zibari) and banned Kurdish newspapers and magazines. For a while, Barzani was content to bide his time in the north, and let Qasim arrest or harass the urban leadership. Thus Ibrahim Ahmad was arrested in March 1961 and the KDP was refused permission to hold its annual congress in July. By September 1961 fighting had broken out in earnest, and this was to continue intermittently until 1975.

By May 1962, Barzani had gained control of the Hamilton road between Ruwanduz and the Iranian border. The Iraqi army was only able to return to this area after the collapse of the Kurdish movement in 1975. When the Ba'th-Nationalist alliance eventually overthrew Qasim in February 1963, the coup leaders had obtained assurances from both Barzani and the KDP leaders that if they were successful the

Kurds would announce a cease-fire, which duly materialised. Ahmad's son-in-law Jalal Talabani was dispatched to Baghdad a few days after the coup to negotiate with the new regime. As might have been foreseen, these negotiations proved futile and fighting broke out again in June 1963.

THE KURDS SINCE 1963

For the next few years the conflict was generally three cornered: between the government, the Ahmad/Talabani dominated KDP and Barzani. Sometimes the KDP would co-operate with the government, sometimes with Barzani and sometimes, though rather more rarely, Barzani and the government would join forces to attack the KDP. Thus in August 1964 Barzani chased Ahmad and Talabani out of Iraq across the Iranian border, in revenge for the KDP's attack on his truce with Arif (February 1964 to April 1965). In July Barzani had set up his 'own' KDP from which all supporters of the Ahmad/Talabani group had been purged. This rupture between Barzani and the 'politicals' had the effect of handing over the day to day control of much of the Kurdish movement on the ground to Barzani; while his military talents were undoubted, his political acumen was so limited as to put the Kurdish cause at a grave disadvantage.

When fighting broke out again in April 1965 virtually the whole Iraqi army was dispatched to the north, but Barzani, who was receiving large supplies of weapons from Iran, inflicted a crushing defeat on the Iraqi army in mid-May 1966. The government began to negotiate seriously with him, and a 'third interlude' began. In July 1968 the Arif government was overthrown and the Ba'th came to power with the tacit support of the Ahmad/Talabani faction of the KDP, some of whom were briefly appointed to the cabinet. Attempts to reach a more durable agreement between Barzani and the Ba'th failed again, and fighting broke out once more. The government replied by sending four divisions to Kurdistan, and the fighting continued for most of that year. In August 1969, a major offensive was launched by the government, once more without any visible success, in spite of atrocities designed to terrorise the inhabitants into submission.

At this stage the Ba'th regime was not yet sufficiently firmly established to continue the campaign indefinitely. It, therefore, approached Barzani with a view to opening negotiations which lasted from mid-December 1969 until March 1970, ending with the publication of an agreement, the March manifesto. This recognised 'the legitimacy of the Kurdish nationality', and promised Kurdish linguistic rights, Kurdish participation in government, Kurdish administrators for the Kurdish area and a new province based on Dohuk. It also envisaged the implementation of the Agrarian Reform Law in the north, and, perhaps most controversially, as future events were to show, stated that 'necessary steps shall be taken ... to unify the governorates and administrative units populated by a Kurdish majority as shown by the official census to be carried out.' The most contentious area here was the town of Kirkuk and the oil wells which surrounded it.

The March manifesto had two important drawbacks for the Ba'th. First it was specifically concluded with Barzani himself, which meant that it recognised Barzani and the KDP as the sole political (and, de facto administrative) authority in an area extending from Zakho to Halabja. Secondly, this recognition had the effect of undermining 'the writ of the Iraqi state in the Kurdish areas'. As events were to show, the manifesto was essentially a device by the Ba'th to gain time to be able to recast its Kurdish policy to its own advantage at some future point. One consequence of the agreement was that the Ahmad/Talabani faction of pro-government Kurds became redundant and in fact dissolved itself in the course of 1970, to reappear, in a somewhat different guise, as the Patriotic Union of Kurdistan (PUK) in 1976.

The government's bad faith became apparent soon after the publication of the manifesto. Large numbers of families were forcibly removed from their homes to change the ethnic balance of particular areas, especially in Kirkuk, which the Kurdish leadership had insisted should form part of the Kurdish area and which the government wanted to retain within Iraq proper. In September 1971 some 40,000 Fa'ili (Shi'i) Kurds were expelled to Iran from the border area near Khaniqin on the specious grounds that they were not really Iraqis. These and other measures showed that the Ba'th were intent on limiting the extent of Kurdistan as far as possible. Also in September 1971, the Ba'th attempted to assassinate Barzani; other attacks on him and his sons took place during 1972 and 1973. Tensions grew and clashes occurred between government forces and the Kurds in Sulaymaniyya and in Jabal Sinjar, where several thousand Yazidis were forced to leave their homes in February and March 1973.

Although a major breakdown seemed inevitable, negotiations continued throughout the end of 1973 and the beginning of 1974. A few members of the KDP (notably Barzani's eldest son Ubaydullah) broke with Barzani and joined the Ba'th dominated National Front, but most Kurds stood solidly behind Barzani and the KDP. In April 1974 fighting broke out once again with the Iraqi air force bombing Qala Diza, Halabja and Jalala, killing 193 civilians and prompting a mass exodus of refugees to Iran. In spite of this, the Kurds maintained the upper hand. The government forces became seriously bogged down and no end seemed in sight.

At this point help arrived from an unexpected quarter. Iraq's concern to get the better of the Kurds coincided with the Shah of Iran's desire to settle the various disputes with Iraq which had inflamed relations between the two countries over the previous decade. In March 1975, in the course of the Organisation of Petroleum Exporting Countries' conference in Algiers, Saddam Hussein and the Shah came to an agreement, which, on the Iraqi side, effectively abrogated the Sa'dabad Pact of 1937, gave the Iranians free rights of navigation in the

Shatt al-Arab, and, on the Iranian side, closed the Iran-Iraq frontier in the north, thus preventing aid reaching the Kurds and also preventing them from regrouping and rearming in and from Iran. The Iranian artillery, which had supported the Kurds, withdrew within 24 hours and the Kurdish resistance collapsed almost immediately. Barzani left for Iran and died in the United States in 1979. He was succeeded by his son Mas'ud.

In the months that followed many of the refugees trickled back to Iraq under a series of amnesties, while the government continued to Arabise the area more forcibly. The inhabitants of the more remote areas were removed from their homes and resettled in newly con-structed concrete villages on the sides of roads where surveillance would be easier. Kurdish was no longer taught in Kurdish schools and Kurdish teachers and administrators were sent to work in southern Iraq and replaced in the Kurdish areas by Arabs. By 1979 an estimated 200,000 Kurds had been deported from the frontier area and some 700 villages burnt down as part of a scorched earth policy, which aimed to clear a strip along the border with Iran and Turkey some 12 miles wide and 500 miles long.

THE IRANIAN REVOLUTION

After the fall of Mahabad, the Iranian Kurdish movement went under-ground, surfacing briefly in 1958 in an effort to take indirect advantage of Barzani's return to Iraq. However, the Iranian government continued to harass and suppress Kurdish activists, and also had a complex rela-tionship with Barzani, whom, as has been mentioned, it armed from time to time against the government in Baghdad. As far as Barzani was concerned, his intermittent dependence on Tehran meant that he was unable or unwilling to assist the Kurdish movement in Iran, even going so far as to hand over to SAVAK (the Iranian secret police) a number of Iranian Kurds who had fled to Iraq. During the Ba'th/Kurdish honey-moon period (1970–74) Iranian Kurdish activity moved to Baghdad, although it was clear that the Shah was continuing to support Barzani. Between 1973 and 1989 (when he was assassinated in Vienna) Abd al-Rahman Qasimlu, a former professor at the Sorbonne, was the leader of the Iranian KDP. It generally lacked the tribal base of the Iraqi KDP and, as a result, was probably more intensely politicised.

The overthrow of the Shah was greeted with great excitement in Iranian Kurdistan, since it seemed to raise the possibility of autonomy once more – and, as one authority points out, the prospects seemed bet-ter than at the time of Mahabad, as no great power interest was involved. However, as the Islamic Republic gradually established itself, it became clear that it too would not support Kurdish se[p]aratist demands, since it was ideologically opposed to the notion of an[y] [e]thnic or other divisions within the Islamic community, recognising only.the canonically sanctioned religious minorities (Christians, Jews and Zoroastrians). On the other hand the situation was so unstable and the control exercised by the centre over the provinces so precarious, that 'creeping autonomy' seemed to be coming in any case.

Unfortunately for the Iranian Kurds, the anti-Iraqi regime in Tehran attracted the support of Mas'ud Barzani and Jalal Talabani, and as a quid pro quo both the Iraqi KDP and the Patriotic Union of Kurdistan (PUK) sided with Tehran against the Iranian KDP and its leftist allies (a step which caused severe convulsions within the Iraqi KDP itself). Sharp clashes took place in the spring and summer of 1979, but by August the Kurds had lost the towns they had previously captured to the Iranian Army. As Kurdish forces continued to control much of the country side an uneasy stalemate persisted until the outbreak of the Iran/Iraq war in September 1980.

THE EFFECTS OF THE IRAN–IRAQ WAR

Again, internal disagreements within the Kurdish movement inside Iran and Iraq and between the Kurdish movements in the two countries resulted in the loss, or the frittering away, of yet another promising opportunity for the Kurdish people. In the first place, the government of the Islamic Republic recruited the Barzanis and the Iraqi KDP to fight against the Iranian KDP. Partly as a result, and partly because of the Iranian army's recovery, the KDP-Iran gradually lost control of the areas it dominated in north-western Iran. At the same time, Jalal Talabani, who had become estranged from the regime in Tehran, made attempts to negotiate some sort of settlement with the regime in Baghdad, which had become uneasy at the large number of Kurdish deserters from the Iraqi army. On 10 December 1983 Talabani actually reached an agreement with Baghdad, ostensibly because of the latter's willingness to admit some of the PUK's demands, but which had the principal effect of releasing Iraqi troops for more effective deployment in the war zone.

As could easily have been predicted, this agreement did not last long. A few months later 24 Kurds were executed in Sulaymaniyya, Talabani's fiefdom, and it was clear that Baghdad was not going to give up its claim to control the area. Such incidents, and what was widely regarded as opportunism on the part of the PUK lost it much credibility and support in the Kurdish areas. By 1987, however, all the main Kurdish groups had formed an alliance against Baghdad and stated that they would press for autonomy within Iraq. Simultaneously, the PUK dropped its opposition to co-operation with Iranian forces, and by the spring of 1987 Iranian and PUK forces were fighting side by side inside Iraqi Kurdistan. KDP and PUK forces now controlled the area between the Great Zab and the Diyala, Ruwanduz and much of the area between Zakho and Aqra. All this took place against a background of terrible brutality on the part of the Iraqi government. Eight thousand members of the Barzani clan were arrested in 1983 and have not been seen since. A further 2,000 hamlets were stripped of their populations, and as many as half a million Kurds were deported to lowland Kurdistan or southern Iraq.

In March 1988 Iranian troops captured Halabja; the next day, the town came under attack from chemical weapons launched by the Iraqi Air Force. Over 6,000 civilians, including large numbers of women and children, were killed. This policy was continued after the Iran-Iraq cease-fire on 20 August; in the face of further Iraqi gas attacks some 60,000 Kurdish civilians fled to Turkey and a similar number to Iran. These attacks, allied to a great wave of repression over the next two years and the forced relocation of much of the rural population had the inevitable consequence that armed Kurdish opposition virtually ceased.

The refugee problem inside Iran and Turkey was considerable, with over 150,000 in camps in Iran and a further 70,000 in Turkey. For its part Turkey, concerned about the effect on its 'own' Kurds, refused to allow the Iraqi Kurds to be described as refugees, insisting that all aid to them be distributed through the Turkish Red Crescent, and generally playing down allegations that many of the refugees had been the victims of gas attacks. At the same time the PKK was gaining support in south-east Turkey, and Kurdish deputies, knowing that human rights issues were an important item on the agenda of Turkey's relations with the EC, made use of the situation to push for further concessions from Ankara.

THE KURDS IN THE 1990S

By far the most significant developments in Kurdish politics over the last few years have taken place in Iraq. Although details only began to filter to the outside world at the end of 1991, it seems that in the period between 1988 and 1990 Saddam Hussein and his circle decided to wreak revenge on the Kurds for their 'disloyalty' during the war with Iran, beginning, perhaps, with the chemical weapons attack on Halabja. In the course of a campaign known as the *Anfal* (booty, plunder), masterminded by Ali Hasan al-Majid, the minister of defence and Husayn Kamil al-Majid, the minister of industry and military industries (both distant relatives of Saddam Hussein), as many as 100,000 Kurds were either taken to encampments on the outskirts of the Kurdish cities or to huge pits in the desert west of Samawa where they were shot and buried. This, in part, may explain the curiously ambivalent attitude to the invasion of Kuwait adopted by some of the Kurdish leadership at the end of 1990. Knowing the fate of so many of their fellow countrymen, they did not wish to side too openly with external forces against Saddam Hussein.

In the event, most of the Kurdish organisations joined the rest of the opposition in declaring their hostility to the Ba'th government. For their part the other opposition groups agreed to accept the principle of autonomy for Iraqi Kurdistan. After the defeat of the Iraqi ground forces in February 1991 two spontaneous risings broke out in Iraq, one in the south, the other in the Kurdish area. For two weeks it appeared that the opposition was decisively in command, and then the tables turned. Kurdish guerrilla forces were driven out of the northern cities, and by the beginning of April 1.5 million Kurdish refugees were camped out on the Iranian and Turkish borders. This human tragedy, unfolding daily on millions of television screens throughout the world, brought the desperate plight of the Kurds to world attention for the first time.

In mid-April 1991 the Coalition forces sponsored a military exclusion zone north of the 36th parallel, and a Kurdish administration was formed in Arbil. On 19 May 1992 elections were held for a 105-seat Kurdish national assembly in which the seats were shared equally between the KDP and the PUK, with a rotating presidency. By July both Kurdish parties were represented in the newly formed Iraqi National Congress, an umbrella movement of opposition parties whose headquarters was established in the Kurdish area.

These developments caused considerable alarm in the interior ministries of Iran, Syria and Turkey because of the potential impact upon their own Kurdish populations. Although the military exclusion zone in Iraq was policed (by Britain, France, Turkey herself and the US) from air bases in southeast Turkey, the Turkish government took every opportunity (and urged its neighbours to do likewise) to stress its support for the territorial integrity of Iraq. In addition, in the autumn of 1993 Turkish bombers attacked Iraqi Kurdistan in pursuit of PKK guerrillas, and Turkish ground forces entered the area on several occasions in 1994. More significantly still, a major invasion of Iraqi Kurdistan took place in March 1995 when a combined air and land offensive was launched, involving some 35,000 Turkish troops penetrating 25 miles into Iraqi Kurdish territory (generating vigorous criticism from Turkey's NATO allies). In the event, both the main Kurdish parties seem to have been sufficiently aware of the need to placate the government in Ankara not to engage in any flirtations with the PKK, and indeed were not above co-operating with the Turkish authorities in 'flushing out' Öcalan and his followers.

A more serious threat to the stability of the fledgling Iraqi/Kurdish regime in the first years of its existence was the apparently ineradicable internecine rivalry between its two main constituent groups, the KDP and the PUK. Although some policy differences certainly exist, the roots of this rivalry are more personal and tribal than ideological and are rooted in the long standing distrust between the two leaders, or at least between Mas'ud Barzani's father, Mulla Mustafa, and Jalal Talabani. It is also true that those who wish the Iraqi Kurdish experiment to fail (the regime in Baghdad among them) are only too eager to manipulate this distrust to their own advantage. Fighting between the militias of the two parties took place for most of the period between late 1993 and mid-1995, in spite of a number of attempts at conciliation by the Iraqi National Congress and outside bodies (perhaps most notably the French government in July 1994). A further explosive element was the Iranian-backed Islamic Movement of Kurdistan, led by Sheikh Uthman Abd al-Aziz, which was involved in attacks against the PUK for much of the first half of 1994. An important casualty of the fighting was the credibility of the Iraqi National Congress. The failure of its efforts at conciliation did not augur well for its capacity to function as an effective umbrella organisation for the Iraqi opposition as a whole.

As the PKK became increasingly active in Turkey in the late 1980s, popular hostility to the security forces' activities grew. Curfews were declared in the southeast, and new decrees forbade press reporting and permitted forcible resettlement. Local support grew steadily throughout 1990 and 1991, fuelled by resentment at the government's generally insensitive handling of the Iraqi Kurdish refugees. At the same time the president, Turgut Özal, pressed successfully for changes which would lift some restrictions on the use of the Kurdish language.

Between 1992 and the end of 1994 the Turkish government was involved in regular regional security meetings with Iran, Iraq and Syria, principally in attempts to ensure that its neighbours understood that they would pay dearly for any favour which they might be tempted to show to the PKK. Thus Turkey and Iran signed a protocol in November 1993 declaring that neither country would allow any Kurdish terrorist organisation to operate on their territory. At a summit in Damascus in August 1994, Syria, which had been sheltering the PKK for several years, publicly pledged not to do so, partly, at least, in an effort to purge itself of the charge of terrorism. It is also the case that commercial and quasi-diplomatic exchanges between Ankara and Baghdad increased in intensity throughout 1994 and 1995. Relationships are thus finely balanced: the Kurdish government depends upon Ankara for its continued existence, but Ankara will continue to support it only as long as it co-operates in the campaign against the PKK and only as long as it does not explicitly proclaim any separatist pretensions.

In Iran hopes for progress towards a Kurdish settlement were dashed with the assassination of Abd al-Rahman Qasimlu in Vienna in July 1989, probably at the hands of agents of the Iranian government, with which he was negotiating at the time. Four other Iranian Kurdish leaders were assassinated in Berlin in September 1992. The generally more pragmatic policies of the post-Khomeini regime in Tehran suggest a greater willingness to compromise, although its anxiety not to offend the Turkish authorities seems to have been paramount. In Iraq, Iranian support for the Islamic Movement of Iraqi Kurdistan has added to the disunity and divisions in the Kurdish autonomous area.

Peter Sluglett and Marion Farouk-Sluglett

8
LEBANON

Until as recently as the late 1960s Lebanon was held up by political scientists as a model of political stability and good neighbourliness in a region of turmoil. The deep divisions which lie so close to the surface, and which have been encouraged and exacerbated to no small degree by the structure of the political system, did not begin to be analysed adequately until after the debacles of the mid 1970s.

The vicissitudes which have afflicted Lebanon for much of the last two decades are deeply rooted in the country's past, and derive largely from the failure to create a political system, even a polity, that is viable or enduring. A great part of the responsibility for this failure must be laid at the door of the institutionalised system of confessional politics and at the door of the Lebanese elite which has perpetuated this system, in that the principle of maintaining a very weak central state structure has been adhered to with remarkable tenacity. However, it is also the case that a number of external forces have done their best to see to it that Lebanon either does not survive or does so in a highly fragmented manner. In that sense the struggles and clashes within Lebanon since the early 1970s are a microcosm of the conflicts taking place in other parts of the Middle East.

One major difficulty is that although most Lebanese support the concept of a Lebanese state there is no basic consensus of the institutional form that this should take, except, generally, that it should encroach as little as possible upon them. In a memorable book published in 1988, the Lebanese historian Kamal Salibi wrote: 'The state has long ceased to exercise sovereign control over its own national territory. There remains an administrative bureaucracy which continues to provide a cover of legitimacy to public and private transactions as well as a minimum of public services of steadily deteriorating quality.' The situation has greatly improved since then, and a great deal of reconciliation and reconstruction has taken place. However, more wide-ranging solutions to Lebanon's problems are unlikely to be achieved before the conclusion of a comprehensive accord between Syria and Israel, and other substantial steps towards an overall Middle East peace settlement.

THE LAST YEARS OF OTTOMAN LEBANON

Lebanon, as it exists today, is a considerable enlargement of a much smaller entity. The *mutasarrifiyya*, or governorate of Lebanon, an autonomous province within the Ottoman Empire, was created by the Ottoman authorities in 1861, after a major outbreak of violence in 1860. This was partly a sectarian clash between Maronite Christians and Druzes, partly a struggle between peasants and landlords, in which some 11,000 people, mostly Christians, lost their lives. Before the creation of the *mutasarrifiyya*, although nominally part of the Ottoman province of Sidon, Mount Lebanon had been more or less independent under a series of mainly Christian dynasties which ruled from the mid-16th century to 1840.

The population of the *mutasarrifiyya* was roughly four-fifths Christian and one-fifth Muslim. It is an important precept of Islam that the 'peoples of the book', as the Qur'an terms Christians and Jews, should be permitted to practise their religion in return for the payment of a capitation fee, or head tax on adult males, to the Muslim authorities. This accounts for the survival of fairly substantial communities of Christians (10 per cent of the population of Egypt, 15 per cent of the population of Syria, for example) and, until the creation of the state of Israel, of Jews, in much of the Arab Middle East to the present day. The mountainous areas of Greater Syria always acted as places of refuge for minority groups or heterodox sects, and Mount Lebanon, traditionally, was the home of two of these, the Maronite Christians and the Druzes.

Simplifying a complex reality, Christians in Lebanon can be divided into members of various Catholic churches in communion with Rome (Uniate), and members of the Orthodox churches. The patriarchs of the Catholic communities are generally cardinals. Apart from the Armenians, the communities are mostly Arab, but they have their own liturgical languages: Syriac for the Maronites and Syrian Catholics; and Greek and Armenian for the Greek and Armenian Catholics. All Orthodox Christians share a common set of beliefs, but have different liturgical languages (Greek, Armenian and Syriac for the Greek, Armenian and Syrian Orthodox). The communities are autocephalous – they are independent of each other and do not recognise any overarching authority beyond that of their own patriarchs: there is no 'Orthodox Pope'

The Orthodox, or Eastern Christians, have tended to associate their political destinies with that of the Sunni Muslims, and to see themselves very much as Arabs. Many individual Arab Greek Orthodox Christians were pioneers of the early Arab nationalist movement, and more recently leaders of nationalist and leftist political organisations, such as Michel Aflaq of the Ba'th Party and George Habash and Na'if Hawatma, leaders of two influential Palestinian political parties. The Catholics and other Uniates, on the other hand, have tended both to be identified with, and identify themselves with, European, and particularly French, culture, often regarding 'Arab' identity as inferior to their own. Hence in any discussion of Lebanon, the notion of a strict Muslim/Christian divide is misleading: there are important divisions *within* the two principal religious communities as well.

In the 18th and 19th centuries, when the Great Powers began to take a closer interest in the political and economic affairs of the Ottoman Empire, Russia, as the major Orthodox power, emerged as the protector of the Orthodox Christians (not just in the Arab Middle East but also in Ottoman Europe, in Bulgaria, Serbia, and so on) while France was the protector of

Ethnic factions in Lebanon

Sunni majority

Christian majority

Shi'i majority

DRUSE Militias

Borders

International

Mutasarrifiyya border (1860-1915)

South Lebanon security zone

Limit of Syrian occupation

Kabir

Homs

Barid

Tripoli

Zghorta

Qurna al-Sawda

Bcharre

1976

Mountains

Asi

Mediterranean Sea

LEBANESE FRONT MILITIA

Baalbek

Bekaa Valley

Mountains

Beirut

DRUSE

Lebanon

Litani

Lebanon

Anti-Lebanon

Zahle

Israeli advance to Beirut 1982

Sidon *1983*

MILITIA

Barada

Damascus

Nabatiya

Jabal Amil

Mar'ayun

A'waj

Hasbaya

Tyre

Litani

SYRIA

Qunaytra

GOLAN HEIGHTS

0   25   50 kms

0   25 miles

ISRAEL

OFFICIAL NAME	The Republic of Lebanon
AREA	10,452 sq. km (4,036 sq. miles)
POPULATION	2,915,000 *(1994)*
CAPITAL	Beirut, population 1,500,000 *(1991)*
LANGUAGE	Arabic
RELIGION	Muslim (57%: Sunni 20%, Shi'i 31%, Druze 6%), Christian (43%: Maronite 25%, remainder Greek/ Syrian/Armenian Orthodox, Greek/Syrian/ Armenian/Latin Catholic and Protestant)
GNP PER CAPITA	US$1,400 *(1991)*

the Catholics. Apart from the Maronites who had long accepted papal supremacy, many Middle Eastern Catholics were the products of a wave of conversion from Orthodoxy in the 18th century – a step many had taken partly because they regarded the protection of France as more secure than the protection of Russia – so there was often little love lost between them and the Orthodox communities from which they had originated.

For their part the Druzes were a heterodox Muslim sect which had broken away from another sect of Shi'i Islam in the 12th century. Other important Muslim groupings in Lebanon are the Sunni Muslims, whose co-religionists form the majority (90 per cent) of all Muslims in the world, and the Shi'i Muslims, living mainly in the south and east of Lebanon, now acknowledged to be the most numerous single sect in the country.

On the whole, this multi-sectarian population lived in reasonable harmony before the explosion of communal violence in Mount Lebanon in 1860. The civil war of 1860 was brought on partly by outside interference by the Great Powers, France supporting the Maronites while Britain supported the Druzes, and partly by economic and social factors related to the way in which entry into the world market had affected Lebanon, whose principal cash crop in the 19th century was silk. As a result of the violence, and to forestall further intervention on the part of the powers (the French immediately sent an expeditionary force) the Ottomans agreed to an arrangement whereby a committee of the powers would assemble at Istanbul and elect a governor of Lebanon, who was to be an Ottoman Christian, usually from some other part of the Empire.

During the 'long peace' between 1861 and 1915 the *mutasarrifiyya* was an autonomous Ottoman province and became prosperous from the silk industry, whose products went mostly to Marseilles. Like other port cities in the eastern Mediterranean, the population of Beirut (itself an administrative enclave separate from the authority of the *mutasarrifiyya* and thus under direct Ottoman control) expanded considerably throughout the rest of the 19th century, from about 35,000 in 1860 to about 130,000 in 1900. The *mutasarrifiyya* had a total population of some 288,000, of whom about 156,000 were Maronites, 59,000 other Christians, and 73,000 Muslims, about half of whom were Druze. Thus, on the eve of the First World War, as well as being the largest single sect, the Maronites formed an absolute majority of the population as a whole.

THE CREATION OF MODERN LEBANON

After the First World War the Ottoman Empire was dissolved, and the Arab Middle East divided into the states which exist today, initially under the tutelage of Britain and France. In this share-out, France was awarded Syria, and Britain Iraq, Palestine and Transjordan. In Syria, France created two separate political entities, Lebanon and Syria, partly in an attempt to control and contain the Arab nationalist movement within the Syrian interior, partly because the Maronites of Lebanon, with whom the French had had links since the 16th century, were the only community in the area on whom they could entirely rely. The new state of Lebanon, created in August 1920, was almost twice the size of the Ottoman *mutasarrifiyya*. It included the town of Tripoli and the Akkar plain in the north, the Bekaa Valley in the east, the districts of Rashaya, Hasbaya and Jabal Amil in the south, and the coastal cities of Tyre, Sidon, and Beirut.

For a long time, many non-Maronite 'Lebanese' considered the formation of a separate and greatly enlarged Lebanon both as a French imperial stratagem and a temporary expedient, and it took some time for them to get used to the idea, let alone accept it. There were many grounds for these objections, the most basic that many Arabs had wanted – and indeed some had fought for – an independent united Arab state, rather than a set of smaller entities under the tutelage of one or other of the victorious powers. In addition, 'Greater Syria' as a geo-political entity had been divided into Lebanon, Palestine, Syria and Transjordan, not to mention the various smaller quasi-autonomous statelets for the Druzes and the Alawites inside what is now Syria. All these divisions rankled, but in the case of Lebanon what rankled particularly was that territories which had traditionally been part of a larger entity thought of as 'Syria' were now detached from it and given to a new state, Lebanon, 'Grand Liban'. Grand Liban was far more viable economically than its predecessor, but large numbers of its inhabitants had always regarded themselves as Syrians, and long continued to do so.

Only the Maronites were generally satisfied with this new arrangement. Many Maronites thought of themselves as the 'real' Lebanese, the descendants of the Phoenicians, forming an island of Christendom, and 'civilisation', in a sea of Muslim barbarism. They believed themselves culturally superior to and were in fact generally better off than the rest of the population around them. Furthermore, many prominent Maronites had actively lobbied for a separate state under French protection. Less satisfactory for the Maronites was that the 'added areas' were largely non-Maronite. The smaller entity had 285,000 inhabitants; the areas added brought another 318,000. Of these only 43,000 were Maronites, while 160,000 were Sunni Muslims and 85,000 were Shi'i Muslims.

Thus, although the Christians formed 55 per cent of the population, and the Maronites were still the largest single community, they no longer formed an absolute majority. In the census of 1932 the Maronites formed some 29 per cent of the population, the Sunnis 22.5 per cent and the Shi'is 20 per cent. Not only were the Maronites reduced from being an absolute majority, but the new state had virtual parity between its Muslim and Christian populations. It is significant that the 1932 census was the last officially taken in Lebanon. Subsequent governments have consistently refused to repeat the exercise, since any new census would have revealed that the Maronites had ceased to be the largest single element in the state.

LEBANON UNDER FRENCH MANDATE, 1920–46

Although the Maronites had lost their numerical preponderance, they saw to it that they did not lose their supremacy. In this they were greatly assisted by the virtual boycott of the new state throughout the 1920s and most of the 1930s by almost all the Sunni Muslims, the only other community which could seriously have challenged them politically. As well as being the principal losers by the separation from Syria, the Sunnis resented their demotion from their status under the Ottomans (the Ottomans themselves were Sunnis), and their subjugation to the Maronites. In consequence they boycotted the 1922 elections, the first to be held on a sectarian or confessional basis. When the Lebanese Republic was officially proclaimed in 1926 it had a Greek Orthodox president and a Sunni speaker of the chamber of deputies, but all the other posts, and finally the presidency as well, were held by Maronites. In time, however, it became clear to what would be the dominant faction among Maronite politicians, that the survival and prosperity of the new state would only be possible if the Muslims, particularly the Sunnis, could be induced to accept it.

In general, the Maronites' educational and economic pre-eminence meant that their community continued to do best out of the new arrangements. The main beneficiaries of the penetration of European capital after 1860 had been the Maronites of Beirut and Mount Lebanon, although a significant stratum of Sunni merchants from Tripoli and Beirut had also participated in the process. At a humbler social level, many of the Maronites of Mount Lebanon in the 1920s were smallholders, while the majority of the Sunni and Shi'i cultivators on the periphery – the Bekaa, Jabal Amil, the Akkar – were sharecroppers on the great feudal estates. The Maronites' head start was also reinforced by their earlier access to modern European-style education. Through most of the period of the mandate (1920–46) education was predominantly in the hands of foreign missions, and thus directed particularly towards the Christian population. As late as 1968, 62 per cent of all school-children attended private, that is mostly Christian, schools. In addition, although the Maronite community was not monolithic, and there were regional and other rivalries among its leaders, the fact that Maronitism itself is centred on Lebanon gave Lebanese Maronitism a particularly strong sense of cohesion.

In contrast, among the Sunni Muslims – the rise of the Shi'is to their present level of political muscle is relatively recent – this sense of cohesion developed in a different way. Since 90 per cent of the population of the Arab world, (and 70 per cent of the population of Syria), is Sunni Muslim, the Sunnis had none of the Maronites' sense of being embattled, and were aware of their membership of a wider Muslim world outside the boundaries of Lebanon, which, in fact, they spent a considerable part of the early years of the Lebanese state trying to join. It was only in 1936, when the French indicated that they were prepared to consider a Franco-Syrian and a Franco-Lebanese treaty, that most Sunnis (in Syria as well as in Lebanon) finally accepted that insisting on reuniting Lebanon with Syria might jeopardise any hopes of obtaining independence for both countries, and reluctantly gave up their boycott of the Lebanese state.

This change in outlook also required recognition on the part of the Maronite leaders that the prosperity of the new entity would require a partnership of a kind between the sects and, particularly in the 1940s and

1950s, between themselves and the Sunnis. The 'historic compromise' was enshrined in the unwritten National Pact of 1943, between the Maronite president Bishara al-Khuri and the Sunni prime minister Riyadh al-Sulh. Essentially, Lebanon was to be independent, neither part of Syria nor a French protectorate, and as such it was one of the founder members of the Arab League in 1945. The National Pact continued the political arrangements of the Republic, enshrining the principle of confessionalism (i.e., the distribution of posts on a religious-sectarian basis to ensure a 'just' representation of each community) in all spheres of public life, high offices of state and at all levels in the civil service and the armed forces.

On the arguable basis that the Maronites were the largest single community, they were given the key posts of the presidency and the commander-in-chief of the armed forces. The Sunnis were given the premiership, and the Shi'is the post of speaker of the chamber of deputies. Notables from the smaller communities were also given appropriate functions in the scheme of things. The Christian-Muslim balance in offices and in the chamber of deputies was maintained by requiring a fixed ratio of six Christians to every five Muslims. The existence of these apparently satisfactory arrangements encouraged the view of Lebanon as a byword for order, stability and tolerance in the 1940s and 1950s.

THE TRADITIONAL STRUCTURES OF LEBANESE POLITICS

One important effect of the way in which the Lebanese political system was organised was that political activity took place along vertical rather than horizontal lines, that is, within confessional boundaries rather than within social classes. It also promoted an acute sense of an individual's own confessional affiliation, and also of the confessional affiliation of anyone with whom he or she might come into contact. This sense of sectarian identification was, understandably, particularly strong at times of political crisis, when the state authority tended to break down.

In consequence, when ideological parties did begin to emerge, the constraints of the Lebanese system were such that they often found it difficult to transcend their sectarian affiliations, and although some did manage to recruit across confessional boundaries most continued to be identified to some extent with a particular sect. Thus the Communist Party when it began to take shape was basically Greek Orthodox and Shi'i; the Nasserists/Arab nationalists were Sunni Muslims almost to a man; the Syrian Social National Party – which advocated Greater Syrian nationalism or national socialism – was largely Greek Orthodox; the Progressive Socialist Party consisted mainly of Druzes, members of the sect of its founder, Kamal Jumblatt; and the Kataib, or Phalanges libanaises were Maronite populists gathered around their founder, Pierre Jumayyil, the father of two presidents of Lebanon.

What emerged as the dominant form in political and public life was a network of horizontal alliances between the leaders of the various communities which gave them the wherewithal to distribute patronage downwards to their clients, who could be co-religionists, political allies or dependents, or all three. This arrangement inevitably perpetuated the divisions between the communities – except at the top, where the power-sharing and most of the power-broking actually took place. An important ingredient, and consequence, was an essentially fragile state structure, in which the state provided a minimum of essential services and promoted a climate of extreme laissez-faire: low taxes; flexible banking regulations; minimal customs and excise dues; and basic social services.

The patronage system, through which these arrangements were mediated, was managed at the lower level by strong-arm men or *qabadays*, petty gangsters and quarter bosses who were the essential link between patrons and clients. Again, the range and nature of their activities implied bypassing whatever rudimentary machinery the state itself possessed. It all worked after a fashion, with a slight hiccup in the civil war of 1958, until the major civil war of 1975–76. The leading notables of the various communities were linked with one another in a complex system of bargaining, whose main objective was to ensure their dominance within their communities, and, as a class, within the system as a whole. They were able to maintain their position because of their monopoly of patronage in the fields of political favours, the direction of contracts, employment, education and so forth and also by means of the ingrained shared ideology which, in addition to stressing the primacy of the sectarian ties already mentioned, also emphasised those of family, clan, and locality.

In a certain sense, the Christian, and in particular the Maronite, political leader had an easier task than his Muslim counterpart in the 1950s, when the Arab world was experiencing major political upheaval and change. The system, with its built in implications of Maronite/Christian superiority, was relatively easy to maintain among a Maronite clientele, which, as a group, had no alternative political arena or external groupings or forces around which its members might rally. Of course, it would be simplistic to suggest that the Maronite community itself was or indeed has always remained entirely monolithic. For example, the Maronites in the north and those in the centre shared in the economic, and to a lesser extent political, rivalry between Tripoli and Beirut, those in the north being more prepared to co-operate with their Sunni fellow townsmen and with Syria than the Beirutis. However, while the system also suited most of the Sunni political leadership, its beneficial effects were less apparent to the rank and file. A similar process was to take place among the Shi'is, when another external factor, the Iranian Revolution, galvanised them into new forms of political mobilisation and awareness.

LEBANESE POLITICS BEFORE THE CIVIL WAR OF 1975

But this is to anticipate. The first signs of a challenge to the status quo came in the 1950s, with Nasser's successful seizure of power in Egypt. This coincided with the beginnings of the oil boom in the Arabian Peninsula, whose general effect was to increase the self-confidence and economic power of the Sunni bourgeoisie, whose links with the Arab hinterland had always remained strong. Here we can see the tensions beginning within the Sunni community. The leaders were consolidating their wealth from their position of advantage within the Lebanese economy, while many of the rank and file were eagerly following Nasser's progress and hoping that a closer integration of Lebanon with the rest of the Arab world, or at least its closer identification with the 'revolutionary' populist aspirations of much of the rest of the Arab world, might result.

Eventually – and the similarities with what was to happen to the Shi'is later is almost uncanny – the greater radicalism of ordinary Sunnis forced at least outward signs of a change of attitude onto the political leadership. Many Sunnis increasingly identified themselves with Arabism and Nasser. There were mass demonstrations against the Baghdad Pact, in support of the nationalisation of the Suez Canal, and against the tripartite aggression against Egypt in 1956. When President Camille Chamoun refused to break off diplomatic relations with Britain and France in November 1956, the two serving Sunni cabinet members were virtually forced to resign. The only way for such leaders to retain credibility among their co-religionists and stay in power was to compete for identification with Nasser.

Such splits, intensified after the creation of the United Arab Republic of Egypt and Syria in February 1958 and reflecting larger divisions between 'progressive' and 'conservative' elements in society, led to a brief civil war in June–July 1958. This was eventually brought to an end by the landing of US troops, and at the end of July the army commander, General Shihab, was elected president of the Republic. The period that followed was the first in recent Lebanese history in which the state became a major actor. Between 1958 and 1970, Shihab and his close associate and successor Charles Hilu (Lebanese presidents have six-year terms of office) were determined to introduce a more reformist style of government, and were particularly keen both to develop the more outlying regions of the country and to curb the powers of the political bosses of all sects, whose 'Byzantine and internecine factionalism', as one commentator has called it, had been an important factor in the clashes of 1958. Shihab also came to a tacit understanding with President Nasser, a sort of second national pact, under which he undertook to follow a generally pro-Egyptian foreign policy while being permitted to contain the Nasserist movement within Lebanon – a task which was considerably eased after the collapse of the United Arab Republic in 1961.

Shihab used the intelligence service he had inherited, the notorious *deuxième bureau*, both to curb the Nasserist movement and to restrict the activities of the political bosses. This caused the leaders themselves to co-operate more fully with each other to try to ward off the increasingly unwelcome encroachments of the state. Almost all Shihab's predecessors as president had been members of the class of political leadership for whom the original spoils system had been designed, so that the office of president had been seen as one of the principal channels through which patronage was distributed. Shihab himself, although a senior member of the Maronite aristocracy, refused to play by what the others had come to consider the rules.

It is possible that Shihabism, as it became known, might have become the norm of Lebanese politics. However, since the basis of both the constitution and the system of patronage were confessional, the structure implied, and of necessity reinforced, confessional solidarity on the part of the participants at all levels while concealing its fundamentally exploitative nature. Partly because of outside events, and partly because of the growth of more populist forms of politics, the system began to totter once more. By the mid-1970s, a combination of galloping inflation, economic dislocation, political frustration, the exigencies of the Arab-Israeli situation and the problems arising from the presence of large numbers of armed Palestinians within the country (most of whom had arrived after the defeat of the Palestine Liberation Organisation, PLO, in Jordan in 1970-71) fused together to deal the system an almost mortal blow.

THE ROOTS OF THE ECONOMIC AND POLITICAL CRISIS

Between the early 1950s and the late 1960s the Lebanese economy was transformed from being based substantially on agriculture to being based mostly on services. In 1970 there were 80 banks in Lebanon, only 15 of which were controlled by Lebanese majority interests. Industrial firms and agro-business were all in the hands of a handful of rich families (about 17 Christian and eight Muslim). While 50 per cent of the economically active population were employed on the land in 1959, only 18.9 per cent were still so engaged in 1970. In addition, the oil price rises of the 1970s encouraged continuously accelerating inflation throughout the region, particularly in the non-producing countries. In consequence, many small holders on Mount Lebanon were forced to sell up because of rising costs and leave the land or become wage labourers – these were to swell the ranks of Pierre Jumayyil's Kataib or Maronite populist movement. Elsewhere, the sharecroppers on the periphery, mostly Sunnis and Shi'is, were driven off the land because of increasing mechanisation. By 1974, half the families of Lebanon lived in greater Beirut.

The effects on the labour market can easily be imagined. An enormous sub-proletariat came into existence, participating occasionally at the lower end of the service sector. Lebanon was to become the battle ground for so many of the other conflicting forces in the Arab world, partly, but by no means entirely because of the presence of some 300,000 Palestinians, (about 12 per cent of the population) on Lebanese territory. There were large numbers of under- and unemployed young men, both Palestinians and Lebanese, eager to be recruited into the various militias, which gave them a more or less regular salary as well as the status derived from the ability to sport a sub-machine gun. Contributions from external sources provided enough money in and around the system to finance the rival militias until the beginning of the 1990s, a state of affairs that the Lebanese state largely lacked the wherewithal to resist.

The Palestinians and the more politically conscious Lebanese had a radicalising effect upon each other, and the attitudes of individual Lebanese or groups of Lebanese towards the Palestinians became effectively the touchstone for a whole set of political ideas and attitudes. Thus there arose the pressing question of the norms which should govern the Palestinians' relations to the Lebanese authorities – especially the Lebanese armed forces. Which was more important: that the Palestinians should not violate Lebanese sovereignty, or that they should be able to pursue the struggle against Zionism and Imperialism from Lebanese soil? Naturally, this raised a variety of acute questions about the nature of the Lebanese state and the legitimacy of its activities.

In the late 1960s and early 1970s, therefore, many of the more radical Palestinians began to join forces, at first ideologically and later militarily, with the more left-leaning Lebanese, pressing for the creation of a secular democratic state which would abolish the confessional political system and all that this stood for. Various radical and leftist groupings had joined together to form the Lebanese National Movement (LNM), a coalition eventually comprising some 18 groups, organised by the Druze Kamal Jumblatt; apart from the Druzes, the LNM was composed primarily, though not exclusively, of Sunni and Shi'i Muslims who had become disillusioned with the inadequacy of their own traditional leaderships. Palestinian raids on Israel were attracting severe reprisals from Israel, and the different resentments felt by the various segments of Lebanese society found expression in clashes between the Lebanese Army and the Palestinian militias which came to a head in November 1969.

Egyptian mediation calmed things for a while, but the various economic and political pressures within and outside the country built up throughout the early 1970s. By the beginning of 1975 various Maronite organisations, most prominently Jumayyil's populist Kataib, had become dissatisfied with what they regarded as the state's incapacity to control or contain the guerrillas (or the forces of the left), and had built up militias of their own to a point where they felt ready to take them on. The crisis came on 13 April 1975, after an incident at a church in Ayn Rummana, where one of Jumayyil's bodyguards was killed by a passing gunman. The Kataib fired back and the civil war began.

THE LEBANESE CIVIL WAR

Over the next few months there were various attempts to patch up a cease-fire, but by the autumn of 1975 the fighting had become more intense. Dialogue proved impossible, as the PLO and the LNM insisted on political and constitutional reform, while the Kataib insisted that the army (which was under Maronite control and influence) should first restore order – in other words, should disarm the PLO and the LNM. By the beginning of 1976 the Kataib, together with other Maronite militias, attacked Palestinian refugee camps in East Beirut, provoking severe retaliation from LNM and PLO forces. At the same time, the increasing intensity of the crisis provoked alarm in Syria, and, later, in Israel, with the latter emerging in time as the principal arbiter of Lebanon's future.

SYRIA AND ISRAEL IN LEBANON

For reasons connected both with its own survival and what it forecast might be the Israeli response, the Syrian government could neither afford to let the PLO and LNM gain an outright victory nor (at least at this stage) let the Maronites set up their own mini-state in Lebanon. Thus Syrian forces, together with contingents of pro-Syrian Palestinians, were despatched to Lebanon early in June. This turned the tide in the Maronites' favour, and enabled them to expel the remaining Palestinian and Shi'i population from East Beirut after the siege of the Palestinian camp at Tall Za'tar. The first stage of the civil war was brought to an end after the Riyadh summit in October 1976 when an Arab Deterrent Force was created, consisting primarily of Syrian forces already in Lebanon. The casualties between April 1975 and October 1976 were estimated at 30,000 killed, while at least a third of the population of some 3.25 million had been forced to leave their homes, either to move to less affected parts of the country or to go abroad. The infrastructure was in ruins.

The main gainers were the Israelis, who supported and encouraged their Maronite allies' desire for partition. The crisis also weakened the PLO, allowed Israel to enter Lebanese territory, and diverted Syria's attention from Israel. A few weeks after the Syrian incursion Israel made it clear that it would prevent any resumption of PLO activity in south Lebanon, and began its open border policy for the inhabitants of the frontier area in association with Major Haddad of the Lebanese Army. The official Lebanese administration was not readmitted to this area after the war ended.

By this time the conflict had created a de facto partitioning of the country. This was most marked in the Maronite-controlled areas in east Beirut and Mount Lebanon, where the Lebanese Front, a rather fractious alliance of Maronite groups, had set up what amounted to a parallel administration, with its United Forces under the command of Bashir Jumayyil, son of the Kataib leader Pierre Jumayyil. However, the end of the first stage of the fighting brought about important changes in attitudes on all sides. Firstly, many Shi'is, who were numerically important in the LNM, were becoming increasingly disillusioned with the activities of the PLO in south Lebanon, where they bore the brunt of Israeli retaliation against the PLO's activities. Some 300,000 Shi'is had become refugees (mostly in the suburbs of Beirut) by the autumn of 1977. Secondly, the presence of the Syrian 'Arab Deterrent Force' came to prove an increasing irritant to both Muslims and Maronites. Thirdly, the LNM was thrown into considerable disarray with the assassination of its charismatic leader, Kamal Jumblatt, in March 1977. Finally, there was a perceptible hardening of sectarianism, visible both within the LNM itself and with the return to prominence of some of the old sectarian leaders, and also, though these were still early days, with the beginnings of the claim of the Shi'i organisation Amal (founded in 1975) to be the sole legitimate focus and representative of Shi'i aspirations, a claim which was to gain added momentum with the Iranian Revolution of 1979–80.

THE ISRAELI INVASIONS OF 1978 AND 1982

An uneasy state of tension and expectation persisted throughout 1977. The tension reflected obvious uncertainties about the likely activities of Israel and Syria, but a certain amount of optimism had been engendered in some quarters by President Carter's apparent willingness at least to recognise that the PLO and the Palestinians had a legitimate interest in any settlement of the Arab-Israeli conflict. There were signs that this cautious American goodwill was beginning to rub off on the more extreme Palestinian groups, and that the PLO was prepared to enter negotiations. On 1 October 1977 the USA and the Soviet Union jointly declared their readiness to call a peace conference at Geneva.

The high hopes invested in this encouraging development were soon to be dashed. On 9 November President Sadat of Egypt, partly in response to the deepening economic crisis at home which he considered could only be solved by total commitment to the West, announced his intention to travel to Jerusalem to initiate direct peace negotiations with Israel. For the Lebanese and the PLO, this had three principal effects. In the first place, Sadat's action effectively removed the only major opposition to Israel from the scene, and thus tipped the military balance in Israel's favour. Secondly, the Palestinians were excluded from any decisions about their future, which was to be decided by Egypt and Israel – and possibly Jordan. Thirdly, Israel was now free to take whatever action it liked in Lebanon, since the threat of Syrian retaliation did not constitute a serious deterrent. Sadat himself remarked in the course of an interview in November 1977 that 'blood will flow in Lebanon and Syria'.

Israel was not slow to capitalise on the new situation, invading south Lebanon (as far north as the Litani river) on 14 March 1978, nominally in response to a brutal PLO attack on a bus in Israel in which 34 Israelis were killed and 78 injured. As a result of the invasion 2,000 Lebanese and Palestinians were killed, and 250,000 new refugees created. Israel was now in occupation of about one-tenth of all Lebanese territory. A United Nations (UN) force, UNIFIL, was given an international mandate to police the area, and various UN resolutions prevailed on the Israelis to withdraw. They did so, but on 12 June 1978 handed over a strategic part of the area to their surrogate, Major Haddad and his South Lebanese Army, which Israel financed and equipped, thus creating a 'South Lebanon security belt' as a permanent buffer zone under their control.

As a result Lebanese politics became polarised once more. On the one hand, there were those (generally the LNM, the PLO, pro-Syrian groups and some older Sunni politicians including Rashid Karami), who saw the main priority as fighting Israel's territorial aims in Lebanon. On the other, there were those who considered that Israel's invasion was entirely due to sins of commission on the part of the PLO, the obvious corollary being that Israeli withdrawal – and thus eventually Syrian withdrawal – required prior PLO withdrawal. This was the view of the Maronite right, and also of some 'traditional' Shi'i leaders who were beginning to regain their former constituency among the southern

Lebanese. It was eventually to bring about a split in Maronite ranks, between those who were steadfastly anti-Syrian – mostly from south and central Lebanon – and those who generally favoured closer relations with Syria – mostly from the Maronite enclave in the north, around Tripoli and its hinterland. The most notable representatives of the latter tendency were ex-President (1970–76) Sulayman Franjiyya and his supporters, and the breach was formalised by the particularly brutal assassination by Kataib militiamen under Bashir Jumayyil and Samir Ja'ja' (Geagea) of Franjiyya's son, Tony, and other members of his family, in June 1978.

Over the next four years the conflict continued to rage on a variety of levels. Israel continued to bombard south Lebanon, and, partly as a result, relations between the Shi'is and the PLO steadily deteriorated. Having silenced his Maronite rivals in the north, Bashir Jumayyil turned on the militia of his father's rival Camille Chamoun, in Beirut in July 1980, and having subjugated them emerged as the de facto ruler of the Maronite enclave centred on East Beirut. All the Maronite militias, now styled the Lebanese Forces (LF), were under his command. Early in 1981 Bashir Jumayyil attempted to expel the Syrians from eastern Lebanon, besieging Zahlé (on one of the main roads to Damascus) for two months. Syria made it unmistakably clear that any attempt on Jumayyil's part to extend his authority beyond the 'traditional Maronite enclave' would be challenged. SAM missiles were deployed in the Bekaa, and there was heavy fighting between Jumayyil's forces and the Syrian army in Beirut, evidently co-ordinated with the shelling of Tyre by Haddad and the Israeli-backed South Lebanese Army.

In July 1981, after a heavy PLO bombardment of northern Israel, an indirect cease-fire was negotiated between Israel and the PLO, which held until the Israeli invasion of Beirut in June 1982. The pretext for this second and far more massive Israeli invasion was the attempted assassination of the Israeli ambassador to London, Shlomo Argov, by Iraqi agents (who had no direct connection with the PLO). In conformity with the July 1981 cease-fire, the PLO itself had not attacked across the Lebanese-Israeli border for over a year. The objectives of this invasion were to set up a pro-Israeli regime (under the Kataib) in Lebanon, to crush the PLO in Lebanon once and for all, and by this means to end Palestinian resistance to the settlement, and perhaps eventually to the annexation, by Israel, of the Occupied West Bank and Gaza.

The Israelis were welcomed by the Maronites, and by some of the Shi'i population of the south. Altogether some 20,000 people, the great majority non-combatant, were killed in the fighting. The Israelis apparently thought they would take West Beirut within a week, but, quite remarkably, given the small number of the city's defenders (perhaps some 15,000 altogether), the relentlessness of the Israeli bombardment and the apparent paralysis of all the Arab states, it took more than three months. Even then, the fact that the PLO fighters were evacuated under safe conduct meant that the Israeli triumph was somewhat less than total.

The evacuation took place at the end of August, with various marine detachments from the USA and the then EC countries to supervise it, and, in theory, to protect the remaining Palestinian civilian population. The massacres of Sabra and Shatila are a terrible testimonial to the lack of seriousness with which this part of the assignment was taken. On 23 August, Bashir Jumayyil had been elected president of Lebanon; 22 days later, the day after the departure of the marines, he was assassinated, either by the Syrians or by the Israelis, concerned that he might not prove quite as docile in office as they had expected. The Israeli Defence Forces promptly surrounded Sabra and Chatila camps, and its commanders effectively allowed the Maronite leaders of the Lebanese Forces, to search out and destroy the 'terrorists' supposedly still in the camps who were held to be responsible for Jumayyil's murder. Between 1,000 and 1,500 civilians were killed in the course of this operation.

DE FACTO PARTITION 1982–90

A week after his brother Bashir's assassination Amin Jumayyil was elected to the presidency. He found it impossible to set up a cabinet of politicians and proceeded to rule by decree. He also appointed Kataib militia commanders to senior posts in the Lebanese army, which was now being supplied with arms and advisers by the USA on the grounds that this was a necessary precondition for national reconstruction. As the army had become little more than an auxiliary of the Maronite militias, 'national reconstruction' was most unlikely to result. Jumayyil only controlled West Beirut, about one per cent of the country's land area, while the Lebanese Forces controlled a further ten per cent, including East Beirut and the coast to the north. His government now attempted to do what the Israelis had been unable to do – to expel all remaining Palestinians from Lebanon. European doctors working in Palestinian hospitals were harassed and some were eventually deported. Palestinians in south Beirut and in Sidon were evicted from the area, and many were killed on their way to and from their homes in the refugee camps in south Lebanon.

At the same time, the Israelis began to convert south Lebanon into a market for Israeli products, dumping citrus and other fruit, at prices with which local producers could not compete, while raising the costs of chemical fertilisers and other essentials landed at Sidon. Israeli sales soon reached $5 million a month, and, according to an International Monetary Fund study in 1985, much of the agricultural land of the south was out of production in 1984 as a result of the deliberate destruction of orchards and meadows. Early in 1984, Israel closed the sole direct crossing point between north and south Lebanon on the Awwali Bridge, diverting traffic through the Shuf mountains and thus virtually cutting the two parts of the country off from each other. By the middle 1980s, according to a Lebanese economist, Lebanon was beginning to lack 'all the elements essential for economic activity'. The Lebanese pound had been devalued by 40 per cent (although far worse was to come); the public debt had risen to a point at which debt service outstripped national income; industry was working at about a quarter of capacity; there was 60 per cent unemployment; and exports had almost ceased. Nearly a quarter of the population had either lost their homes or moved between 1975 and 1984.

In May 1983 Israel negotiated an agreement with Jumayyil to withdraw from Lebanon on draconian terms, including the creation of a buffer zone extending 30 miles into south Lebanon. Having reached agreement without Syrian involvement, however, the deal was effectively rendered void almost immediately and sparked off another furious round of fighting between the LNM and the Lebanese Forces. This time the LNM had been reconstituted as the National Salvation Front (NSF), a grouping loosely allied with Syria, consisting principally of the Druze leader Walid Jumblatt (whose militia formed the nucleus of the fighting forces), the Sunni politician Rashid Karami, and (until his defection in 1984) ex-President Sulayman Franjiyya. In addition the Amal leader, Nabih Berri, who repeatedly declared that his movement had no sectarian goals, had an informal alliance with Jumblatt, albeit outside the NSF. At this stage the Shi'is (organised along both 'secular' and 'religious' lines, *see* below) had re-emerged as a vital element on the political scene, much feared by the Maronites who realised the implications of their numerical supremacy within the population.

As Israel withdrew from the Shuf and the LF attempted to take its place, Jumblatt's Druze forces, with Syrian assistance, fought effectively against the LF. At the same time, Amal initiated a campaign of resistance against the Israelis in south Lebanon, where, apart from Major Haddad and his successor Antoine Lahd, Israel had found it impossible to maintain credible collaborators. By the end of September 1983 the cease-fire left the Druze forces in control of the Shuf, and brought the Druzes' Syrian allies back into negotiations. At the beginning of 1984 Amin Jumayyil had been obliged to rescind the agreement of May 1983 with Israel, and Syrian forces remained in the Bekaa, demonstrating clearly that no settlement could be imposed on Lebanon without Syrian consent. US involvement in Lebanese affairs was dealt a severe blow in October 1983. A few days after the apparently gratuitous Israeli disruption of the Shi'i *ashura* procession in Nabatiya, some 240 US marines were killed when a commando drove a truck full of explosives into their barracks. By 1984, Amal was in virtual control of West Beirut.

In spite of US attempts to paint the Syrians as Soviet puppets, and thus legitimise their own support of Israel and its Lebanese allies, the next few years saw a gradual strengthening of anti-Israeli forces in Lebanon, to the extent that by the summer of 1985 Israel was forced to withdraw from the south. However, the PLO, some of whose fighters were slowly infiltrating back into Lebanon, also suffered great losses during this period especially after Abu Musa's 'defection' to Damascus, Arafat's break with Asad in June 1983 (at a time when Asad feared that Arafat and King Husayn were about to enter Palestin-ian/Jordanian negotiations with Israel under the aegis of the 1982 Reagan Plan), and the intra-Palestinian fighting around Tripoli in the autumn of 1983.

At the end of 1985 some sort of settlement seemed in the offing, partly because of the apparent end of the PLO's role as a serious contender for power (or as a key ally of the various contenders for power) in Lebanon. The leader of the LF, Elie Hubayqa had negotiated this agreement, the Damascus Accord with Berri and Jumblatt. If implemented, it would have abolished the confessional system over a threeyear period, given equal Muslim and Christian representation in parliament, and enhanced the powers of the prime minister at the expense of the president, all within the framework of fairly close involvement with Syria. However, Amin Jumayyil and another powerful militia leader, Samir Ja'ja' (who had previously split the LF off from the Kataib), managed to unite their forces against Hubayqa and expel his forces from Beirut in January 1986, thus wrecking the arrangement.

A further dimension to the Lebanese conflict in the early and middle 1980s was the growing influence of Islamic fundamentalist groups. Their rise in the 1970s had been boosted by the Iranian Revolution, as well as by the general moral and practical failings of declaredly secular progressive political movements in Lebanon and elsewhere in the Arab world. The fundamentalist campaign in Syria, and the terrible events of Hama in February 1982 (*see* Chapter 14, Syria), meant that many members of the (Sunni) Muslim Brotherhood fled from Syria to Tripoli. Others gathered in Sidon, while among the Shi'is an 'Islamic Amal' was founded in Baalbak, and a Hizbullah movement was established in 1982 in Beirut and the Bekaa (although a similar organisation had been founded in 1978). In spite of her support of Iran in the war with Iraq, the existence of more extreme (and thus not easily controllable) Shi'i groups was anathema to Syria, which assisted Amal but not Hizbullah. Such groups were fiercely opposed to political movements on the left, as was shown by the massacres of communists by Sunni fundamentalists in Tripoli in 1983.

The rise of fundamentalism was another reason for the 'return of sectarianism' in the mid-1980s, but was also presented, in another context, by the USA, Israel and their Lebanese Christian allies as irrational 'Islamic terrorism' against which virtually unlimited force could be directed. Hizbullah became the principal channel through which the Islamic Republic of Iran attempted to influence events in Lebanon, not always to Syria's liking.

The gradual increase in the military power of Amal brought great tensions throughout 1985–87, with fierce fighting between Shi'i and Druze militias representing a struggle for territorial conquest and supremacy rather than a clash of ideologies. As always, Syria was concerned to prevent any individual party to the conflict reaching a position where it could not be checked by a combination of Syrian and other forces ranged against it. In this case the imbalance in the numbers of the Shi'i and Druze 'constituencies' (respectively perhaps 35 per cent and seven per cent of the population) made it likely that Amal's forces would ultimately prevail. Thus the Syrian army was despatched to occupy West Beirut in March 1987 to put an end to the fighting between Syria's main allies. This period was also one of fierce fighting between Shi'is and the reconstituted Palestinian movements, partly with Syrian encouragement, as well as between pro- and anti-Syrian factions in the Maronite militias, all indications of the folly of trying to identify the various parties in this apparently endless conflict according to neat ideological or sectarian categories.

Nevertheless, although almost mortally wounded, the Lebanese state managed to survive, and the question of the succession to the presidency when Jumayyil's term of office would expire in September 1988 was vigorously discussed, indicating that most parties and factions in Lebanon were fundamentally opposed to partition and wanted the existing system to continue. The names of several prominent personalities, including Dany Chamoun, Ja'ja', the army commander Michel Awn, and even the Maronite patriarch, as well as the incumbent, Amin Jumayyil, were ventilated as possible candidates. Jumayyil was constitutionally excluded from standing again, but he clearly had ambitions in that direction.

Both the largest communities continued to be torn by internal dissent. Jumayyil was at loggerheads with the LF commander Ja'ja' and Amal was fighting both Hizbullah and the PLO. The cabinet did not meet at all in the course of 1987, but the Chamber of Deputies, which had been elected in 1972, formally abrogated both the Cairo Accord of 1969 (which formalised the PLO presence in Lebanon) and the May 1983 agreement with Israel. Although the Damascus Accord of December 1985 had proved a dead letter it was clear that some sort of arrangement on these lines (between moderate Druzes, Maronites and Shi'is, with Syrian backing) would be necessary if any permanent settlement were to be reached. Jumayyil himself certainly understood this, and tried, unsuccessfully, to mend his fences with Asad throughout 1987.

A major disadvantage for Jumayyil was the highly circumscribed nature of his authority and his inability to exercise control over events on the ground in Lebanon. Attempted and successful assassinations, killings of prominent personalities and kidnappings had become nightmarishly routine. The list of murders and attempted murders in 1987 encompassed individuals from all sides of the political spectrum, including the Prime Minister, Rashid Karami, closely identified with Damascus, on 1 June. By July 1987, some 130,000 people had been killed in Lebanon since April 1975, and 14,000 kidnapped, of whom 10,000 were subsequently murdered. On 20 January the Archbishop of Canterbury's envoy, Terry Waite, was abducted by Hizbullah. Some 25 other Europeans were being held by various militia groups at the same time, including the highly respected French academic Michel Seurat, later murdered by his captors.

CHAOS AND STEPS TOWARDS RECOVERY, 1988–95
The presidential elections of 1988 provoked a new political crisis, as the Lebanese parliament (which elects the President) failed to elect a

successor to Jumayyil. Just before his presidential mandate expired, Jumayyil himself nominated the commander of the Lebanese army, General Awn, as Prime Minister, in contravention of the National Pact, under which this office always goes to a Sunni. The incumbent Sunni Prime Minister, Salim al-Huss, supported by Syria, refused to give up his post. This development, which came shortly after the end of the Iran/Iraq war, signified the reappearance of Iraq as a major actor in Lebanese politics. Iraq wanted to undermine its bitter enemy Syria through Lebanon, and had been supplying Awn with weapons for this purpose since the summer of 1988. For reasons connected with his own hostility to Syria (and his increasingly close relations with Iraq), Yasser Arafat also gave his tacit support to Awn. Awn also gained tentative recognition from France and the USA because of his hostility to Syria, then seen as the West and Israel's principal foe in the region.

Awn had gained a certain popularity as commander in the course of 1988 and 1989 for his apparent ability to control the Maronite militias, notably the LF under Samir Ja'ja', whom he managed to subdue early in 1989. This meant that the LF's control of (and thus income from) the port of Juniya and part of the port of Beirut was assumed by 'the state', in so far as Awn could be said to represent it. Such activities brought a swift response from Syria, and the fighting in and around Beirut between Awn and his supporters, and the Syrians and theirs, reached new levels of intensity, to the extent that all those inhabitants of Beirut who could leave the city tried to do so. On 30 June 1989 the UN Disaster Relief Organisation announced that in the preceding 16 weeks in Beirut, 438 people had been killed, 2,300 wounded, and 500,000 had left the city. The struggle continued until the end of September 1989, when Awn was obliged to give up, at least for the time being, as his Iraqi suppliers had been persuaded to stop delivering arms to him.

The lull brought new efforts to find a solution on the part of the Arab League, Syria and Saudi Arabia. The surviving members of the (1972) Lebanese parliament were flown to Taif in Saudi Arabia, where a fairly modest political agreement (the Taif Accord) was hammered out in the course of October. In brief, the powers of the President of the Republic were to be reduced and those of the Prime Minister enhanced. Muslims and Christians were to have parity (54 seats each) in a new parliament, replacing the former 6:5 ratio in favour of the Christians. Syrian troops would be withdrawn two years after the adoption of 'constitutional reforms'.

Reaction in Lebanon itself was not particularly favourable. Jumblatt, Berri, Hizbullah and the Iranians disapproved, largely because the Accord seemed too generous to the Maronites, and, as far as the Shi'is were concerned, did not provide them with sufficient additional representation, although Syria's commitment to the Accord meant that Amal gradually came to accept it. On 4 November 1989 parliament met again in Beirut and elected the Maronite deputy, René Mu'awwad, President. Eighteen days later he was assassinated, and succeeded by Ilyas Harawi, who declared himself in favour of 'good and solid relations with Syria'.

For his part Awn declared himself president on 7 November. Throughout late November and early December there were demonstrations in his favour, largely because of his continuing anti-Syrian stance. He continued to hold out against the Taif Accord in his virtually separate state in East Beirut well into 1990, and his forces (units of the Lebanese Army) were involved in bitter fighting with the Lebanese Forces under Ja'ja', who declared himself ready to participate in any government formed by Harawi. However, as always, Syria was also anxious to ensure that Ja'ja' and the LF were not in a position to defeat Awn outright, since this would put the latter in too powerful a position in Lebanon. Syria was anxious that the two factions should exhaust themselves rather than that the one should triumph over the other. The economic effect of this was that the dollar exchange rate fell from some 45 Lebanese pounds (LL) in late 1985 to LL650 in May 1990, and to LL1040 in October 1990.

It is impossible to estimate how long Awn could have held out had Iraq not invaded Kuwait and thus ceased to be able to supply him. Syrian ground attacks and aerial bombardment of his headquarters eventually forced him to take refuge in the French Embassy on 13 October. In the course of the next few weeks, the Druze, Hizbullah and Amal militias gradually withdrew from Beirut. On 24–25 October the capital was formally reunited and on 19 December a cabinet uniting most shades of political opinion was formed. Syrian orchestration of these arrangements could not have been carried out without US approval, given in a number of high level visits to Damascus and underlined by a cordial meeting between Hafiz al-Asad and George Bush at Geneva on 22 November. While certainly consolidating Syrian influence within Lebanon, these new measures also produced a state of affairs closely approximating to peace in most parts of the country. The Lebanese Army, now about 30,000 strong, and firmly under the control of a relatively representative government, substantially outnumbered the various militias, whose total membership was about 15,000.

Coupled with the resolution of the hostage crisis at the end of 1991, these developments combined to restore a degree of stability to the Lebanese polity. Lebanon also became an active participant in the Middle East peace process which started in October 1991. On the other hand Israel continued to bomb south Lebanon in response to rocket attacks by Hizbullah and Fatah throughout 1992. The economy remained very weak, the Lebanese pound dropping to 2,100 to the dollar in May 1992. After a series of cabinet crises the Sunni multi-millionaire Rafiq Hariri was appointed Prime Minister in October 1992, at the head of a cabinet approved by the Syrian president Hafiz al-Asad; the Shi'i leader Nabih Berri had been elected speaker of the chamber of deputies a few days earlier. It was hoped that Hariri, with his strong ties to Saudi Arabia as well as to Syria, might be particularly well qualified to launch Lebanon along the road to reconstruction. The task was formidable. An estimate made in 1994 showed that between 1975 and 1990, out of a total population of about 3.5 million, some 150,000 to 200,000 had been killed, 300,000 had been wounded and nearly 900,000 had emigrated.

Although a fair amount of reconstruction and reconciliation were indeed hallmarks of the early 1990s, this was achieved largely at the expense of an almost total sacrifice of the country's independence to its political masters in Damascus. For the Maronites in particular this was difficult to stomach. Hizbullah, now somewhat more closely influenced by Syria, remained almost entirely outside the remit of the Lebanese government (although by 1992 it had eight members or sympathisers in the Lebanese parliament), and its activities in the south continued to attract heavy reprisals from Israel. At the end of July 1993, for example, some 130 Lebanese were killed, 500 wounded and 300,000 forced from their homes in the south as the result of a week of Israeli attacks. With all its limitations, however, Hizbullah's fire power remained an important bargaining counter for Syria in its negotiations with Israel.

In 1994 Hariri's government, self-evidently with Syrian backing, attempted to put an official end to the lawlessness of the previous two decades by trying some of those allegedly responsible for political crimes and assassinations. Samir Ja'ja', who had been accused of involvement in the bombing of a church in Juniya in February 1994, was also tried for the assassination of Dany Chamoun in 1990; in June 1995 he was found guilty and sentenced to death, but subsequently given life imprisonment. Critics of the government pointed out that Elie Hubayqa, another former militia leader whose hands were probably at least as bloodstained as Ja'ja's, had escaped prosecution simply because he held a cabinet portfolio. In spite of these and other incidents, however, a peace of sorts had been in place since 1990, and developments elsewhere in the region have combined to make further outbreaks of internecine violence unlikely. At the time of writing (October 1995), however, Beirut is still looking over its shoulder waiting for Tel Aviv and Damascus to make the final crucial moves towards a 'permanent' resolution of the Middle East conflict.

Peter Sluglett and Marion Farouk-Sluglett

9
LIBYA

WHEN LIBYA was granted independence by the United Nations in 1951, it faced a bleak future. With Libya essentially a desert state, many of its problems were geographical. Only slightly more than one per cent of its land area is arable, while only a further four per cent can be used for pastoralism. The rest forms part of the Sahara desert, stretching west to east across the country, except for the Gefara Plain and the Jabal al-Akhdar regions, and actually reaching the Mediterranean in Sirtica, at the base of the Gulf of Sirte.

Water was the major problem facing the new state, however. Rainfall rarely reaches eight inches per annum and then only in the northern coastal areas of the Gefara Plain and the Jabal al-Akhdar. Limited underground water reserves were really all that were available for drinking and for agriculture. Not surprisingly, therefore, the new country was one of the poorest states in Africa and its 1.1 million-strong population seemed to have little prospect of escaping its chronic poverty.

The situation had been worsened, however, by what had happened to Libya during the first half of the 20th century. Between 1911 and 1927, the country had been ravaged by war, as Italy tried to impose colonial rule. Italy had then created a settler colony in Libya, bringing in 110,000 Italians to add to the 800,000 Libyans who had survived the war.

Despite modest British and French aid when they jointly administered Libya after 1943, Libya's essentially subsistence economy at independence was still trying to recover from the three decades of Italian Fascist colonisation and the damage caused by three years of warfare during the Second World War. Within ten years, however, the economic picture had completely changed, as Libya entered the oil era at the beginning of the 1960s. The political situation was also transformed at the end of the decade, when the Idrisid monarchy, which had ruled the country since independence, was suddenly overthrown by an army coup – the 'Great September Revolution'. Its authors turned out to be junior army officers, powerfully affected by the Arab nationalist ideology of Egypt's president, Gamal Abdel Nasser, and under the leadership of a communications officer, Mu'ammar Qadhafi.

Colonel Qadhafi has since created one of the world's most idiosyncratic political systems and, aided by the country's oil wealth, has also attempted to carve out an international role for Libya in the modern world. Yet even if Libya's economic status has been transformed, its international reputation has been clouded by the Qadhafi regime's notorious involvement in international terrorism – although the media

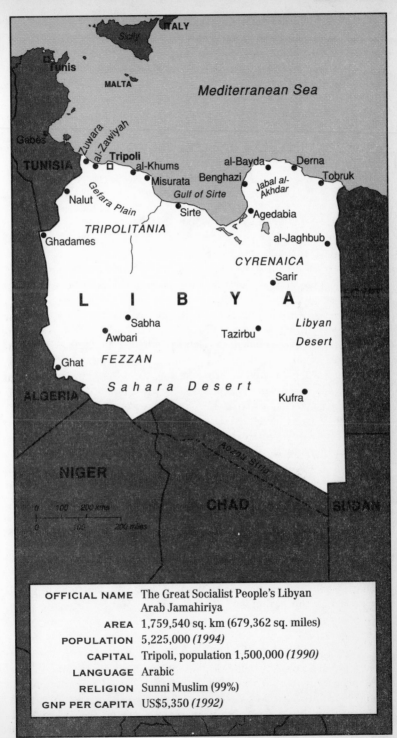

OFFICIAL NAME	The Great Socialist People's Libyan Arab Jamahiriya
AREA	1,759,540 sq. km (679,362 sq. miles)
POPULATION	5,225,000 *(1994)*
CAPITAL	Tripoli, population 1,500,000 *(1990)*
LANGUAGE	Arabic
RELIGION	Sunni Muslim (99%)
GNP PER CAPITA	US$5,350 *(1992)*

image tends to be far more impressive than the reality. The policies and means that the Libyan leader has chosen to achieve these objectives, however, reflect as much Libya's own past as they do the diplomatic and political freedom of manoeuvre bequeathed by oil or the inspiration generated by an ideological imperative.

LIBYA BEFORE THE COLONIAL ERA

The name Libya – first applied to the modern state in 1934 when the Italians created a single administration for their colony of Libya – derives from the name Lebu or Rebu given by the Egyptians of the Old Kingdom in 2700–2200 BC to marauding Berber tribes that penetrated from Cyrenaica into the Nile Delta. Even then, pressure on the scanty resources of a marginal environment forced the population of Libya to migrate. The modern form of the name, however, was first applied to the coastal regions by Greek and Roman settlers in Classical times, when Tripolitania and Cyrenaica formed part, first, of the Carthaginian empire in Tunisia and Tripolitania, together with Greek colonies in the east, and, later, of the Roman Empire.

The reality of political control up to the Italian occupation in 1911, however, highlighted the fact that population settlement concentrated on four separate and separated locations. These were the Jabal al-Akhdar region of Cyrenaica; the Gefara Plain of Tripolitania; the oasis complexes of the Fezzan; and, to a much lesser extent, the oases of Kufra, al-Jawf, Sarir and Tazirbu. Around these settled regions were nomadic hinterlands that stretched down towards the desert and controlled the trade routes across the Sahara towards the Sahel, Egypt and the Maghrib (*see* Chapter 10, The Maghrib).

The Islamisation of Libya, which began in the late 7th century, initially touched only the Christianised and Judaised coastal Berber populations. Thereafter, the country tended to be polarised politically, with Cyrenaica falling under the control of Islamic dynasties based in Egypt and Tripolitania being part of Ifriqiyya, the Islamic political entity created in modern Tunisia. The Sahara desert fell under the control – direct or indirect – of central African empires, such as the Zaghawa and the Safawa in Kanem. It was only in the 11th century that Islam penetrated into the hinterland and Libya became an essentially Arab-speaking region, as a result of the invasions of the Banu Hilal and the Banu Sulaym – tribal populations from the Nile Delta who had been ordered westward by the Fatimids in Cairo in an attempt to discipline their rebellious governors in Ifriqiyya.

THE OTTOMANS AND THE QARAMANLIS

Libya's independent history really begins with the expansion of Ottoman naval power into the western Mediterranean to counter Hapsburg influence there in the 16th century. In 1551 Tripoli was captured by the Ottomans from the Order of the Knights of St John of Jerusalem who had originally been given the city, along with the island of Malta, in 1530 by Charles V. The Ottomans soon established an effective administration of their new province of Tarablus al-Gharb (Western Tripoli) and, by the 1580s, had extended their control into the Fezzan. Their presence in Cyrenaica, however, was nominal and limited to Benghazi, while the hinterland was intermittently controlled from Egypt. Tripoli became a significant Mediterranean base for the *corso* – the corsairing tradition that pitted Islam and Christendom against each other in a form of naval warfare that masqueraded as legalised piracy.

Ottoman control from Istanbul was rarely more than formal and power increasingly devolved onto the local administration, dominated – as elsewhere in the Ottoman world – by the janissaries. Ottoman Turks also intermarried with the local population, producing a warrior-caste known as the *kulughlils*. In 1711, a popular *kulughlil* leader, Ahmad Qaramanli, seized power and extracted formal recognition as pasha from Istanbul. His successors formed the Qaramanli dynasty, which ruled over the Regency of Tripoli – one of the three Barbary states familiar to European history from the 17th to the 19th centuries because of their role in the *corso* – until 1835, when the Sublime Porte in Istanbul seized power in Tripoli again. During their rule, the Qaramanlis asserted effective control over Cyrenaica for the first time, while extending their power in the Sahara and making the Regency of Tripoli into a leading corsairing state.

THE SECOND OTTOMAN OCCUPATION

The Ottoman reoccupation in 1835 came hard on the heels of France's occupation of Algiers in 1830. It resulted from a rebellion in Tripoli that pitted factions of the Qaramanli family against each other in which each enjoyed the support of France or Britain. Istanbul feared a European colonial takeover as a result and acted to forestall such an event. The Ottomans found themselves in charge of an unruly country, without the proper resources to control it. Nonetheless, tribal rebellions in the Gefara Plain were suppressed, small garrisons were left in the Fezzan oases and a rudimentary administration was set up in the coastal towns.

THE SANUSIYYA

In Cyrenaica, however, the Ottomans came up against a new problem. Two years after they took over the regency, a new Islamic religious order, the Sanusiyya, was founded at Mecca in Saudi Arabia by an Algerian scholar, Muhammad ibn Ali al-Sanusi. The purpose of the order was first, to revive Islamic values in the face of the growing European cultural and technological onslaught and second, to resist European occupation of the Muslim world – particularly in North Africa.

In 1843, the first *zawiya*, or 'lodge' was set up in Cyrenaica, at al-Bayda. The order rapidly gained support amongst the Cyrenaican tribes and in 1859, to avoid conflict with the Ottoman authorities along the coast, established its headquarters at the desert oasis of al-Jaghbub. In 1895, as the order's influence spread into Egypt and Sudan, the headquarters were moved down to Kufra and, in 1902, to Gourou in northern Chad. By then, there were 146 *zawiyas* in Libya (mainly in Cyrenaica), western Egypt, northern Sudan, northern Chad and Saudi Arabia.

The order's success in garnering universal tribal support lay not just in its ideological and religious message but in its unique organisational abilities. *Zawiyas* were set up at the boundaries of tribal territories, at local markets and on the major trade routes. In addition to providing shelter, education and religious guidance, they also provided a neutral arena for the settlement of tribal disputes and, thereby, a focus for administrative authority. Eventually they also became the focus of indigenous resistance to European occupation, particularly in Chad. In short, the order provided an informal but cohesive alternative administration with which the Ottomans, given their own weakness as their empire began to disintegrate elsewhere, had to collaborate.

COLONIALISM AND INDEPENDENCE

By the start of the 20th century, the decline of Ottoman authority made the conversion of Ottoman Libya into a colony only a matter of time. In an agreement between France and Italy in December 1902, the French government made it clear that it was prepared to allow Italy to satisfy its own colonial ambitions in Libya. Paris had come to this decision in order to avoid further difficulties over French and Italian borders in Europe or over Italian claims to Tunisia – where Italians had long formed the majority of the European community.

Italy was a latecomer to the colonial scene, largely because of its own belated development as a modern nation-state. Nonetheless, Italian politicians as far back as Mazzini in 1838 had cast eyes on North Africa as a strategic key to the central Mediterranean and as a means of recovering the classical grandeur of Imperial Rome. More pragmatically, Italy coveted control of trans-Saharan trade and saw in Libya an empty land to absorb its poverty-stricken peasantry in the dispossessed south, the *mezzogiorno*. As a result – and even though trans-Saharan trade was being rapidly undermined by the construction of railways in west and central Africa – a press campaign popularised Italy's claims to Libya. Italian economic penetration into Tripolitania also proceeded apace.

THE ITALO–SANUSI WARS

In 1911 a crisis with Tripoli was engineered by Rome and war erupted. However, the Italian invasion of the coastal towns soon bogged down and, although Ottoman Turkey abandoned the struggle in October 1912 when, through the Treaty of Ouchy, the sultan renounced all territorial claims on Cyrenaica and Tripolitania, the Sanusiyya maintained a vigorous resistance, particularly in Cyrenaica. Ottoman Turkey maintained clandestine support for the Sanusiyya struggle during the First World War, until, as a result of British pressure from Egypt, a truce was arranged in 1917.

The Sanusi leader, Idris al-Sanusi, was recognised as Amir of Cyrenaica. A separate group of Tripolitanian nationalists in Misrata also, attempted to persuade Italy to recognise an independent republic, as did the Berber community of the Jabal Nafusa. In 1922, however, all these initiatives collapsed and the disparate groups attempted instead to rally behind Idris al-Sanusi as the Amir of both Cyrenaica and Tripolitania.

Italian hostility to this development coincided with the creation of a more efficient military command in Libya itself under Count Giuseppe Volpe and the arrival of the Fascists to power in Rome. The second Italo-Sanusi War, which began in 1923, was to prove to be a much more serious affair. The principal theatre of operations was to be Cyrenaica and, although Amir Idris soon fled to Egypt, where he was to stay for 25 years under British protection, the leadership of the struggle devolved onto a Sanusi sheikh, Umar al-Mukhtar, one of the greatest figures of the anti-colonial struggle in the Islamic world. In September 1931 Umar al-Mukhtar was captured and hanged before 20,000 unwilling Arab spectators. The final resistance collapsed a few months later when the methodical and calculated brutality of the local Italian field commander, Rodolfo Graziani, brought the struggle to an end in 1932.

ITALIAN FASCIST COLONIALISM

The following decade of Fascist colonisation of Libya saw a determined attempt to realise the dream of converting Libya into Italy's Quarta Sponda (Fourth Shore). By 1942, there were 110,000 Italians living there, of whom 40,000 were directly involved in agriculture. The creation of a modern infrastructure and the settling of the colonial arrivals had cost Italy 1.8 billion lira, in what appeared to be only the beginning of a constant drain on the finances of metropolitan Italy.

Libyans played little part in these grandiose plans. Instead, they were to become 'economic collaborators' and 'coparticipants' without the benefit of state aid. Instead they continued to survive in considerable poverty, as land was alienated for colonisation, as a modern Italian-dominated economic sector was created and as the economy of Libya overall was integrated into that of Italy. Nonetheless, the Italian colonial experience did, for the first time, create the administrative structures and the infrastructure for a unitary Libyan state.

Italian colonialism also established internationally recognised borders for its African colony. The borders were even rectified, with the Sarra Triangle being ceded from the Anglo-Egyptian Sudan to Libya and the cession of the 500-mile-long and 60-mile-deep Aozou Strip by French Equatorial Africa to Libya being proposed in 1935.

The secession of the Aozou Strip was a French response to Italian irredentist demands for border rectification in Europe and to other demands over the Italian community in Tunisia, as well as being an attempt to prevent formal treaty links developing between Fascist Italy and Nazi Germany. Although the transfer in the Mussolini-Laval Treaty, was ratified by both countries, the instruments of ratification were never exchanged. By 1938, Italy – by then in the Axis (the Pact of Steel) with Nazi Germany – no longer had any interest in what was being offered. Nonetheless, the modified border was internationally accepted for the next two decades, until Libya obtained independence and signed a border treaty with France in 1956, in which, under duress, it tacitly tolerated border revision. The Aozou Strip dispute, together with similar disputes with Algeria, have continued to bedevil Libya's relations with its neighbours ever since.

Italy's colonial presence in Libya was destroyed by the Second World War. British forces occupied Cyrenaica and the Tripolitanian littoral, while Free French forces from Chad occupied the Fezzan in early 1943. Separate British military administrations were set up in Cyrenaica and Tripolitania, while France created an indirect system of administration based on the Sayf al-Nasr clan – the traditional tribal notability of the Ait Sulayman, the dominant tribe in Fezzan. Although the administration was designed to operate on a 'care-and-maintenance' basis, as required by international law, British administrators began to create a Libyan civil service, while France integrated parts of Fezzan into its Algerian colony.

In 1947, Italy renounced its colonies and Libya became the protégé of the newly founded United Nations (UN), although both Britain and France maintained administrative trusteeship. A search for a permanent solution then began. Several countries expressed interest in a UN mandate for Libya before full independence was granted, although popular pressure inside Libya was for immediate independence. Although there was a strong nationalist movement in Tripolitania that sought a unitary republican state for independent Libya, it was eventually persuaded to accept a federal solution under a Sanusi monarchy, with Idris as king. Independence was proclaimed in Libya on 24 December 1951.

INDEPENDENCE UNDER THE MONARCHY

The newly independent state started with a series of handicaps over and above its harsh geographic environment and poor resource base. The political system bequeathed to it proved extremely difficult to operate, not least because local and provincial loyalties continued to be stronger than loyalties to the new state itself. In Tripolitania, resentment at a Cyrenaica- and Sanusi-dominated government intensified and, after elections in mid-February 1952, all political parties were abolished. Popular dislike of the Sanusi monarchy continued to strengthen during the 1950s and 1960s, particularly in Tripolitania and Fezzan. These sentiments were fed by popular sympathy for the Arab nationalist Nasserism of neighbouring Egypt. This was also fostered by the large number of Egyptian teachers who had been brought in to bolster Libya's educational system and by the inflammatory broadcasts of Radio Cairo.

Egyptian antagonism towards the Sanusi monarchy was, in turn, intensified by the pro-Western option adopted by King Idris's government. Britain and the United States maintained large military bases in Libya, while France's military presence in the Fezzan was ended only in 1956. Libya depended heavily on foreign aid, particularly from the Anglo-Saxon world, and tried to avoid being dragged into the complex and increasingly anti-Western politics of the Middle East and the Arab-Israeli dispute, a stance which in turn increased the government's unpopularity at home.

In 1959 the discovery of oil dramatically altered the options open to Libya's government. Oil came on stream in 1961; almost overnight, Libya began to be transformed by oil revenues. Concomitantly, it also began to play a more assertive role in regional affairs, not least because of domestic pressure for a more pro-Arab and less pro-Western attitude. This came to a head with the 1967 Six Day War, when rioting in Libya forced the government to take a more active role in support of the Arab cause. Increasing domestic repression in response to popular unrest led to disaffection in the army and, eventually, to the junior officer coup on 1 September 1969.

The coup, organised by the Union of Free Officers, took everybody by surprise. It had been evident for some time that the monarchy faced serious problems of credibility and an army-based coup had been long anticipated. However, the senior officer corps was expected to organise it and, apparently, even had a degree of tacit support from Libya's main Western allies. Although there was plenty of evidence of discontent amongst junior officers and the government had taken some desultory steps to curb it, nobody was aware of the degree of organisation that had taken place in secret and that had ensured success.

MU'AMMAR QADHAFI

It gradually became clear that the dominant influence in the new government was a 27-year-old Signals captain – soon to be appointed colonel – Mu'ammar Qadhafi. He was born in 1941 into the transhumant Qadhadhfa tribe, located along the Gulf of Sirte, where his father had been a client of a local notable from the Sayf al-Nasr family. After a mosque-based primary education, the future Libyan leader attended secondary school in the Fezzanese centre of Sabha, as the family followed their patron who had been appointed to a high administrative position there. His secondary-school career was relatively short-lived; Qadhafi soon became a political activist, publicly espousing the Arab nationalism of President Nasser.

His expulsion from secondary school was followed by recruitment into the military academy in Benghazi in 1961. With his military education completed in 1966, he was transferred away from elite army units, such as the Cyrenaican Defence Force, into the communications branch in the mistaken belief that his political radicalism could be safely contained there. Instead, it provided him with an excellent cover for the creation of the Free Officers Movement and, eventually, with the means necessary to launch a successful coup d'état while King Idris was on holiday in Turkey.

Although the new government promised to be a typical army-backed radical Arab nationalist regime – it dramatically expanded the armed forces, arrested and sentenced its predecessors for corruption, insisted on an immediate end to British and American military bases and soon forced the remaining 13,000 Italians out of Libya – it also quickly developed characteristics typical of its leader and his background. In imitation of its Egyptian mentor, the new regime founded a mass movement to provide popular backing for the role of the army within the regime –

the Arab Socialist Union (ASU) – and dedicated itself to radicalism in inter-Arab affairs, to confrontation with Israel and to Arab unity, as well as to state-directed economic development. Libya was to undergo a unique ideological evolution over the next decade.

That evolution mirrored the experiences, attitudes and beliefs of its leader. Mu'ammar Qadhafi had grown up in the strongly Islamic, egalitarian and communal environment of tribal Libya. His political views had been profoundly influenced by this experience and by the wider currents of Nasserism. They also reflected, however, a series of resentments; resentments of the tribal groups of Sirtica against the dominant tribes of Cyrenaica; resentments of rural Libya against the merchant communities of Tripoli and Benghazi; and resentments of many Libyans over the arrogance in the Middle East and North Africa towards them because of supposed Libyan backwardness and primitiveness. It has been a combination of these three factors of personal background, Arab nationalism and national sensitivities that has formed the idiosyncratic ideology of Colonel Qadhafi's revolution, as enshrined in the doctrines of the Third Universal Theory and as described in the colonel's *Green Book*.

DOMESTIC POLITICS

Up to the publication of the *Green Book* in 1976, Libya's domestic politics were largely a question of experiment and a quest for stability as the regime grappled with the twin problems of discrediting its predecessors and of finding a viable political structure for the new state. Then, in 1975, after major disagreements within the Revolutionary Command Council (RCC) over economic management, Major Umar Mihayshi, an RCC member and minister of planning, suddenly fled abroad after trying to organise an abortive coup of his own. He had tried to recruit other RCC members to support him and had also expected support from his home town of Misrata in order to force Colonel Qadhafi to resign.

Three attempted coups made clear the alienation of the new regime from important groups within Libyan society. A December 1969 coup marked the breach between the RCC – all junior officers – and their military superiors, still tied to the policies of the monarchy. A July 1970 coup marked a final breach between the Sanusi movement and traditional tribal elites, which had been the backbone of the monarchy, and the RCC. The Mihayshi coup in August 1975 marked the collapse of consensus within the RCC and the reduction of the regime's geographic and social powerbase, as the Misrata region became disaffected by its loss of influence with the disgrace of Umar Mihayshi himself. In part, this development was an inevitable reflection of the regime's attempts to create an authentic base of radical popular support. During the previous five years, it had attempted to supplement the effectiveness of the Nasserist ASU, which it had created in 1971. It had done this by appealing to traditions of popular consensus inherent in Libya's Islamic heritage, appeals supplemented by laws repeating the ban on political parties and limiting the freedom of trade unions and the press. Tribalism and regionalism were also attacked.

By 1973, however, it was clear that none of these measures had worked. Tensions inside the RCC, had intensified and, after a threat to resign from his positions of RCC chairman, head-of-state and comman-der-in-chief, Colonel Qadhafi suddenly radicalised the government by bringing in Major Abd al-Salam Jallud, his closest collaborator in the RCC, as premier and then announced a 'cultural revolution'. In April, in a speech at the coastal town of Zuwara, the colonel warned that the Libyan revolution was threatened and proposed a five-point programme to revive it. These included the suspension of the legal system, arming the population to protect the revolution, purging the country of the 'political-ly sick', the destruction of the bureaucracy and the bourgeoisie and the destruction of all aspects of culture contrary to the Qur'an. In place of the existing institutions of government there were to be popularly elected committees, responsible for administration, while a purified Islamic culture would determine Libya's cultural environment. In the event the 'cultural revolution' had petered out by August 1973, with the collapse of a proposed union agreement with Egypt. However, it had set the stage for the next radical shake-up of the political system in March 1976.

THE *JAMAHIRIYYA*

A year after the 'cultural revolution', Colonel Qadhafi resigned his posi-tion in the RCC and devoted himself to preparing for the final stage in the evolution of Libya's new political system – the creation of the *jamahiriyya*, 'the state of the masses'. Its proclamation was foreshad-owed by the publication of the colonel's Third Universal Theory in late 1973, in which he argued that Islam represented the source of the only viable political philosophy for the Third World, superior to both capi-talism and communism.

The *Green Book* proposed a political system based on direct popular consensual democracy, with popular control of the means of produc-tion, and limited private ownership set within the context of an austere collective social structure. It was a vision that owed much to Islamic legal and moral precursors and the collective social order of tradition-al rural nomadic life.

The new political system was installed in March 1977, after the 'people's authority' (popular sovereignty) had been proclaimed in Sabha at the final meeting of the now defunct ASU which, thereby, transformed itself into the new embodiment of popular sovereignty, the General People's Congress (GPC). The new system was based on a series of Basic Popular Congresses (BPC) to which all Libyans belonged. The 187 BPCs (enlarged to 2,150 in 1984) were structured in terms of population location, and their elected chairmen, secretaries and assis-tant secretaries became delegates to the GPC. The GPC also included an equal number of delegates designated by trade unions, and by trade, social and professional organisations. The GPC thus represented all shades of opinion, both by population location and by economic activity. Delegates were mandated by their nominating organisations, thus ensuring that the ultimate political decision should reflect the direct democratic views of the population at large.

Daily administration was to be carried out by a series of popular committees which, at least in theory, were elected by those who were to be administered – the organisations which provided delegates to the GPC, whether BPC or another occupational organisation. The popular committees were under the ultimate control of the General People's Committee, itself elected by the GPC and answerable to the General Secretariat of the GPC, which maintained continuity in GPC policy between its biannual sessions. The General People's Committee was, in short, the equivalent of a cabinet and its secretaries the equivalent of ministers. The GPC General Secretariat was the key body, as far as the regime was concerned, for its members were the five remaining members of the original RCC which had organised the 1969 overthrow of the monarchy – with Colonel Qadhafi at its head and with Major Abd al-Salam Jallud, Colonel Abu Bakr Yunis Jabr, Major Mustafa Kharrubi and Major Khuwayldi Hamidi as its other members. They have since been joined by Khalifa Khanash, a cousin of Colonel Qadhafi. Their presence ensured political continuity, for, as the 'people's authority' was declared, they abandoned all other formal positions of power.

This political system has been formally in operation in Libya since 1977, but lacked genuine popular support. Within a year of the establishment of the *jamahiriyya*, the Qadhafi regime found it necessary to modify the basic structure. During 1978 revolutionary committees began to appear, apparently spontaneously, in reality under central direction by the small group of former RCC members around Colonel Qadhafi. Their function was to radicalise the BPC and popular committee system and to 'guarantee the revolution' – in short, to ensure that the system worked and that dissent was excluded. Their membership was clandestine and under the direct control of Colonel Qadhafi and Major Jallud. By February 1980, the revolutionary committee system had spread throughout the political structure, paralleling it at every level, and with its own annual congress. At the congress in February 1980, Colonel Qadhafi gave the movement an additional function, that of eliminating what he called 'the stray dogs of the revolution', those Libyans who rejected the *jamahiriyya*, both inside Libya and abroad. The most important elements of the revolutionary committee movement – those who took over responsibility for eliminating the 'stray dogs of the revolution' – also had another mode of identity with the regime: they were members of tribal groups that were themselves linked to leading members of the regime around the colonel himself.

In fact, the irony was that the Qadhafi regime, in seeking a popular mandate, had alienated such large sections of Libyan society that it had to fall back on its most basic element, the tribe. It was a notable fact that most of those who held real power inside the regime were linked to the major tribes of Sirtica – the Qadhadhfa, the Maghara and the Warfalla. Others were linked to the Fezzan. They include relatives of

Colonel Qadhafi, such as Said Qadhaf Adhm (the military commander of Sirtica) and Ahmad Qadhaf Adhm (seen as Qadhafi's heir apparent), Abd al-Hafid Mas'ud (commander of the southern military region) and Abd al-Hafid Yunis (commander of the eastern military region). They had also included Hasan Ishkal, who was executed after an abortive coup in December 1987. Others include Musa Kursa, the former diplomatic chief in London until his expulsion in 1980, and Abdullah al-Sanusi and Said Rashid of the Maghara, which is Major Jallud's own power-base.

This process of 'retribalisation' of Libya through the revolutionary committee movement has effectively created a third level of political control, which, although informal in nature, is the real repository of political power. It extends into every key area of society and the economy and, by this process of fragmentation of Libyan political, social and economic structures into a series of personalised fiefs, ensures that the core of the Qadhafi regime maintains effective personal control. The five close collaborators of the colonel up to 1995 controlled the oil industry (Major Jallud); the army, which is now also penetrated by revolutionary committees and is threatened with replacement by a popular militia movement (Abu Bakr Yunis Jabr); the security services (Khalifa Khanaish); the popular militia movement (Mustafa Kharrubi); and the police system (Khawaildi Hamidi). All except Khalifa Khanaish have now been forced into retirement and Colonel Qadhafi increasingly relies on his immediate family for support.

It is largely because ultimate control depends on this informal system that the Qadhafi regime has been able to survive the vicissitudes of the 1980s, including the United States bombing of Tripoli and Benghazi in April 1986 and the catastrophic defeat of the Libyan army in Chad in March 1987. It is typified by the colonel's decision, in late 1987, to decentralise the administration away from Tripoli and to create a new capital on the Gulf of Sirte under the direct control of the Qadhadhfa. It even ensures the regime's survival despite the current UN sanctions against it because of the Lockerbie crisis – the destruction of a Pan Am aircraft over the Scottish town of Lockerbie in December 1988 for which the Qadhafi regime has been held responsible.

OPPOSITION TO THE REGIME

This system has also generated a massive popular discontent, both inside Libya and abroad. It has resulted in at least seven major exile dissident organisations, of which the best-known is probably the National Salvation Front for Libya, organised in 1980 by the former Libyan ambassador to India, Muhammad al-Mughariaff but which split in a welter of disagreements in 1995. It has also engendered a growing anti-regime Islamic movement, against which the authorities have reacted savagely.

Much of the basis for the discontent has been engendered by the campaigns waged by the regime against what it considered disaffected elements of Libyan society during the 1970s. Royalists left, of course, in

1969. They were followed in 1973 by the bulk of Libya's intellectuals, and in 1977 they were followed, in turn, by much of Libya's business class, who took fright at the implications for the economy of the political changes introduced under the *jamahiri* system. In essence, these required enterprises to be taken over by workers' popular committees; domestic trade was centralised progressively under state control, as was foreign trade. Wage employment was formally banned; instead, employees became the owners of the means of production. Private ownership and personal property were limited by decree. In effect, although Libya was supposed to be a 'stateless state', it was the state that took over control of the economy.

Islamist opposition to the Qadhafi regime has, strangely enough, been engendered by the regime's own assumption of an Islamic mantle. In 1977, the religious leadership in Libya had the temerity to question the religious orthodoxy of the *Green Book*. Colonel Qadhafi reacted by claiming that true Islam required no mediation between Allah and man and that, therefore, the religious authorities had no function. He went on to claim that Islamic law was valid only insofar as it was a restatement of the principles of the Qur'an and had no intrinsic validity because of its status as authoritative interpretation of Islamic doctrine. He finally concluded that each Muslim had an equal capacity to interpret the Qur'an in the light of modern conditions. The colonel rammed home his convictions by altering the starting date of the Islamic calender from the date of Muhammad's migration to Medina to the date of the prophet's death. The result has been growing Islamic opposition to his regime. The colonel's individualistic attitudes towards Islam, however, are exactly paralleled by his attitude towards foreign affairs.

FOREIGN AFFAIRS

Foreign policy under the Qadhafi regime has been influenced by the principles of radical Arab unity, a Libyan conviction of its primordial role within the Third World and an opportunistic determination to maximise benefits to the Libyan state. Arab nationalism bequeathed to Libya a profoundly confrontational attitude towards Israel over the Arab–Israeli dispute and the Palestinian problem, as well as justifying Libya's constant search for partners for projects of political and economic unity within the Middle East and North Africa. Libyan perceptions of its anti-imperialist role, as the embodiment of the principles of the Third Universal Theory, led to confrontation with the West and a concomitant attempt to ensure security by an alliance with the Soviet Union. Opportunism has forced the Qadhafi regime into a series of irresponsible actions towards its neighbours, not least its intervention in Chad during the 1980s.

Libyan attempts at achieving unity reflect both ideological and practical preoccupations. The original attempts in 1970 and 1973 to create such agreements with Egypt and Sudan and then with Egypt alone were both rational attempts to match Egypt's population or Sudan's agricultural potential with Libyan oil wealth as much as they were ideological imperatives.

For Libya, however, unity with neighbouring states also offered a means of guaranteeing the security of a state that otherwise had little means of ensuring its own security. Despite massive spending on armaments – $14 billion with the Soviet Union alone during the 1980s – Libya's armed forces have not acquitted themselves well in any of the major armed clashes in which they have been involved: in Chad in 1987; in Uganda in the mid-1980s; or in the border war with Egypt in 1977. In fact, Libya has had to use states such as Algeria to ensure its territorial integrity; it was Algeria, after all, that prevented Egypt from prosecuting the 1977 conflict.

It is this concern over regional security that explains Libya's constant search for allies within North Africa. It did so unsuccessfully with Algeria, Tunisia and Mauritania in 1983; temporarily with Morocco in the Arab–African Union between 1984 and 1986; and now it is part of the Arab–Maghrib Union with all four countries since February 1989. It is also this concern, together with anger at the failure of North African states to oppose the UN sanctions over the Lockerbie affair, that has now led Colonel Qadhafi to seek, once again, close links with the Mubarak regime in Egypt, as much as any lingering ideological preference that reflects the remnants of the Nasserist vision.

Unity can, however, follow ideological prejudice as well. It was undoubtedly because of Syria's and Libya's common opposition to Egypt's acceptance of the Camp David Agreement with Israel in 1978 that the two states, which had formed part of the Confrontation Front along with Algeria and Iraq, actually declared formal unity in 1980. This decision also brought Libya into the pro-Iranian camp during the Iran–Iraq War, a move which earned considerable hostility for the Qadhafi regime in the rest of the Arab world and was also the cause of intensifying hostility between Tripoli and Washington during the Reagan administration of the 1980s.

The other main cause of American hostility was the growing perception in Western capitals that Libya was heavily involved in promoting international terrorism. Statements by leading Libyan politicians only encouraged this belief. Libya's insistence on its role as an anti-imperialist leader, its support for national liberation movements, particularly in the Middle East and Africa, above all its attitude towards Libyan political dissidents abroad, all encouraged this attitude. In 1980, 1982 and again in 1984, Libyans connected with the diplomatic service or with the Foreign Security Bureau were involved in assassinations and assassination attempts in London, Athens, Rome and Vienna and in the United States.

The terrorist crisis culminated in April 1984 in the murder of a policewoman, Yvonne Fletcher, in London during an attempt to machine-gun anti-Qadhafi Libyan demonstrators from the Libyan People's Bureau (embassy) in St James' Square. British diplomatic relations with Libya were severed and American hostility towards Libya, which had already resulted in a military confrontation in the Gulf of Sirte in August 1981, was racked up a notch. Two years later, Washington accused Libya of being involved in terrorist attacks on United States servicemen in Berlin and, in March 1986, attacked military installations in the Gulf of Sirte. One month later came the bombing attack on Tripoli and Benghazi.

Ironically, the American attack on Libya had precisely the opposite effect from that intended. Instead of rallying against the Qadhafi regime, Libyans, outraged that they should have been made personally responsible for the vagaries of a leadership they could not control, initially rallied behind it.

Libya also renewed massive aid to the IRA in Northern Ireland in revenge for the role played by Britain in the bombings. Libya had supplied limited aid to the IRA between 1973 and 1975, in the mistaken belief, so officials in Tripoli later claimed, that it was a genuine movement of national liberation. Now Libya's support was without any ideological coloration, and, until it ended in 1988, Tripoli is believed to have supplied five shiploads of weapons and explosives to the IRA.

American hostility towards Libya also touched on another area of Libyan foreign policy: that concerned specifically with Libya's own opportunistic advantage. Libya's claim to northern Chad had never been abandoned, despite the 1956 treaty with France, which was ostensibly meant to rectify the border situation. By 1980, the Chadian civil war had degenerated into a struggle between two northern factions, one of which headed the provisional government placed in N'Djamena by the Organisation of African Unity (OAU) in 1979. In June 1980, Libya responded to an appeal from this group, headed by Goukouni Oueddai; by December of that year, Libyan troops were present in the Chadian capital. Although the leader of the opposing faction, Hissan Habré, was forced to flee, he returned triumphantly to Chad two years later, now with Egyptian, French and American support. Libya continued to support the defeated Oueddai faction in the hope of making its presence in the Aozou Strip permanent, until its forces were forced out with massive losses – $1.4 billion-worth of equipment was abandoned and thousands of Libyans killed in early 1987. Eventually Libya accepted an International Court of Justice ruling in February 1994 that the Strip should be returned to Chad.

The Habré regime's success was due in no small part to French and United States perceptions of the need to humiliate the Qadhafi regime in Libya. Libya, however, had its revenge. Three years later Tripoli was to finance a successful overthrow of the Habré regime and to see a more sympathetic government installed in its place.

THE ECONOMIC DIMENSION

One crucial reason why Libya has been able to engage in its domestic political experiments and its risky foreign policy has been its access to substantial oil income during the past three decades. In 1985, 41 per cent of Libya's gross domestic product (GDP) was derived from oil production.

Despite the fall in international oil prices over the intervening years, 27 per cent of GDP was still attributable to oil in 1989. If manufacturing industry, which is largely petrochemical in nature, is included, the proportion of GDP attributable to the oil sector rises to 45 per cent and 35 per cent respectively.

Oil also generates 99 per cent of Libya's export revenues, with oil production currently running at around one-million barrels per day, compared with a maximum of two-million barrels per day in 1979. The actual level of oil revenues has varied greatly, however, depending on the level of international oil prices, from a maximum of $22 billion in 1979 to as little as $5.8 billion in 1986. Revenues are currently estimated to be around $8-9 billion and Libya's oil reserves, although shrinking, are expected to last for 60 years.

Interestingly enough, Libya is almost unique amongst Organisation of Petroleum Exporting Countries (OPEC) members in that its oil industry has always involved joint ventures with foreign companies. This pragmatic approach towards oil exploitation and exploration is all the more surprising since Libya played the key role in the radicalisation of OPEC at the start of the 1970s. It was a Libyan decision unilaterally to force up prices in 1971 that eventually destroyed the international oil companies' control of world oil prices and their control of national oil industries in the Middle East. Colonel Qadhafi took a straightforward approach to the oil companies operating in Libya, most of them 'independents' and therefore without access to worldwide crude that would have allowed them to face Libya down. He pointed out that Libyans had done without oil revenues for 5,000 years and could, therefore, do so again if need be.

Oil revenues have funded Libya's massive arms purchases. One analyst has calculated that these and other hidden expenditures over the past 25 years have cost Libya between 32 and 67 per cent of its total oil revenues of around $150 billion. Nonetheless, sufficient has been left over to pay for development of an elaborate infrastructure and for industrial and agricultural development, including a petrochemical industry and a steel industry at Misrata. Oil revenues have also financed Libya's sizeable foreign labour force, made up mainly of Egyptians and Tunisians and providing up to 60 per cent of the total labour force. It has also paid for Libya's chronic food deficit: over 65 per cent of all the food required by Libya's 3.6-million-strong population, now growing at a rate of around 2.8 per cent annually, has to be imported.

Most strikingly, oil has provided Libya with the hope that it could achieve food self-sufficiency by irrigating the desert. Since the mid-1980s, Libya has tried to overcome its inadequate water supply to coastal cities – now saline through over-use – by constructing a massive water pipeline from Kufra and Sarir oases in the east and from the Fezzan in the west to supply the Gefara Plain and Jabal al-Akhdar areas. This, the Great Manmade River Project, is ultimately expected to cost between $18 and $21 billion. Water from the scheme is also to be supplied to Sirte, in the hope of creating an agricultural base there.

Expert opinion varies as to the utility of the scheme, but few doubt that urban and industrial demand for water will soon vitiate the objective of food self-sufficiency.

Libya is, in short, an oil-rich state with a high absorptive capacity which is becoming ever more oil dependent. Its ambitions of economic self-sufficiency are, no doubt, delusions, and Libyan planners are looking more and more towards the Kuwaiti example of foreign investment and downstream integration of their oil industry with expansion of marketing networks into Europe.

RECENT EVENTS

Since its defeat in Chad in 1987, the Qadhafi regime has attempted to moderate its domestic and international reputations. Within Libya, the rigours of the *jamahiri* system have been significantly eased. Private enterprise has been permitted in agriculture, retail trade and small-scale manufacture. Barriers to foreign travel and to private importing from abroad have been abolished. Borders have been opened and Libyan political prisoners have been freed. Most important of all, virtually all Libyan exiles have been permitted to visit Libya and even to return if they wish.

In international affairs, Libya has gone out of its way to demonstrate that it is a responsible international partner. It has sought to improve links with Europe, its major trading partner, particularly with Italy, France and Germany. It has also attempted, unsuccessfully, to improve relations with Britain and the United States. Until the Lockerbie crisis, it had successfully integrated itself into North African regional political and economic structures. It has also moderated its attitude towards inter-Arab affairs. The most striking example of this new moderation occurred during the Gulf War. Despite widescale popular antagonism to the Western intervention, the Qadhafi regime condemned Iraq's invasion as 'injurious to the Arab world' and even offered to supply troops to the coalition.

Many Libyans view this conversion with suspicion, believing that, once the opportunity is right, Colonel Qadhafi will revert to his preferred persona as a radical political visionary and that the full rigours of the *jamahiri* system will be reimposed. In 1992–93 Libya saw its diplomatic gains reversed by its alleged complicity in the bombing of flights PA 103 over Lockerbie in 1988 and UTA 772 over Niger in 1989. Requests from France, Britain and the US for the handing over of those allegedly responsible were turned down by the Libyan authorities. In consequence sanctions were imposed against Libya which are still in place at the time of writing (September 1995). Now all the regime's energies are turned towards reversing the sanctions imposed upon it and to countering Western hostility to it – with little hope of success!

George Joffé

10
THE MAGHRIB

THE THREE STATES OF THE MAGHRIB – Algeria, Morocco and Tunisia – in some ways form a neglected and isolated corner of the Arab world. Despite their rapid integration into the religious culture and society of Islam shortly after the Prophet Muhammad's death in AD 632, all three states long resisted a concomitant integration into the linguistic universe of Arabic. Even today, substantial minorities in the Maghrib speak languages other than Arabic – basically one of the Berber group of languages, such as Tarifit, Tamazight and Tashilhit in Morocco and Taqbilt, Mzabi and Tamarshak (a Touareg language) in Algeria – as their mother tongue. The Maghrib's geographical location, furthermore, excluded it from the great events that shaped the Mashriq – the Middle East. It was indeed, as the Arabic version of the name given to the region today suggests, the Far West of the Arab world. At the same time, however, the Maghrib forms a significant demographic component of that world; with total populations of 58.632 million (mid-1990 estimate), it provides 27.7 per cent of the total population of the Arab world, as defined by the members of the Arab League.

Even in religious and cultural terms, the Maghrib differs significantly from the Mashriq. In place of the religious confusion of the Mashriq, where Islam's dominant position is split between Sunni and Shi'i and exists alongside significant Christian and Jewish minorities, the Maghrib's religious character is predominantly Sunni Islam. Colonialism, too, has left a different mark on each region: while France and Britain vied for influence in the Middle East, the Maghrib was the preserve of France and today French is almost as important a language as Arabic or Berber. Nor did the Maghrib have to deal with the divisive effects of the creation of the state of Israel, just as the era of independence was beginning to dawn.

Yet, from another point of view, isolated though it may be from the Middle East by the deserts of Libya and by distinct cultural differences, the Maghrib also forms a vital part of two other worlds. Traditionally, the states of the Maghrib have seen themselves, and have been seen, as an integral part of Africa, for the vast Sahara desert, now seen as a barrier to communication, used to be viewed as the equivalent of an inland sea, crisscrossed from time immemorial by trade routes. At the same time, the confrontation between Islam and Christianity in the Mediterranean since the Spanish Reconquista in the 15th century has made them into Mediterranean states. That northward dimension of their historical and cultural experience has been profoundly intensified in modern times as a result of colonialism.

The colonial experience differed considerably between the three modern states, however. Algeria, for example, which had not had a sovereign existence as a state before the colonial period, was occupied by France from 1844 and was administratively integrated into France for much of its subsequent colonial period. There was also massive European settlement in Algeria, with the result that independence was only gained in 1962 after eight years of intense warfare which cost up to one million lives. Indeed, independence was granted as much because of changes in metropolitan perceptions in Paris of the utility of colonial empires as because of Algerian successes in military conflict.

In Tunisia and Morocco, by contrast, the basic structures of unitary states existed before the colonial period. Indeed, in the case of Morocco, the state can claim an unbroken one thousand-year-old tradition of independent government. The two countries were colonised in 1881 and 1912 respectively, however. Having learnt from its experience in Algeria, France created 'protectorates' in both countries, whereby the French presence was supposed to assist indigenous authority in modernising the administration and the economy, while France took over responsibility for external affairs. In reality, French colonial interests dominated. Nonetheless, far more of the innate fabric of indigenous society was preserved than was the case in Algeria.

Yet, at independence, which came to Morocco and Tunisia six years before it was granted to Algeria, all three states were endowed with the structures of a modern European-style nation-state. They had modern-style administrations, defined territorial borders and the rudiments of a modern economy, created by European settlers during the colonial period. They also had comprehensive links with the economy of metropolitan France, for which they had served during the colonial period as sources of cheap raw materials and food. Those distortions in commercial links have persisted since independence, reflecting the preferential position occupied by Europe in the Maghrib's economic horizons today.

In short, it is the Mediterranean dimension of the Maghrib which is of most immediate importance to it today. All three states are acutely dependent on Europe for trade and for economic survival. In 1989, 53 per cent of the Maghrib's total trade was with the countries of the European Union (EU). Algeria is a major hydrocarbon supplier; Morocco and Tunisia sell agricultural goods; Morocco is also Europe's major source of phosphate. The EU, in turn, supplies most of the region's consumer goods and much of its grain. More importantly, perhaps, Europe has traditionally absorbed excess labour from the Maghrib. Now, with Europe facing the challenge of the collapse of communism in Eastern Europe and the Soviet Union and with greater European economic unity since 1992, the Maghrib is anxious about the consequences of these momentous changes for its own future. The resolution of this dilemma, however, will be as much a consequence of history as it will be of economic, social and diplomatic change.

In fact, given their pre-colonial experiences, the political divides between Maghribi states run across an underlying sociological reality which emphasised a common historical and cultural experience. Indeed, until the 16th century, few Maghribis would have noticed a significant difference in society and culture anywhere in the region. It was only with the penetration of Ottoman power into modern Tunisia and Algeria in response to European attempts to dominate the Mediterranean – Morocco was never part of the Ottoman Empire – that specific cultural distinctions began to emerge. Even then, they were essentially limited to the Maghrib's Mediterranean littoral. Inland, society continued to follow its region-wide norms.

THE IMPOSITION OF COLONIALISM

The 19th century was a period of gradual disillusionment for the Maghrib, as its rulers came to understand the implications of European dominance. In the immediate aftermath of the Napoleonic wars, however, European interest appeared to have been diverted away from the region. Apart from lingering irritation over commercial misbehaviour, particularly in Algiers, where deliveries of cereals to the Napoleonic armies had never been paid for, the Maghrib seemed to have relapsed into the somnambulism of the pre-Napoleonic period.

The picture was to change dramatically in 1830 when, ostensibly in revenge for an insult offered to the French consul by the Bey of Algiers in 1827, France decided to occupy the beylik. In reality, the decision represented a desperate attempt by the government of the Bourbon monarch of France, Charles X, to avoid a military coup against him. The Algerian adventure was supposed to distract the army; it failed to do so and the Bourbon monarchy soon disappeared into oblivion.

France, however, having neglected to formulate a plan of occupation, was dragged into the political vacuum it had created in destroying the bey's administration. By the end of the decade, French troops were forced to suppress the beyliks of the interior and to create a country-wide administration to replace them. In western Algeria, the French army soon found itself confronting a tribal federation under the leadership of the Amir Abd al-Qadir. It was only when a ruthless scorched-earth policy was instituted that resistance was broken.

As France was sucked into its first territorial acquisition in the Maghrib, so it had to manufacture a system of administration and determine what it would do with the territory it now administered. Colonial settlement was encouraged as land was confiscated from the rural tribes. After initial hesitation, the new colony was integrated into the metropolitan administration of France. Algerians, however, were merely colonial subjects in their own land, denied virtually all rights, their culture marginalised.

By 1870, as the Second Empire was being destroyed by Prussia, eastern Algeria burst into rebellion. It was to be the last such outburst until independence almost a century later. The rebellion was suppressed with great brutality, and European control, particularly by the local settler population – the *colons* – was powerfully reinforced.

Thereafter, it would be colonial Algiers, with its one million *colons* – the *pieds noirs* – which would call the tune that Paris would have to follow, whatever the official nature of the relationship. It was to be a relationship that would, eventually, lead to the destruction of France's North African empire.

In Tunisia, the Husainid beylik had taken note of what had happened in Algiers. Ahmad Bey had also realised, like Muhammad Ali in Egypt some years before, that European success was based on an efficient military machine supported by an effective industrial base. He tried to modernise Tunisia on similar lines, both to create a powerful modern state and to counter the growing privileges extracted from his government by the European consuls in Tunis.

Tunisia, however, was still an Islamic state, in which the basic tax structure could not sustain the costs of modernisation. To counter the financial weakness of the state, the government began the disastrous policy of borrowing from European powers and mortgaging its tax revenues in repayment. Soon Europeans took over control of the state finances and government power weakened. In 1859, the bey was forced, in imitation of European practice, to concede a formal constitution – the Destour – the first to be granted in the Arab world. The following year he was obliged to permit European land and property ownership in Tunisia. Attempts to restructure the government were thwarted by European pressure. Finally, in 1881, on the ostensible grounds of incursions into eastern Algeria by a Tunisian border tribe, the Khrumir, but in reality to prevent other European powers from intervening, France invaded the beylik.

Under the treaties of Bardo and La Marsa, France instituted a novel form of control. It did not wish to repeat the expensive mistake of direct rule on the Algerian model. Instead, it created a structure of indirect rule, in which France was supposed to 'aid' and 'modernise' the administration of the beylik alongside the existing authorities. France would also take over responsibility for security and foreign affairs. This 'protection' system, in effect, became a cover for the slow assimilation of the Tunisian economy into that of metropolitan France, while a significant 100,000-strong, mainly Italian, settler colony was introduced.

The process of colonial assimilation in Morocco was to take a further 30-odd years. Although Morocco had been rudely shocked by its defeat in the Battle of Isly in 1844 and the sultanate's authority had been threatened by a series of tribal rebellions in consequence, France was not anxious to exploit its weakness, though pressures from Britain made it unlikely that it could have done so anyway. Nonetheless, Morocco was forced to grant economic privileges to both countries and to introduce a variant of the 'Capitulations system' – the protégé system – to protect foreign nationals.

It was only in 1860 that the process of colonisation began to lumber into action. The spark that set it off was provided by tribal unrest along the borders of two Spanish coastal enclaves, Ceuta and Melilla. War broke out, which Spain easily won, demanding, in consequence, a massive indemnity.

The payment of this, in turn, led to the disastrous process of Moroccan borrowings from Europe – first from Britain, later from France – and to the opening of Morocco to European commercial exploitation. By 1906, under the terms of the Treaty of Algeciras, Morocco had lost control of its taxation system to a European debt commission and Europeans administered its customs system in order to pay off its accumulated debts. France took over control of the state financial system.

Although Britain had entertained ambitions for colonial control in Morocco, these were abandoned in the Entente Cordiale of 1904, when France offered, instead, a free hand in the eastern Mediterranean and in Egypt. Despite German objections France continued to expand its presence in Morocco, with military encroachments from Algeria and from the coastal port of Anfa, later, as Casablanca, Morocco's economic centre and port. Tribal anger at constant European encroachment sapped the sultanate, which in turn encouraged ever deeper European penetration.

Finally, in 1912, under the provisions of the Treaty of Fez, France imposed a protectorate system on Morocco, similar to that imposed on Tunisia 30 years before. Eventually, 500,000 European settlers moved in. The protectorate was shared with Spain which took over control of northern Morocco and the province of Tarfaya in the south. Spain also instituted a separate colony over the Western Sahara, which it had begun to create after 1884.

It was, however, to take a further 22 years before the country was brought under French control. The complex process of pacification was also to cost Spain massive losses in the Rif War. That, in turn, led directly to the Spanish civil war and, following his victory, to Franco's Fascist government. It was a political system which, ironically, ended only in 1975, as Spain abandoned its last colony in Africa in the Western Sahara.

THE NATIONALIST RESPONSE

The French colonial experience was to alter profoundly the physical appearance and the social structure of the Maghrib. Widespread agricultural settlement – settlers took over two million acres in Tunisia, six-and-a-half million acres in Algeria and around two-and-a-half million acres in Morocco – created a modern cash-crop agricultural system. This was encapsulated within a traditional subsistence farming and pastoral system that had to support rapidly growing rural populations. Despite massive and accelerating rural drift, particularly after the Great Depression of the early 1930s, urban populations remained a minority overall. At the same time, a modern industrial sector grew up in some urban centres, particularly along the coast, under European ownership and management. The French administrations, in addition to pacifying even the most remote corners of the countryside and the desert, created modern communications and infrastructural systems.

Even though indigenous populations were largely excluded from the benefits of modernisation, life expectancies and population growth increased significantly. Nonetheless, the overall balance of the colonial experience for Tunisians, Algerians and Moroccans must be negative, not least because it was marked by massive population dislocation and famine as the countries of the Maghrib were, first, integrated into centralised monetary economies and, second, linked into the European regional economy.

Tunisians, Algerians and Moroccans were also well aware of what was being done to their societies and they developed their own responses to it. These fell into two categories and were, at first, the prerogative of the elite groups that dominated national society, although the movements they initiated were later to win much wider support. Initially, however, the elites both wished to participate in and benefit from the innovations introduced by France, while at the same time reaffirming the Maghrib's Islamic and historical heritage. They desired, in short, to adapt and adopt European modernism within the indigenous cultural and sociological framework and sought co-operation with Europe, not exclusion from it.

In this respect, the initial movements of proto-nationalist protest were similar to the Young Ottoman and Young Turk movements which, from the 1880s onwards, had done so much to reform and, eventually, to replace, the sultanate in Ottoman Turkey. The Young Tunisian, Young Algerian and Young Moroccan movements were also inspired by the revivalist movements sweeping the Middle East, particularly by the Salafiyya movement, and they began to reaffirm also the Maghrib's conscious political and cultural identification with the Mashriq.

The early nationalists were optimistic about the French response to their demands. During the First World War, for example, all three countries generously provided manpower and resources to France's war effort. Indeed, the tradition of labour migration into Europe actually began as a result of French calls on Maghribi labour to make up for the shortfalls caused by conscription. Nationalists assumed – and were persuaded by French propaganda – that France would reward the Maghrib after the hostilities were over by encouraging political and economic participation.

These hopes, however, were disappointed, for during the 1920s nothing changed. Admittedly, this would have been difficult in Morocco, where, between 1921 and 1926, France was engaged with Spain in crushing the Riffian tribes of the northern Mediterranean littoral. In reality, however, the French administrations were deaf to indigenous protest. By 1930, furthermore, the Great Depression caused vast economic damage to settler societies and indigenous communities alike, so that France was even less disposed to consider political reform as economic hardship engendered growing popular anger and protest. Towards the end of the decade, the nationalist movements in Tunisia and Morocco began to widen their popular support by assuming the leadership of such protest. In consequence, colonial repression intensified.

In any case, indigenous protest did not speak with a single voice. The *assimilationistes* argued that North Africans should integrate fully into French political life on a basis of formal equality. Others, the *associationistes*, argued that integration was to be avoided in favour of parallel development so that Maghribi society could preserve its identity while taking from Europe what it required for the purposes of modernisation.

In Tunisia and Algeria, these different points of view convulsed the nationalist movement. In Tunisia, the Young Tunisian movement in the Destour party, founded in 1920, had called for the restoration of the 1859 Destour (constitution). Such a move by the bey would have forced the French administration to accept political partnership. However, the party's failure forced it to concede the leadership of the nationalist movement in 1934, at the Ksar Hellel conference. Habib Bourguiba, a young French-trained lawyer, thereafter successfully created a far more activist political movement, the Neo-Destour, which was eventually to lead the struggle for independence after the Second World War.

In Algeria, the *assimilationistes*, led by Ferhat Abbas and Ben Djelloul, confronted the *associationistes*, dominated by the moderate Islamist movement of the Algerian *ulama* and led by Ibn Badis. The French administration ignored them. Real nationalist sentiment, however, was gathering steam amongst Algeria's migrant populations in France, where the *Etoile Nord-Africain* group, led by Messali Hadj, demanded complete independence. It was only after the Second World War, however, that an effective nationalist movement, the *Front de Libération Nationale* (FLN), developed, demanding full independence from France for which it was prepared to fight.

In Morocco, the nascent nationalist movement of the 1920s had realised that the country's political and cultural traditions would not allow a fully secularist option. Under the leadership of Allal al-Fasi, in 1930 the movement fought a successful campaign to prevent the French administration from limiting the role of Islamic religious law in Berber areas and, thereby, splitting the nascent Moroccan body politic. After the French authorities rejected a plan for Moroccan participation, the movement rallied itself behind the political legitimacy of the sultanate. After the exiling of its leaders at the end of the decade, the movement reformed in 1944 and, under the banner of *Istiqlal* (Independence), demanded the ending of the protectorate and the restoration of Morocco's sovereignty under Sultan Mohammed V.

In fact, the Second World War was a crucial turning point in the nationalist struggle. France's defeat by Nazi Germany and the installation of pro-Nazi Vichy administrations throughout the Maghrib, together with continuing conflict with Free French sympathisers, shattered the myth of French omnipotence. Nazi propaganda also persuaded some nationalists that colonialism was not an immutable fact. However, probably the most profound experience was the extension of fighting into the region and the Torch landings in the Maghrib in late 1942, which brought United States and British servicemen into the region. Despite Free French attempts to reassert colonial control, United States leaders made it clear that they had no wish to see the French colonial presence prolonged.

THE STRUGGLE FOR INDEPENDENCE

Immediately after the war, France moved to suppress nationalist aspirations throughout North Africa. In Tunisia and Morocco, steps were taken to modify the protectorate system – which left sovereignty fully in indigenous hands – by a new concept of 'co-sovereignty' in which France and the country concerned would share full sovereign rights. Such a development would have made the removal of France legally impossible and the proposal was powerfully resisted. The French authorities imposed new governmental structures in both countries at the start of the 1950s, expelling Neo-Destourians from power in Tunisia in 1952 and exiling the sultan of Morocco to Madagascar in 1953.

The result was an immediate outbreak of violence in Morocco and Tunisia. By 1955, the French government had come to realise that compromise was essential. French politicians decided that the colonial presence in Morocco and Tunisia could be abandoned in order to safeguard France's colonial control of Algeria. Morocco was offered negotiations in 1955 and independence was granted on 2 March 1956. Tunisia was offered autonomy in 1955, which Habib Bourguiba, as leader of the Neo-Destour, accepted. This was converted into full independence in 1956, while at the same time the beylik was abolished and the new independent government transformed Tunisia into a republic.

The French hold on Algeria remained, however. Both the nature of French rule there, which was manipulated by the leaders of the *colon* community, and the metropolitan reluctance to abandon control after the debacle in Vietnam made it impossible for Paris to repeat what it had done in Morocco and Tunisia. In addition, the discovery of oil in the Sahara and French ambitions for nuclear weapons – for which the Sahara made an ideal testing ground – intensified French determination. However, against France was ranged a new kind of clandestine resistance movement in the FLN, led by individuals from modest rural or urban petit bourgeois backgrounds, with familiarity with nationalist aspirations from their pre-war connections with the Messalist movement and with experience of military action from the war.

They formed the FLN in October 1954 and, on 1 November 1954, initiated a guerrilla campaign. Although the FLN was not initially a mass movement, it moved rapidly and ruthlessly against all other Algerian nationalist groups, forcing them into line behind its own policy of armed struggle. It capitalised on the destruction of Algerian traditional society to impose its own structures and paid special attention to the massive Algerian migrant community in France. The result was that by 1956 it had become a genuine mass movement and the authentic voice of Algerian nationalist aspirations. Its leadership also realised that armed struggle alone could not win independence and, as a result, the movement sought to win international support for its demands.

In fact, by the end of the decade, it had become evident that military victory was impossible. New recruits to the FLN's military bases in Tunisia and Morocco were kept out of Algeria by elaborate border defences – the *Ligne Challe* – and the exhausted guerrillas inside were hunted down by an ever-more efficient and brutal French army, while millions of Algerian peasants were uprooted from their villages to improve military control. At the same time, however, the continuing guerrilla campaign in the cities and *colon* suspicion of the commitment of successive French governments to the struggle led to a political collapse in France.

In 1958, a combined *colon*-army revolt in Algiers led to the return to power of General Charles de Gaulle in Paris. The French Algerian population anticipated that the general would safeguard it in Algeria by maintaining the French presence there: the general quickly realised that this would be impossible. However, he moved cautiously, seeking out Algerian 'moderates' with whom to negotiate and attempting to isolate the FLN while prosecuting the military campaign to the full. His policy was frustrated, however, by *colon* hostility to compromise and by the FLN's complete control over the nationalist movement itself.

By 1961 de Gaulle had accepted that the FLN would have to be the partner for negotiations and, after obtaining a popular mandate by referendum in January 1961, negotiations began. Their course was disturbed, however, by a revolt amongst France's leading generals – the 'generals' revolt' – and by the outbreak of violent guerrilla actions against the government by a clandestine military organisation within the French army in Algeria, the OAS. The negotiations continued, however, and France eventually recognised full Algerian independence, despite its anxieties over access to Algerian oil and over its Saharan nuclear-testing sites. With the signing of the Evian Accords on 18 March 1962, the war was over – at the cost of over one million killed and apparently unbridgeable hostility between *colon* and Algerian. Within six months, virtually all the *colon* community had fled Algeria, leaving the country to start its independent existence with no specialist experience to manage agriculture or industry.

INDEPENDENCE – TUNISIA

Independence presented the new Tunisia leader, Habib Bourguiba, with a dual problem, that of asserting his control over both party and state. The Neo-Destour, the political vehicle through which independence had been achieved, was to become Tunisia's single political party, now renamed as the Destourian Socialist party (DSP). At the same time, all other state-wide organisations in effect became subordinated to it. The DSP also acquired a parallel position within the institutions of the state, so that the bureaucracy also acted as a party machine.

Other factors of political organisation – such as Islam – were coerced into acquiescence or bypassed. In 1961, for example, President Bourguiba outraged religious opinion by proclaiming a legal end to the month-long annual Ramadan fast, on the grounds that fasting was excused during *jihad*, or holy war, and that economic development was a form of *jihad*. Although public opinion forced the government to moderate its position, the incident showed just how far the president was prepared to go in trying to create a secularist, pro-Western regime through his own charisma. He was, for example, the first Arab statesman to call for peace with Israel in the mid-1960s, a time when such a statement was unthinkable for any Arab statesman who wished to remain in power.

It also underlines the peculiarly personal nature of Bourguiba's rule in Tunisia. As a result, his period of office, which lasted until he was deposed (although in theory he was president-for-life) in November 1987, was marked both by his personal capriciousness and his skill in weathering political crises. Furthermore, the crises were also peculiarly personal in nature, for they have reflected popular and party perception of the role that Habib Bourguiba played in government. Each has involved potential rivalry from a ministerial colleague.

The first crisis, in fact, even pre-dated the full achievement of independence. The autonomy agreements negotiated by Bourguiba allowed Paris to control foreign affairs and security matters, as well as leaving French civil servants in key positions. Both the Neo-Destour secretary-general, Salih Ben Youssef, and the head of the UGTT, the powerful trade union organisation, Ahmed Ben Salih, objected to the agreement. Ben Salih eventually acquiesced, but Ben Youssef denounced it and was expelled from the party. He fled abroad and tried to organise armed resistance from Cairo. In 1961, he was assassinated in Frankfurt.

Ben Salih, however, was rewarded by being given the planning portfolio in the new government in 1961, just after France had agreed to abandon its last military base in Tunisia at Bizerta. The Bizerta crisis had developed as a result of French bombing of a Tunisian border village, Saqiat Sidi Youssef, because of Tunisian support for the Algerian independence struggle. Armed incidents between French military and Tunisian volunteers outside the Bizerta base eventually led to an agreement for a French evacuation by 1963. At the same time, French capital in Tunisia began to be withdrawn and, in 1964, Tunisia retaliated by nationalising all French-held land there.

The crisis forced a radical approach to Tunisia's economic problems. The Bourguiba administration wanted to counter the loss of French investment by encouraging popular participation in industry and agriculture through the creation of co-operatives. These were also expected to enhance output and improve efficiency, and Ben Salih was put in charge of the co-operative experiment. Fishing, crafts and construction co-operatives were set up in 1960, agricultural co-operatives in 1962 and expanded onto former French and now state land in 1965. By 1968, however, it was clear that popular resistance had caused the experiment to fail; despite massive state investment, output was stationary and there were widespread anti-government demonstrations. By September 1969 Bourguiba had accepted that the experiment was a failure; when Ben Salih protested, he was removed from his post, and, later, arrested.

Tunisia now radically altered its economic course and, under Hedi Nouira as premier, introduced liberal policies. Political control, however,

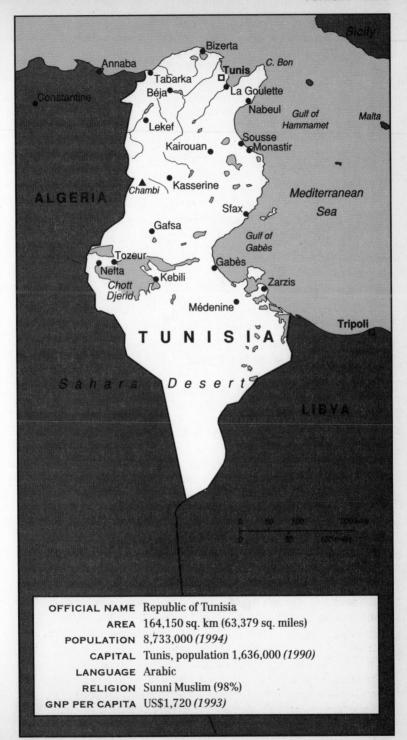

OFFICIAL NAME	Republic of Tunisia
AREA	164,150 sq. km (63,379 sq. miles)
POPULATION	8,733,000 *(1994)*
CAPITAL	Tunis, population 1,636,000 *(1990)*
LANGUAGE	Arabic
RELIGION	Sunni Muslim (98%)
GNP PER CAPITA	US$1,720 *(1993)*

remained firmly in the president's hands. The next decade was marked by two significant developments; heightened tension with the new radical Qadhafi regime in Libya and the growth of Islamic fundamentalism in Tunisia itself in response to growing urban poverty, particularly in the south, and to the DSP's domination of the political scene.

The crisis with Libya revolved around Colonel Qadhafi's anxiety for political unity with neighbouring states. Although Bourguiba rejected such advances in 1971, in 1974, in a surprise move, he signed a unity agreement with Libya. The president's decision had been strongly influenced by Tunisia's Arab nationalist foreign minister, Mohammed Masmoudi. Once news of the decision reached the premier, however, it was swiftly overturned. The union treaty was, as a result, still-born, much to the Libyan leader's irritation. Tensions between Tunisia and Libya intensified, and Libya began to support Tunisian dissidents.

Among those dissidents were young Tunisian fundamentalists who sought the violent overthrow of the Bourguiba regime. Moderate forms of Islamic fundamentalism had appeared in Tunisia in the early 1970s, as economic disparities increased as a result of Hedi Nouira's liberal policies. Foreign investment, particularly from Germany, sought to exploit cheap Tunisian labour, while the 1973 explosion in oil prices caused rapid inflation. Agriculture continued to stagnate and Tunisian labour sought opportunities for employment abroad – not in Europe, where the barriers had already begun to descend, but in the Middle East, particularly in Libya. In Tunisia itself, demonstrations began in January 1978 and were violently suppressed, a process that began to estrange labour leaders from the Bourguiba regime.

Quite apart from the looming economic crisis, the Arab defeat in the Six Day War in 1967 by Israel had both discredited Arab nationalism and had estranged many from the West, now apparently committed to Israel's preservation as a Western strategic bastion. Islamic fundamentalism appeared the obvious alternative. These two developments came to a head in January 1980, with an abortive Islamic rebellion in the southern town of Gafsa. In the middle of the crisis, the Tunisian government was suddenly incapacitated when the prime minister suffered a disabling stroke.

A new political moderate was appointed as premier, Mohammed Mzali, a former school teacher who had made a name for himself as an ideologue of Bourguibism. However, the president's growing interference rendered Mzali virtually impotent. In November 1981, the regime's intention of holding on to power was made clear in the legislative elections in which officially tolerated opposition parties failed to win a single seat, largely because of electoral irregularities.

The 1981 elections marked the beginning of a slow dissolution of the Bourguiba regime. It had already forfeited labour support after the January 1978 riots. Now a prolonged confrontation between the UGTT and the government began, which, in 1985, resulted in a lengthy prison sentence for the veteran labour leader, Habib Achour, on trumped-up charges, and his replacement at the head of the UGTT by a DSP party hack. Economic policy provided the next arena for discord, when the respected planning minister, Mohammed Moalla, and the finance minister, Abdelaziz Lazram, resigned in a row over proposed consumer subsidy cuts. Basic food prices rose at the start of 1984 when all subsidies on flour and bread were removed – to the accompaniment of countrywide riots.

Although the president annulled the price rises, his premier's authority was virtually destroyed by the crisis. Mzali's remaining credibility was undermined by an attempt to blame the minister of interior, Driss Guiga, for the riots. Although the hapless minister fled abroad, Mzali had, by his action, managed to offend the president's powerful wife, Wassila Bourguiba, who had been patron of both of them. The consequent crisis forced the president to take control of the government and to replace the cabinet by a cabal around the president as the major executive arm of government. Within two years, Mzali himself had fled abroad.

The latter period of Mzali's period of office had seen a new crisis with Libya, when 30,000 Tunisian migrant workers were suddenly expelled in August 1985, and political tensions rose. In large measure this was because of Libya's disappointment at being excluded from a new 20-year treaty of fraternity and concord signed between Tunis and Algiers in March 1983. Tunisia had continued to play a moderating role in Arab affairs. In 1980, it became the home for the Arab League after the pan-Arab organisation had moved from Cairo in the wake of Egypt's peace treaty with Israel. In 1982, Tunisia also agreed to accept the PLO leadership after its expulsion from Lebanon but, in October 1985, Tunisia suddenly found itself the victim of an Israeli bombing raid against the Palestinian organisation, an experience repeated in 1988 when an Israeli commando assassinated a leading PLO official in Tunis.

Bourguiba himself began to behave increasingly irrationally. Rapid changes in government personnel were accompanied by the sudden disgrace of his wife. He also clearly felt that Tunisia's growing fundamentalist movement – itself a consequence of his government's economic failure – was a major threat to stability. As result, government actions against the major Islamist movement, the *Mouvement de Tendence Islamique* (MTI), were intensified and its leaders were either arrested or fled abroad.

By now, however, other members of the government had come to the conclusion that it was the president himself who was the major threat to stability. Under the leadership of Premier Ben Ali, Bourguiba was deposed on 7 November 1987 on the grounds that he was incapable of discharging his official functions and the prime minister stepped into his shoes. The changeover in government came in the midst of a major economic crisis, as Tunisia, in return for International Monetary Fund (IMF) support, finally began to remove consumer subsidies and to restructure its economy.

The new president sought a new political consensus. He liberalised the political system, tried to persuade political leaders to rally around a national political charter and held general elections in 1989. He was unable, however, to accept that the fundamentalist movement should be allowed to join the formal political arena, even though it reorganised itself as the *Nahda* party, in accordance with regulations that forbade political parties to adopt religious platforms. The exclusion of the *Nahda* party from the elections led to an increase in Islamist opposition and agitation against the government, culminating in December 1989, after the departure of party leader Rashid Ghannouchi into voluntary exile the previous April, in violent clashes between police and demonstrators. Similar tensions erupted once again over the municipal elections held in June 1990 which were boycotted by the opposition parties including the *Nahda*. In October 1990, Amnesty International reported that human rights abuses continued as a result of a growing official campaign against Islamist activists and, a year later, claimed that over 8,000 persons were, effectively, political prisoners. Over the next six months this campaign continued, culminating in the execution of three militants in October 1991. Although foreign observers continued to criticise Tunisia's human rights record, the government denied their claims and, furthermore, argued that the back of the Islamist movement had been broken.

The anti-Islamist campaign ran alongside the international effort to force Iraq to abandon annexation of Kuwait in August 1990. During this crisis, Tunisia temporarily abandoned its traditional pro-Western diplomatic approach when the president initially denounced Western hostility towards Iraq and refused to join Saudi and Egyptian support for Western policy. Although Tunisia was formally neutral, Gulf retribution was swift to make itself felt. Kuwait, which had been a heavy investor, cut all links and the Gulf states did not restore normal relations with Tunis for two years.

The official Tunisian position was, in part, predicated on public hostility towards Kuwait, as elsewhere in North Africa. As evidence mounted of Western intentions to punish Iraq, Tunisian popular anger was increasingly directed against the West. In consequence, tourism collapsed in late 1990 and throughout 1991, and foreign aid was cut back. The Tunisian government, however, had to authorise demonstrations by the opposition parties to defuse popular tensions but re-asserted its political control once the crisis was over. Nonetheless, it was clear that some form of multi-party system would have to be introduced and preparations to this end went ahead in 1993.

By March 1992, Tunisia was again ready again for legislative elections, this time under a new electoral law guaranteeing parliamentary access for opposition parties. Although the *Nahda* party was excluded from the electoral process, the other parties participated, winning only 2.27 per cent of the vote but, nevertheless, obtaining their first taste of parliamentary power. The Tunisian authorities, once the elections and simultaneous presidential elections – which President Ben Ali, who was the only candidate, won outright – were over, reverted to their usual authoritarian stance, rejecting applications for new political party registrations and imprisoning leading human rights activists for criticising the government.

There was no doubt, however, that by 1994, the Tunisian political and domestic scene was marked by an apparent calm. In part this was a result of authoritarian official attitudes, but it was also a consequence of the progress made by the Tunisian economy. Gross domestic product (GDP) growth continued to vary between eight per cent (1992) and five per cent (1994) despite continued difficulties in the agricultural sector as the result of prolonged drought. Direct private foreign investment also continued to arrive, as Tunisia began a privatisation programme designed to reduce significantly the public sector's control of 40 per cent of the economy. The oil sector showed renewed vitality, thus postponing the day when Tunisia would become a net oil importer. This economic revival culminated, in 1995, in Tunisia being the first south Mediterranean state to sign a new partnership agreement with the EU designed to usher in the Union's new Global Euro-Mediterranean Partnership policy.

As Tunisia moved into the last five years leading up to the millennium, the Ben Ali regime could congratulate itself on achieving a significant economic recovery and placing Tunisia in the forefront of south Mediterranean states in their new relationship with Europe. As far as foreign affairs were concerned, the damage done by the war against Iraq seemed to have been repaired and the country enjoyed the support of Algeria and Egypt and even, to some extent, of Libya for its anti-Islamist policies. On the domestic front, however, there were growing anxieties that repression could not be maintained indefinitely and that the authorities would eventually have to come to terms with political plurality that also provided space for Tunisia's Islamists. It remains to be seen if the Ben Ali regime has sufficient imagination to achieve this without social and political unrest and discord.

ALGERIA

The signing of the Evian Accords on 18 March 1962 marked the end of the Algerian war of independence but not the beginning of a smooth transition to independence. Not only did the European *colon* population virtually disappear over the next six months, while a vicious secret war was fought out in Algeria and France by the OAS, but the FLN itself was in disarray. Nonetheless, an economic programme was drawn up in May 1962 during FLN discussions in Tripoli. The Tripoli Charter, as it was called, proposed a socialist economic future for independent Algeria and attacked the wartime provisional government for 'feudalism' a clear reference to the moderate policies of its leader, Ferhat Abbas.

The political problems of the FLN were more severe, however, for its membership fell into four distinct factions, which now lined up to contest the leadership of the victorious movement. In addition to the moderate provisional government, there were the *vilayet* guerrilla groups inside Algeria, which had borne the brunt of the war against the French army and felt, thereby, that they were the legitimate FLN leadership, and the leadership of the *Armée de Liberation Nationale* (ALN), a military force created in Morocco and Tunisia which had not participated in the military struggle because of the French army's successful border campaign to keep it out. Its leadership under Houari Boumedienne now represented a formidable military force. Finally, there was a group of five of the nine *chefs historiques*, the nine original organisers of the FLN. They had been imprisoned in France early in the war but were released to participate in the negotiations over independence.

In the aftermath of the Evian Accords, battle over the leadership was joined. Ben Bella, leader of the *chefs historiques*, obtained the support of Houari Boumedienne and the ALN. The new allies turned, first, against the *vilayet* leaders, whose forces were crushed by the ALN. Then Ben Bella dealt with the provisional government; Ferhat Abbas was forced out of office but Mohammed Khider, the FLN's secretary-general, had an independent power-base. He eventually resigned his post in April 1963 while Ahmed Ben Bella became president of the newly independent state.

Finally, the new Ben Bella–Boumedienne coalition turned on the dissident *chefs historiques*, led by Hoceine Ait Ahmed, Krim Belkacem, Mohammed Boudiaf and Mohand ou el-Hadj. Under the leadership of Ait Ahmed, a native of the Berber stronghold of Kabylia, a rebellion against the central government was organised in 1963. By 1964, however, resistance had been eradicated and the dissident leaders had either been arrested or had fled abroad. A separate rebellion in the Sahara under Colonel Chaabani was also suppressed.

Ahmed Ben Bella was not to enjoy presidential power for long, however, for he was overthrown by an army coup on 19 June 1965 and replaced by his former ally, Houari Boumedienne. One major reason for the coup was the apparent chaos and economic disarray of his period in office. The other was that army leaders suspected that Ben Bella was about to move against them to cut the army's political power. In fact, the chaos in Algerian affairs under Ben Bella merely reflected the condition the country had been left in after eight years of war and the subsequent departure of virtually all its technocratic elite.

One short-term response was workers' self-management. The workforce of the enterprises in agriculture and industry abandoned by their French managers and owners took over control of operations. The movement was initially spontaneous, but the government soon saw its utility and began to take it over. Central control was slowly imposed both to rationalise economic activity and to crush a dangerously anarchic development in the revolution. The price paid, however, was a halt in growth.

Ben Bella's move against the army began when, in late 1964, Mohammed Medeghri, the army-backed minister of the interior, was stripped of his powers over provincial administration. The government

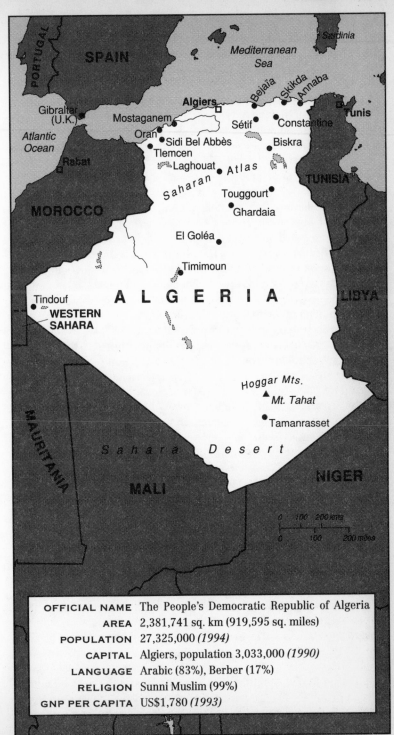

OFFICIAL NAME	The People's Democratic Republic of Algeria
AREA	2,381,741 sq. km (919,595 sq. miles)
POPULATION	27,325,000 *(1994)*
CAPITAL	Algiers, population 3,033,000 *(1990)*
LANGUAGE	Arabic (83%), Berber (17%)
RELIGION	Sunni Muslim (99%)
GNP PER CAPITA	US$1,780 *(1993)*

then began to seek support from the trade union movement and from the clandestine Algerian communist party (PAGS, or *Parti de l'Avant-Garde Socialiste*), which, although formally banned, was well represented within the FLN. Other ministers backed by the army were then sacked or demoted. Inevitably, Boumedienne reacted by removing Ben Bella from power with support from the army and from the security services. Ahmed Ben Bella was confined to prison for the next 15 years.

Houari Boumedienne came to power on the promise of the restoration of order and of progress after the sacrifices of the war and the chaos of the Ben Bella period. The new regime soon made its priorities clear: domestic conformity and order, and national social and economic development. In return, Algerians were to obtain basic social services and education, while international respect was to be achieved from a neutralist foreign policy. Oil revenues were to pay for this and for a programme of industrialisation that would lay the foundations for Algeria's future prosperity. The state would direct development through state companies, which would develop the basic sectors of the economy, with heavy industry receiving priority.

The austere future proposed by the Boumedienne regime did little to improve its popularity initially. It was only after the Six Day War, in which the regime took an uncompromising pro-Arab stance, and after French oil interests in Algeria were nationalised in 1971, that a degree of popular support was achieved. The oil and gas nationalisation programme was, needless to say, extremely unpopular in France and clouded relations between the two countries until the latter half of the decade. Algeria justified the move, however, by claiming that it needed complete control of these resources to finance its development plans. Its actions anticipated similar decisions by the Organisation of Petroleum Exporting Countries (OPEC) in 1973 and ensured that Algeria captured all the benefits of the international energy price rises of 1973–74 and in 1979–80. Boumedienne also increased Algeria's international reputation by his speech to the UN in 1974, in which he called for a new economic relationship between the developed and the developing worlds.

The regime then moved to consolidate its support and to counter growing factionalism in political life. It sought to do this by providing greater democracy in the workplace, limited participation in government and improved access to land in agriculture. The last objective was to be achieved by an agrarian reform programme which began in 1971. Large landowners had their holdings restricted and land was distributed to the peasantry. The programme, however, turned out to be a failure, largely because of inadequate financing and a failure to reform distribution systems. The result was that urban drift continued unabated and that Algeria continued to import up to 65 per cent of its food.

The political reforms were intended to revive the FLN which, as a result of the factional struggles of the first decade of independence, had become moribund. They were also intended to create a hierarchy of representative assemblies, culminating in an elective National Assembly. Before this was instituted, however, a new political compact between government and populations had to be forged. This was done in 1976 by the promulgation of a National Charter, in which the principles for the next stage of national development were laid down. After extensive public debate, the document was approved by referendum, and National Assembly elections were subsequently held in February 1977.

Within a year, however, the Algerian president died from an unexpected illness and, since the constitutional changes envisaged by the National Charter debate were not fully implemented, the army again became the arbiter of Algeria's political future. Despite a challenge from within the FLN by the incumbent secretary-general, Mohammed Salah Yahyaoui, and from the liberal foreign minister, Abdelaziz Bouteflika, the army imposed its choice as successor, the commander of the Oran military region, Chadli Ben Jedid. His selection was confirmed by a national election in February 1979 and he was re-elected in January 1984 and in December 1988.

The new president confronted a complex set of problems. The Algerian economy was riven by inefficiency, particularly in the state sector, which accounted for 70 per cent of the economy. Despite the National Charter, the Algerian population was increasingly disaffected with the austere regimen still in force. New generations had come to maturity who were no longer prepared to delay the benefits of independence and who were not prepared to accept the strict Islamic and Arab cultural character that the regime had defined for Algeria.

The initial official response was to liberalise the economy, particularly in the agricultural sector. In April 1980, however, the government had to face a major crisis when rioting occurred in the Berber stronghold of Kabylia. This, sparked by a clumsy administrative decision to ban cultural events involving Berber languages, spread into a general attack on the regime's cultural and religious policies. The regime's policy of Arabisation – whereby French was to be reduced in favour of Arabic – came under attack because it excluded Algeria's indigenous languages, such as Berber and *darija* (Algerian dialectic Arabic). The official support of Islam was also attacked, as an aspect of the regime's attempt to enforce conformity and because of the implied official support for the growth of Islamic fundamentalism.

By 1984, the regime had to deal with a growing popular disaffection. Cautious political liberalisation – which did not touch the formal institutions of government, however – was partnered by a growing pragmatism in economic affairs. The 90-odd massive state sector companies were split into over 300 autonomous institutions and freed from direct state control. In 1985 the National Charter was revised and liberalised in a further attempt to win popular support.

In foreign affairs, the Chadli Ben Jedid regime tried to follow the example of its predecessor and sought to play a role as an international mediator. It did this successfully in 1981, when it helped end the

siege of the American Embassy in Tehran. It also sought, less successfully, to play a mediating role in the Gulf War. Algeria also improved
relations with the United States, after the president made the first official visit by an Algerian leader to Washington in May 1985.

In regional affairs, Algeria had to moderate its support for the
Polisario Front, engaged in war with Morocco for control of the
Western Sahara, seeking a solution through diplomatic means rather
than by armed conflict. In fact, Algeria's growing economic weakness
has imposed a self-denying ordinance on Algiers in this respect. At the
same time, the Chadli Ben Jedid regime attempted to improve its
regional role by signing a mutual support treaty with Tunisia in March
1983, which Mauritania joined in the following December. In the past
five years, however, Algeria's diplomatic freedom has been severely
hampered by its growing economic weakness.

As a result of declining oil prices after 1980, Algeria found increasing difficulty in maintaining its ambitious development plans. Even
though natural gas has played an increasingly important part in its
export revenues over the past decade, heavy investment in uneconomic
gas liquefaction technology, together with too sanguine a view of international gas prices, continued to hamper its ability to maximise revenues. The consequence of this was that, since the government was not
prepared to abandon its plans, nor to service its growing foreign debt,
which had risen from $14 billion in 1984 to $23 billion in 1989, domestic consumer imports were severely cut back.

In 1986, however, Saudi Arabia's decision to increase production,
and thereby to allow oil prices to fall, coupled with a rapid decline in
the dollar, produced an 80 per cent shortfall in Algeria's oil revenues –
equivalent to around half of its total export revenues. The Algerian government set its face against increasing its foreign debt and, instead,
compressed imports. Although its economic management seemed to be
successful, social tension was rising dangerously. In October 1988, a
wave of strikes exploded into a frenzy of countrywide riots and the
army had to be brought in to restore control.

Chadli Ben Jedid, shaken by the strength of popular feeling,
promised widespread political liberalisation (while also exploiting the
situation to remove his opponents within government). The major
benefactors of the riots, although they had not been involved in their
initial organisation, turned out to be Algeria's growing Islamic fundamentalist movement, the *Front Islamique de Salut* (FIS). Almost
overnight, Algeria was transformed into the most liberal of Arab states
and the original single political party, the FLN, lost its privileged status.
In addition to the fundamentalists, Berberist groups began to appear
and former political exiles returned to the country as constitutional
reforms guaranteed a multiparty system in future. Eventually over 40
political parties were recognised by government.

In June 1990, municipal elections were held under the new conditions. Most of the new parties abstained, on the grounds that insufficient

time had been provided to prepare for elections. The result was a sweeping victory for the FIS. The FLN was humiliatingly beaten into second place, retaining its hold only in the south and in rural regions. The way appeared to have been cleared for national elections in 1991, but the Hamrouche government, determined to prevent a FIS victory, tried to gerrymander constituency boundaries.

By spring 1991, the FIS had begun to protest, its leaders fearing government attempts to prevent a potential FIS victory in the planned national elections. The protests turned into a trial of strength. The Hamrouche government was forced from office, but the new Ghozali regime had FIS leaders Abbasi Madani and Ali Bel Hadj arrested in June. The army moved into the streets and the FIS was formally disbanded, although its leadership reformed in time for the legislative elections in December 1991.

In the first round of the electoral process, the FIS won 188 of 430 seats in the National Assembly. Fearing an overall FIS win and the threat of an Islamic Republic, the authorities cancelled the next round. Ben Jedid resigned and a five-man Council of State under Mohammed Boudiaf took over on 10 February 1992, when a state of emergency was declared. Thereafter the domestic situation continued to deteriorate, with up to 8,000 persons being held as militant Islamists in hastily constructed detention camps in the Sahara. The growing tensions culminated in the assassination of President Boudiaf in June 1992.

His death, in Annaba, brought to an end his attempt to create a popular consensus for a mass political movement outside both the FLN and the FIS. He had proposed the creation of an *Assemblé Patriotique* in the hope that this would permit a peaceful evolution of the crisis created by the January 1992 coup. Instead, the confrontation between the FIS, now forced underground after it was banned in March 1992, and the military-backed government worsened. Not only was the government implicated in the assassination in the public mind, but the outlawed Islamic movement began to organise armed resistance to the security forces.

Public opinion believed that the shadowy Algerian mafia together with the equally shadowy *hizb fransa* had collaborated to destroy Boudiaf because he was seen as a threat to their interests. The mafia was the term popularly given to the network of corrupt functionaries and military personnel who had reaped massive personal benefit from the former regime. There was little doubt that this had occurred and one former premier, Dr Abdulhamid Brahimi, claimed that as much as $26 billion had been embezzled from the state. The *hizb fransa* was the term given to the network of modernist francophone Algerian officials who sympathised with and supported French policy towards Algeria and were violently opposed to the Islamic movement. The official explanation was that he had been killed by the nascent Islamic opposition which had infiltrated his own bodyguard. One of the leading military members of the government, Larbi Belkhair, was forced to resign in consequence.

The High Council of State, charged with ensuring the continuity of political leadership, sought to focus popular support on the government by bringing back another venerable FLN activist, Belaid Abdessalam, as premier. The move worsened relations with France, already concerned because of the interruption of the electoral process in January 1992 despite its dislike for the Islamist FIS. Nor did it improve Algeria's economic performance or popular support for government. Despite the introduction of special military courts, violence throughout the country worsened.

By 1993, it was evident that government attempts at outright repression had failed but there was no willingness within army and security circles to consider the alternative of negotiation and compromise. In government, however, the group around the premier – *the conciliateurs* – realised that there was no other way forward. In August 1993, the last remaining senior figure of the FLN, Kasdi Merbah, who like his colleague Belaid Abdessalam knew that compromise with the FIS in the end would be inevitable, was assassinated. Belaid Abdessalam left power shortly afterwards, thus ending the old-guard attempt to resolve the crisis and leaving the field open to the modernists who rejected compromise, the *eradicateurs*.

During 1993, the clandestine resistance gradually evolved into two major groupings: the *Group Islamique Armé* (GIA) and the *Mouvement Islamique Armé* (MIA). The former, which was located in central northern Algeria, including the capital, Algiers, brought together the most extreme elements in the Islamic movement and was believed to be heavily infiltrated by Algerian military security. It engaged in a campaign of spectacular assassinations, targeting civil servants, security and military personnel, journalists and government officials. Many of these adversely affected the Islamist cause and, conversely, allowed the authorities to underline the violence and extremism involved. At the end of 1994, the GIA expanded its campaign outside Algeria, with a spectacular Christmas hijack of an Air France aircraft in Algiers which they apparently intended to destroy over the French capital, Paris. The hijackers were killed by special French forces during a stop-over in Marseilles. During the summer of 1995, a bombing campaign, attributed to the GIA, broke out in Paris and spread to other major cities in France – an indication of Algerian perceptions of French involvement in Algerian affairs.

The activities of the GIA, however, were of less significance to the authorities in Algiers than were those of the MIA, which extended its control over vast tracts of western and eastern Algeria. During 1995 the armed forces organised massive clearing operations in an attempt to recover control of the interior. Their success was difficult to judge since media access to regions outside the major towns was strictly controlled. What evidence there was suggested that the MIA and its successor, the *Armé du Salut Islamique* (AIS) had been successful in wresting control of considerable areas of rural Algeria from the government. Only in the south, in the all-important oil and gas field regions of the central Sahara, had Islamic activity been confined to a minimum.

This, no doubt, reflected the vital importance of Algeria's hydrocarbon sector. The political crisis had been accompanied by a worsening economic situation in which Algeria's massive foreign debt – around $26 billion in 1994 – forced the government into accepting formal debt rescheduling in 1993-94. At the same time, after a final burst of economic autarchy under Belaid Abdessalam, his successor premier, the modernist Redha Malek, accepted the need for an IMF-inspired reform programme and a severe devaluation of the Algerian currency in early 1994. During 1995, the economic crisis eased as the effects of debt rescheduling and currency depreciation began to take effect and foreign aid from France and multilateral organisations began to flow again. Much hope was placed in a new gas pipeline to Spain via Morocco, which was expected to radically improve foreign exchange earnings in 1996.

At the start of 1994, the constitutional situation required the appointment of a new president and, with the reluctant backing of the *eradicateurs*, the defence minister – a former army general, Lamine Zerouel – was selected. He made it clear that he would seek negotiations with the FIS, releasing some members of the imprisoned leadership and transferring the paramount leadership, Ali Bel Hadj and Abbassi Madani, to house arrest. It proved impossible, however, for the two sides to find common ground, not least because the extremists on both sides viewed the idea of compromise with great suspicion. The *eradicateurs* within the army hindered the president's initiatives and GIA sympathisers amongst the FIS undermined the leadership's search for a viable compromise.

At the same time, the other legal political parties in Algeria began to seek new opportunities for dialogue and, with the help of the Sant Egidio community in Rome, formulated a negotiating platform in January 1995. Although the FIS accepted their proposals, which received cautious backing from France, the Algerian government was unable to do so. It proposed instead presidential elections for the end of the year, an initiative which the FIS vowed to prevent. The result was that, by autumn 1995, both negotiations and repression were at a stalemate which seemed likely to endure, since neither side was strong enough to dominate the other, unless the necessary concessions were made.

MOROCCO

The advent of independence in Morocco was characterised by the fact that the ultimate victor had been given the sultanate. Because it had been supported as a symbol of national legitimacy by the nationalist movement, *Istiqlal*, it stood at independence as the sole guarantor of the victory that had been achieved. In addition to support from *Istiqlal*, the sultanate could also call on the loyalty of the traditionalist countryside and much of the population of Morocco's newly expanding cities.

Sultan Mohammed V (to become King Mohammed V in 1957 when dynastic succession was based on primogeniture) was determined, however, that there should be no competitors for power in the future and that *Istiqlal* – which believed that it, too, had a claim to power – should be reminded of its real place in the monarchical scheme of things.

In addition to its new-found legitimacy and potential monopoly of power, the monarchy had several other advantages, which stemmed directly from the changes made during the colonial period. Most importantly, it possessed a modern administration. It also possessed defined territorial boundaries. Since these excluded territory in Algeria that had been traditionally part of Morocco, as well as the Western Sahara that Morocco claimed as part of its pre-colonial territories, they could always serve as a rallying call when popular support was required. Indeed, in 1963, Morocco and Algeria fought a six-month border war over their common frontier and there is still a dispute over the Western Sahara. Although the Algerian–Moroccan border was delineated by treaty in 1972, the actual treaty was not ratified until 1989.

The monarchy also had considerable economic power at its disposal. Large sections of the Moroccan economy, as a result of French colonial administration, were in the hands of the state, including the crucial phosphate industry. The independent state would also be interventionist, despite the monarchy's preference for liberal economic theory. The problems it faced were too large for it to take any other course.

Demography was the greatest problem, then as now. The Moroccan population was exploding at 2.7 per cent annually, with the urban population growing even faster. From 15 per cent of the population in 1912, it had grown to be 35 per cent in 1956 and over 45 per cent 30 years later. New cities, such as Casablanca which had hardly existed in 1912, had been created. Casablanca itself, then the second largest city in Africa, was the new economic capital of Morocco and typified the way in which colonialism had reoriented the country's economy from integration inside the Maghrib towards Europe.

Immediately after independence, the monarchy chose to collaborate with *Istiqlal*. It was only biding its time, however, and, in 1959, Mohammed V seized on splits within the movement to end its hegemonic control over government. The radicals in *Istiqlal*, under Mehdi Ben Barka, broke away to form a new party, the *Union Nationale des Forces Populaires* (UNFP). The palace invited both parties to participate in government, but with the UNFP being given the major governmental posts. At the same time, its radical wing was disciplined by arrests. A year later, the UNFP-dominated government was dismissed.

The new government was dominated by the royal family, with Crown Prince Hasan the new premier. He had long been groomed for government and, in addition to sharing his father's exile in 1953, he had been educated in France, at the University of Bordeaux. At independence he had taken over Morocco's armed forces and had played a leading role in suppressing a rebellion in the Rif. He succeeded

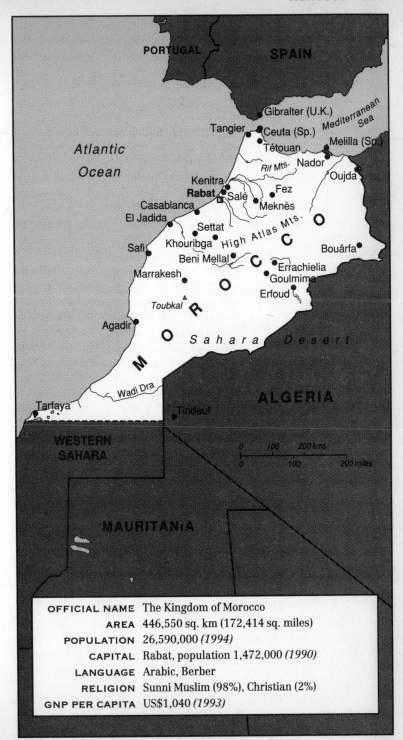

OFFICIAL NAME	The Kingdom of Morocco
AREA	446,550 sq. km (172,414 sq. miles)
POPULATION	26,590,000 *(1994)*
CAPITAL	Rabat, population 1,472,000 *(1990)*
LANGUAGE	Arabic, Berber
RELIGION	Sunni Muslim (98%), Christian (2%)
GNP PER CAPITA	US$1,040 *(1993)*

unexpectedly to government in 1961 when his father died during a minor operation.

King Hasan II made clear that he was anxious to introduce a limited democratic system under royal tutelage through a constitutional monarchy and a limited multiparty political system. The experiment was a failure, however. Parliamentary politicians exploited their positions for personal gain, and the extremist positions adopted by the political parties prevented parliament from carrying out its obligations under the constitution. In November 1963, the UNFP was accused of plotting against the monarchy with help from Algeria and its leaders, including Mehdi Ben Barka, were arrested or fled.

Palace attempts to form a government of national union were frustrated by the refusal of left-wing parties to co-operate and, when riots occurred in Rabat, Fez and Casablanca in March 1965, the king seized the opportunity to suspend the constitution and declare a state of emergency. Over the next five years, government was directly controlled by the palace, aided by a non-political cabinet of ministers. A new constitution was planned and elections were held under it in 1970. The new parliament was one with which the palace could work, for the centre-right parties and independents – in effect, supporters of the monarchy – marginalised the left. However, within ten months this constitutional experiment also collapsed.

The cause was a coup attempt, mounted from within the army, at the summer palace at Skhirat, just outside Rabat, on 10 July 1971, the king's birthday. It was partnered by a simultaneous army attempt to take over government centres in Rabat itself. The coup, which had been masterminded by General Medboh in response to growing evidence of widespread corruption in government, collapsed when the general himself was killed and Hasan was able to restore control over the army. Ten senior officers were executed for their involvement in the plot and many other soldiers were imprisoned (some have only recently been released, according to Amnesty International). The composition of the officer corps, which had been based on Berber groups, was also gradually changed, so that members of the Fasi urban elite, with a stronger tradition of loyalty to the palace, replaced them.

There were also claims that the UNFP had been involved, and party members were put on trial in Marrakesh. The new constitution was again suspended. A non-partisan government was brought in and a new constitution was drafted. Care was taken on this occasion to address the growing social and economic inequalities inside Moroccan society. Once again, however, the process was disrupted by another attempted coup. On 16 August 1972, King Hasan's personal aircraft was attacked by Moroccan air-force fighters. The attempt failed largely because the king persuaded the attacking aircraft by radio that he had been killed in the initial attack.

Once order had been restored, it was discovered that the defence minister and *éminence grise* of the regime, General Oufkir, had organised the attempt, in order, he claimed, to forestall a left-wing coup from within the army. According to official sources, he committed suicide; 11 other officers were later executed. Government sources also claimed that Libya had been involved. A violent war of words subsequently developed between the two countries.

In March 1973 there was new evidence of public disaffection with the Hasan regime. UNFP militants, trained, according to the Moroccan government, by a veteran Ba'thist opponent of the government, 'Fqih' Mohammed Basri, who had fled to Algeria in 1969, infiltrated Morocco and attempted to start a guerrilla campaign. Bombings in Oujda, Nador and Casablanca were followed by a small revolt at Tinehrir and Goulmima, in the southern High Atlas mountains. The government lost no time in decimating the UNFP by arrests; 13 people were condemned to death for involvement in the plot.

In the wake of the government's wave of repression, the UNFP split, with the new splinter group, led by Abderrahim Bouabid, taking the name *Union Socialiste des Forces Populaires* (USFP). It has since replaced its predecessor in popular support and the UNFP has dwindled into insignificance. Student protest now appeared and a clandestine pro-Marxist-Leninist opposition formed. Known as the *Front Progressiste* (FP), it brought together three left-wing groups: the March 23 Movement; *al-Alam*; and *al-Mutaqatilun*. Government repression soon dismantled the groups and leading intellectuals began to populate Morocco's prisons.

The trials of the FP coincided with a new development in Morocco's already complicated political scene. This was the government's decision, in 1974, to make the integration of the Western Sahara into Morocco a national priority. The government's claim to the Western Sahara, then still under Spanish control, was based on arguments that it had been part of the pre-colonial Moroccan state and thus could be recovered legally without a referendum over self-determination. Spain had been most reluctant to accept this, even though the Franco government had been under considerable pressure to abandon its last African colony.

In mid-1974, Spain announced that it was prepared to put the issue of decolonisation to a referendum in the Western Sahara, largely as a result of military pressure from the newly founded national liberation movement, the Polisario Front. Morocco, in turn, insisted that the matter be placed before the International Court of Justice at The Hague. The court's judgment, handed down in October 1975, satisfied no-one. It accepted that there had been links with Morocco in pre-colonial days, but decided that these did not amount to sovereignty. Morocco, nonetheless, occupied the region; Spain, by then gripped by the succession crisis as Franco lay dying, acquiesced under protest.

By early November 1975, Morocco was tied into a major military commitment, as the Polisario Front shepherded thousands of Western Saharans into refugee camps around the Algerian border town of Tindouf and then began a widespread guerrilla campaign, with

Algerian and Libyan support, to force Morocco out. Mauritania, which had occupied the southern part of the territory, was forced out in 1979, whereupon Morocco took over the former Mauritanian claim. Nonetheless, until 1980, Morocco was seriously disadvantaged by Polisario guerrilla activity. Thereafter, however, a new strategy of fixed defences enabled the Moroccan army, by then 180,000-strong, of which two-thirds were deployed in the Sahara, to re-assert control over 80 per cent of the territory.

Morocco has suffered in diplomatic and economic terms from the conflict. In 1982 it withdrew precipitately from the Organisation of African Unity, when that organisation recognised the Polisario Front as a national liberation movement. The Moroccan boycott lasted until 1986, when it finally accepted the principle of a referendum for self-determination in the disputed territory. At the same time, King Hasan knows that neither the Moroccan army nor the population of Morocco would tolerate any abandoning of the territory and it is therefore likely that a referendum will only be held when Morocco is certain of success.

The Western Saharan operation has also been an expensive undertaking, with the war costing an estimated $1 million a day. Much of the cost has, however, been borne by friendly Gulf states. Morocco has, nevertheless, had to spend heavily on arms, around $250 million annually. Considerable sums have also been expended on improving the infrastructure of the Sahara, an operation estimated in 1988 at $1 billion. There has also been significant migration into the region, which depends entirely on southern Morocco for essential supplies. Of the 170,000-strong population, up to 90,000 are believed to have come from Morocco itself. There are also around 170,000 refugees in the camps around Tindouf, although many of them are believed to come from other parts of the Sahara.

The Western Sahara issue did create a degree of consensus within Morocco in support for the monarchy, not least because the political parties were bought off by a promise of renewed democratic activity. Indeed, since 1976, there have been elections every six years and the Chamber of Representatives has been allowed a limited executive role. It cannot question basic economic policy, the role of the palace in government, or basic policy towards the Western Sahara issue. Yet, outside these limits and as a result of parallel measures to decentralise the administration, Morocco has enjoyed relative political calm.

The result has been that since the mid-1980s there have been no further attempts to overthrow Hasan. Morocco has still had to weather severe problems, however. Many of these are economic in origin, for, in 1975, Morocco attempted to exploit its quasi-monopoly over world phosphate exports to quadruple international phosphate prices. The enlarged revenues were to pay for ambitious development plans. Unfortunately, Florida phosphate producers increased output dramatically, forcing prices down to their previous levels. Since then, phosphate prices have been stagnant.

The Moroccan government, faced by the collapse of its export revenues, gambled. It did not cut its development plans but instead borrowed the required funds, on the assumption that, by the time the loans had to be repaid, improved output as a result of development would enable the additional revenue to be raised. By 1983, it was clear that the experiment had failed and Morocco was forced to reschedule its $11 billion-worth of foreign debt in September of that year. The Moroccan government then gambled again, agreeing to accept IMF and World Bank requirements for economic restructuring and reform: the removal of consumer price subsidies, export-oriented growth, trade regime liberalisation, and the reduction of public sector expenditure through privatisation.

Although Morocco's debt has continued to rise and is now around $22 billion, the economic restructuring is considered by international organisations to have been a success. The privatisation programme is in full swing and Morocco benefits from the provisions for debt relief in the Brady Plan. The reforms have not been without economic cost, how-ever. In January 1984, as consumer subsidies were cut, there were countrywide riots involving over one hundred deaths. The riots were not as intense as riots in Casablanca in June 1981 over economic hardship, which developed out of a political confrontation between two trade union organisations and led to over 630 deaths in a single after-noon. Nonetheless, they were a salutary warning to the government of the limits of popular tolerance; the subsidies were partly restored in consequence. Tensions still run high, however, and new rioting occurred in Fez in December 1990.

Despite these tensions Morocco has been spared the kind of intense Islamic fundamentalism which has characterised Tunisia and Algeria. In part, this is because the king himself, through his claim to direct descent from the Prophet Muhammad, monopolises the sphere of religious legitimacy. It is also the case, however, that the Moroccan government has been skilful at diffusing tension through effective security monitoring and use of the courts to stamp out religious protest. Nonetheless, there is a growing fundamentalist movement, partnered by a violent clandestine wing, which observers fear may become a serious problem. Serious human rights abuses have been curtailed.

In foreign affairs, Morocco has astutely ensured the support of the West throughout the 1980s. It has been prepared to provide facilities for United States strategic military planners concerned over rapid deployment facilities to the Gulf. Furthermore, King Hasan has been only the second Arab leader after the late President Sadat formally to meet Israeli leaders. In summer 1986, the then Israeli premier, Shimon Peres, visited Morocco and was received by King Hasan. Nothing came of the visit, because of Israeli reluctance to compromise over the Palestinian issue. Nonetheless, the king's willingness to break ranks caused considerable anxiety elsewhere in the Arab world.

Nowhere was that anxiety greater than in Libya, where Colonel

Qadhafi seized on the news of the king's initiative to attack Morocco for the first time in two years. His attack allowed King Hasan to break off a formal relationship with Libya which had become an embarrassment. In 1984, Morocco and Libya, in a riposte to the Algerian–Tunisian treaty of concord and fraternity signed the previous year, proclaimed their own African–Arab Union. The arrangement quickly served Morocco's purpose of detaching Libya from its support for the Polisario Front in the Western Sahara dispute and of demonstrating to Algeria that Morocco was still its most potent adversary in the Maghrib. The Libyan condemnation in 1986 provided the ideal opportunity to break off a relationship which had served its purpose.

The 1990s dawned with the Moroccan government offering all-out support to the United States in the latter's response to Iraq's invasion of Kuwait. This rapidly proved to be one of King Hasan's rare miscalculations, for popular sentiment was wholly opposed to government policy. The king rapidly recovered the initiative, taking a much more cautious line in support of the integrity of Saudi Araba but avoiding military involvement in the campaign against Iraq. At the same time, popular tensions were released by officially permitted demonstrations of support for Iraq, particularly after hostilities were over.

The monarchy realised in the wake of the conflict, however, that a more democratic form of government would now be necessary in Morocco. Phased constitutional change over the next four years reduced the palace's interventionist role in government and introduced a dual chamber parliamentary system. At the same time, many political stalwarts, such as the veteran minister of the interior, Driss Basri, saw their power curtailed as the king prepared for the transfer of governmental power to the opposition parties for the first time in many years. The Moroccan media were also given greater freedom of expression with the result that there was an explosion of new publications. These moves were in part designed to curb Morocco's growing fundamentalist movement; in part, to counter the chronic economic difficulties faced by most of the population. Despite the reforms, however, King Hasan remained firmly in charge of Morocco's political and economic future.

The Moroccan economy continued its innovative path within North Africa by initiating a major privatisation programme in 1992. Foreign debt began to decline to $21 billion in 1995 and foreign investment continued to increase. Problems still faced the country, however, not least a major drought in 1995, growing tensions with the EU over fishing rights on Morocco's shores and the adjustment terms for an agreement within the framework of the Global Euro-Mediterranean Partnership policy. Overall, however, Morocco's future seemed brighter than those of either of its two North African partners, particularly because the long-promised referendum in the Western Sahara was now due to be held in early 1996 and Morocco expected a positive result to confirm its annexation of the territory in 1975.

THE MAGHRIB TODAY

The aftermath of the war against Iraq has dramatically changed the current situation and the outlook in the Maghrib. The Maghrib Arab Union (UMA), which seemed to hold out so much hope for regional economic development and political harmony when it was formed in February 1989, is now moribund. Although Tunisia is still anxious to promote the idea of regional unity as a means of negotiating from strength with Europe and as a device for defusing the traditional tensions between Morocco and Algeria for regional hegemony, its partners are now more concerned over quite different issues.

Libya has abandoned its North African partners and has turned, instead, towards Egypt because of their failure to support it over the issue of UN sanctions because of the Lockerbie affair. Algeria is preoccupied with its internal difficulties and feels disadvantaged over the Western Saharan affair. Morocco, for its part, is more concerned about relations with Europe than with the regional scene. Thus, although negotiations continue over future regional structures, the UMA concept seems to be more and more irrelevant to the new geo-economic zone that Europe is creating in the southern Mediterranean.

Events in the Middle East, too, have altered North African priorities. With the advent of the Middle East peace process in October 1991 and the signature of the Oslo Accord in September 1993, Morocco and Tunisia were able to establish formal diplomatic relations with Israel. Libya, after an abortive attempt to curry American favour by sending pilgrims to Jerusalem, has relapsed into a sullen acceptance of the reality of the peace process. All North African states, Libya included, now seem to feel that their priority lies within the Mediterranean basin and in relations with Europe.

Strangely enough, Europe, too, has rediscovered its interests in North Africa, despite the anti-Western hostility universally manifest throughout the region in 1991. The major reason for this is European anxieties over the spread of fundamentalist violence across the Mediterranean, as has now occurred with France, and concomitant anxieties over migration, legal or illegal, into Europe. Given the levels of xenophobia now manifest in most European countries, all governments are anxious to prevent the anticipated flood of migrants from entering their frontiers. Yet Europe is not prepared to face the fact that, if it wishes to avoid this crisis, it must provide a more active response to the economic difficulties facing the Maghrib states. In part, the new Global Euro-Mediterranean Partnership initiative is an attempt to do this, but it is inadequate for the goals it has set itself. Europe has yet to face the real measure of what must be done in North Africa if a major economic crisis is to be avoided.

George Joffé

11
THE PALESTINIANS

THE QUESTION OF PALESTINE has haunted the Middle East for the entire 20th century, causing numerous wars, acts of terrorism, coups d'état, and widespread human misery and suffering. More than any other single issue, the problem of Palestine and the Palestinians has determined the political and social contours of the contemporary Levant. Indeed, its impact has been felt throughout the Middle East and the world, twice almost threatening global nuclear wars. The Palestinian question has helped produce a level of militarisation in the region unmatched in the world, with states preparing for war instead of development. In short, Palestine and the Palestinians have constituted a defining issue of this century, and may continue to do so into the next.

Ever since their dispossession in 1948, Palestinians have lived all over the Middle East and the world. Of the approximately five million Palestinians – there is no consensus on their exact number – three million live in historic Palestine: today's Israel, the West Bank and Gaza Strip. The other two million are widely dispersed, with large concentrations in Jordan, Lebanon and Syria. Before the 1990–91 Gulf war, Kuwait also had a substantial number of Palestinians, most of whom were technocrats, teachers and businessmen who had effectively built that country.

Palestinians evoke highly emotive and contradictory images. On the one hand, they are generally an educated and industrious people, responsible for a great deal of the economic and social development of the Middle East. Like many unwanted minorities before them, they have developed a strong commitment to education as a means of advancement when other avenues are shut. In fact, they are among the most highly educated national communities in the world. Conversely, Palestinians evoke images of terrorism for some, from the violence at Munich in 1972 to current Hamas attacks on civilians. It is fair to say, however, that they have been the victims of violence at least as often as they have perpetrated it, indeed probably more. They are a complex people with a tragic history, briefly sketched below.

PALESTINE IN THE LATE OTTOMAN PERIOD

Palestine did not exist as such under Ottoman rule, in the sense that there was no administrative or political unit whose borders matched those of what became Mandatory Palestine. This was not exceptional, since no contemporary state in the area can trace back its borders even to the 19th century. Like Israel, Jordan, Lebanon, Syria and Iraq, Palestine (and by extension Palestinian national identity) is a creation

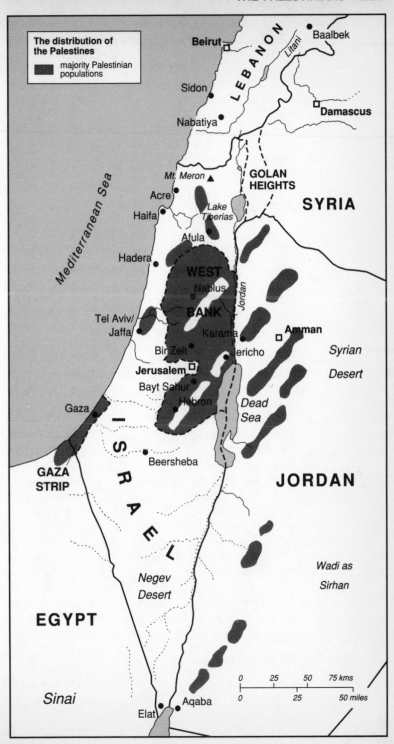

The distribution of the Palestines

■ majority Palestinian populations

of the 20th century. To speak of Palestine in the 19th century is a somewhat erroneous if convenient shorthand to refer to an area that even in
this early period was becoming increasingly central to world events.

The latter half of the 19th century marked a period of rapid change
in Palestine. Reforms undertaken by the Ottoman Empire since the
1840s had transformed Palestinian society, and exacerbated social
inequalities. Of particular consequence were changes in the collection
of taxes and in land tenure. In order to finance its modernisation drive,
Istanbul empowered prominent local families in Palestine (and
throughout the Levant) to collect provincial taxes for the empire. As
Istanbul was more interested in the amount of taxes transferred back
to the capital than the total collected or the means of collection, abuse
was rampant. At the same time, the Ottoman Empire legalised the possession of private property, making the creation of vast estates possible
for the first time in Ottoman history.

The most important consequence was the formation of a landed
urban elite in Palestine. Ottoman reforms transformed local dignitaries
into a powerful elite – the *ayan*, or notable class – which was to dominate Palestinian politics for a century. The gradual introduction of a
cash economy led to a further transfer of wealth upwards, as peasants
in Palestine were prone to indebtedness and, ultimately, the forfeiture
of their lands.

While the distribution of wealth in Palestinian society was increasingly unequal, the aggregate level of economic activity in Palestine grew
dramatically. The penetration of European capitalism in the area, in
conjunction with Ottoman reforms and local investment, led to a relatively high rate of overall economic activity in the country. Growth in
coastal cities such as Jaffa, Haifa and Acre was particularly pronounced.

In hindsight, the most important change was the new level of attention by Europe. It was during this period that Christians in western
Europe rediscovered the 'holy land' and European Jews invented
Zionism. Numerous Christian institutions – many with overlapping
religious and political significance – were established in Palestine.
Simultaneously, the advent of the Zionist movement, with its goal of
creating a Jewish state, led to the establishment of a small but important
Jewish immigrant community in Palestine. Zionist migration, in conjunction with growing anti-Turkish and anti-European feelings, sowed
the seeds for the earliest expressions of a Palestinian national identity.

At the beginning of the 20th century, Palestinian society was characterised by an increasingly fragmented social structure, a political
elite born of dubious Ottoman reforms, a peasantry partially alienated
from its land, capitalist transformation and growth, and the fear of a
powerful European competitor for its land.

PALESTINE UNDER THE BRITISH MANDATE

Even before the end of the First World War and the establishment of the
Mandate, Britain was intimately involved in Palestine. In particular, to

aid the war against the Ottomans, Britain made a series of conflicting promises to different groups concerning the future of Palestine.

To the Arabs, and specifically to Sharif Husayn of Mecca, Britain promised most of the Levant as an independent Arab kingdom, although for reasons mentioned above, the documents make no specific mention of Palestine. In exchange, Sharif Husayn promised to initiate a revolt against the Ottomans in order to force Istanbul to divert scarce resources to suppress it. The Arab revolt, made famous in the West through the writings of T.E. Lawrence (Lawrence of Arabia) began in June 1916 after several month's exchange of letters between the British High Commissioner in Egypt, Sir Henry McMahon, and Sharif Husayn. Later, when the provisions of the agreement were alleged to have been breached, some British officials argued that the Arab kingdom men tnioned in the McMahon/Husayn correspondence had not included Palestine, and that an exception had been made for those areas lying to the west of Damascus, Homs, Hama and Aleppo. A brief look at the map reveals the spurious nature of this argument, since no part of geographical Palestine is located west of these four cities.

At the same time as the negotiations with Sharif Husayn, Britain was negotiating with its three main allies, France, Italy and Russia, the postwar status of the Ottoman Empire in the event of an Allied victory. The Sykes-Picot Agreement of 1916 divided the Arab Middle East into British and French spheres of influence, with an international regime for 'Palestine and the Holy Places'. The Bolsheviks, after their seizure of power in Moscow in 1917, published the Sykes-Picot Agreement which was never repudiated. In the event, under the arrangements for international trusteeship vested in the newly created League of Nations, Britain gained the mandate for Iraq, Palestine and Transjordan, and France the mandate for Lebanon and Syria.

In addition to these conflicting promises, Britain announced the Balfour Declaration in November 1917, offering support for the 'establishment in Palestine of a national home for the Jewish people' (*see* Introduction, page 10). The mandate, formally established in 1922, contained within it the principle as set out in the Balfour Declaration, thereby virtually guaranteeing Palestinian-Arab rejection of its goals.

Palestinian society under the Mandate was marked by political fragmentation, rural discontent and urbanisation, and the growth of Palestinian nationalism in the face of Zionist colonisation and British colonial rule. The fragmentation was seen particularly in the intense rivalry between elite families. The major schism pitted the Husayni clan and their allies (known as the *majlisiyya*) against the Nashashibi clan and its allies (the *mu'arada*). The British worked initially with both sides, but in the early 1930s clearly sided with the Nashashibi clan against the more politically strident Husaynis, led by the Mufti of Jerusalem, Hajj Amin al-Husayni. The harm to Palestinian society caused by the factionalism of these notable families cannot be overestimated. The clans were in open competition with each other for virtually the entire period of

British rule; at times they engaged in barely concealed warfare. This rivalry undermined any chance of forging a united front to oppose effectively the increasingly large and powerful Zionist presence in Palestine.

In spite of British efforts to ease rural hardship, the Palestinian peasantry – by far the largest segment of society – continued to face dispossession, poverty and death. Many migrated from the countryside to search for jobs, swelling the size of Palestine's cities. Loss of land through debt and forfeiture, or through the sale of village lands by absentee landlords to Zionist concerns, combined with stagnant rural incomes to produce a high degree of rural discontent in Palestine. This anger was manifested in the 1935–39 revolt against the British and Zionist presence. While the revolt was ultimately put down with great loss of life (and with Nashashibi assistance), its ferocity compelled Britain to rethink the nature of its mandate in Palestine. The revolt, in addition to the coming war in Europe, led Britain essentially to renounce the Balfour declaration in the 1939 White Paper.

While most Palestinian opposition to Zionism and the British Mandate cannot properly be described as nationalism, this period did see the growth of a Palestinian national identity. As with all nationalisms, its first proponents were urban intellectuals, followed by some members of the urban middle and upper classes. Most elite opposition was not based on nationalism as such but rather the protection of threatened notable interests. Likewise, peasant political activism was based primarily on the tangible deterioration of rural life, not national identity.

The 1939 White Paper notwithstanding, British rule effectively empowered the Zionist presence in Palestine and hampered Palestinian state-building. This was not the intended result of British policy, which sought institutional partners from both communities. However, since the terms of partnership – the Mandate – included support for the implementation of the Balfour declaration, the British found willing partners among the Zionists, but not among the Palestinians.

In the early years of the Mandate, which coincided with the world economic slump of the 1920s, Jewish immigration appeared to have reached a natural peak. By 1926 about 100,000 immigrants had arrived in Palestine from Europe and by 1931 the Jewish population numbered 175,000, out of a total of just over one million (about 18 per cent). By 1939, however, the picture had changed dramatically – there were now some 429,000 Jews in Palestine, 27 per cent of a population of 1.6 million.

1948: DISASTER AND EXILE

The year 1948 contained the defining experience of the Palestinian people: the loss of Palestine and the mass expulsion of its people. The events surrounding the country's loss were so traumatic that Palestinians refer to them simply as *al-nakba* – the disaster.

In the aftermath of the Second World War, Britain made clear its inability to continue shouldering the burden of the Palestine Mandate, referring the issue to the newly established United Nations (UN) in 1947. The UN Special Committee on Palestine charged with recommending a solution to the Palestine question submitted two plans. The majority report recommended partitioning Palestine into separate Jewish and Arab (Palestinian) states, with Jerusalem maintaining an international status; the minority report recommended a federated state shared between Jews and Arabs. On 29 November, 1947, the UN voted to accept the majority report and partition Palestine into two independent states, with Jerusalem as a *corpus separatum*.

The partition resolution pleased no one. The Palestinians rejected it outright, primarily because they believed that the UN did not have the moral right to surrender any portion of Palestine to the Zionists. A second Palestinian objection was more pragmatic: the Jewish community constituted one-third of the total population in Palestine and owned about eight per cent of the land, yet would receive over half of the land under the partition scheme and an even greater percentage of the cultivable area. The projected Palestinian state would have only a minuscule Jewish minority while the envisioned Jewish state would barely have a Jewish majority, effectively disenfranchising large segments of Palestinian society.

The Zionist community was likewise displeased with the outcome. While the Zionist leaders publicly accepted the partition resolution, they were, in fact, actively seeking to undermine it. As recent historical research has shown, the Zionist leadership was then in collusion with King Abdullah of Transjordan – with the knowledge of Britain – to partition between themselves the land allocated for the Palestinian state. Neither Transjordan (soon to be Jordan) nor the Yishuv (soon to be Israel) favoured the establishment of an independent Palestinian state. Thus, David Ben Gurion publicly accepted the UN partition resolution and actively worked for its non-implementation, while King Abdullah publicly condemned the creation of Israel and vigorously assisted in its founding.

Fierce fighting immediately followed the passage of the partition resolution. For all the changes that had occurred in the preceding decades, Palestinian society was still primarily a traditional, peasant society and was no match for transplanted Europeans familiar with modern weaponry, strategy and systems of command and control. The Palestinians were easily routed by the Zionists, as were the ill-trained and ill-equipped, if numerically far superior, Arab forces which attacked in May 1948 following the termination of the Mandate and the unilateral proclamation of the state of Israel. The only Arab army capable of confronting Israeli power, Transjordan's Arab Legion, avoided clashes altogether with Israel's army, the Haganah, as required by the secret agreement between the two parties. Only in Jerusalem – where there was no agreement – did the Arab Legion inflict serious casualties on the Zionist side. Almost everywhere else, Zionist forces had their way with whatever combination of Arab forces they encountered.

Not only were the Palestinians thoroughly defeated in the 1948 war, but hundreds of thousands of Palestinian civilians found themselves in exile as a result. As the Zionist forces advanced, they usually expelled those Palestinian civilians who had not fled at their approach. After the fighting had ceased, the Palestinians were not permitted to return to their homes and were expressly prevented from doing so by subsequent Israeli legislation. As a result of the expulsions, approximately 700,000 Palestinians were made refugees. Most ended up in Lebanon, Syria, Jordan, the Egyptian-controlled Gaza Strip or the Jordanian-controlled (and eventually annexed) West Bank. Only 20 per cent of Palestine remained outside Israeli control, and none was under the sovereign power of Palestinian authority.

The problems stemming from the diaspora created in 1948 (and exacerbated in 1967) remain burning issues today. Palestinians constitute a majority of Jordan's population, and significant minorities are found in Lebanon and Syria. The West Bank and (especially) Gaza are populated in large measure by Palestinians exiled in 1948. In spite of numerous calls for their repatriation, including UN Security Council Resolution 194 of December 1948, the Palestinians expelled in 1948 were never permitted to return to their homes, nor were they ever compensated for their losses. Such is the origin of the Palestinian's bitterness, their demands for justice and their later acts of political violence.

The events of 1948 so traumatised and ruptured Palestinian society that it was incapable of launching a serious response for two decades. To be sure, there were some feeble political and military actions during this period, such as the short-lived All Palestine Government, based in Gaza, or sporadic small-scale raids across Israel's new borders. Even the creation of the Palestine Liberation Organisation (PLO) in 1964 was a half-hearted effort led by Egypt's Gamal Abdel Nasser, designed more to control Palestinian resistance than to promote it.

Palestinian political quiescence was also desired by the states in which Palestinians lived. As far as they could, the Arab states surrounding Israel strictly controlled Palestinian incursions into Israel, either forbidding them altogether or, on occasion, allowing such incursions only for their own political purposes. Jordan, which acquired the bulk of the Palestinian refugees, granted citizenship rights to the Palestinians when it annexed the West Bank in 1950. However, the Hashemites demanded that no separate nationalist activity occur in Jordan – that Palestinians leave any opposition to Israel to the Arab states. The same applied in Gaza under Egyptian control, as well as to Lebanon's and Syria's Palestinian populations, although these states did not grant citizenship rights to Palestinians. Even in Israel, where a significant Palestinian minority remained, there was little Palestinian nationalist activity for decades, probably because the Arab community in Israel lived under martial law until 1966.

The years between 1948 and 1967 were marked by a lack of significant Palestinian political activism. In addition to the social rupture caused by the 1948 war and life under authoritarian rule, there is a third explanation for this relative political quiescence. The states in which the Palestinians lived used the political strategy of supporting the notable elites as intermediaries to the larger Palestinian population. Jordan, Israel and Egypt, in particular, funnelled resources to the Palestinian population through this old Ottoman elite, thereby creating dependence on it for all kinds of day-to-day living requirements. In turn, the notables understood that they would maintain their privileged position only in so far as they could ensure the political quiescence of their communities. The co-optation of the notable elite was a remarkably successful policy, pursued by states of different political persuasions.

THE 1967 WAR AND AFTER: THE DIASPORA RESPONSE

Israel's conquest of the remainder of Palestine (and more) in the 1967 war changed political calculations in the Middle East in a number of ways. For the Palestinians, the most important consequence was the reunification of all of Palestine, albeit under Israeli domination. While the 1967 war swelled the number of Palestinian refugees living in surrounding Arab countries, for the first time since 1948 most Palestinians lived in one polity in their historic homeland as the West Bank and the Gaza Strip came under Israeli occupation.

The immediate results of the war were the discrediting of existing Arab states and the radicalisation of the emerging Palestinian national movement. The three years following the 1967 defeat represented the heyday of Palestinian radicalism and revolutionary rhetoric. Palestinian guerrillas (fedayeen) had virtual political and military carte blanche in Jordan to conduct the revolution against Zionism and Arab reactionary regimes. While most of this was bluster, occasional limited successes against Israeli forces, such as the battle of Karama, gave sustenance to the revolution. At the same time, guerrilla factions, led by Yasser Arafat's Fatah, took over the PLO, transforming it into a meaningful national liberation organisation. This period also marked the apex of Palestinian terrorism, undertaken in particular by Wadi Haddad and the Marxist Popular Front for the Liberation of Palestine (PFLP).

In fact, it was an infamous multiple hijacking of international jumbo jets in the autumn of 1970 which precipitated the next defeat in Palestinian history. The jets were commandeered to a seldom-used airstrip in Jordan, where they were blown up, to the great embarrassment of King Husayn of Jordan. This humiliation was the last straw in the growing resentment by the Jordanian regime of the challenge posed to its sovereignty by the virtual state-within-a-state that the PLO had created in Jordan. In response, the king unleashed his bedouin army troops to smash the PLO infrastructure in the refugee camps and elsewhere. The civil war in Jordan between Palestinians and East Bankers was a one-sided affair, leading to the expulsion of the fedayeen to Lebanon. Resulting in tens of thousands of casualties, Black September (as it came to be called) was a turning point in Palestinian history because it showed unambiguously that – in spite of the rhetoric of solidarity and mutual struggle – Arab states were more than ready to act in their own interests, even to the point of massacring large numbers of

Palestinians. Black September also led to further acts of terrorism as the Palestinians grew even more desperate.

Palestinian radicalism of the late 1960s and early 1970s was tamed by the mid-1970s for two reasons. First, the dramatic discrediting of Arab states after their disastrous showing in the 1967 war was mitigated by the performance of Egypt and Syria in the 1973 war. More important, the rise to prominence of the conservative Gulf states shifted the balance of power away from radicalism. Some believed that God had rewarded the conservative Islamic states – not the self-proclaimed revolutionary republics – with oil. More tangibly, the tremendous resources at the disposal of Saudi Arabia and others gave those countries vastly enhanced power to shape the political and cultural contours of the Middle East. In the end, Saudi oil was able to buy off political radicalism – at least of the secular variety.

The retreat of Palestinian radicalism was seen in a series of decisions made by the PLO and Arab League during this period, in particular the 1974 PLO decision to establish a 'Palestinian national authority in any area liberated from Israeli control'. This was the intellectual origin of the PLO's formal adoption in 1988 of a two-state solution to the question of Palestine, with its concomitant implicit recognition of Israel. It would also provide the internal justification for the post-Oslo establishment of the Palestinian National Authority in the Gaza Strip and Jericho in 1994. The move away from radicalism in favour of a more typical nationalist movement was capped by Yasser Arafat's invitation to address the UN General Assembly in 1974.

After its expulsion from Jordan, the PLO established its headquarters in Lebanon, in part because the weakness of the Lebanese state assured the PLO a great measure of autonomy. While the PLO's presence in Lebanon was not the sole cause of that country's civil war which began in 1975, it did help to inflame a volatile situation. In spite – or because of – the civil war in Lebanon, the PLO was able to establish a virtual Palestinian mini-state, particularly in southern Lebanon. In addition to its sporadic military clashes with Israel, the PLO ran schools, paved roads and administered a variety of social services: in short acting as a proto-state during the decade it remained in Lebanon. While the PLO had little choice as to where it could go, its presence in Lebanon – as with the large Palestinian refugee population there – engendered resentment from some Lebanese, including the large Shi'i population in southern Lebanon.

THE 1967 WAR AND AFTER: PALESTINIANS IN THE WEST BANK AND GAZA STRIP

The course of Palestinian events inside the occupied West Bank and Gaza Strip after 1967 differed markedly from that in the Palestinian diaspora. While the diaspora was engaging in radical politics, civil war and displacement, the Palestinians in the occupied territories went through a period of relative political quiescence and even experienced a degree of economic growth. Then, as the PLO gradually moved toward accommodation with its Arab hosts and mainstream nationalism, the 'inside'

Palestinians increasingly radicalised and mobilised. In particular, three developments little commented upon at the time helped transform Palestinian society, and pave the way ultimately for the Palestinian uprising: the opening of Israeli labour markets to Palestinians; the massive confiscation of Palestinian lands by the Israeli government; and the establishment and expansion of the Palestinian university system.

In the wake of its conquest of the West Bank and Gaza Strip in 1967, Israel opened its domestic labour market to Palestinians from the Occupied Territories. The often unskilled or semi-skilled jobs that Israelis refused to do themselves – principally in the agricultural and construction sectors – Palestinians were recruited to do. This pool of cheap labour was a boon to Israeli businesses, which grew rapidly in the late 1960s and early 1970s. For their part, these jobs appealed to Palestinians both because they paid relatively well in comparison to jobs in the Occupied Territories, and because there was an endemic shortage of local jobs, so any available work was desirable. The Palestinians employed in Israel tended to come from the lower classes, primarily the peasantry and refugee camp dwellers. They came in large numbers: within a few years of the opening of Israel's labour market, one-third of the Palestinian labour force in the West Bank and Gaza Strip was employed in Israel. By the 1980s, over 120,000 Palestinians – fully 40 per cent of the Palestinian labor force – worked in Israel.

The result of this massive shift of labour was the virtual disappearance of the Palestinian peasantry and appearance of a large working class. This upheaval destroyed many patron-client networks, especially in the West Bank, seriously undermining one of the pillars of social power for the Palestinian notable elite in the Occupied Territories. Like working classes everywhere, Palestinian labourers were less likely to be bound to traditional forms of activity, and more likely to be mobilised politically. In fact, this pool of recruits proved crucial in the general political mobilisation campaign of the 1980s and the subsequent Intifada.

A second change which helped transform Palestinian society in the West Bank and Gaza was the massive confiscation of land by the Israeli military government. The first act of confiscation came in the immediate wake of 1967 when Israel tripled the size of the municipal boundaries of East Jerusalem and then annexed it. Large areas within the new boundaries of East Jerusalem were unilaterally declared state lands and taken by Israel, often for use as Jewish settlements. Other land in East Jerusalem was confiscated on security grounds, while other parcels were awarded to Israelis who had claims dating from before 1948. In addition, those lands not confiscated in one manner or another were in essence frozen, so that any natural expansion of Palestinian neighbourhoods in the new East Jerusalem was virtually impossible.

Confiscation of land in the West Bank and Gaza Strip was even more extensive. The most common forms of confiscation were to declare parcels of land as state land or needed for security reasons, although outright confiscation of recognised private property also occurred. More often than not, Jewish settlements would then be built on the land seized. While large tracts of land in the West Bank and Gaza were confiscated in the first decade of military occupation, the confiscations were accelerated and were often deliberately provocative after the conservative Likud party came to power in Israel in 1977. In all, on the eve of the Palestinian uprising in 1987, over half the West Bank and one-third of the Gaza Strip had been confiscated or otherwise made off-limits to Palestinians.

In addition to antagonising the Palestinians, such confiscations directly attacked a second pillar of notable power – control over land – further undermining this elite's legitimacy in the eyes of most Palestinians. They were shown to be powerless to stop or even slow down Israel's seizure of their lands. Land confiscations also made the land-owning elite less willing to co-operate with Israel.

The third change which gradually transformed Palestinian society in the West Bank and Gaza was the creation and expansion of a Palestinian university system. Prior to 1972, higher education was a privilege reserved for the elite, as only those families could afford to send their children to university in other Arab states or in Europe or the USA. In 1972, the first fully fledged Palestinian university, Birzeit, was established in the premises of a former teachers' training school. In subsequent years, other universities were established in Bethlehem, Nablus, Hebron, Jerusalem and Gaza. While Israel did not encourage this proliferation of universities, it did not prevent it. In the decade preceding the Intifada, the Palestinian university student population went from a few thousand to 15,000–20,000 annually. The effect cannot be overestimated, as tens of thousands of Palestinians who would not have been eligible a generation before, went through the university system and its concomitant politicalisation.

The composition of the student population at these new universities was striking: 70 per cent of the students came from refugee camps, villages and small towns. It was from this student population that a new Palestinian elite emerged in the 1970s and 1980s, one that was larger, more diffuse, from lower social strata, more activist and less urban than the notable Palestinian elite it began to replace. As a result, Palestinian politics in this period became more confrontational with Israel's military occupation of the West Bank and Gaza.

The major strategy of this rising Palestinian elite in the 1980s was to build grassroots organisations to mobilise the population against the occupation. In turn, these institutions would act as proto-state structures, designed to vest authority in Palestinian hands and away from the military government. This was the time for the building or expansion of most labour unions, women's committees, agricultural and medical relief committees, voluntary works committees and student blocs.

Two pertinent international events helped spur the mobilisation campaign in the West Bank and Gaza. First, the 1979 peace agreement between Israel and Egypt removed the Arab world's strongest state from the Arab-Israeli conflict, shifting the regional balance of power dramatically in Israel's favour. The result for Palestinians was the recognition – given Israel's enhanced power – that any positive solution to their dilemma would be a long way off. Thus, the first order of business was to make the West Bank and Gaza difficult for the Israelis to rule and absorb. Palestinian leaders hoped to complicate Israeli rule by mobilising their community in opposition to the occupation.

Second, Israel's 1982 invasion of Lebanon – designed to destroy the PLO and, by extension, make Israeli rule over the Occupied Territories permanent – had the unintended consequence of invigorating the emerging elite in the West Bank and Gaza. It was clear they could no longer rely on the 'outside' PLO for salvation, as the PLO was defeated and dispatched to far-off Tunisia. If even a fraction of Palestine was to be salvaged, it was believed, it would have to be by those Palestinians still living there. While this new elite was widely affiliated with the major factions of the PLO – Fatah, PFLP, Democratic Front for the Liberation of Palestine (DFLP) and the Palestine Communist Party (now the Palestinian People's Party) – it was significant that the political initiative clearly lay with those on the inside.

THE INTIFADA

In December 1987, sparked by a car accident in the Gaza Strip in which four Palestinians were killed, a mass uprising against Israeli occupation began. The uprising, or Intifada, was a spontaneous event in so far as no person or faction planned its ignition. However, without the structural changes and the mobilisation campaign described above, the Intifada would not have been possible.

The Intifada was not an armed uprising, nor was it even particularly violent. Virtually all the violence employed by Palestinians came in the form of thrown rocks, bricks and the occasional Molotov cocktail. Demonstrations, marches and rallies were certainly employed, especially in the first six months. However, the Intifada was primarily about mass organised disengagement from Israel. In political terms, Palestinians denied Israeli authority on any number of issues, and created alternative authoritative bodies to govern Palestinian society. For over two years the principal locus of authority was the Unified National Leadership of the Uprising (UNLU), an ever-changing body of local PLO activists which published periodic leaflets directing the Intifada. The UNLU's first confrontation with the military government came over the closure hours demanded of commercial establishments. The UNLU would instruct merchants to close their businesses at certain hours, while the military government commanded that the businesses stay open those hours and close other hours. The confrontation went on for weeks, until finally the Israelis relented, and the UNLU was free to set strike hours and days. Their authority in these matters was recognised and widely obeyed during the Intifada, especially in its first two years.

Political disengagement was not limited to the UNLU. Alternative structures of authority sprang up everywhere in the occupied territories in the form of popular and neighbourhood committees. These would provide the social services hindered by the Intifada, including distributing food during curfews, organising 'popular education' when the schools were closed, planting 'victory gardens' to diminish dependence on Israeli agricultural products, organising guard duty to watch for military or settler attacks, ensuring compliance with strike days and the like. Some committees undertook more violent activities, particularly the interrogation and execution of alleged collaborators.

Other forms of disengagement were also used. Economic disengagement was seen in the boycott of Israeli-made goods sold in the Occupied Territories and the refusal to pay taxes to Israel in a number of communities, especially the town of Bayt Sahur. Institutional disengagement was illustrated by the mass resignation, at the UNLU's urging, of the Palestinian policemen employed by the military government. Perhaps most important of all was the psychological disengagement undertaken during the Intifada. The uprising was a vehicle of individual and communal empowerment, where at least for a time Palestinians believed they could actually roll back the occupation, that fatalism and dependence did not have to be the norm.

After an initial period of confusion, Israel responded to the Intifada harshly, using, in the words of then-defence minister Yitzhak Rabin 'force, might, beatings' to crush it. Well over one thousand Palestinians were killed by Israeli forces, with many thousands more injured and tens of thousands imprisoned – many without charge or trial. Most important was the strategy of collective punishment, where many were punished – through house demolitions, curfews, destruction of crops and similar means – for the alleged crimes of a few. But if bringing disproportionate force to bear was a reasonably successful strategy in containing the Intifada, it could not solve the underlying problems.

The Intifada was also responsible for significant changes in Palestinian society. First, the traditional respect for elders in Arab society was largely dissolved. Neither the young people who were throwing stones nor the more important 'mid-generation' which was building popular institutions had much time for what were regarded as the compromises and concessions of their elders to Israel. This was seen clearly in the liberalisation of family structures, where clan patriarchs carried little weight in decision-making during the Intifada. Second, and related to this development, was the anti-notable flavour of the Intifada. While Israel was the primary target of the Intifada, the old Palestinian elite was the secondary target. The same families which had held local power for generations were largely marginalised by the Intifada, continuing a process begun before the uprising.

Third, the Intifada facilitated the rise to prominence of a powerful Islamic alternative to the secular PLO. The largest Islamic group, the Muslim Brethren, had been politically discredited in the years before the uprising because of their co-operation with the Israeli authorities. The Intifada radicalised the Islamist movement, giving birth in its early days to the Islamic Resistance Movement, or Hamas. Hamas (and the

Islamic Jihad group) brought to Palestinian resistance a new level of violence against Israeli targets in the West Bank and Gaza, gaining converts and splitting Palestinian society. The Islamic challenge to the PLO was so great that, early in the autonomy period, Palestinian society was on the brink of civil war, a danger which has still not passed.

The 'outside' PLO in Tunis was as surprised as Israel when the Intifada broke out. Nor was the PLO in Tunis particularly important to the unfolding of events during the uprising. Rather, Tunis sought to capture and control the Intifada, something it was never able to do completely. The PLO did funnel resources and advice to the occupied territories in support of the Intifada and did what it could to give the Intifada greater attention on the world's stage. Also, the PLO had not lost its legitimacy in Palestinian eyes. However, Tunis was geographically and psychologically too far removed from the course of events in the West Bank and Gaza to matter much.

Clearly, though, the PLO was not enamoured of the alternative bodies of authority – the popular committees – in the Intifada, and viewed them and any autonomous political activity as potential threats to its position. As a rule, the PLO undermined those political actions in the Intifada over which it had little control, while endorsing those activities it could control. Thus, while the PLO supported the Intifada in principle, it often acted to demobilise Palestinian society in the West Bank and Gaza.

The one area the PLO in Tunis could control completely was the diplomatic sector. In the historic November 1988 meeting of the Palestine National Council (in effect the PLO's parliament in Algeria), the PLO declared the birth of an independent Palestinian state, living side by side with Israel. By adopting formally a two-state solution to the question of Palestine, the PLO completed a diplomatic process it had begun in 1974. In the hopes of beginning negotiations with the United States, Yasser Arafat subsequently clarified the PLO's recognition of Israel and renounced the use of terrorism. In what was seen as a humiliation by many Palestinians, Arafat was rebuffed twice. American officials then wrote for him exactly what he needed to say to gain a US dialogue, and he uttered the precise words. A flurry of not very serious diplomatic activity occurred over the ensuing 15 months, until Israel's prime minister, Yitzhak Shamir, put an end to further diplomatic discussions over the future of the West Bank and Gaza Strip in March 1990.

THE SECOND GULF WAR

If the Intifada's main accomplishment was to break the status quo and Israel's complacency over its military occupation of the Palestinian people, then the Gulf war did likewise for the world's remaining superpower, the United States. Saddam Hussein's hypocritical political use of the Palestinian question for his own ends showed clearly to the Bush administration that American interests in the Arab world could not be well served with the Palestinian wound unhealed. Only by solving the Palestinian question would larger American interests in the Arab world be better protected.

Iraq's manipulation of the Palestinian issue gave false hope to many Palestinians during the 1990–91 Gulf crisis. While some Palestinians felt that Saddam Hussein was the kind of strong Arab leader who might be able to balance Israel's power and help the Palestinian cause, other Palestinians were simply pleased to see some Arab state launching first rhetorical and then actual missiles at their oppressor. The Palestinian position was hardened following the October 1990 massacre of at least 17 Palestinians on the grounds of the Dome of the Rock and al-Aqsa mosque in Jerusalem. Yet though more prescient Palestinians warned against an emotional and political alliance with Iraq, their voices were not heeded.

In the biggest blunder of its existence, the PLO tacitly sided with Iraq during the Gulf war. The failure of the PLO leadership to evaluate properly either the strategic or moral implications of their choice led to disaster. Kuwait and Saudi Arabia had provided the lion's share of PLO revenues, and these monies were quickly cut off by the former patrons. The PLO went broke virtually overnight. PLO diplomatic institutions were shut down, administrators' salaries were not paid on time or in full, and the families of Palestinians killed or imprisoned during the Intifada no longer received financial assistance – a major source of support for families who had lost their breadwinners. Before long, the viability of the organisation itself was threatened. The severe, almost fatal financial difficulties of the PLO brought on by such poor judgment explains in part the PLO's later acceptance of peace terms that it had long rejected.

The Bush administration pushed hard for some kind of diplomatic breakthrough on the Palestinian front after the war. The result of its efforts was the historic October 1991 Madrid Conference. The PLO acquiesced to the demand that it not participate formally in the Madrid Conference, although it clearly had considerable influence on who did participate and what was to be said on its behalf. All the other major parties to the conflict also participated. The Palestinian presentation at Madrid was made by Haydar Abd al-Shafi, a respected senior statesman from Gaza, and was widely listened to in the West Bank and Gaza. Although technically part of the Jordanian team, for the first time the Palestinians were in attendance at a major peace conference.

The Madrid conference gave way to a series of parallel bilateral talks in Washington. Like the others, the Israel-Palestinian talks went on periodically for months without significant progress. Agreement proved elusive. While the Palestinians negotiated for an Israeli withdrawal from the occupied territories and the establishment of a Palestinian state in the West Bank and Gaza, the Israelis demanded permanent Israeli control of those areas. As Prime Minister Shamir later stated, he was willing to drag out the negotiations for ten years until enough settlers were present in the territories to make territorial compromise impossible.

The election in June 1992 of a Labour government in Israel bought new impetus to the talks. In fact, the labour leader Yitzhak Rabin had made such a settlement a cornerstone of his election campaign. Initially, however, little changed in the Washington rounds of negotiations. On the ground, in contrast, the failure of the PLO-backed negotiators (the PLO continued to be excluded formally from the negotiations) to win any diplomatic concessions strengthened the opposition, particularly the fundamentalist movement Hamas. Hamas intensified its political attacks on the PLO and its physical attacks on Israel. In December 1992, after a series of provocations, Prime Minister Rabin ordered the expulsion to Lebanon of over 400 Hamas and Islamic Jihad activists for two years.

The mass expulsion in December 1992 briefly eased the polarisation of Palestinian society between the PLO, primarily Yasser Arafat's Fatah group, and their fundamentalist opposition. While both sides (and the international community) denounced the expulsion, it was not long before Arafat ordered his negotiators back to Washington for the ninth round of talks, a decision that proved extremely unpopular among Palestinians, and led the chief negotiator, Haydar Abd al-Shafi, to resign in protest. While Abd al-Shafi was eventually persuaded to withdraw his resignation, the negotiators were not then told the real reason for their return to Washington: to divert attention from the more important secret talks being held in Oslo between Israelis and Palestinians.

THE OSLO ACCORDS AND THE BEGINNING OF LIMITED AUTONOMY

In the spring of 1993, while Palestinians were debating the merits of returning to the Washington talks, Israeli and PLO negotiators were already constructing a secret agreement to end their conflict. There were several reasons for bypassing the Washington talks. First, the Washington talks had produced no breakthrough, and it was thought that the public nature of the sessions was not conducive to real diplomatic movement. Second, while both parties were anxious for a settlement, the PLO was particularly desperate for one because of its empty treasury and its marginality after the Gulf war. Third, the new Clinton administration in Washington was seen by both parties as too one-sided in the conflict to be of any use as a facilitator and mediator.

Though rumours of secret talks in Europe persisted through the spring and summer of 1993, the August announcement of the near-conclusion of an agreement between the PLO and Israel was nonetheless startling. In September, following formal mutual recognition, the PLO and Israel signed a Declaration of Principles – the Oslo accords – designed to guide the two parties through the final resolution of their conflict. Even though Washington had nothing to do with crafting the agreement, both Arafat and Rabin wanted the signing ceremony to be at the White House to insure superpower support and involvement in implementing it.

The accords were far more important symbolically than substantively. In fact, they ignored any discussion of the shape of the final arrangements, instead relying on a few basic principles and the goodwill of the parties involved. The Oslo accords outlined a two-stage settlement consisting of an interim period that would begin almost immediately and lead to a final settlement in five years. While reaffirming the territorial integrity of the West Bank and Gaza Strip, the interim section of Oslo accords called for, among other things, an Israeli withdrawal from parts of the West Bank and Gaza; Palestinian self-rule in a number of functional sectors; and the holding of Palestinian elections. They also specified the deadlines for these events. The truly difficult issues – the future of Jerusalem, and Israeli settlements in the West Bank and Gaza, for example – were deliberately left for the negotiations over final arrangements.

The euphoria generated in Palestinian circles by the Oslo accords quickly abated when circumstances on the ground did not change, and the first Oslo-mandated deadlines for army withdrawal were ignored by Israel. Apprehension increased in early 1994, when a Jewish settler opened fire on Palestinians in the Ibrahimi mosque in Hebron, killing at least 29 Palestinians (bodies are often taken quickly and buried by their families, making casualty figures inexact). Fearful of retaliation against the approximately 400 settlers in Hebron, Israel kept the 100,000 Palestinians in Hebron under curfew for months.

In May 1994 in Cairo, Israel and the PLO signed a partial interim agreement, initially limiting self-rule to the Gaza Strip and Jericho. The degree of autonomy called for in the 'Gaza-Jericho first' agreement was far more limited than that which most Palestinians had expected from the Oslo accords, with Israel maintaining control of all borders as well as overall security. The settlements in the Gaza Strip and the main roads there were also to remain in Israeli hands. The limited degree of autonomy was made worse in the eyes of most Palestinians by further settlement expansion and land confiscations throughout the Occupied Territories following the Cairo signing.

Opposition to the Gaza-Jericho agreement was strong among Palestinians, and not only among those groups (such as Hamas and the PFLP) which had consistently rejected the whole process. In a startling display of no-confidence in the agreement, many former Palestinian negotiators who were long advocates of peaceful resolution, signed a petition rejecting the agreement. The petition drive, led by Haydar Abd al-Shafi, included prominent members of factions which had strongly supported the Oslo accords (in particular, the Palestinian Peoples' Party and FIDA, an offshoot of the DFLP) as well as well-known independents. Indeed, only a small segment of the Palestinian political establishment continued to support a process that had gone awry.

In spite of such opposition and the collapse of optimism in Palestinian circles, the implementation of the Gaza-Jericho agreement went forward, with the arrival in Gaza that summer of Palestinian security forces, outside PLO members and, finally, Yasser Arafat. Negotiations to reach a full interim agreement continued slowly.

Finally, in September 1995 the PLO and Israel signed the long-delayed full interim agreement which is to govern life on the West Bank until May 1999. The interim agreement called for rapid IDF redeployment away from most Palestinian cities (excluding Hebron), with redeployment away from Palestinan villages and some other lands to follow. The percentage of land to be turned over to the PLO is under some dispute at the time of writing (September 1995), but will probably not exceed one third of the West Bank. Overall control will remain with Israel until the final status negotiations are completed. Those talks will begin, in theory, by May 1996. Like Oslo I and the Cairo Accords, Oslo II did not deal with the major issues of the conflict, especially Jewish settlements in the West Bank, the status of Jerusalem, Palestinian refugees and sovereignty.

Like the earlier accords, Oslo II badly split the Palestinian community (as it did Israel, too). Its proponents argued either confidently that this was the next step to an independent Palestinian state, or with a degree of resignation that this was the best deal possible given the circumstances. Alternatively, opponents of Oslo II argued that the process was leading to the creation of Palestinian cantons or Bantustans – unconnected entities without real sovereignty. But the opposition itself was split between those who rejected the agreement but were committed to co-operate with the Palestinian National Authority (PNA) to make a bad deal better, and those who rejected any co-operation with institutions of autonomy. Given the divided opposition, it seems clear that the PNA will be able to implement the agreement.

The performance of the PNA in Gaza and Jericho in its first year was not inspiring, even considering the daunting tasks it faced. The long occupation and the Intifada had remade Palstinian society in the West Bank and Gaza into something quite separate from Palestinian society in the diaspora. After such a long separation, the PLO in Tunis correctly assumed that the social bases for its rule in Palestine were limited. The grassroots empowerment and autonomous political activity which had underminded Israeli military rule during the Intifada posed a similar potential threat to Arafat and the PNA. In essence, Arafat could not rely exclusively on local Palstinians for his rule. His more loyal followers were Palestinians from the diaspora, to whom he naturally turned for support.

Arafat and the PNA relied on three pillars for their rule in Gaza and Jericho. First and most important were the extensive police and security services established under autonomy, composed of individuals largely recruited from outside the West Bank and Gaza, many of whom had never set foot in Palestine prior to 1994. Their political loyalty was strongly focused on the outside PLO, and on Arafat in particular. The second pillar of PNA rule were the most loyal cadres of Fatah. Many Fatah activists who were viewed as too independent from Tunis and Arafat were dismissed or otherwise marginalised at the outset of self-rule. In some cases, people accused of collaboration during the Intifada have joined Fatah and assumed positions of local authority. Third, Arafat politically resuscitated members of the old notable families who had been relegated to the sidelines of Palestinian society during the Intifada. This has given them a renewed legitimacy, but their more recent marginalisation makes them dependent on Arafat for their political survival. There is no significant political force with an independent base in Palestinian society which shares power with Arafat.

The drive toward creating a Palestinian police state in Gaza and Jericho has been helped indirectly by the actions of Hamas. Hamas has engaged in a series of violent acts against Israel to the embarrassment of the PNA. Hamas threatened retaliation for the 1994 Hebron mosque massacre and carried out several acts of terrorism in Israel, including attacks on civilian buses in Afula and Hadera. As self-rule got under way in 1994–95 Hamas continued its attacks, again bombing civilian (and military) buses. In response to these attacks – and under heavy Israeli and American pressure to crack down hard on Hamas – Arafat checked Hamas' activities through greater police powers, including the establishment of special security courts. These courts would routinely try and convict suspected Hamas activists in sham court sessions in the middle of the night, unwatched by neutral observers. Such measures won praise from Israel and the US for their effectiveness, although they horrified Palestinians concerned with the rule of law and democracy.

THE DIFFICULTIES AHEAD

In spite of the problems which have plagued the post-Oslo period and dashed hopes for a rapid settlement of the Palestinian problem, the greatest difficulties still lie ahead. The Oslo accords deliberately left the trickiest issues for the negotiations on permanent arrangements. Four particularly problematic topics remain: Jerusalem, settlements, the Palestinian diaspora and sovereignty.

Israel expanded and annexed East Jerusalem after it captured the city in 1967, although the international community has never recognised the annexation. Since then Israel has built vast Jewish settlements encircling the city, making territorial concessions virtually impossible. Today, Jews constitute a slight majority of the population of East Jerusalem, and the government – whatever its promises in the Oslo accords – routinely rejects any hint of compromise on permanent Israeli control over East Jerusalem. There is an equally strong Palestinian consensus that no permanent deal can be arranged which does not include Palestinian political rights over East Jerusalem. While a number of creative plans of shared sovereignty or dual sovereignty over Jerusalem have been devised which satisfy the main interests of both parties in Jerusalem, there is little reason for optimism that such an emotional issue will be solved equitably.

The fate of Jewish settlements, particularly in the West Bank, is also potentially insoluble. Even discounting settlements in East Jerusalem, there are well over 120,000 Jewish settlers in the Occupied Territories, with the vast majority in the West Bank. The Rabin government has been unwilling to relocate even the most problematic settlements, such as those in Hebron, and no Israeli government will have the domestic political support necessary to remove over 100,000 settlers. To meet Palestinian demands, many settlements will have to be dismantled, and the ones that remain must fall under Palestinian jurisdiction. It is unlikely that Israel would agree to such arrangements. While settlers constitute only a fraction of the Israeli body politic, they have enough political support to make any decision on their future difficult. The Rabin government seems to recognise this, and instead of diminishing the number of settlers it has instead built a series of bypass roads to lessen friction between settlers and Palestinians in the West Bank. The expansion of settlements and the concomitant land confiscations have continued in the post-Oslo period.

The third major issue is the fate of the diaspora Palestinians. While most Palestinians live in historic Palestine, about two million live elsewhere, many in refugee camps. Will they be able to return to a rump Palestinian state if that transpires? If not, how will their host states treat them? Only Jordan has legally incorporated its Palestinians, and even there pressure is great to have many of them returned to their homeland. However, neither Israel nor the PNA is keen to have hundreds of thousands of Palestinians flood the West Bank and Gaza in the coming years. If the diaspora is made to feel alienated from a final agreement between Israel and the PLO, as appears likely, then it may well constitute a force for regional instability for years to come.

Finally, ultimate sovereignty of the West Bank and Gaza is still to be determined. The Palestinians have said constantly that their goal is an independent state in the West Bank and Gaza. Israel continues to oppose that development. Such opposition would intensify if any proposed Palestinian sovereignty were to include East Jerusalem and Jewish settlements, as Palestinians insist should be the case. Israel may accept limited Palestinian sovereignty over much of the West Bank and Gaza, but with overall security remaining in Israeli hands. This in turn would not be acceptable to most Palestinians.

Thus, while optimism ran high after the signing of the Oslo accords, reality has greatly dampened such hopes. The Israelis have not helped matters by showing callous disregard for their time-table commitments outlined in the Oslo accords, and by their continued settlement activity and land confiscations. Likewise, the Palestinians have done little to gain Israeli confidence (or the confidence of committed Palestinian liberals and democrats) with the creation of a security state in Gaza and Jericho, and with the plethora of terrorist attacks carried out by Hamas. More ominous for the Palestinians, the PLO may discover in a couple of years when final status negotiations are under way that it has lost the little leverage it used to have. By agreeing to Oslo, the PLO opened the door for other Arab states – notably Jordan – to make their own peace with Israel. It is quite possible that all frontline states will be at peace with Israel by the time discussions of Jerusalem and settlements begin between the PLO and Israel. Without any viable leverage, Palestinian rights in these crucial areas will likely be ignored, which would greatly threaten the viability of any peace settlement.

Glenn E. Robinson

SAUDI ARABIA

I N 1902, Abd al-Aziz ibn Abd al-Rahman Al Saud led a group of kins-
men and followers in a daring raid on Riyadh, the major city of Najd
(central Arabia). Eleven years earlier, his father had been driven from
the city by a rival Arabian dynasty, an event which marked the nadir of the
political fortunes of a family that had been the dominant players in central
Arabian politics since the mid-18th century. Abd al-Aziz, known in the
West as Ibn Saud, proceeded over the next 32 years to recover the patri-
mony of his ancestors through military force, political skill and deft diplomacy. The centrality of his, and his family's, role in the construction of the
state is evident in the name he gave it – the Kingdom of Saudi Arabia.

ESTABLISHING THE STATE

Modern Saudi history begins in 1744, with a political pact between
Muhammad ibn Saud, the ruler of the Najdi oasis town of Dir'iyya, and
Muhammad ibn Abd al-Wahhab, a zealous and puritanical Muslim
reformer. The two agreed that the ruler would enforce the principles of
the preacher in his realm, and the preacher would place his movement at
the service of the expansion of that realm. Thus were combined the dynastic fortunes of the Al Saud (House of Saud) and the rigorous Islamic interpretation of 'Wahhabism'. Being standard bearers of this religious
ideology has allowed Saudi rulers to engender loyalty to their rule across
the family, tribal and regional divisions that had kept Arabia divided for
centuries. But the demanding strictures of the Wahhabi interpretation of
Islam have often clashed with the practical demands of diplomacy and
governance. Religiously inspired critics of the Saudi regime have pointed
to that gap between ideology and reality as a rallying point for opposition.

The fortunes of the new Saudi-Wahhabi alliance waxed during the latter part of the 18th century. The successors of Muhammad ibn Saud were
able to bring under their control Hasa (eastern Arabia), Asir (southwest-
ern Arabia) and parts of Yemen, northern Arabia as far as the Syrian and
Iraqi deserts and Hijaz (western Arabia), including the holy cities of Mecca
and Medina. Their forces raided as far north as Damascus and Baghdad.
The depredations of this new, expansionist Arabian power attracted the
attentions of the Ottoman empire, which in 1811 ordered the governor of
Egypt, Muhammad Ali, to retake the holy cities from the Saudis. In a
seven-year campaign the Egyptian forces drove the Saudis back into central Arabia, captured the reigning Saudi prince and razed Dir'iyya. Family
dissension and tribal defections helped to weaken the Saudis during the
long war. This marked the end of the first Saudi Arabian realm.

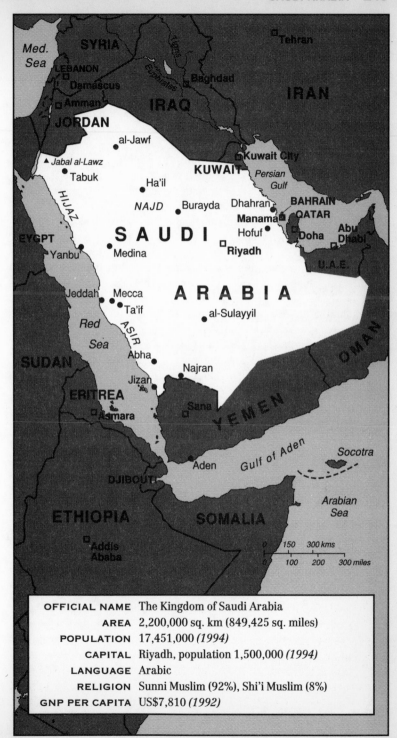

OFFICIAL NAME	The Kingdom of Saudi Arabia
AREA	2,200,000 sq. km (849,425 sq. miles)
POPULATION	17,451,000 *(1994)*
CAPITAL	Riyadh, population 1,500,000 *(1994)*
LANGUAGE	Arabic
RELIGION	Sunni Muslim (92%), Shi'i Muslim (8%)
GNP PER CAPITA	US$7,810 *(1992)*

By 1824, a grandson of Muhammad ibn Saud re-established the family's rule in Riyadh, a central Arabian town near the ruins of Dir'iyya. This second Saudi realm never reached the geographic extent of the first, being limited to Najd and Hasa. The state was wracked by intra-family feuds, which allowed outside powers such as the Egyptians and the Ottomans to meddle in its politics. In 1887 a rival dynasty, the Rashidis from Ha'il in northern Arabia, allied with a dissident member of the Al Saud to capture Riyadh and put an end to the second Saudi realm.

It was from the detritus of the second Saudi realm that Abd al-Aziz fashioned his new state at the turn of the 20th century and set out to re-establish his family's control in Najd. It was 20 years before he was able to capture the Rashidi capital of Ha'il. In the meantime, he restored Saudi rule to Hasa, reclaimed by the Ottoman empire, in 1913. The First World War brought British recognition and some British financial and military support, which helped Abd al-Aziz subdue rebellious tribes and finally defeat the Al Rashid, who had sided with the Ottoman Empire in the War.

While British recognition was an important political achievment for Abd al-Aziz, London was hesitant to provide him substantial military support. It worried about Saudi intentions toward the British-protected sheikhdoms of the Persian Gulf coast, and about the growing tensions between Abd al-Aziz and Sharif Husayn, the ruler of Hijaz, another British client. Abd al-Aziz needed to build his own military strength to consolidate and expand his realm. He found the means to do so in a revival of the Wahhabi religious ideology that animated the first Saudi realm. He sent preachers to the central Arabian tribes, who organised Wahhabi communities where the residents theoretically abandoned tribal allegiances in favour of intense devotion to Islam. These communities, provided a vastly expanded source of manpower for Abd al-Aziz's army. The Ikhwan (Brethren), as this Wahhabi-inspired force was called, allowed Abd al-Aziz to gain the upper hand over his Arabian rivals. They were the shock troops in his final defeat of the Al Rashid and in his conquest of Hijaz in 1926, bringing the holy cities of Mecca and Medina (and the revenue that pilgrimage to them brought) under Saudi control again.

The Ikhwan, emboldened by their military successes, quickly challenged Abd al-Aziz's control over his newly expanded territories. Ikhwan leaders criticised his tolerance of 'un-Islamic' practices. Ikhwan raids into the new mandates of Transjordan and Iraq threatened to bring Abd al-Aziz into a direct confrontation with the British, something he had skilfully avoided in the past. Matters came to a head in 1929, when Abd al-Aziz raised a force of Najdi townspeople and loyal tribesmen and defeated the rebellious Ikhwan units. Their settlements were razed and the movement brought more strictly under Abd al-Aziz's control.

In 1934 Saudi forces attacked Yemen, consolidating Abd al-Aziz's hold on the disputed territory of Asir and capturing large sections of the Yemeni Red Sea coast. In the treaty concluding the war, the Imam of Yemen recognised Saudi sovereignty over Asir and the towns of Najran and Jizan, now on the Saudi-Yemeni border. With that Abd al-Aziz reached the extent of his territorial ambitions, which were prudently circumscribed by British power to the north (Iraq and Transjordan), east (the protected sheikhdoms) and south (British-protected Oman and Aden Colony). He now turned to the task of bringing his far-flung realm under stable, centralised rule. In 1932 he declared his territories a unitary state – the Kingdom of Saudi Arabia. But declaring them so was only the first step. No one since the Prophet Muhammad had been able to forge a united state in Arabia that survived beyond his death.

The four major regions of Abd al-Aziz's kingdom had distinct histories and particular social structures. Najd was the basis of Abd al-Aziz's support, the home of the Wahhabi movement and of his family. Its tribes and towns were keys to the maintenance of stability in the new Kingdom. Hijaz was much more cosmopolitan than Najd, with a long history of contact with the outside world through trade and the pilgrimage to Mecca. Urban Hijazis generally did not accept the puritanical Wahhabi doctrine and viewed Najdis as bumptious, if not dangerous, country folk. Asir was the most densely populated area of the Kingdom, and the least politically mobilised. Hasa contained a sizeable Shi'i minority, whom strict Wahhabis viewed as unbelievers. Hasa also was the location of the natural resource that would provide the glue that kept these disparate territories linked – oil.

THE ADVENT OF OIL

Before oil, Saudi Arabia was a dirt poor place. Most of its inhabitants survived by subsistence farming, by fishing or by pastoral nomadism. This was hardly an adequate tax base for the new state, particularly as distributing money and gifts to the tribes was a major element in maintaining their loyalty. The only reliable and substantial source of income was the revenues from the annual pilgrimage to Mecca, and the 1930s world depression severely reduced the number of pilgrims. The King's confidant, St John Philby, reported him saying, 'If anyone offers me a million pounds now, he would be welcome to all the concessions he wants in my country'.

That offer came in 1933, when the Standard Oil Company of California (Socal) was granted a concession to search for oil in the Kingdom. Oil in commercial quantities was discovered in 1938, but exports did not commence until 1946. Until that time the Kingdom relied on royalty payments and loans from Socal, British subventions and, from 1944, American aid to maintain the minimum government functions it provided. Socal quickly discovered that it was sitting atop the largest oil reserves in the world, and brought in other United States' oil companies to assist in their development. In 1938 Texaco entered into the partnership, and in 1948 Mobil and Exxon joined what became the Arabian American Oil Company (Aramco). Aramco developed, produced and marketed Saudi oil, paying the Saudi government (after 1950) 50 per cent of the profits after expenses. Saudi government revenue from oil grew from $10 million in 1946 to $212 million in 1952, the last full year of King Abd al-Aziz's reign. While at times profligate, the Saudi government would not again be poor.

The advent of oil changed the relationship between state and society in Saudi Arabia. The government now had the means, limited through the 1960s and nearly unlimited in the1970s, to provide benefits to Saudi citizens. Those means came not from taxing the citizens, but from a foreign-operated enclave of the Saudi economy that transferred revenue directly to the state treasury. Most states engage in *redistribution* of wealth – extracting it from society and giving at least some of it back. In Saudi Arabia the state simply *distributes* wealth,having obtained it not from society but from the international oil market.

Saudi leaders have been able to use that wealth to privilege certain groups in their society, giving them a financial and political stake in the Saudi regime. First and foremost among those groups is the Al Saud themselves. The extensive ruling family is the ultimate basis of any Saudi king's support, and keeping them happy is a political necessity. The Wahhabi religious establishment controls a vast array of educational, legal and cultural institutions funded by the Saudi state. Najdis have been disproportionately represented in the Saudi military and in the civilian bureaucracies, which were instituted in the 1950s and mushroomed with the oil boom of the 1970s. Merchants from all parts of the Kingdom benefited from state contracts, import franchises and the vast increases in economic activity during the oil boom.

For much of its history the Saudi distributive state allowed the rulers to suppress, co-opt and ignore voices demanding greater political participation in the Kingdom. Since citizens have not been taxed, the nexus between taxation and representation that fuelled demands for democracy in the West has not existed in Saudi Arabia. Oil revenues funded generous welfare programmes for citizens, particularly from the 1970s, decreasing the likelihood of political opposition. Oil revenues have also allowed the Saudis to build a large and relatively efficient coercive apparatus, aimed at identifying and repressing domestic political opposition.

BUILDING A MODERN STATE: THE 1950S AND 1960S

The death of King Abd al-Aziz in 1953 was a turning point in Saudi history. His successors had none of the historical aura or personal charisma of the founder of the Kingdom. They did have increasing amounts of oil money, but how to use it was an unsettled question. Abd al-Aziz had run the country out of his pocket; one of his aides kept the state account book under his bed at night. A ministry of foreign affairs was created in 1930, a ministry of finance in 1932, and other ministries later on, but Abd al-Aziz's style of rule remained personal and idiosyncratic. His sons confronted the need to build a modern bureaucratic state at a time when Arab nationalist ideology, personified by Egyptian president Nasser, presented a direct challenge to the legitimacy and stability of Saudi rule. The other major challenge faced by Abd al-Aziz's successors was to work out among themselves how succession would pass through the family. These two challenges became tied up in the contest for power between two of Abd al-Aziz's eldest sons, Saud and Faysal.

Saud, the eldest of the old king's 43 sons, succeeded his father in 1953. His brother, Faysal, who had served as foreign minister, became Crown Prince. The two initially worked together, but their different approaches to domestic and regional politics soon drove them into open competition for power. Saud governed much in the style of his father, with little concern for bureaucratic procedure or budgetary constraints. By 1958 the Kingdom was in a serious fiscal crisis, as uncontrolled spending had outpaced the substantial but still limited oil revenues. Originally an ally of President Nasser, Saud began to fear Nasser's growing power in the region after 1956. In 1958 Nasser revealed that King Saud had paid a Syrian politician to have him assassinated, actually producing at a press conference a copy of the personal cheque Saud had signed. The combined fiscal and regional crisis led a council of elder members of the Al Saud to transfer governing power to Crown Prince Faysal, who was seen as a more sober leader and more experienced at dealing with the outside world. Saud, however, retained his title as king.

While Faysal's fiscal austerity brought financial order, it alienated important constituencies both inside and outside the ruling family. Saud reclaimed effective leadership of the government in 1960, allying temporarily with a faction of family members who advocated a more liberal (domestic) and Arab nationalist (foreign) policy. Quickly jettisoning the 'free princes' (who took refuge in Cairo), Saud reverted to his previous patterns of rule and came under intense attack from Nasser. With the arrival of Egyptian troops in North Yemen in September 1962, invited by the army officers who had overthrown the Imamate, the challenge from Nasser to Saudi security became more than rhetorical. Egyptian jets bombed Saudi territory on the border, and Saudi pilots ordered to defend the Kingdom's airspace defected with their planes to Cairo. Faced with this new challenge, the family again turned to Faysal. He assumed effective control of the government in late 1962, and the title of king in 1964, when a council of the senior members of the Al Saud formally deposed Saud. The transfer of power was confirmed by the senior members of the religious establishment. Faysal moved energetically to meet the dual challenges presented by the Arab nationalist threat domestically and the Egyptian military threat in Yemen. On the foreign policy front, he reaffirmed relations with the USA and with Britain that had been strained during the previous years of instability in Riyadh. Both Washington and London provided political support and military equipment to the Saudis. Faysal also gave substantial financial support and a base in Saudi Arabia to the Yemeni royalist forces fighting against the Egyptians and the new republican regime. The Egyptians became tied down in a debilitating guerrilla war, which Nasser called his Vietnam.

The domestic challenge was not as easily met. Immediately upon assuming control in November 1962, Faysal published a ten-point reform and development programme meant to launch the Kingdom into the modern age. While it took 30 years to redeem one of Faysal's promises – to promulgate a basic law, or constitution, for the Kingdom –

his commitments to improved educational and social welfare opportunities for Saudi citizens and to a more rational and bureaucratic approach to governance did gradually come to fruition. Faysal's reforms were more bureaucratic than political. They involved greater efficiency in governing Saudi society, in providing benefits and maintaining social control, not greater participation by Saudis in political life. By combining the offices of king and prime minister, Faysal in fact concentrated power almost exclusively in his own hands. He used that power to set Saudi Arabia on the course of the modern welfare state that it is today.

Faysal's reforms did not end political discontent. There were reports of failed coup attempts at various times in the 1960s, and Nasser remained a popular figure to many Saudis. But the reforms did allow the Saudi government to stabilise its control over the country and to provide more Saudis with tangible benefits. The Nasserist tide crested in 1967. His defeat in the 1967 Arab-Israeli War led to the withdrawal of Egyptian forces from Yemen and to a steep decline in his popularity in the Arab world. Moreover, Saudi annual oil revenues climbed steadily, from $334 million in 1960 to $904 million in 1967 and $2.7 billion in 1972, even before the oil boom of 1973. This added revenue allowed Faysal to realise many of his development plans, expand the government bureaucracy and the military, and provide more benefits for both the bulwarks of his constituency (the ruling family, the religious establishment and the merchant class) and for the general population. As the threat to Saudi stability posed by Arab nationalism subsided, the Saudi state's financial resources were increasing. Saudi Arabia was getting richer, but the real riches were yet to come.

THE OIL BOOM OF THE 1970S

Before 1973 Saudi Arabia was a moderately rich state. After 1973 it was a fabulously rich state. The quadrupling of world oil prices in 1973-74, an event in which Saudi Arabia played a major role, increased government revenue enormously. Between 1972 and 1974 Saudi annual oil revenue increased ten-fold to $22.5 billion. The second oil shock, initiated by the Iranian Revolution of 1979, further increased the Saudi take from oil sales. In 1981 Saudi annual oil revenues peaked at $102.1 billion, and hard currency reserves were estimated to be over $100 billion.

As the largest oil producer in the Middle East, Saudi Arabia was at the centre of events in the 1973-74 oil crisis. In October 1973 Egypt and Syria attacked Israel, looking to recover the territories lost in the 1967 Arab-Israeli War. Since the political changes of 1970, which brought Anwar Sadat and Hafiz Asad to power in Cairo and Damascus, Egypt and Syria had courted the support of Saudi Arabia. This was a welcome change for King Faysal, whose regime had been fiercely attacked by the previous Egyptian and Syrian leaders. He was thus willing to pay a substantial price to support Sadat and Asad, including putting at risk his relations with the USA. As Israel turned the tide in the 1973 War and American aid poured into Israel, Saudi Arabia declared an embargo on oil shipments to the USA on October 20 and its intention to cut oil production every month that Israel retained control of the occupied territories.

This announcement electrified the oil market, which had seen substantial increases in oil prices (from $1.80 per barrel in 1968 to $3.01 in September 1973). OPEC producers had already announced their intention to raise prices further in October before the war started. Upward pressure on prices was the result of significant increases in world demand for oil in the 1960s, and by the early 1970s demand had reached the level of existing supplies. The prospect that Saudi Arabia would cut production and embargo a major oil importer set off a wave of panic buying. By January 1974 prices had settled at $11.65 per barrel.

The irony of the 1973-74 oil crisis is that world oil production declined only marginally, for a few months, during this period. The threats of monthly production cuts were withdrawn after the USA became actively involved in mediating the end of the war. Other producers increased production. The international oil companies shifted delivery schedules to abide by the embargo decision (lifted in March 1974) and still supplied the USA with over 90 per cent of its pre-embargo levels of imported oil. But the higher prices stuck because world demand for oil continued to increase in the 1970s, despite the enormous jump in price.

Saudi Arabia used this new revenue to inaugurate a vast expansion of the reach and role of the state in the lives of Saudi citizens. Five new ministries, aimed at providing services to the population, were created in the 1970s. The government provided free medical care and education through to post-graduate level, and subsidised food, water, petrol, electricity, land purchases and rents. The public education system grew exponentially, and secular and religious universities were built throughout the Kingdom. The state created two industrial cities, Yanbu on the Red Sea coast and Jubayl on the Persian Gulf coast, to develop petrochemical and other oil-related industries. It bought the controlling interest in Aramco, formally shifting decision-making power on oil questions from the oil companies to the state. Subsidies were provided to Saudi agribusiness to grow wheat in the desert at a cost vastly higher than the world market price. Employment in the state sector expanded to the point that over 50 per cent of the Saudi work force are now employees of the state or of parastatal enterprises. Even Saudis in the private sector – merchants, contractors, other businessmen – relied on government contracts, concessions and licenses for much of their income.

A state that gives so much also expects to control much of the everyday life of its citizens. Television, radio and print media expanded during the oil boom, but under strict state control. Freedoms of speech and association for political purposes were then, and now, extremely limited. The budgets of the coercive arms of the Saudi state – the military and the police – grew enormously during the 1970s and early 1980s. In 1970 the budget of the Saudi Defence Ministry (excluding the National Guard) was less than two billion Saudi riyals; in 1981 it was 65 billion Saudi riyals. The combined expenditures on internal security – the Interior Ministry and the Intelligence Bureau – in 1970 were less than 600 million Saudi riyals; in 1980 they were over 12 billion Saudi riyals. The political equation was clear: the state would provide a comfortable life, but in exchange you owed it your loyalty, or at least your aquiescence.

Two important social consequences flowed from the oil boom. The first was the vastly increased urbanisation of the Saudi population. For decades Riyadh had been encouraging the settlement of formerly nomadic tribes. The new influx of oil money in the 1970s created overwhelming economic incentives for Saudis to settle in the Kingdom's major cities, where most government jobs and spending was concentrated. By the 1990s over 80 per cent of the Saudi population was urban. While tribalism remains an important element of personal identity and social relations, the associated lifestyles – pastoral nomadism, long-distance caravan trade and oasis farming – have largely disappeared.

The second social consequence of the oil boom was the influx of foreign labourers to support the Kingdom's growing economy. The official Saudi census of 1991 counted 4.6 million foreigners in the Kingdom, over a quarter of the total population. Foreign workers occupy positions at the top and the bottom of the labour hierarchy. Western advisers help the Saudis run their businesses, their oil industry and their military. Labourers from south and southeast Asia sweep the streets, drive many of the taxi cabs, cook the meals and tend the shops. The largest group of Arab foreign workers had been the Yemenis, whose number may have reached as high as one million during the early 1980s, but most of them were forced to leave during the Gulf crisis of 1990-91. Egyptian manual labour has taken the place of some of the Yemenis, but the decade-long trend in Saudi Arabia is to rely on non-Arab guest labourers.

Saudi intellectuals debate the consequences on their Arab and Islamic identities of so many foreigners in their country , but the long-term cultural impact is unclear. Politically, foreign labourers have no rights or voice, and their direct impact on the Saudi polity has been limited. The fact that the Yemenis – fellow Arabs and Muslims – could be so easily forced out in 1990 is an indication of the political marginality of foreign labourers in the Kingdom. The greatest political impact has been the 'de-Saudisation' of the working class, elimating the potential for indigenous labour organisation and agitation in Saudi politics.

The enormous social and economic changes of the 1970s occurred in a climate of surprising political stability. The Saudi-US relationship, strained by the embargo of 1973-74, was quickly put right. US contractors and military advisers played the major role in building the infrastructure of roads, airports and military bases that transformed the Kingdom. US oil companies continued to provide technical advice and marketing outlets for the oil industry. Much of the surplus capital that flowed into the Kingdom was invested in the US. Even the assassination of King Faysal in 1975, by an embittered and mentally unstable junior member of the Al Saud, did not shake the political system. The family management team, all sons of King Abd al-Aziz, which Faysal had put in place, continued to run the Kingdom's affairs. His crown prince, Khalid, became king. Fahd, the interior minister, became crown prince, taking charge of the day-to-day operations of government. Sultan and Abdullah remained heads of the Defence Ministry and the National Guard respectively, and Fahd and Sultan's full brother, Na'if, became interior minister. The most important technocrats, finance minister Muhammad Aba al-Khayl and oil minister Muhammad Zaki Yamani, continued in their posts.

THE CHALLENGES OF THE 1980S

The oil crisis of 1979-81, caused by the Iranian Revolution of 1979 and the beginning of the Iran-Iraq War in 1980, inflated Saudi oil revenues yet again. But the political consequences of these events presented new problems. The success of Khomeini's Islamic revolution in Iran was both an ideological and a security challenge to the Saudi regime. For years the Saudis were the uncontested bearers of the banner of Islam in regional politics, battling with secular nationalists and leftists for the hearts and minds of Arab Muslims. The Islamic revolutionaries in Tehran not only challenged Riyadh's leadership of regional Islamic movements, but also contended that monarchy itself was an un-Islamic form of government. They condemned the Saudis' close ties with the USA, the Great Satan.

The effects of Iran's revolution on Saudi Arabia were numerous. Saudi Shi'is, emboldened by Iranian propaganda, staged demonstrations in Hasa in 1979 and 1980. The Saudi government met this challenge at first with force, and then with increased government spending in Shi'i areas. The mix of carrot and stick successfully quelled overt Shi'i discontent in the Kingdom. Less directly, the success of the Iranian revolution inspired Sunni Islamic activists throughout the Middle East to become more visible and vocal in their opposition to their own governments. While Sunni Islamic movements rejected much of the particulars of Iran's Shi'i revolution, the model of popular Islamic activism toppling an entrenched, pro-American monarchy was powerful. In November 1979 a group of Wahhabi zealots took control of the Grand Mosque in Mecca, Islam's holiest site, and held it for two weeks as a protest against what they said was the Saudi regime's deviation from the path of true Islam. The incident was an indication that religiously inspired political discontent existed in the Kingdom, and a precursor of problems the Saudis would face in the 1990s.

The fall of the Shah also drastically altered the Saudis' security environment. While Riyadh had always been nervous about the Shah's military might, he was a fellow monarch and closely allied to the USA. The new Iranian regime sought out confrontation with Washington and attempted to spread Islamic revolution throughout the region. Moreover, as the growing tensions between Iran and Iraq led to war in September 1980, the Saudis found themselves in a position where the outright victory of either side could be very damaging to their interests. As the Iran-Iraq War spread to the waters of the Persian Gulf, Riyadh also had to worry about the security of its oil exports. These external security issues pushed the Saudis toward Washington. Bilateral relations, which had cooled over the Saudi refusal to support the Camp David accords of 1978 and over the oil price increases of 1979-80, returned to their historical level of closeness. The USA sent an airforce squadron to Saudi Arabia in 1980 to symbolise its commitment to support the Kingdom, and new arms deals were signed. In 1987 American naval forces began to escort and protect Saudi and Kuwaiti shipping in the Gulf.

Along with these new security challenges, in the 1980s the Saudis began to run up against the limits of their oil wealth. The oil price increases of 1979-81 led to decreased world oil consumption and to the development of new oil resources outside the Middle East. Oil prices began to decline in 1982, falling briefly in 1986 to below $10 per barrel. Saudi oil revenues declined precipitously, to below $20 billion in 1987 and 1988. To maintain the expensive welfare state built during the 1970s, the high levels of defence spending and the generous outlays to the members of the ruling family now cost more than the Saudis' yearly oil income. Moreover, Riyadh committed itself to providing between $10 and $20 billion in 'loans' to Iraq to support its war against Iran. The Saudi government met these financial burdens by drawing down the reserves built up during the previous decade. This was a successful short-term strategy, but the real financial crunch was yet to come.

The 1980s, like the 1970s, were characterised by stability at the top of the Saudi political system. King Khalid died in 1982, and was succeeded by Crown Prince Fahd. The new king appointed his half-brother Abdullah, commander of the National Guard, crown prince and his full brother Sultan, the defence minister, second deputy prime minister and successor presumptive to Abdullah. The major figures, both from the Al Saud and the technocratic class, who ran the Saudi government in the 1970s continued to do so in the1980s. The only change of note was the dismissal of Zaki Yamani as oil minister in 1986. It was Yamani's strategy of increasing Saudi oil production, aiming to recover lost market share, that drove oil prices below $10 per barrel that year.

DESERT STORM AND AFTER

The Iraqi invasion of Kuwait in August 1990 faced the Saudis with a stark choice: accept the overthrow of a fellow monarch and Iraqi dominance of the Arab side of the Persian Gulf, or activate the US security connection that, for domestic and regional reasons, they had always preferred to keep in the background. They chose the latter, opening up the Kingdom to hundreds of thousands of US and other foreign troops and, in a very public way, linking their security to the US. The liberation of Kuwait in February 1991 and the decimation of Iraq's military capabilities removed the major external threat to Saudi security. But the Gulf crisis had profound consequences for Saudi politics.

In foreign policy the crisis had the effect of ending Saudi hesitations about publicly following the US line on Middle East questions. Riyadh had always been reluctant to be seen as co-operating too openly with Washington. Sensitivity about American policy on Arab-Israeli issues and a desire to assert their independence to domestic and regional audiences led the Saudis to prefer that their American ally be 'over the horizon'. Desert Storm changed that. Palestine Liberation Organisation (PLO) support for Saddam Hussein made it easier to back the US-sponsored peace process. Saudi Arabia has participated with Israel in the multi-lateral talks begun at the Madrid conference of 1991, supported the Israeli-PLO agreements, and dropped its secondary and tertiary economic boycotts of Israel – all out of deference to the US.

While both Washington and Riyadh are careful to emphasise that there are no US military bases in Saudi Arabia, the US military presence is considerable. US airforce squadrons are stationed at Saudi air bases and large US training and support missions are attached to branches of the Saudi armed forces. The great bulk of Saudi arms purchases and civilian contracts (particularly the purchase of airliners and telecommunications systems) since Desert Storm have gone to US companies.

The domestic consequences of Desert Storm have been even more far-reaching. As the crisis escalated the Saudi government allowed an unprecedented amount of public discussion of politics to occur within the Kingdom. Petitions were circulated during and immediately after the crisis, among both liberal and Islamist Saudis, calling for political reform. Responding to these demands, in March 1992 King Fahd issued three decrees: 1) the 'Basic System of Government', a constitution-like document outlining the rights and responsibilities of government and citizens in the Kingdom; 2) the statute for an appointed consultative council (*majlis al-shura*); and 3) a system of regional government for the Kingdom's 14 provinces. These innovations in no way challenge the ultimate power of the king individually and the Al Saud as a family. They are, however, the first acknowledgment by the ruling family of the need to develop formal participatory institutions in Saudi politics.

King Fahd appointed the first *majlis al-shura* in August 1993. Among its 60 members are a cross-section of the elite of the Kingdom, including former army officers, religious scholars, businessmen, technocrats and tribal leaders. Over one-third of the members have received PhDs from Western universities. What remains unclear is how much influence the *majlis* actually has on government decision-making. Its proceedings are not public. It can suggest laws and modifications of laws to the government, but cannot enact legislation. The development of the *majlis*, either as a powerless rubber stamp or a real deliberative body, will speak volumes about the character of Saudi politics in the future.

Another domestic consequence of Desert Storm has been the emergence, for the first time since the Ikhwan revolt of the 1920s, of organised Islamic political opposition to the Saudi regime. After the crisis, criticism of the regime in religious circles escalated. In the summer of 1992 a 46-page 'memorandum of advice' signed by over 100 Islamic activists set out in great detail a critique of all aspects of the government's policy, from economics and cultural issues to defence and foreign policy and the close US-Saudi ties. The core of its criticism was that the Saudis had abandoned their commitment to the Wahhabi interpretation of Islamic law.

King Fahd's response to the Islamist critique was swift. He reaffirmed the centrality of Islam to the political life of the Kingdom while moving to reassert the state's control over the religious establishment. In May 1993 a group of Islamic activists founded the 'Committee for the Defence of Legitimate Rights' to monitor the regime's fidelity to Islamic principles. The Saudi authorities arrested a number of the organisers and orchestrated a condemnation of their activities by senior members of the *uluma*. One of the founders, Muhammad al-Masari, escaped to London and has conducted a skilful propaganda campaign against the regime from there. In September 1994 two prominent Islamist critics of the regime were arrested with about 100 of their followers. Opposition groups have reported other arrests of Islamic activists subsequently. The car bombing in November 1995 of a building in Riyadh housing an American training mission for the Saudi National Guard is an indication that underground opposition movements still exist in the Kingdom.

The growth of Islamic opposition is abetted by serious economic problems, the third consequence of Desert Storm. The Saudis spent over $50 billion on Desert Storm, largely depleting their financial reserves. The Saudi government can no longer maintain levels of spending in excess of its revenues. The Kingdom has taken some important steps to re-establish fiscal discipline, cutting the budget in 1994 by nearly 20 per cent and imposing price increases on a number of subsidised consumer goods. There is also discussion about privatising state enterprises, though few concrete measures have been taken. Fiscal discipline, however, means short-term economic hardship for many citizens – price increases, fewer jobs in the public sector, fewer government contracts to the private sector.

The current retrenchment is only a first step in addressing the long-term problem of maintaining the welfare state in a time of flat oil prices and a rising population. Saudi population growth, 3.2 per cent per year, is among the highest in the world. To continue to provide schooling , jobs and healthcare for an increasing population – the implicit promises of the welfare state built by King Faysal – will be a difficult challenge.

How the Saudis handle the twin challenges of economic management and Islamic opposition will determine the future of the regime. The tactics chosen to deal with these issues will depend upon who is leading the family, and the state. The current top leadership – King Fahd, Crown Prince Abdullah, Defence Minister Sultan – are all over 70 years old. The younger sons of Abd al-Aziz could move up to take their places, but at some point leadership in the family will pass to the next generation, the grandsons of Abd al-Aziz. There are no guidelines for how that transition will occur. Managing it will be a necessary prerequisite for successfully dealing with the larger challenges facing Saudi Arabia.

F. Gregory Gause, III

13
SUDAN

MODERN SUDAN, bordering eight other states, may be divided geographically into three broad zones. The northern third is mainly desert, the central band mainly semi-desert and savannah, the southern third savannah and forest. The dominant feature, crucial to the economic and political history of Sudan, is the Nile and its tributaries. Rising in the Great Lakes of Africa, the White Nile, having been joined by the Bahr el-Ghazal, the Sobat, and other feeders, itself joins the swifter, silt-laden Blue Nile at Khartoum to form the main Nile, the lifeline of northern Sudan and Egypt. It was the Nile system that presented motives and avenues for the Turco-Egyptian conquest of Sudanese lands in the 19th century. Lured by the promise of slaves and gold, the armies of Muhammad Ali Pasha and his successors easily subdued the decrepit states and tribal confederacies of the northern Sudan and pushed gradually south, west and east until, by the mid-1870s, Egypt had extended its nominal control even beyond today's Sudanese borders. In doing so, the Turco-Egyptian regime imposed itself on a wide variety of peoples in greatly varying stages of development: the northern riverain Sudanese, who mostly resembled (and some were akin to) the Nubians of Upper Egypt; the Arabs of Kordofan and the Bayuda, largely camel and cattle nomads who chafed at outside control; and the enormously variegated African peoples of the south, who in language, culture and political and economic development differed widely not only from their Turco-Egyptian conquerors and northern neighbours, but also from each other. No less than the European creations elsewhere in the Middle East and Africa, Sudan's borders are the result of imperialism, albeit in this case mainly Ottoman-Egyptian rather than western European.

THE MAHDIYYA: REACTION AND REFORMATION

Ironically, the Middle East's most determined and successful resistance to imperialism occurred in Sudan. That this assumed a religious – indeed messianic – form should not obscure its social and political nature, nor the foreign innovations and intrusions against which it reacted. In 1881, significantly at a time when the Egyptian government at home was in the throes of a nationalist movement that would end in British occupation, Muhammad Ahmad Abdullah, a Dunqalawi Sufi, proclaimed himself Mahdi – the Expected Deliverer of the Muslims. Gradually gaining strength over several years, his movement scored stupendous successes against the poorly led and demoralised Egyptian forces at Shaykan in 1883 and, famously, at Khartoum in January 1885. Viewing Sudan as a waste of money that Egypt, in bankruptcy, could ill afford, its new ruler, Sir Evelyn Baring (later Lord Cromer), agent and consul-general from 1883 to 1907, argued successfully for a purely defensive policy. The death of the Mahdi in June 1885, and the destruction of the Mahdist invasion force at Tushki in 1889 punctuated a period of watchfulness on the Sudan-Egypt border where, however, no serious Mahdist threat again appeared. Indeed, it was the changing fortunes of the European Powers that dictated Britain's adoption of a more aggressive policy in 1895–96. An Anglo-Egyptian force first took Dongola in 1896, then, with massive technological superiority, pushed southwards in a campaign that ended in the rout of the Sudanese at Karari in September 1898. Two weeks later Kitchener, the Anglo-Egyptian commander, confronted the less well-armed but yet more dangerous Major Marchand at Fashoda. Though the British now understandably viewed Mahdism as an 'exploded cult', it survived: in the sect itself, which formed the nucleus of a powerful political movement, and, less obviously, in its unifying, 'nation-building' effects – the Mahdi has come to be called Abu'l-Istiqlal, the Father of Independence.

THE ANGLO-EGYPTIAN CONDOMINIUM

The formula devised to salvage French honour at Fashoda was to dominate the political development of Sudan throughout the age of European imperialism. Rather than claim the upper Nile for Britain, Kitchener claimed it for Britain's ward, Egypt, thus allowing the French to defer to the unenforceable claims of the khedive rather than to dispute the firepower of the Royal Navy. Likewise Lord Cromer, having been hampered in Egypt by the Capitulations, Mixed Courts, and other machinery of internationalism, devised a 'hybrid form of government' for Sudan, by which Egypt and Britain would in theory be joint rulers. The so-called Condominium Agreement(s) of 1899 enshrined this principle; in fact, until 1956 Britain was the dominant partner. Great power was invested in a single individual, the governor-general of Sudan, who was always British, while Sudan's budget and development debts were assumed by an Egyptian government fearful of total exclusion. Thus a regime was created that was unique in the Middle East, indeed nearly so in the world. The interplay of the co-domini with each other, and with the various Sudanese interest groups, complicated Sudan's political development, with results all too apparent today.

Sudan was under direct colonial rule longer than any other Middle Eastern state. Although the device of condominium deeply affected the character of the regime and acted as a brake on the British, it did not result in economic, social or religious policies very different from those pursued in other British dependencies. Thus to conciliate Muslim opinion direct taxes were kept low, the concurrence of the *ulama* (religious experts) was won for major initiatives, the pilgrimage to Mecca was facilitated, government funds were ear-

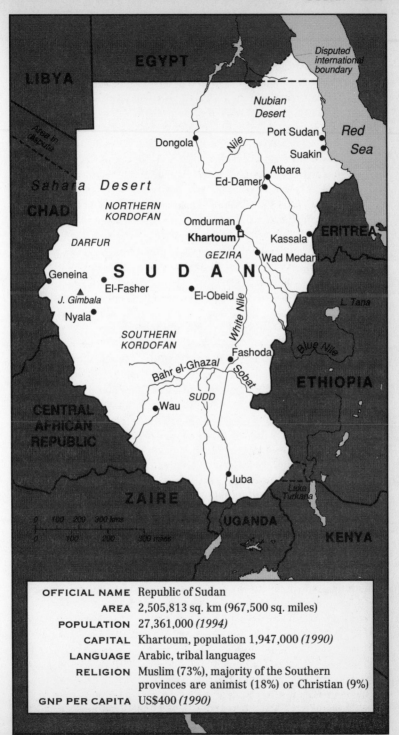

OFFICIAL NAME	Republic of Sudan
AREA	2,505,813 sq. km (967,500 sq. miles)
POPULATION	27,361,000 *(1994)*
CAPITAL	Khartoum, population 1,947,000 *(1990)*
LANGUAGE	Arabic, tribal languages
RELIGION	Muslim (73%), majority of the Southern provinces are animist (18%) or Christian (9%)
GNP PER CAPITA	US$400 *(1990)*

marked for mosque construction and repair, slavery was not prohibited (and, although the slave trade itself was banned, it, too, continued), new Mahdist and similar cults were suppressed, and Christian proselytisation in the northern Sudan was virtually prohibited. While Sufi *turuq* (religious brotherhoods) were at first deeply suspected – the Mahdi had begun his religious career as a Sufi, and Sudanese Sufism was, in British eyes, 'fanatical' and therefore unpredictable – individual Sufi sheikhs who proved amenable were cultivated and supported. Notable among them were the Mirghani family, hereditary sheikhs of the Khatmiyya *tariqa*, who had opposed the Mahdi and now openly sided with the new rulers. As correct as British policy was towards Islam, however, it could not reorient the loyalties of northern Sudanese towards orthodoxy: the *ulama* were soon recognised as respected but not widely influential, while Sufi sheikhs retained and expanded their hold on popular opinion. Recognition of this came most obviously during the First World War, when not only Sufi sheikhs, but even the son of the late Mahdi, Sayyid Abd al-Rahman, were recruited to exhibit publicly among the Sudanese their support for Britain against the Ottoman sultan and self-proclaimed caliph of Islam. Conciliation of the Mahdists, however, was resented by both *ulama* and Sufi sheikhs, and resulted in a polarisation that would match, among the ruled, the divergence that increasingly marked their Anglo-Egyptian rulers.

That divergence, present from the start, grew to breaking point after the First World War. The Egyptian revolution of 1919 led inexorably to Britain's unilateral declaration of Egyptian independence in 1922, after which Sudan, as one of the four 'reserved points', came to dominate, even to symbolise, Anglo-Egyptian relations. As Britain withdrew direct control from Egypt, so control in Sudan (and, through the Nile, therefore indirectly still of Egypt) assumed greater importance; to Egyptian nationalists the Unity of the Nile Valley and independence became irreducible aspects of Egyptian sovereignty, negotiable only in so far as negotiations might lead to their unequivocal acceptance. In 1924 the dispute turned violent. The British governor-general of Sudan (who was still, anomalously, also commander-in-chief of the Egyptian army) was assassinated in Cairo. The British reacted by demanding evacuation of the Egyptian army from Sudan, and this was taken in hand. Some Sudanese troops, suffering from divided loyalties, were engaged by British forces in a shoot-out in Khartoum, with heavy casualties. The Egyptian units were evicted, as were many Egyptian civilian officials, and a new Sudan Defence Force (SDF), responsible to the governor-general alone, was set up. That the Egyptians went quietly was not lost on Sudanese public opinion which, however, was now preoccupied with a reactionary British policy that sought to combat the danger of Sudanese nationalism by curtailing modern advance.

Thus during the 1920s and early 1930s education stagnated, and administrative functions were increasingly assigned by the British to conservative tribal leaders rather than to the 'class' of educated

Sudanese that had been created to assume subordinate posts in the government. This policy of indirect rule or 'native administration' had its origins and echoes as far afield as Nigeria and Iraq; in Sudan it was proclaimed with particular emphasis but not in fact seriously implemented because it proved impracticable. The return of Egyptian troops in 1937, symbolic of the relations restored in the Anglo-Egyptian Treaty of 1936 (itself the result of complex British and Egyptian regional and international interests), marked the resumption of rivalry between the codomini for sole dominion in Sudan.

From the late 1930s that rivalry was heightened and complicated by direct Sudanese involvement. In 1938 the Graduates' General Congress was established as an ostensibly social but obviously political organisation to represent the interests of the small, Western-educated northern Sudanese elite. The British welcomed, even encouraged, this development in the hope that it would foster a Sudanese nationalism distinct from the Unity of the Nile Valley. In fact what emerged was a dichotomy in the nascent nationalist movement mirroring the split between the co-domini. One Sudanese faction eventually sided with Egypt, and proclaimed its unalterable (though never clearly defined) demand for union, while the other upheld the goal of Sudan for the Sudanese, if necessary in temporary co-operation with Britain to combat Egyptian pretensions. The continuing resilience of traditional tribal and religious authority and the numerical insignificance of the nationalists meant, however, that they had to ally with sectarian forces in order to win mass support. Thus, by the end of the Second World War, two opposing lines were discernible. On the one hand was a pro-independence group, dominated by Sayyid Abd al-Rahman al-Mahdi and deriving its mass support from his followers, the Ansar, in loose tactical alliance with the British. On the other hand were the unionists, in alliance with Egypt and supported, though much less openly, by Sayyid Ali al-Mirghani of the Khatmiyya, the long-standing rival of the Mahdists. Although this dichotomy greatly complicated political development, it both helped and hindered the British in retaining effective control. Significantly, however, it led to a debasing of those parliamentary institutions that were created in the post-war decade, as each side saw these in terms of its sectarian advantage rather than of consequence to the national good.

THE 'SOUTHERN PROBLEM'

That we come only now to consider developments in the southern Sudan is itself a reflection of the peripheral nature of the region during the 19th- and 20th-century colonial periods. The Turco-Egyptian regime had seen the south as a source of slave labour and natural resources, notably ivory. Such administration as existed was designed to facilitate extraction of those commodities, and was often indistinguishable from mere raiding. The period of the Mahdiyya was if anything even more disastrous, as the rudimentary Turco-Egyptian administration was destroyed but not replaced: the region degenerated into a chaos from which recovery would be slow and fitful. This was in turn because the next wave of foreign conquerors, the Anglo-Egyptians, again saw the south in largely negative terms, as territory that had to be occupied in order to safeguard the Nile basin. Thus again only very basic administration was set up, largely military in character and personnel, and with limited goals. Indeed, so loose was the control that the period from 1898 to 1929 was punctuated by a depressing series of local 'risings' and 'punitive expeditions' launched to assert government authority.

Whereas in the northern riverain Sudan some government resources had been invested in social services, little was spared for the south. In the north, for example, primary and elementary schools were established, albeit on a limited scale, and the Gordon Memorial College in Khartoum provided secondary education in order to supply the government with subordinate officials. In the south, however, education was left entirely in the hands of foreign Christian missionaries who, while long-suffering and admirable in their dedication, necessarily enhanced the separateness of the region and provided education to a lower standard. Again, whereas in the north medical care was increasingly available, especially in the towns but even in important rural areas like the Gezira, in the south health was a matter for missionaries or the army. Indeed, in the whole wide field of social and economic development, the first three decades of the condominium witnessed in the north such massive (if problematic) projects as the Gezira Scheme, the Sudan Railways, and the construction of Port Sudan; in the south no such investment was made. The result was a widening gap that was recognised, indeed formalised, in the famous Southern Policy of 1930.

The Southern Policy was designed to allow a breathing space during which the south would be allowed to develop free from the dangerous influences of the more advanced north, while indigenous political institutions were strengthened and modern education extended, so that the peoples of the region could stand on their own. In practice, however, the prescribed educational advances were not made, but the reactionary, exclusionary aspects of the policy were ham-fistedly enforced. The result, of course, was that by the end of the Second World War, when the northern Sudanese embarked on the road to self-government and self-determination, the south was still mired – indeed arguably more deeply – in backwardness. The British decision, taken in 1946, that the south should remain part of a unitary Sudanese polity (rather than, as had from time to time been mooted, being attached to Britain's East African dependencies) was itself never matched by real attention to the urgent social and economic advances that successful implementation of that decision required. By 1946 northern Sudanese politicians saw British concern for the south as cynical foot-dragging rather than belated paternalism, and this coloured their views on the constitutional disputes ahead.

INDEPENDENCE

Decisions taken in 1946 hardly took into account the prospect of self-government in 1953, still less of full independence in 1956. That such rapid advance took place was the result of the interplay of Sudanese politics and Anglo-Egyptian relations, which in turn were affected by Western interests in the Middle East. An Advisory Council of the Northern Sudan, established in 1944, was superseded in 1948 by a Legislative Assembly representing the whole country. Its powers were limited, and its efficacy further damaged by the refusal of the unionists to take part in it. Indeed, it is a telling comment on the politics of the period that the main constitutional bodies had little to do with major political advances. Thus continuing Anglo-Egyptian negotiations, concentrating on Sudan and the Suez Canal Base, were mirrored in the Sudan by heightening rivalry between the independents and unionists. This was, in turn, only the 'modern' face of the old sectarian rivalry of the Mahdists and Khatmiyya. The hollowness of political discourse – for the only 'issue' of moment remained union or independence – in fact suited the British and continued until the overthrow of the Egyptian monarchy in 1952. The successor regime called the British bluff: abandoning the old Egyptian claim to sovereignty in Sudan, the government of General Najib publicly recognised the Sudanese right to self-determination, confident that the eventual decision would favour union. The promise of immediate self-determination was one around which all Sudanese parties could unite, for against it the British policy of eventual independence paled even for the Mahdists.

Events moved quickly. An Anglo-Egyptian Agreement enshrined the main points of separate deals made by Egypt and the Sudanese political parties. That agreement called for a period of self-government during which prescribed steps would be taken towards self-determination. Elections to a Sudanese parliament were held in late 1953. To the shock and dismay of the British, these were swept by the unionists; the close association of the Mahdist Umma party with the British, and even more its obvious subordination to the dynastic ambitions of Sayyid Abd al-Rahman al-Mahdi, had turned public opinion towards a unionism that really meant the disappearance of the British rather than their replacement by the Egyptians. Indeed, 'union' was still a vague concept susceptible of interpretations ranging from a complete absorption to mere consultation of independent states. Thus the first Sudanese government, formed in early 1954 by the unionist leader Isma'il al-Azhari, was more anti-British than pro-Egyptian: its ultimate ambitions had yet to be decided.

A number of factors and developments led eventually to independence rather than union. In 1954 the Mahdists made clear, through violent demonstrations, their absolute opposition to union – even unto civil war. The eclipse in Egypt of General Najib, personally popular in Sudan, by Nasser was achieved at a cost of Sudanese support. This was made worse by the suppression of both the Egyptian communists and

Muslim Brotherhood, raising further fears among the Sudanese. Finally the true views of al-Azhari and his sometime patron, Sayyid Ali al-Mirghani, were crucial. Sayyid Ali had never favoured union, but had backed the unionists in order to oppose his rival, Sayyid Abd al-Rahman; with the Mahdists now in unaccustomed parliamentary opposition and considerable disarray, Sayyid Ali could turn against Egypt's Sudanese allies. And among those allies, including especially al-Azhari himself, unionism had evidently been a strategy, not an end in itself. He now moved adroitly to preside over Sudanese independence, which was achieved with British enthusiasm and Egyptian acquiescence on 1 January 1956.

PARLIAMENTARY AND MILITARY REGIMES 1956–69

Although the end of the condominium and creation of a republic appears as a clear demarcation in the political history of Sudan, in fact the more important dividing lines are in 1953, when the Anglo-Egyptian Agreement sealed the demise of the condominium, and 1958, when the regime established under that agreement was overthrown by the Sudanese army. The period from 1953 to 1958 was in fact largely out of continuity, during which the Sudanese government assumed the attributes of sovereignty but failed to achieve a depth of legitimacy sufficient to withstand the winds of change in the Muslim Middle East.

Faced with a deteriorating economy, growing disaffection in the southern Sudan, and the probable combination of his parliamentary enemies, Abdullah Khalil, the Umma politician who had succeeded al-Azhari in 1956, handed power to the army in 1958. Intended as a manoeuvre to win temporary respite from mounting difficulties, this flouting of the (still provisional) constitution opened the door not only to a six-year military regime but to all the coup-makers who followed. The demonstrable frailty of parliamentary government in turn has been a major difficulty in settling Sudan's north-south problem, because formal arrangements inspire little public confidence. In any event, the military regime of General Ibrahim Abbud failed ultimately in the major tests it faced, economic and political, and was itself overthrown. In what has become a peculiarly Sudanese phenomenon, he and his generals were driven from power in 1964 by a wave of popular disaffection, fed by economic malaise and, importantly, by the inability of the military to defeat rebellion in the south.

That rebellion, as we have seen, had its roots in the colonial period and even earlier. In 1955, on the eve of independence, the insensitivity of northern politicians – and the intrigues of Egypt – led to a mutiny of southern units of the SDF. This spread quickly across Equatoria and resulted in some 300 deaths, mostly of northern civilians. Although the rising was suppressed, its warning was never heeded in Khartoum, and disaffection merely simmered thereafter. Southern support for independence had been won by the promise of northern parliamentarians to consider a federal system of government; that promise was shelved as soon as independence was won and southerners saw themselves at the mercy of northern politicians. The Abbud regime was even more misguided than its civilian predecessor. It pursued an unabashed policy of Islamisation, thus fomenting the opposition – indeed helping to create the separate southern identity – its ostensibly 'nation-building' measures were supposed to combat. By 1964 open civil war was under way, and the generals were disastrously exposed as no more effective in the military sphere than in the civilian.

The transitional government that administered Sudan from October 1964 until elections in 1965 was one of unfulfilled promise, still wistfully recalled to this day. The broad coalition of trade unions, professional groups, and illegal political parties that brought down the Abbud regime was dominated by progressives who wished to avoid a return to the sterile politics of the old parties. In this they were foiled by their own disunity and the strength of the parties' sectarian bases. The Sudanese Communist party, for instance, although instrumental in the movement against the military regime, and prominent in the transitional government, had only a tiny following in the country; its hopes depended on a long transition period rather than on early elections. A promising Round Table Conference held to help settle the civil war fell victim, too, to the jockeying of the old parties, none of which would make concessions to African southerners on the eve of parliamentary elections. Thus the war continued, elections returned a government dominated by the Mahdist Umma party, and the structural changes envisaged by the New Forces were either still-born or rescinded.

If the fall of military governments is a theme of post-independence Sudanese politics, so is the failure of their parliamentary predecessors and successors to learn from their own mistakes. The second parliamentary regime (1965–69) witnessed heightened in-fighting between the sectarian parties, constant manoeuvring within them for personal advantage, splits over issues of little substance, and a partly consequent decline in the country's economic and social life. The war in the south worsened, as Khartoum politicians, now prisoners of their own rhetoric, dared make no concessions to the rebels. It proved impossible, too, to devise a permanent constitution, as such knotty problems as the nature of the state – secular or Islamic – took precedence over the practical concerns of the mass of the people. It was with relief, even satisfaction, that public opinion welcomed the military coup that overthrew the regime in May 1969.

THE 'MAY REGIME'

The young officers who took power in 1969 saw themselves as successors not of Abbud and the old-style soldiers of 1958–64, but of the visionaries of the transitional government of 1964–65. The May Regime, as it came to be called, was thus consciously reformist, even radical, in its ideology, which it derived in part from that of Nasser in Egypt and progressive regimes elsewhere in the non-aligned world.

Although it would survive longer than any government in Sudan's independent history, it, too, failed to fulfil its initial promise, and by the time that it, too, was overthrown, Sudan was set on a downward spiral from which it has yet to recover.

The new government acted quickly to assert itself in a potentially hostile political environment. In 1970 the open opposition of the Mahdists was suppressed violently: thousands died, including the leader of the Ansar, the Imam al-Hadi al-Mahdi, killed while trying to escape; his nephew, the former prime minister, Sadiq al-Mahdi, went into exile. In this suppression of the religious right wing, the fledgling government was helped by the active support of the left; now the regime turned on them. Increasingly emboldened, the leader of the junta, Ja'far Muhammad Numayr, made bitter public attacks on the Communist party and removed its sympathisers from the government; the party itself was split over whether to subsume itself in a new one-party organisation the regime was planning, or to maintain its independence. In the event, a disastrous miscalculation played into Numayr's hands. In July 1971 leftist junior officers led by Hashim al-Ata staged a coup, arrested Numayr, and occupied key installations. Their announcement of socialist goals preceded their consolidation of power: Numayr escaped, and with Egyptian and Libyan help rallied to defeat the rebels. A violent purge ensued, and the May Regime, destined to last another 14 years, turned its back on the left. Foreign and domestic policies were adjusted accordingly, as Numayr acted to solidify his personal position through alliances with the West and by conciliating both the religious right wing and the southern rebels.

The Addis Ababa Agreement of 1972 ended the war in the south. Although the May Regime had developed from the outset a new attitude towards the south, it had failed to achieve a settlement and indeed had turned towards military means. But the nearly successful coup of 1971 and, more importantly, the new unity of the Southern Sudan Liberation Movement (SSLM) under Joseph Lagu allowed both Khartoum and the rebels to approach peace talks with considerable momentum. Secret meetings led to formal talks, and in March 1972 agreement was reached by which the war would end, the south would be granted a degree of autonomy and the rebel forces would be integrated into the national army. Although some elements of the rebel movement never accepted it and its terms were soon dishonoured, the Addis Ababa Agreement brought the war to an end, allowed the start of an experiment in southern autonomy, and shored up Numayr's personal position both at home and abroad.

The abandonment of the May Regime's self-proclaimed socialism was accelerated in the 1970s by Numayr's renewed need to placate the religious right wing. Coup attempts punctuated his presidency (which was formalised by a spurious plebiscite in 1972). In July 1976 Mahdists almost succeeded in bringing down the regime; hundreds were killed, and Numayr himself escaped only by luck. He resolved therefore to conciliate and thus de-fang the Mahdists, and after secret talks with Sadiq al-Mahdi he announced a policy of 'national reconciliation', by which Sadiq would be allowed to return to Sudan and re-enter public life; in return he would recognise the institutions of the May Regime. Thus the opposition to Numayr was again split, as Sadiq al-Mahdi returned, the promised reforms were slow in coming and Numayr successfully played a masterly role in exploiting his opponents' weaknesses. Yet lip service on 'Islamic' issues was paid at a cost in southern and other secularist support, and in any case could not itself suffice indefinitely. By the early 1980s Numayr's measures to protect his personal position rekindled southern opposition, and this led to a new civil war and the eventual downfall of the regime itself.

THE REVOLT OF THE SOUTH AND THE FALL OF NUMAYR

The autonomy enjoyed by the southern Sudanese between 1972 and 1983 was vitiated by the ineptness and corruption of southern politicians and by the manoeuvres of Numayr and his government in Khartoum. Cynical exploitation of the perquisites of power in the south played into Numayr's hands and allowed many of the practical benefits of autonomy – especially rapid social and economic development – to be postponed indefinitely. Numayr's national reconciliation, promising, for instance, country-wide implementation of the *shari'a*, or Muslim law, could not be so long postponed, and by the early 1980s southern disaffection had been recharged. The final straw came when, in 1983, Numayr proclaimed the 'redivision' of the south into three separate 'regions' corresponding to the old southern provinces of colonial days and, a few months later, the implementation of the *shari'a*. In fact the spark of southern revolt had already been applied to the tinder in May, when units of the army rebelled and took to the bush.

In allowing this Numayr reckoned without important changes in the southern radical leadership. The new rebellion was spearheaded by the Sudan People's Liberation Movement and Army (SPLM/SPLA), an organisation with a tightly knit political-military command (in contrast to the disunity that bedevilled earlier movements) and with the vehemently asserted goal not of secession but of bringing down the Khartoum regime and replacing it with a new democratic and socialist one. After suppressing rival movements supported by Khartoum, the SPLM/SPLA quickly emerged as a formidable political-military adversary, and won adherents even among secularist northern Sudanese.

Civil war was a decisive factor, but hardly the only one, in bringing down Numayr in April 1985. A disastrous economic collapse, attended by a series of catastrophes of almost biblical proportions – drought, famine, pestilence – brought Sudan to bankruptcy and the verge of collapse. The black humour of the Sudanese expressed itself in the view that a coup was unlikely because there was no longer anything worth taking over, but this belied the continuing failure of the opposition to unite against a discredited regime. The SPLM/SPLA, despite its protests to the contrary, was tellingly seen even by most northern intellectuals as a southern movement, and thus perhaps as an ally but never as the object of their primary personal or factional support. The old parties, having successively collaborated with Numayr, were reduced to their core support of 'holy families' and their economic dependents. The communists had not recovered from 1971. Indeed, the most coherent political grouping left in northern Sudan was the Muslim Brotherhood, and it was to them that Numayr turned in the early 1980s. They were glad to co-operate with a weakened president who was willing to implement some of their own programme; Hasan al-Turabi, the brilliant leader of the Muslim Brotherhood, occupied important posts in the government. When, however, in late 1984 Numayr tried to curb their power, he was left with only the army to support him. In April 1985, as mass protests escalated and Numayr haughtily went on a foreign tour, the army leadership acted to save itself and deposed him.

It is important to note that the Transitional Military Council that ruled until the spring of 1986 was essentially a continuation of the Numayr regime without Numayr. No radical departures were taken by the generals or by the weak civilian cabinet they appointed. The infamous September Laws, whereby Numayr had made the *shari'a* the law of the land, went largely unenforced but were not repealed. The war therefore continued: absurd rumours that the SPLM/SPLA leader, Dr John Garang de Mabior, would lay down his arms or even join the new government showed the depth of misunderstanding of both that movement and the disaffection it had tapped. Hopes among northern secularists, trade unionists, members of professional associations and other progressives, that a lengthy transition period might be used to prepare thoughtfully for a new, democratic political system, were dashed. Just as they had in 1965, so in 1985–86 the old sectarian parties re-emerged to retake power. Elections were held as early as possible and, as predicted, the Umma party formed a government under Sadiq al-Mahdi. Yet even this sequence of events, coming as it did after the debacle of the May Regime, seemed to promise a new start.

Despite 20 years out of power, during which he had endured exile, prison, impoverishment and the enormous strain of coup and countercoup, Sadiq al-Mahdi returned to the premiership with no clear policy. Perhaps more than any other Sudanese, he had by virtue of intellect and traditional sanction the means to forge a truly national programme, one that might end the war, win over the northern Sudanese to a secularist constitution and resume by slower processes the very nation-building that stubborn northern chauvinism had prevented. Yet he did not exploit the opportunity. Instead he presided over a series of weak coalitions, the survival of which seemed always to depend on lip service to the *shari'a*, an Islamic constitution, the defeat of rebels (rather than the conciliation of fellow opponents of Numayr) and other discredited policies. As the country's economic situation worsened, the war was effectively lost in the south (but continued to drain the treasury), and the government frittered away the goodwill that had attended a return to parliamentary rule. By the spring of 1989 the army, in an unprecedented move, publicly warned the government to break the impasse in the south or face overthrow. Sadiq finally acted but, characteristically, too late: just as an important preliminary agreement was about to be signed, which promised real progress towards a peaceful settlement of the war, elements of the army stepped in and overthrew the regime in June 1989.

SUDAN SINCE 1989

The composition and aims of the group of officers who took power in 1989 were not immediately clear. At first it was thought that the army, having publicly warned the prime minister, had simply fulfilled its promise. It gradually became evident, however, that the coup had been staged by middle-ranking and junior officers against the army leadership itself and without any fixed programme or underlying ideology; the officers timed the coup to subvert arrangements for a cease-fire in the south, not to guarantee it. The weakness and inexperience of the junta was an opportunity for Hasan al-Turabi and the National Islamic Front (NIF), the party vehicle of the Muslim Brothers. By the time the junta had consolidated its power it had also exhibited the Islamic orientation that became its hallmark.

Despite the minority status of the NIF, many Sudanese were pragmatically willing to judge the new regime by its results, as indeed they had been after the 1958 and, especially, the 1969 military takeovers. It soon became clear, however, that the doctrines of Hasan al-Turabi were no substitute for a government programme. In important areas – economic policy, constitutional reform, the war in the south, and foreign relations – the National Salvation Revolution, as the regime called itself, lurched from crisis to crisis and soon held power by force rather than consensus.

In redoubling Khartoum's efforts to crush the SPLM/SPLA the new regime differed from its predecessors mainly in degree. To be sure, its repeated invocation of jihad and welcome of support from other Arab and Muslim states, including Iran, was innovative, but the policy of repression was not. More important than that assistance, moreover, was the fall of the Mengistu regime in Ethiopia, and the subsequent loss to the SPLM/SPLA of its main foreign base and backing. There followed a disastrous split in the rebels' ranks, fulfilling the worst fears and persistent expectations of their respective supporters and enemies. Personal and tribal rivalries, born in part of reaction to the iron hand with which John Garang had held the movement together, brought the whole southern resistance near to defeat by 1993. Khartoum's total disregard for the civilian masses caught up in the war was both a tactic in its policy and a clue to its strategic design, the Islamisation (or, as some would say, Sudanisation) of the south.

While northern Sudanese support of the Islamic regime was never contingent on the conduct of the war, the economic consequences of the war were a different matter. At base, the teachings of Hasan al-Turabi are socio-religious nostrums unencumbered by economics. Inflation – the Sudanese pound declined in value from about $0.25 in 1985 to $0.0013 in 1995 – has ravaged the economy. Skilled workers, ranging from drivers to engineers and doctors, have emigrated in large numbers and with a sense of permanency absent during previous troubles. Donor countries have cut off aid, in protest against both Sudan's economic policies and its widely publicised human rights abuses.

In foreign affairs the NIF regime has won a degree of international notoriety. It supported Iraq in the Gulf War, and has aligned itself with Iran. It has alienated some Arab states by supporting their armed domestic opponents. It has been widely condemned by Western governments for harbouring individual terrorists and helping to establish terrorist base camps in the country. The alleged involvement of Sudanese in the World Trade Center bombing in New York in 1994 has left Sudan on the State Department's list of rogue governments. Relations with Egypt have continued to worsen; an assassination attempt in Ethiopia on President Mubarak of Egypt in June 1995 led to mutual recriminations and border violence. Meanwhile relations with Uganda and Kenya, immediately important because of cross-border aspects of the civil war, improved in the early 1990s only to deteriorate again in 1995, when there was fresh evidence that supplies were channelled through those states to the southern rebels. While Sudan's very weakness vis-à-vis Egypt and the West has won it a degree of sympathy in world bodies, and has served at moments of crisis to rally the faithful in Sudanese towns, the regime's isolation remains an important factor in its long-term prospects for survival.

Finally, in the area of constitutional reform, the NIF regime had by 1995 faltered over the same obstacles as its predecessors. Successive rebel movements in the south had always elicited a degree of northern support because of their opposition to the idea of an Islamic state; the politically important northern middle class, whether tending towards the right or the left, has been essentially if not admittedly secularist. Once the orientation of the post-1989 regime was clear, therefore, it became a mere junta holding power by force and enjoying the support of a tiny minority. The regime's institutions are redolent of impermanence. Elaborate and expensive devolution schemes are conduits of patronage rather than of power. Interest in carefully staged local elections is low.

The outlook for Sudan remains bleak. The country shares with others in the region the lack of a unifying principle under which its many ethnic, religious and social differences might be reconciled; an Islamic state of the NIF variety has not provided a focus for nation-building. While the end of the cold war lessened foreign interest in the country's ideological orientation, the NIF's forays on the world stage have won Sudan little discernible benefit. The south, ravaged and decimated as it is, shows no signs of surrender and some evidence of revival; even the SPLM/SPLA, since its inception adamantly a national rather than separatist movement, has opted for self-determination for the region. Already one of the poorest states in the world, Sudan grows poorer; the educated elite, trained at great cost, continue to vote with their feet and emigrate.

The NIF's best hope of remaining in power is the disunity of its enemies. The only armed opponents are southern rebel groups, and while these have made occasional alliances with northern parties and politicians, it has been the rare northener who has been willing to accept southern leadership. The old northern parties retain some automatic sectarian support, but understandably have lost credibility and inspire no enthusiasm. The army was systematically and ruthlessly purged after 1989, and its current leadership has no support outside the NIF. The appearance of foreign bullying, whether American denunciations or Egyptian threats, is likely in Sudan – as it would be elsewhere – temporarily to rally support for the regime rather than embolden its opponents. Foreign subversion is another matter, and a combination of internal factions with covert external support, not unprecedented in Sudan's turbulent history, remains a possibility. But the likeliest scenario for change is a steady draining of support that culminates in mass action; the examples of 1964 and 1985, when military dictators were toppled after popular uprisings, are often rehearsed by hopeful Sudanese. The ideological character of the present regime suggests, however, that another such uprising would be much more violent than those almost bloodless affairs. Moreover the failure of the parliamentary regimes that came after them raises the question of whether Sudan's problems are indeed intractable.

Martin W. Daly

14
SYRIA

O N 30 SEPTEMBER 1918, with Damascus surrounded by Australian and British Indian troops, the Northern Arab Army under Faysal ibn Husayn was allowed to enter the city and to take control. Faysal subsequently proclaimed 'an absolutely independent government embracing all Syria'. This was the beginning of the Arab Kingdom of Syria, which lasted from October 1918 until 25 July 1920, at which point Faysal and his supporters were ejected from Syria by the French, and the French mandate administration installed.

By the end of October 1918, the British had penetrated as far north as Aleppo. The whole of Greater Syria had been detached from the Ottoman Empire and was now under British military control. The area was divided into three zones, the Occupied Enemy Territory Administration (OETA), south, west and east – corresponding to Palestine, the Syrian coast and the Syrian interior – all under the command of General Allenby. Of crucial importance at this stage was that in spite of France's well publicised territorial ambitions in the area, there were only a few small detachments of French troops in Greater Syria at the end of 1918, and only one senior diplomat, François Georges-Picot, former Consul-General in Beirut.

Much of the confusion of the next few years, and the fact that the ultimate 'disposal' of Syria took place in circumstances of great rancour and bloodshed, can be ascribed to intense suspicions on the part of the French as to the intentions of Britain and its Hashemite protégés. The British Foreign Secretary Sir Edward Grey had declared to the French Ambassador in London in December 1912 that Britain had no territorial designs on Syria, and the Sykes-Picot agreement (*see* page 10) of February 1916 had effectively assigned the Syrian coast and 'influence' over the potentially Arab-administered Syrian interior, to France. However, the situation on the ground at the end of 1918 seemed to threaten the security of these guarantees. It was in what is now Syria that the latent contradictions between the aspirations of 'the Arabs' and the French surfaced with the greatest violence. Faysal, relying on his interpretation of Britain's promises to his father, Sharif Husayn, insisted on his claim to rule Syria, while the French demanded the fulfilment of the agreements made between themselves and the British.

Since Anglo-French co-operation was essential in other areas of the post-War settlement, the French government eventually got its way, in the face of strenuous objections from Faysal and his supporters. After the announcement that British troops would be evacuated from Syria

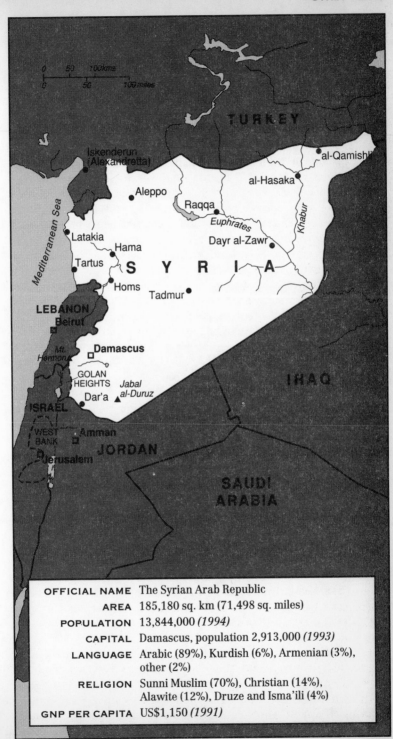

OFFICIAL NAME	The Syrian Arab Republic
AREA	185,180 sq. km (71,498 sq. miles)
POPULATION	13,844,000 *(1994)*
CAPITAL	Damascus, population 2,913,000 *(1993)*
LANGUAGE	Arabic (89%), Kurdish (6%), Armenian (3%), other (2%)
RELIGION	Sunni Muslim (70%), Christian (14%), Alawite (12%), Druze and Isma'ili (4%)
GNP PER CAPITA	US$1,150 *(1991)*

and Cilicia in November 1919, Faysal rushed to Europe in a desperate effort to have the decision reversed. When he realised he would not make any headway he tried to come to an accommodation with the French before returning to Syria at the beginning of 1920.

Syria was then in great ferment, since contradictory rumours held both that liberation was imminent and that a great struggle with the French was about to take place. It gradually became clear that the latter was the reality. In February Faysal announced that independence would be won 'by the sword', and on 8 March the Arab National Congress proclaimed him king of all Syria. This further galvanised the British and French into action. On 25 April the mandates for Mesopotamia, Palestine and Syria, and the approximate boundaries of these states, were decided upon at San Remo. At this Faysal's supporters took the law into their own hands, and launched a series of raids into the French controlled area on the Syrian coast. By early July, following a Franco-Turkish armistice under which the Turks finally withdrew from northern Syria, the French commander General Gouraud delivered an ultimatum to Faysal, who accepted it. In a brave but quixotic act of defiance, a few of his supporters attacked the French at Khan Maysalun, on the road between Beirut and Damascus. They were defeated, and Faysal was sent into exile.

SYRIA UNDER FRENCH MANDATE 1920–46

Although Faysal's rule had not been universally popular, the provocative and often brutal nature of the French mandatory regime was vigorously opposed by wide sections of the population for much of the mandate. In the first place, Lebanon, considerably enlarged by the addition of areas traditionally considered parts of Syria, was constituted by the French as a separate state (*see* Chapter 8, Lebanon). What remained of Syria was then further divided into three administrative units: one including the four main cities of Aleppo, Hama, Homs and Damascus; one for each of the 'compact' minorities, the Druzes and the Alawites; and finally the *sanjak* of Alexandretta, which the French eventually ceded to Turkey (in violation of the terms of the mandate) in 1939. The thinking behind the divisions was that the religious minorities living mostly in the rural areas would become bound to France by ties of loyalty and gratitude for having saved them from the domination of the Sunni majority, considered to be infected by the virus of Arab nationalism. The extent to which this failed can be gauged from the fact that the Druze area in particular was the source of some of the most vigorous opposition to the French during the mandate period, and that the rural minorities regularly made common cause with the people of the cities against those whom they regarded as their colonisers and occupiers.

The first major revolt of the period actually began in the Druze area, under the leadership of the Druze notable Sultan al-Atrash, in 1925. Starting off as a tribal revolt against the French administration in the Jabal Druze, it became a national rising when al-Atrash was joined by a number of Damascene notables centred around Abd al-Rahman al-Shahbandar and his People's Party, who called for national independence. Although the uprising was defeated in 1926 it led eventually to some relaxation in French policy, in that the French showed themselves prepared to countenance a constitution and the gradual withdrawal of French troops. Negotiations continued well into 1928, and the nationalists were successful to the extent that a national assembly was elected and asked to draw up a constitution for Syria.

Although the assembly was dominated by 'moderate' rural and tribal notables and other pro-French elements, the constitutional committee itself was outnumbered by the better educated and generally more enlightened representatives of the urban elites. The draft constitution that emerged recommended the transfer of all powers to the (non-existent) polity of Greater Syria (that is, an entity which was to include Lebanon, Palestine, Syria and Transjordan), reflecting the widely felt anger and resentment at what was seen as the arbitrary division of Syria by Britain and France. The draft was rejected and France introduced its own constitution by decree under which Syria was declared a constitutional republic. Negotiations for a Franco-Syrian treaty, generally on the lines of the Anglo-Iraqi Treaty of 1930, which provided for an independent Iraq under strong British influence, continued until stalemate was reached in 1933. Negotiations were resumed in the spring of 1936, mainly as the result of a seven week general strike in Aleppo and Damascus. The election of the Popular Front government in France later in the year seemed to presage a more favourable atmosphere for the talks.

Unlike in Iraq, where the 'nationalists' around Nuri al-Sa'id had generally been in partnership with Britain and the Iraqi monarchy, most Syrian nationalists continued to oppose the French Mandate. They did not constitute a unified body, however, but continued to be divided into regional factions. These were centred around the urban-based absentee landowning families of the great cities – Damascus, Aleppo, Hama and Homs – where they maintained their political base and their social networks. Although rivalries persisted they joined together in 1931 to form the National Bloc, an independence movement rather than a political party, which was to dominate Syrian politics until independence in 1946.

Although the Bloc had not instigated the general strike in 1936 and many of its members were alarmed when it seemed to get out of control, its apparent ability to contain the strike became an important asset. When it did manage to assume leadership and take control of the strike, the French showed their preparedness to negotiate and invited its representatives to Paris. The leader of the Syrian delegation to Paris was Jamil Mardam Bey, a moderate inclined to accommodate French interests. In September 1936 a draft treaty was initialled, which provided for a form of qualified Syrian independence while guaranteeing French hegemony. The Alawite and Druze regions were to be integrated into the Syrian state while keeping a certain degree of autonomy, as was the case at this stage for the *sanjak* of Alexandretta. By 1939, however, the new French government had not yet signed the treaty. The Alawite and Druze regions were still autonomous; and the Jazira, in the northeast of the country and recently settled mostly by Christians and Kurds, had been put under the direct rule of the high commissioner. Parliament was dissolved, martial law declared and Syria fell once again under direct French rule. In June 1939 Alexandretta was annexed by Turkey, causing a tremendous loss of prestige to the nationalists and great economic damage to the city of Aleppo.

Thus, by the start of the Second World War the Syrian nationalists' efforts to free themselves from the French had come to nothing. In the end, independence was only achieved with British support. British and Free French troops invaded Syria and Lebanon in 1940 in a successful attempt to prevent Axis forces from gaining a foothold in the Middle East. But although the constitution was restored and the minority areas integrated into the Syrian state, the Free French seemed in no more of a hurry to grant independence than their predecessors. The nationalists, however, now under the leadership of Shukri al-Quwwatli, continued to push for unconditional independence. In clashes between the Syrian leaders and their French opponents, Britain began to back the leaders of the National Bloc, particularly al-Quwwatli.

During the mandate, the French High Commission and its representatives in the various administrative subdistricts took all major decisions and controlled the country's principal sources of revenue. The Syrian pound was linked to the franc, which, given the precarious state of the French economy in the interwar period, meant that the currency was highly unstable. The French also controlled the bank of note issue, the Banque de Syrie et du Grand Liban, whose gold reserves were kept in Paris.

No Syrian national army was created during the French mandate. The French controlled Syria by means of the Armée du Levant, consisting mainly of colonial troops from Africa and Madagascar, and the Troupes Spéciales du Levant (TSL), mostly recruited from the minority communities in Syria and Lebanon, particularly the Alawites, Armenians, Circassians, Druzes, Isma'ilis, Kurds and Turcomans, as were many of the rural gendarmerie. The preponderance of minorities in the TSL was to have an important impact when the TSL became the basis of the Syrian army after independence. Generally, few urban Sunnis, and very few Sunnis from prominent families, opted for a military career, so the minorities were proportionally over-represented in the officer corps.

THE EARLY YEARS OF INDEPENDENT SYRIA 1946–63

When independence was finally gained in 1946, those who came to power were the old urban absentee landowning notables who had dominated the National Bloc. Although generally more progressive than the rural and tribal notables who had been the mainstay of French rule, the new political leaders were mostly too short-sighted to realise that things could not simply continue as before. The country desperately needed major reforms to solve its most outstanding social and economic problems. Competition and personal rivalries weakened the new government and the political situation continued to be precarious. In 1949 Syria experienced three military coups: the first led by Husni al-Za'im; the second by Muhammad Sami al-Hinnawi; and the third by Adib al-Shishakli, who managed to cling to power until he was brought down by provincial revolts in 1954.

Nevertheless, the old nationalist leaders who came back to power after al-Shishakli was ousted in 1954 had not lost legitimacy and in fact gained a landslide victory in the famously free elections held in the same year. However, they were too divided and too set in their ways to be able to take up the new challenges and expectations of change both in Syria and in the Arab world. In addition, preoccupied with the threat of communism and the rise of the left, they did not fully appreciate the immediate threat to their own interests posed by the military. But if the old elite was generally incapable of coping with the new sociopolitical circumstances, some of its leading figures, notably Khalid al-Azm, did make serious attempts to lead the country towards social reform and the creation of a democratic pluralist political system. Khalid al-Azm came from one of Syria's wealthiest and oldest families and had no intention of establishing some kind of communist state. But the mere fact that he had good relations with both the Soviet Union and the Communist Party and was attempting to introduce a number of social democratic reforms, laid him open to charges of communism from his Pan-Arab rivals. The misunderstanding, overestimation and exaggeration of the threat of communism was a major feature of the years of the Cold War, fuelled by the Eisenhower doctrine, and deeply embedded in the political ideology of many of Syria's Arab neighbours.

Several new political parties and organisations had emerged, some in the 1930s and others after the Second World War. These included the Syrian Social Nationalist Party (SSNP) founded by Antun Sa'ada, the Communist Party led by Khalid Bakdash, the Muslim Brotherhood, and the Ba'th Party founded by Zaki Al-Arsuzi, Salah al-Din al-Bitar and Michel Aflaq in the early 1940s. The SSNP represented 'Greater Syrian' nationalism, calling for the unity of geographical Syria, Iraq and Cyprus; it was founded by, and drew most of its support from, Greek Orthodox Christians in Syria and Lebanon. The Ba'th Party advocated Arab unity, claiming to be a truly pan-Arab party with branches in each Arab country seeking to unify the whole Arab world. During the 1950s the Syrian Ba'th was able to widen its appeal, moving to the left after its merger with Akram Hawrani's Arab Socialist Party in 1952. It gained 16 seats in the 1954 elections.

However, none of these parties gained ground in the presidential elections of 1955 which brought Shukri al-Quwwatli back to power. The government fell in 1956 and Sabri al-Asali formed a government of national unity with representatives of most of the parties, including Khalid al-Azm's Democratic Bloc and the Ba'th. Early in 1958, when al-Azm, who was already Minister of Defence and of Finance, became Deputy Prime Minister, his political rivals began to regard the growth in his power and personal popularity as a serious potential threat to their own ambitions.

THE UNITED ARAB REPUBLIC

Accordingly, fearing al-Azm might win a landslide victory in the impending parliamentary elections, Salah al-Din al-Bitar hit on the expedient of a United Arab Republic of Egypt and Syria (UAR). This had the double advantage of satisfying the Pan-Arab aspirations of many Syrians and of advancing the prospects of Aflaq, al-Bitar and the Ba'th as the principal authors of this grand gesture. Furthermore, it was anticipated that unification would effectively check the perceived threat of communism, although in the absence of free elections no accurate measure of communist support at the time is possible.

The 14-man military delegation which left Damascus for Cairo on 12 January 1958 had no clear authority from the civil government; indeed their action was in effect a coup d'état. Nevertheless, on 1 February 1958 al-Quwwatli and Nasser proclaimed the creation of the United Arab Republic of Egypt and Syria, and, as a political entity, Syria disappeared temporarily from the scene. The union with Egypt created an atmosphere of euphoria in Syria and other parts of the Arab world, but this soon wore off, and the UAR experiment only lasted three years. Frustrated by Egyptian domination and exploitation, many former advocates of unity became disillusioned and came to favour secession, and in the autumn of 1961 a military coup in Syria put an end to the United Arab Republic. Civilian rule was restored and elections held, bringing back the old elite of the pre-1958 period. Apart from Akram Hawrani's wing, which had opposed union with Egypt and was able to gain 15 seats, the Ba'th around Aflaq and al-Bitar did very badly in the elections. Independents gained the highest number of seats (62) and Ma'ruf al-Dawalibi and Nazim al-Qudsi, both from the old elite, became respectively premier and president of the republic.

Over the next two years, members of the old notability, particularly al-Azm and al-Dawalibi, pressed for the restoration of democratic liberties and the creation of a mixed economy. A fierce jockeying for power behind the scenes ensued, expressed in three minor military coups in Damascus, Homs and Aleppo in 1962. In spite of this the civilian leadership survived, and in September 1962 the National Assembly asked Khalid al-Azm to form a National Union Cabinet, in which the Ba'th refused to serve.

One important consequence of the UAR episode was a general lowering in the standing and reputation of the Ba'thists and Pan-Arab nationalists for having taken Syria into the Union, although Pan-Arabism continued to have a certain appeal. Their poor showing in the elections clearly indicated that they would only be able to regain power by extra-parliamentary means, that is, through a military coup. Al-Azm's efforts to establish a functioning democratic parliamentary system and to keep the army at bay, therefore, constituted a direct challenge to the ambitions of the Pan-Arab nationalists and their allies in the army.

ECONOMIC TRENDS AFTER INDEPENDENCE

Although it does not possess the extensive natural resources of its richer neighbours, Syria was able to sustain one of the most integrated and productive economies in the region for several decades after the Second World War. Perhaps the lack of such resources was not entirely unfortunate, in that the country was forced to make prudent use of what it had. An additional feature distinguishing it from most of the oil states is that Syria possesses many cities of great antiquity, well endowed with skilled labour and with an expanding and educated middle class. Both urbanisation and population growth accelerated increasingly (3.5 per cent per annum) after the mid-1960s, and the economy had some difficulty in keeping ahead of these developments. Nevertheless, it was only after the Arab-Israeli war of 1973 that Syria began to rely heavily on external resources, partly expatriate remittances but mostly aid from the oil rich Arab states.

During and immediately after the Second World War both industry and agriculture prospered. Industrial and agricultural development were left to private initiative, while the state concentrated on infrastructural projects, including building new roads, the port of Latakia and the Homs oil refinery, the latter with the help of a Soviet loan. Syria produced a range of light consumer goods such as textiles (based on local cotton), processed food, soap, glass and cement. In 1960 industry accounted for 15 per cent of gross domestic product (GDP) and employed 12 per cent of the labour force, agriculture employing 60 per cent.

THE RISE OF THE BA'TH

In spite of al-Azm's serious illness, the government stood firm when tensions mounted in the spring of 1963. Radio Cairo intensified its campaign against reactionary and secessionist (that is, from the UAR) elements. Socialist and Muslim Brotherhood ministers continued to quarrel and the military command squabbled over proposals to promote or dismiss various officers. Although the Ba'th-Nasserist coup in Iraq in February 1963 had been directed by the CIA, as King Husayn of Jordan later confirmed, the Iraqi coup was hailed as progressive by both the Pan-Arab nationalists and the Ba'thists. Clearly encouraged by events in Iraq, a group of Ba'thist and Nasserist officers engineered a military coup in Damascus on 8 March 1963 and asked the Ba'th to take over. The Ba'th agreed and integrated the officers into the party structure. Salah al-Bitar, whose party had failed miserably in the 1961 elections, was asked to form the government.

Real power remained with the armed forces, and it was within the military that the struggle for key positions and control which characterised the period until 1970 took place. Although a few Sunnis maintained their positions, all key posts in the armed forces were gradually taken up by members of the non-Sunni minorities, the Alawites, Druzes and Isma'ilis, all of whom came mainly from the rural areas. The Ba'th, which had only about 400 members in March 1963, substantially increased its membership, especially among these same communities.

In the relentless infighting which ensued between the various Ba'th factions, political actors began increasingly to seek support among their own immediate kin and within their own communities.

The Alawites, a heterodox Shi'i community constituting some 12 per cent of the Syrian population, came originally from the mountainous northwest of the country where they worked as peasants or sharecroppers on the land of Alawi landowners or on the plains, where the landowners were either Sunni or Greek Orthodox. They did not form a uniform entity but consisted of a number of loosely linked tribal confederations and included several smaller religious sects. Thus Hafiz al-Asad, President of Syria since 1970, originates from the Matawira tribe from the village of Qardaha and belonged to the Qamariyya sect. One of the attractions of Ba'thism for the Syrian minorities was that, at least in theory, a secular state would diminish the importance of sectarian affiliation and enable them to be integrated into the state of Syria as citizens rather than as members of a particular sect.

During the second half of the 1960s control over the state became increasingly concentrated within the Alawite community, although some of its most severe critics came from within its own ranks. However, instead of diminishing its sectarian identity, Ba'th rule became almost exclusively identified with Alawite rule. On 23 February 1966 a military coup ended the long struggle for dominance between the old Ba'thists, notably Amin al-Hafiz and Salah al-Din al-Bitar, and the Neo-Ba'th, mostly from the provinces and provincial towns, centred around Salah al-Jadid and Hafiz al-Asad, in favour of the latter. While both the new President and the new Prime Minister were Sunnis, real power lay in the hands of Jadid and Asad. Subsequently the two began to compete with each other for control of the key positions within the state. Jadid tried to do this by controlling the Party machine, while Asad built up his network within the army and the air force and, in November 1970, managed to oust Jadid, who died in prison in August 1993.

THE BA'TH'S ECONOMIC POLICIES

The Ba'th takeover in 1963 led to a complete transformation of the Syrian state structure and of its social base. Both the land reform, inaugurated under the UAR and subsequently carried out more effectively during the 1960s and 1970s, and the wholesale nationalisations of the same period, substantially weakened both the political and economic power of the established elites. They found themselves compelled either to leave the country with as much of their capital as they could take with them (as many did) or to co-operate with, or at least acquiesce in, the new structures of power. As a result the success or failure of particular businesses became increasingly dependent on the degree to which those running them managed to manipulate various social and political networks within the state and its institutions.

After Asad came to power in 1970 there was a certain degree of economic liberalisation. Restrictions were lifted and exchange and trade regulations were relaxed. The repatriation of Syrian capital from abroad, together with substantial aid to Syria from other Arab states after 1973, increases in oil revenues and transit trade, and remittances from Syrians working in the Gulf, led to an economic boom which lasted until the late 1970s. At the same time, the state began to launch some of its most ambitious industrial development schemes, earmarking almost half of total investment for industry. As most of these industries required a volume of investment far beyond the capacity of local private capital, all major industries soon became state owned.

Private manufacture benefited indirectly from the infrastructural improvements, and more generally from the expansion of the market and of purchasing power. Most private manufacturing enterprises – some 85,000 – continue to be of small or middling size employing fewer than ten people, often family members; only a small proportion (about 2,000) employ more than ten workers. The most profitable businesses are in construction and in contracting in which private individuals act as middlemen between private companies – both foreign and domestic – and the government.

In order to make Syria more self-sufficient in food, the Ba'th began to promote agriculture more systematically. As well as receiving much more investment, price controls for vegetables and fruit were also lifted. In spite of the land reform, 70 per cent of land is still worked privately. In order to stimulate agricultural investment further during the 1980s the government began to support new mixed public/private sector ventures, many of which were concerned with vegetable growing and poultry farms. This has resulted in improved supplies of fresh vegetables, fruit, eggs and chicken on the local markets but has also meant substantial price rises. Farms employing wage labour, utilising modern machinery and production methods coexist next to small traditionally run family farms. Another lucrative business is livestock raising which is entirely in private hands. The value of animal produce constitutes almost one-third of total agricultural output.

POLITICAL DEVELOPMENTS SINCE THE 1970S

The most striking political development of the 1970s was the transformation of the state in favour of the presidency. The president, elected every seven years, is supreme army commander and determines the overall outlines of government policies. He appoints and dismisses ministers and cabinets and makes the key appointments in the judiciary. Hafiz al-Asad was elected in 1971 and re-elected in 1978, 1985 and 1992 with over 99 per cent of the vote. Real power continues to lie with the army, the security services and a group of trusted men who report directly to the president. Asad was grooming his eldest son Basil to succeed him, but since his death in a car accident in January 1994, Basil's younger brother Bashar seems to be being trained to replace him. However, his inexperience and lack of political clout suggest that, unless it is a long time coming, the succession is likely to be problematic.

Apart from the interior, foreign and defence ministers (Abd al-Halim Khaddam, Faruq al-Shara' and Mustafa Tlas) who have the ear of the president, individual ministers generally carry little political weight and are there to carry out executive decisions; nevertheless, they include both party members and technocrats. Parliament, which has largely symbolic powers, consists of a single chamber People's Council with a Ba'th majority but also includes members of other parties and a number of independents. The Ba'th Party reputedly has almost a million members of a population of some 13 million. In 1972 the Ba'th co-opted a number of rival political parties (including the Communists) into a National Progressive Front, thus ensuring a minimum degree of pluralism.

Hafiz al-Asad became ruler of Syria at a time of mounting tensions in the Middle East. An important consequence of the 1967 war for Syria, when it lost the Golan Heights, was that its role in the Arab-Israeli conflict was greatly enhanced, and that the conflict itself came increasingly to dominate its internal affairs and its regional and foreign policy. Here Syria's role was almost inevitably ambiguous. On the one hand, the leadership was probably genuinely committed to the Arab cause. On the other, more mundane and immediate considerations of *realpolitik* caused it to act in ways which were motivated more by self-interest and regime consolidation than by the best interests of 'the Arabs'. Syria's role in Lebanon since 1976 and its alliance with Iran during Iran's war with Iraq are two striking examples. In addition, because of its role as a front line state, Syria obtained considerable aid from the richer Arab states after 1973, which enabled it to expand its armed forces, mainly through purchases of arms from the Soviet Union.

SYRIA'S INVOLVEMENT IN LEBANON

In 1973, Syria took part in the war against Israel alongside Egypt, but Sadat's failure to give adequate logistical support exposed Syrian forces to a dangerous extent. In consequence relations between the two states deteriorated sharply, especially when it became clear in the latter part of the 1970s that Egypt was prepared to enter separate negotiations with Israel. A further important consequence of both the Arab-Israeli wars was the rise of the Palestine Liberation Organisation (PLO) as a political and military force which could and did challenge national armies and national governments, as happened in Jordan and Lebanon. In 1974, at the Rabat summit, the PLO was recognised as the sole legitimate representative of the Palestinian people, a development which both enhanced its own political role and altered the position of other actors in the region, especially King Husayn of Jordan.

Early in 1976 the Lebanese National Movement (LNM), led by Kamal Jumblatt in close co-operation with the PLO, was beginning to gain the upper hand in the Lebanese civil war (*see* Chapter 8, Lebanon). At this point a fortuitous community of interest developed between Syria and the USA, both of which were alarmed (though for different reasons) at the prospect of a future radical leftist government transforming the balance of power in Lebanon. In these years of superpower confrontation the USA was particularly concerned about Soviet influence in Lebanon increasing if the LNM and the PLO were to succeed. It was thus intimated to Syria that neither the USA nor Israel would oppose Syrian intervention. Thus reassured, Syria sent a detachment of its own army as well as troops from Saiqa, the Syrian-financed Palestinian militia, into Lebanon in June 1976. This intervention was crucial in turning the tide against the PLO and its Lebanese allies. Most immediately, it enabled Maronite forces to attack Palestinian and LNM areas in East Beirut, with fearful consequences, notably at Tall Za'tar, where some 3,000 civilians were massacred.

The Syrian incursion had taken place without consultation with the Soviet Union, Syria's principal arms supplier. In spite of the conventional wisdom and the Syrian/Soviet Treaty of 1980, Syria was never a true Soviet satellite; throughout the relationship, Syria insisted on maintaining its political autonomy. Soviet arms shipments, reduced drastically in 1976, were only resumed in March 1978, when Syria became concerned that the Israeli invasion of south Lebanon was the prelude to an attack on Syria.

YEARS OF POLITICAL TURMOIL

The late 1970s and early 1980s were years of great turmoil in Syria. The involvement in Lebanon continued, causing a huge drain on the economy, especially after the Israeli invasion of Beirut in 1982. Relations with Iraq, which had been less than cordial since the late 1960s, deteriorated steadily after Saddam Hussein's formal assumption of power in 1979 and Syria's support of Iran in the Iran/Iraq war. The improvement in Jordanian/PLO relations, and the possibility that King Husayn might obtain a mandate to negotiate with Israel on behalf of the PLO caused great anxiety in Damascus, which feared that such a *démarche* would leave Syria isolated and vulnerable. In addition, violent events within Syria, which external forces, particularly Jordan and Israel, were widely suspected of attempting to orchestrate, caused a major crisis of confidence in the Asad government.

Ba'thism is a form of secular pan-Arabism with strong statist, or in Ba'thist terminology, socialist, connotations. Although the government attempted to incorporate the Sunni population (as long as control of the centres of power remained in its own hands), resentment at what could easily be labelled secular and minority rule grew, and found expression in the activities of the Muslim Brethren, with whom some members of the majority Sunni community began to identify. This meant that political opposition to the status quo was expressed in sectarian rather than political terms. In June 1979 some 60 Alawite officer cadets were killed at the Aleppo artillery school, the first of a series of sectarian attacks on individuals and groups over the next three years. These culminated in a major rising, instigated by Islamic militants in the city of Hama in February 1982. This was brutally put down by government forces over a period of three weeks, in the course of which the city was shelled repeatedly and many thousands of its inhabitants killed.

Though the massacre effectively ended the Islamic threat to Asad's government (indeed, there has been none since), its situation remained precarious, especially when Asad himself became seriously ill in the autumn of 1983. At this point his younger brother Rifa't, the flamboyant commander of the well-armed 55,000 strong Defence Brigades, began to think of himself as a suitable candidate for the presidency, for which he received some support among senior military officers. Once Asad began to recover, support for Rifa't evaporated, but the latter's continuing ambitions brought him into a conflict with the heads of other paramilitary units. Eventually Rifa't was sent on a semi-official visit to Moscow at the end of May 1985, after which, although returning to Syria from time to time, he has lived mostly in France and Spain.

POLITICAL AND ECONOMIC CRISIS DURING THE 1980S

During the second half of the 1980s Hafiz al-Asad's health improved, and he was able to exercise all his former authority. This was a time of great economic and social crisis and galloping inflation, aggravated by Syria's continuing involvement in Lebanon and the loss, or substantial reduction, of much Arab aid. Asad had to steer a delicate course when most of his Arab neighbours began to rally behind Iraq in the Iran/Iraq war. In fact he somehow managed simultaneously to maintain friendly relations with Iran and to re-integrate himself into the mainstream of Arab politics. This found its expression in a number of meetings with various Arab leaders (including a secret meeting with Saddam Hussein in Jordan in 1987), a more conciliatory Syrian line vis-à-vis Egypt and resumption of diplomatic relations in December 1989, and participation in various Islamic and Arab summits.

Syria had generally kept a low profile in Lebanon during the mid-1980s, while PLO forces had gradually infiltrated the country. However, sensing that the Amal militia was gaining the upper hand to an undesirable extent, Syrian forces reoccupied West Beirut in February 1987 (*see* Chapter 8, Lebanon). At the end of the Iran/Iraq war in July 1988, Iraq sought to weaken and destabilise Syria by interfering on the side of its enemies in Lebanon. Iraq sent arms to the commander of the Lebanese Army, General Michel Awn, who was nominated Prime Minister of Lebanon by the outgoing President, Amin Jumayyil, in October. Syria's regional standing was further weakened by the PLO's acceptance of UN Resolution 242 (and thus its de facto recognition of Israel) in December 1988.

In spite of the heavy military opposition which it engendered, Awn's defiance of Syria and his claim to represent Lebanon against Syria gained him considerable popularity in Lebanon, extending to outside the Maronite community. In the spring of 1989 the main pro-Syrian factions and militias in Lebanon joined forces with the Syrians to try to dislodge Awn and his supporters from their positions. Between July and

September, a virtual blockade was imposed on the area he controlled, which was only lifted after pressure had been brought to bear on both Awn and Iraq by the USA. The ending of this round of fighting enabled Syria and Saudi Arabia to arrange an interim settlement, the Ta'if Accord, in October. Members of the Lebanese parliament were taken to Ta'if in Saudi Arabia where they elected a new president, René Mu'awwad.

Mu'awwad was assassinated shortly afterwards, but his successor, Ilyas Harawi, undertook to maintain the Ta'if process. Awn continued to hold out in his stronghold in East Beirut, denouncing Ta'if and its supporters as Syrian lackeys. This confrontation persisted until October 1990 when Iraq's preoccupations elsewhere meant that it was no longer capable of supplying Awn. On 13 October the general fled to the safety of the French Embassy and, some months later, to exile in France. Syria then proceeded to impose a *pax Syriana* on Lebanon, which, with all its evident shortcomings, has brought about a period of tranquillity unknown to most of the country since the late 1960s.

Although a small country with few raw materials and substantially dependent on foreign aid, Syria has generally managed to maintain a fair degree of autonomy. In spite of what often appeared virtually unsurmountable obstacles (its identification by Israel and the West as a supporter of international terrorism, its friendship with Iran), Syria managed to maintain autonomy more or less successfully throughout the latter 1980s, restoring full diplomatic relations with the USA and all EC countries except Britain (broken over the 1986 Hindawi affair) during 1987. At the same time Syria managed to overcome some of the ambiguities of its relations with Moscow and to ensure Moscow's continued support within the newly emerging framework of international and regional alliances.

However, one consequence of *perestroika* and *glasnost* in Eastern Europe was that relations with friendly states were to be based more firmly on commercial criteria, that is, on their ability to pay for goods and services, rather than simply on the Soviet Union's geopolitical interests. In 1990 Soviet sources estimated Syria's debts to the Soviet Union to be in the region of $9 billion. An indication of the continued importance of the Soviet Union to Syria was the fact that, in 1990, it was the destination for over a third of its exports. At the same time (before the start of the peace process) the Soviet Union made it clear that Syria must abandon the idea of strategic parity with Israel and instead pursue defensive rearmament in a way which would restrain Israel. The Soviet Union was itself then engaged in talks with Israel in order to re-establish diplomatic relations (broken off in 1967). By 1990 the emigration of thousands of Soviet Jews to Israel could be seen on Syrian television, watched in awe and amazement by the audience.

One by-product of Syria's 'outsider' role during the 1980s was a drastic decline in Arab aid, which, together with the costs of its activities in Lebanon as well as the reduction in remittances resulting from the falling price of oil, brought about a major economic crisis. This manifested itself in high inflation, a severe fall in the value of the Syrian pound, a lowering in living standards particularly for those on fixed incomes, and a number of austerity measures, all of which created great discontent. This was aggravated by widely believed and most probably accurate reports of large-scale corruption in high places. The regime tried to absorb some of the palpable dissatisfaction which this caused in various ways. No obstacles were put in the way of those who wished to emigrate – there were long queues at the US and Canadian consulates. Some instances of corruption were detailed in the state media and a number of individuals were given long prison sentences. However, the economic situation was soon to improve.

SYRIA AND THE GULF WAR

A fortuitous combination of Hafiz al-Asad's keen sense of self-preservation and many years of intermittent Syrian hostility towards Iraq meant that there was little hesitation on the regime's part over the attitude that it should take to the invasion of Kuwait. Although Syrian forces played a relatively insignificant role in the war, Syria's anti-Iraqi line was of major political significance and resulted in the enhancement of the role of Hafiz al-Asad as a crucial player in the politics of the region. His increased standing became clear when he met George Bush in Geneva in November 1990 and was given the green light to move into Lebanon. In July 1991 the Syrian government indicated its acceptance of the US proposals for an international peace conference to establish a lasting settlement of the Arab-Israeli conflict, thus putting Israel into a position where it was difficult for it to refuse to do the same.

The indirect effects of the Iraqi invasion of Kuwait were also generally beneficial to the Syrian government. On the negative side, there was an immediate decline in remittances caused by the forced return of thousands of Syrians from Kuwait. In addition, the government's decision to condemn the invasion and subsequently to send forces to Saudi Arabia did not meet with universal approval, especially from Syria's substantial Palestinian community. On the positive side, as has been described, Syria was able to stabilise the situation in Lebanon to its own advantage, and also profited from the rise in oil prices. On the wider political front the decision to support the coalition forces brought immediate and substantial financial rewards, in the form of large injections of aid and credits from Saudi Arabia, the Gulf States, the USA, the EC and Japan, all of which acted as a great boost to the economy and to the Asad regime itself.

SYRIA AND THE MIDDLE EAST PEACE PROCESS

Syria continued to participate in the peace process throughout 1992 and 1993, although the major stumbling blocks remain (as of October 1995) Israel's unwillingness to commit itself to evacuating the Golan Heights and Syria's continuing if not particularly enthusiastic support of Hizbullah in south Lebanon. Between mid-1992 and early 1994 the

Syrian government granted exit visas to all those members of the Syrian Jewish community who wanted to leave the country. Like King Husayn, Asad was taken by surprise and far from delighted at the signature of the PLO/Israeli accords in September 1993. However, while castigating Yasser Arafat for not keeping his Arab partners informed of the secret negotiations in Norway, Asad made it clear that he would not interfere with the process. After a meeting with President Clinton in Geneva in January 1994, Asad declared that he looked forward to the establishment of 'normal and peaceful relations' in the region. A few days later Yitzhak Rabin announced that any decision to return the Golan Heights would need to be ratified by a referendum in Israel.

The massacre of worshippers at the mosque in Hebron in February 1994 effectively stalled official talks between Israel and Syria, although these were resumed in Washington in June 1995. A few weeks earlier Asad referred to Israel by name in public for the first time. The Damascus office charged with the Arab League's boycott of Israel has virtually ceased to function since April 1994. In general, as in much of the Arab world, there is a sense of cautious optimism in Syria over the peace process, and especially from the economic dividends which might follow, including, if Jordan's experience is anything to go by, undertakings on the part of foreign creditors to write off a substantial portion of Syria's external debt. In the spring of 1995, this was estimated at about $20 billion. However, in spite of measures to liberalise the economy, the backwardness of the banking system and the rest of the economic infrastructure, together with a complex three tier foreign exchange system, are major barriers to foreign investment.

As in so many other Middle Eastern states, inflation and the political instability resulting from an acute overcentralisation of power pose major problems for Syria's future. In addition, greater cordiality in US/Syrian relations (and Syria's public disavowal of support for the PKK) has still not led to Syria's being removed from the US list of countries sponsoring terrorism. This may, in part, be due to the continuing presence in Damascus of the headquarters of Palestinian groups opposed to the peace process in its entirety. The signing of the Palestinian-Israeli accord on 28 September 1995 means that Syria and Lebanon are particularly isolated. Clearly, Lebanon cannot negotiate a settlement with Israel without Syria, and time is of the essence: there are elections in the USA and Israel in 1996 in which, on present showing, further advances for right-wingers and hard-liners may well result. The governments of Israel and Syria seem interested in coming to a settlement, although both countries have so long regarded their adversary as the devil incarnate that it seems difficult for them to find the appropriate psychological moment to do so.

Peter Sluglett and Marion Farouk-Sluglett

15
TURKEY

WITHIN THE MIDDLE EAST, Turkey has a distinctive but sometimes ambiguous status. The Ottoman Empire, from which the
modern Turkish state evolved, was one of the superpowers of
Renaissance Europe, embracing a huge territory running as far as
Hungary in the northwest, to the Red Sea and the Persian Gulf in the
south and east and to Algeria in the west. Within this vast empire, ethnic
Turks formed the ruling class, but proportionally they were only a small
minority in a patchwork of diverse nationalities. The empire collapsed
during the 19th and early 20th centuries, leaving modern Turkey a relatively compact and ethnically homogeneous unit in the Turkish heart-
lands of the old empire. In the 1920s, under Kemal Atatürk, a concerted
effort was made to redefine its political identity as a nation-state on the
European model, committed to secular political values and institutional
and economic modernisation. As a result, most modern Turks tend to see
their country as being more a part of Europe than of the Middle East, or
else as being balanced between the two, both culturally and politically.

Turkish culture is also distinctive. Turkish tribes, who were only recent
converts to Islam, moved into Anatolia from central Asia between the 10th
and 13th centuries. Their language and religion gradually supplanted
those of the Byzantines, while absorbing elements from the ancient past of
the region. As Muslims, the Turks added a large number of Arabic and
Persian words to their language, but its basic structure and vocabulary
remains distinct: linguistically, the Turks are closer to the Turkic people of
central Asia than to the other nations of the Middle East. Ethnically, there
is a high degree of homogeneity. Following the deportations and massacres of the Armenians during the First World War, and an exchange of
minority populations with Greece in the 1920s, the Kurds remain the only
important ethnic minority in Turkey. They probably account for about 15
to 20 per cent of the total population, though classification is difficult, as
there are many people of mixed descent and identity.

Turks are sometimes apt to exaggerate their national unity. Turkish
society is divided, like those of the other Middle Eastern states, between
a westernised and urban middle class and the millions of villagers who
mix western and traditional values in their social and cultural life. Urban
workers and artisans lie culturally between the two. Economically, the
relatively prosperous and industrialised regions of western Anatolia are
a world apart from the poor and neglected regions of the east. The division between the Sunni Muslim majority and the minority of Alevi Shi'is
(probably around 15 to 20 per cent of the total) is also an important social

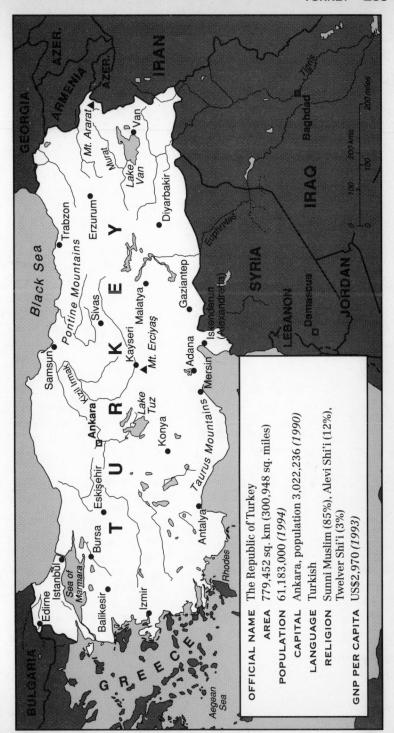

OFFICIAL NAME The Republic of Turkey

AREA 779,452 sq. km (300,948 sq. miles)

POPULATION 61,183,000 (1994)

CAPITAL Ankara, population 3,022,236 (1990)

LANGUAGE Turkish

RELIGION Sunni Muslim (85%), Alevi Shi'i (12%),
Twelver Shi'i (3%)

GNP PER CAPITA US$2,970 (1993)

cleavage. Nevertheless, it is probably true to say that Turkey is nearer to being a unitary political community than most other states in the region, and closest of them to the European model of a nation-state.

OTTOMAN LEGACIES

The Ottoman Empire reached its apogee during the 16th century, but by the end of the 18th century was clearly in decline. Faced with the danger of defeat by the rising power of Russia and, later, by their nominal vassal Muhammad Ali Pasha of Egypt, a succession of sultans began to modernise their army and administrative machine. The janissary regiments – the professional core of the old Ottoman army – were suppressed in 1826 by Mahmud II, the greatest of the reformist sultans, and were replaced by a new model army, organised and trained on European lines. New schools to train army officers and civil servants were opened, and in the 1860s the administrative system was reconstructed on a centralised French model.

The sultans' intentions were that the process of reform (known as the Tanzimat or regulation) would stop short at their own thrones. Nevertheless, the new education system opened the eyes of the military and bureaucratic elite to the idea of constitutional rather than just administrative or military reform. This, combined with pressure from the states of western Europe for better treatment of the Empire's Christian minorities, led to a virtual coup d'état in 1876 and the proclamation of a constitution under a new sultan, Abdul Hamid II. The Empire's first elected parliament convened in March 1877. Unfortunately, internal reforms did not prevent a disastrous war with Russia in 1877–78, as a result of which the Ottoman-ruled territories in the Balkans were reduced to Thrace and Macedonia. In February 1878 the sultan seized the opportunity of the war to suspend parliament indefinitely. For the following 30 years he ruled the Empire as an absolute monarch.

Discontent at Abdul Hamid's autocracy came to a head with the so-called 'Young Turk' revolution of July 1908, when the army in the Balkans rose in revolt. The sultan gave ground by promising to reconvene parliament, which was duly elected at the end of the year, but his attempt to retain his throne proved unavailing: in 1909, following an unsuccessful counter-revolt by conservatives in the army and their clerical supporters, he was finally deposed and sent into exile. His brother Reshad took the throne as Mehmet V, but with the constitution altered to reduce the royal powers. However, the events of 1909 did not lead to a liberal or stable regime. Instead, the Young Turks divided into rival groups in a confused period of instability and struggle. In the meantime, in 1912–13, Greece, Bulgaria and Serbia launched yet another war against their former Turkish overlords, which finally ended Ottoman rule in the Balkans. The internal struggle for power ended in January 1914 when Enver Pasha, one of the leaders of the original revolt of 1908, became minister of war. He imposed himself as the head of a three-man junta, consisting of himself, Ahmed Jemal (the minister of the navy) and Mehmet Talat (minister of the interior). The sultan and grand vizier were reduced to insignificance. This triumvirate dragged the empire into its final defeat, by entering the First World War on the German side. In the ensuing struggle, the Turkish army put up a far stiffer resistance than many outsiders had expected. Nevertheless, by the autumn of 1918 the empire was in ruins. Its existence as an imperial entity was ended by an armistice with the Entente powers, signed on 30 October 1918.

THE TURKISH REPUBLIC 1919–38

In the 1920s, Turkey's internal structure and external relations were transformed by the foundation of a secular national state, but this outcome was only achieved by yet another war. After their victory, the Entente powers put together a complex and sometimes vague partition plan to divide Anatolia among themselves, reducing Turkey to a rump of territory in northern and central Anatolia. This scheme, formalised as the Treaty of Sèvres, was officially accepted by the government of the last sultan, Vahdettin (Mehmet VI) in August 1920. But it was decisively rejected by a movement of national resistance, led by Mustafa Kemal (later Atatürk), which effectively set up a rival government in Ankara. Greece was the only Entente power prepared to back its claim to territory in western Anatolia by force of arms. However, in the summer of 1922 the Turkish forces counter-attacked, driving the Greeks out of Anatolia by October 1922. The verdict of the battlefield was confirmed by the Treaty of Lausanne of July 1923, which established Turkey within what are virtually its present frontiers (the only subsequent frontier change occurred in 1939, when the province of Hatay, or Alexandretta, was transferred from Syria to Turkey). Since then, the idea of re-establishing Turkish rule in the Middle East has never been seriously resuscitated.

The victory of 1922 swept Atatürk into a position of virtually unchallengeable national authority. He used it to effect a sweeping reconstruction of the state and to mount a determined campaign of cultural reorientation and economic development. Vahdettin was deposed and the sultanate abolished in November 1922. Less than a year later, Turkey was declared a republic, with Ankara as its capital and Atatürk its elected president. The office of the caliphate, previously occupied by the sultans and the principal constitutional link between the state and the Muslim religion, was abolished in March 1924. The Islamic legal system was swept aside in 1926, and replaced by secular criminal, civil and commercial codes copied from western Europe. In 1925 even the fez – the symbol of attachment of male Turks to Islam – was banned, while in 1928 the Arabic script was replaced with a version of the Latin alphabet. The change in the script was part of a determined attempt to nationalise culture: to promote the principle that the Turks were culturally and historically separate from the rest of the Muslim world. Among the rural masses, the campaign was never entirely successful, but it had a significant effect on the educated elite and, as time went on, among non-elite groups as well.

Atatürk's regime was culturally progressive but politically authoritarian. Apart from two brief experiments with a multi-party system, in

1924–25 and 1930, Turkey was ruled as a single-party state under the Republican People's Party (RPP) and organised dissent was outlawed. At the same time, the government made determined moves to develop the national economy, and enhance its own role within it. Under the first five-year industrialisation plan, implemented between 1934 and 1938 and introduced as part of the official policy of étatism, Turkey began to acquire a range of basic industries (textiles, sugar, steel, chemicals, paper and coal) most of which were dominated by state enterprises, competing in some sectors with private firms.

CHALLENGE AND CHANGE 1938–60

Kemal Atatürk died in November 1938, to be succeeded by his principal and faithful lieutenant, Ismet Inönü. The new president carefully steered Turkey through a difficult path of neutrality during the Second World War, maintaining – indeed, tightening – the single party regime. In November 1945, however, he took the momentous step of announcing that he favoured the formation of an opposition party. Under the leadership of Adnan Menderes, the Democrat Party rapidly emerged to play this role in Turkey's first post-war elections, held in July 1946. It then swept to power with a massive majority in the next elections of May 1950.

Besides the need to create a safety valve for domestic discontent after years of heavy-handed rule by the RPP, foreign policy considerations contributed to Inönü's dramatic change of course. In 1945–46 Stalin launched a diplomatic campaign for revision of the Montreux Convention of 1936, with the aim of establishing Soviet-controlled military bases at the Straits. The defeat of fascism in the Second World War, allied to the need to strengthen Turkey's moral claim for Western assistance against the Soviet Union, helped to create the climate for internal political liberalisation. It also laid the basis for Turkey's overriding foreign policy alignments since then, signalled by its admission to NATO in 1952.

The election of 1950 brought about a fundamental shift in political power. Resting on the votes of millions of peasant farmers, a new elite of businessmen, landowners and professionals took over power from the state-centred metropolitan elite which had held the dominant position under the RPP. As prime minister, Adnan Menderes fully realised his debt to the peasants, and repaid it by putting new emphasis on agricultural development, granting easy loans and subsidising crop prices to farmers. In industry, greater emphasis was put on private investment. During the second half of the decade, however, the economy deteriorated: the growth of national income slowed to a crawl; inflation rose; and a large trade deficit developed. Menderes responded with a return to heavy-handed political tactics, rigging the elections in some constituencies in 1957 and restricting opposition political activity.

The political crisis came to a head in the spring of 1960, when the government voted to establish a special commission, with arbitrary powers of search and arrest, 'to investigate the activities of the Republican People's Party'. The result was widespread disturbances in

Ankara and Istanbul, with fierce fighting between students and police, and the imposition of martial law in the two cities. Hitherto, the army had abided by Atatürk's principle that it should stay out of politics. However, the declaration of martial law forced it back into the political arena for the first time since the Young Turk period. In a virtually bloodless coup, launched and completed in the early morning of 27 May 1960, the government was overthrown, and Turkey's first post-war military regime was installed. The titular leader of the coup, General Cemal Gürsel, became Turkey's temporary head of state, leading a 38-man junta known as the National Unity Committee.

GENERALS AND POLITICIANS 1960–83

The military junta of 1960 stayed in power for 18 months. In spite of conflicts within its ranks, it endowed Turkey with a new constitution, with a wider definition of civil liberties. Its greatest mistake was the execution of Menderes and two of his colleagues for allegedly breaking the previous constitution, which created a legacy of bitterness over the following three decades. However, in November 1961 it duly handed over power to a newly elected parliament. Since no party had won an overall majority in the elections, Ismet Inönü was forced to soldier on until 1965 at the head of a series of three coalition governments. Meanwhile, the Justice Party (JP) had effectively emerged as the Democrat Party's successor. In 1964 a newcomer to politics, Süleyman Demirel, took over the leadership of the JP, winning an overall majority in general elections held in October 1965. He renewed this majority in the following elections, held in 1969. Until 1971, he provided Turkey with a rare interval of stable government as well as economic advance.

Demirel's first period as premier ended in March 1971, after a confused putsch by the military forced him to resign. During the preceding months, Turkey had been wracked by a wave of urban terrorism carried out by extremists of both left and right, and the army evidently hoped that a 'supra-party' government, following their directions, could restore law and order. However, they failed to find an effective proxy as prime minister, and the result was a series of weak coalitions. In the meantime, the leadership of the Republican People's Party shifted from Ismet Inönü to Bülent Ecevit, who moved the party in a social democrat direction. In October 1973, realising that indirect control was unworkable and that a fully fledged military regime would be equally unacceptable, the military chiefs returned to their barracks and free general elections were held. Again, no party won an overall majority. This result was repeated in the next elections, held in 1977. Although Ecevit won wide popularity through his ordering of the invasion of Cyprus in 1974, following a botched attempt to take over the island by the then Greek junta, he failed to win sufficient authority in parliament. Consequently, power see-sawed between Ecevit and Demirel no less than six times between 1974 and 1979.

The weakness of government during the 1970s had devastating effects. By 1980, the failure of successive administrations to limit their expenditure and to promote effective foreign trade policies had produced triple-digit inflation and a huge balance of payments deficit. Meanwhile, an upsurge of terrorist violence by extremists of left and right as well as among Kurdish guerillas in the southeast brought the country to the verge of civil war. The long-expected takeover by the military, on 12 September 1980, was greeted with general relief. Under General Kenan Evren, the military regime rapidly re-established law and order and put the economy back on the rails, though only by drastic methods. The suppression of normal political rights allied to the frequent use of torture against political suspects produced mounting international criticism. Nevertheless, Evren and his colleagues pressed on with their project to return Turkey to civilian rule, under conditions of their own choosing. Having closed down all existing parties in 1981, they introduced yet another constitution, which was accepted in a national referendum in November 1982. Under the new constitution, Evren was declared elected president for the next seven years while Demirel, Ecevit and the other pre-1980 party leaders were forbidden to return to politics until 1992.

To compete in the following elections, which were scheduled for November 1983, Evren encouraged the creation of two new parties: the Nationalist Democracy Party (NDP) on the right; and the Populist Party (PP) on the centre-left. However, he did not prevent the formation of the Motherland Party by Turgut Özal, who had himself served under the military as deputy premier, in charge of the economy, between 1980 and 1982. Two other parties entered the fray, in the shape of the Social Democrat Party (Sodep), headed by Ismet Inönü's son, Erdal Inönü, and the True Path Party (TPP), set up by Demirel under a proxy leader. Both parties were prevented from competing in the elections by a legal loophole. As a result, the Motherland Party won a clear majority, capturing 211 of the 400 seats, compared with 117 for the PP and 71 for the NDP. Özal duly formed the new government.

THE ÖZAL ERA 1983–93

As prime minister, Özal buttressed his success over the following years. His free market policies continued to bring growth to the Turkish economy, as well as a dramatic improvement in the balance of foreign trade. The 1980s also saw a steady withdrawal of the military from the political scene. The process of military disengagement was aided by President Evren, who stuck strictly to a neutral role as president.

The strength of Özal's government was reinforced by the simultaneous division of the opposition. An artificial creation from the start, the NDP withered away and was formally dissolved in 1986. Meanwhile the PP avoided the same fate by merging with Sodep to form the Social Democrat Populist Party (SDPP) in November 1985 under Erdal Inönü's leadership. Its position as the standard bearer of the centre-left was challenged by Bülent Ecevit, who soldiered on at the head of his own Democratic Left Party (DLP) which was nominally led by his wife Rahşan. Besides Demirel's TPP, Necmettin Erbakan sponsored the

Welfare Party (WP), as the representative of the Islamic viewpoint. Turkey thus had no less than four discordant opposition parties, and no credible alternative government.

By 1987 it had become clear that the ban on the pre-1980 party leaders was both undemocratic and unworkable since it had not prevented them from setting up front parties under the nominal leadership of close colleagues or relatives. Accordingly, a referendum to decide whether to remove the ban was held in September 1987. The motion in favour was carried by a hairsbreadth margin of 50.2 per cent to 49.8 per cent. Demirel, Ecevit and Erbakan were thus able to take over the official leadership of their respective parties. However, the result suggested that the old leaders did not have overwhelming support. Accordingly, Özal decided to call a snap general election, on 7 November 1987. His gamble paid off handsomely: the Motherland Party won only 36 per cent of the vote (compared with 45 per cent in 1983) but changes in the electoral system, as well as the split opposition vote, enabled it to retain power with 292 of the 450 assembly seats. The SDPP finished in second place, with 99 seats, followed by the TPP with 59 seats. Since they failed to clear the 10 per cent barrier, the DLP and the WP were left with no parliamentary representation.

An important watershed was passed in November 1989 when Kenan Evren's term as president expired. It was significant that Evren was not succeeded by a retired military commander, as all presidents had been since 1961. However, by deciding to run for the presidency himself, Özal further strengthened his personal position. Like its predecessors, the present constitution provides that the president should be elected by an absolute majority in parliament. Thanks to the Motherland Party's large majority, Özal was easily able to win the election, and took office on 9 November 1989. He immediately appointed Yıldırım Akbulut, previously speaker of the assembly, as his successor as prime minister.

Akbulut was chosen as premier primarily because, as a comparatively little-known and neutral figure, he would be unlikely to challenge the new president. However, his evident weakness and lack of government experience were clearly a liability, and led to growing calls for his replacement. These were further intensified by the government's failure to control inflation, which severely eroded its popularity. In local elections, held in March 1989, the Motherland Party scored only 22 per cent of the vote, compared with 28 per cent for the SDPP and 26 per cent for the TPP. In June 1991 Mesut Yılmaz replaced Yıldırım Akbulut as prime minister and nominal leader of the Motherland Party, though Özal continued to exercise effective control. But the party was ousted from power after early general elections in October 1991, having gained 24.1 per cent of the votes and 112 seats. In November Süleyman Demirel formed a coalition government in which his TPP shared office with the SDPP. Erdal Inönü, the SDPP leader, became deputy prime minister. Meanwhile, Özal carried on as president, until his sudden death from a heart attack on 17 April 1993. He had certainly not been without his critics, but he should be given credit for his role in aiding the remarkably smooth return to civilian politics after 1983, as well as his re-orientation of the Turkish economy and his successful conduct of Turkish policy in the Gulf crisis of 1990–91. His career thus represented an important chapter in Turkey's recent history.

TURKISH POLITICS SINCE ÖZAL

Turgut Özal's death presented Süleyman Demirel with the unexpected opportunity to have himself elected to the presidency. Supported by the SDPP as well as by his own party, he easily secured this on 16 May 1993. As in the case of Özal's election to the same office, this temporarily left Turkey without a prime minister. The vacancy was filled on 13 June when a special convention of the True Path Party elected Tansu Çiller to the party chair and hence to the premiership. Mrs Çiller announced her cabinet on 25 June: essentially, it was a continuation of the TPP-SDPP coalition formed by Demirel, though with a new team of ministers from the TPP.

Mrs Çiller's election brought a fresh face to the forefront of Turkish politics, quite apart from its significance as the first occasion on which a woman, who was not a member of a political dynasty, had won the political leadership of a Muslim country. Nonetheless, her power as premier was constrained by her own inexperience of parliamentary politics and her weak control over the levers of power in her own party. Previously a professor of economics at Istanbul's Bosphorus University, she had not even been a member of parliament until 1991, when Demirel had promoted her as someone who could bring relative youth and presumed economic expertise to his front-bench team. Although she had won overwhelming support among the convention delegates, she was almost certainly not the first choice of her party's MPs, who would probably have preferred a more conservative leader. By instinct, she appears to have had liberal views on the Kurdish and other questions but was constantly liable to be driven in a more restrictive direction by her conservative backbenchers. Her government was further weakened by frictions between the two parties in the coalition and by internal rivalries within the SDPP. The apparently endless war in the southeastern provinces between the security forces and the Kurdish insurgents of the PKK, and the government's lack of effective control over the economy were other sources of serious weakness.

All these problems became evident in the first 18 months of Mrs Çiller's premiership. In September 1992 a group of 18 SDPP MPs under Deniz Baykal, who had long chafed at Erdal İnönü's leadership of the party, had broken away from the party to re-establish the Republican People's Party, thus reducing the government's nominal majority in parliament to around a dozen. In September 1993 İnönü then decided to step down, to be succeeded as party leader and deputy premier by Murat Karayalçın. At the time of his election, Karayalçın was well regarded in the party as a popular and successful mayor of Ankara, but he had little experience of national politics. This weakness showed through during 1994, as he failed to prevent constant rebellions by the left wing of his party who felt that the coalition was doing nothing to protect the interest of the urban working class or to improve human rights.

These complaints were strengthened during the first half of 1994 when Turkey entered one of its periodic economic crises, forcing the government to introduce an emergency retrenchment package which brought a sharp reduction in real wages and a severe industrial downturn. Popular discontent was clearly demonstrated in the nation-wide local elections held on 27 March 1994, when the two ruling parties lost votes heavily and the pro-Islamic Welfare Party made striking gains. In the run-up to the elections, Mrs Çiller had also attempted to win ultra-nationalist sympathies by backing the expulsion from parliament of six MPs from the Democracy Party (DeP), formed in 1992 by a splinter group from the SDPP as Turkey's only legal pro-Kurdish party. The party was closed down in June 1994 and all 13 of its MPs automatically lost their seats. In the following December, the 'DeP six' were sentenced to long terms of imprisonment for alleged links with the PKK and for statements held to have endangered the territorial integrity of the state. This may have won Mrs Çiller the plaudits of the ultra-nationalist right but she was opposed by most of the SDPP and also provoked severe criticisms from Turkey's western allies.

After these failures, events during the first half of 1995 suggested that the outlook for the government might be brightening up, as the economy returned to growth. In March 1995 the SDPP and the Republican People's Party reunited, under the latter's title, adding a useful 15 seats to the government's parliamentary tally. The leader of the merged party was Hikmet Çetin, formerly foreign minister, who now succeeded Karayalçın as deputy premier. Erdal İnönü also returned to the cabinet as foreign minister. In the same month, representatives of the European Union (EU) signed an agreement with Turkey providing for the establishment of a customs union between Turkey and the EU to begin in 1996, although implementation of this agreement would depend on its ratification by the European Parliament. This was far from certain, given the European Parliament's strong criticism of Turkey's policy on the Kurdish question and the country's shaky human rights record. Nevertheless, if achieved, it could be accounted an important success for the government. Some four months later, on 23 July 1995, Mrs Çiller managed to win an important victory over the conservatives in her own party, when parliament agreed to amend a number of articles of the constitution which had previously restricted civil liberties. However, she suffered an unexpected reverse in September 1995 when Deniz Baykal was elected leader of the RPP. Baykal failed to agree with Mrs Çiller on the continuation of the coalition, forcing her resignation. It was expected that she would probably carry on in a caretaker capacity until general elections early in 1996. In the longer term, a merger – or at least a coalition – with the Motherland Party seemed the most viable outcome, but it was far from certain that this could be secured.

KURDS, HUMAN RIGHTS AND ISLAM

Since the beginning of the 1990s, the struggle between the Turkish state and the Kurdish militants of the PKK has become by far the most serious security problem in Turkey. By the end of 1994, it had already cost around 13,000 lives, and was reported to be adding some $6 billion per year to the government's security expenditure. Meanwhile, the economy of the southeastern provinces, where most of the fighting took place, had been severely damaged by the loss of agricultural production and the interruption of trade. Although exact figures are impossible to establish, it is likely that around one million people had been forced to leave their homes, either through fear of the PKK or through enforced evacuation by the army, which in many cases burnt down their villages. When these internal refugees are added to the large number of Kurds leaving their villages every year for economic reasons, it is likely that around half the total Kurdish population of Turkey, which can be very roughly estimated at around 9–12 million, now lives outside the original Kurdish heartland in the southeast, having moved to the big cities of western Turkey. Serious human rights abuses by the armed forces, including a string of unsolved murders of Kurdish activists, have been a constant source of complaint by Amnesty International and other human rights organisations as well as by western governments. At the same time, the PKK has itself been responsible for the murder of thousands of civilians and other brutal abuses of human rights. Nor has it responded to complaints on this issue by Amnesty International. It also appears that the PKK leader Abdullah Öcalan, who is based in Syria, has sometimes had little control over his own local commanders.

Defenders of the Turkish government's policies are likely to point out that the state does not distinguish between its citizens on an ethnic basis, that as Turkish citizens the Turkish Kurds have full voting and other rights and that they can rise to the highest positions in the land. This claim is justified to the extent that several members of Mrs Çiller's cabinet have been of Kurdish stock, as are many army officers and civil servants. Against this, it has to be said that such individuals may not claim a separate Kurdish political identity, and that any kind of separatist political activity is strictly forbidden. Following closure of the pro-Kurdish Democracy Party in 1994, a successor was established under the title of the People's Democracy Party, but this was also closed down. The previous ban on the use of the Kurdish language was withdrawn in 1991, at Turgut Özal's instigation, and printed material in Kurdish is now allowed, but Kurdish-language broadcasting and education are still outlawed. Although regional economic disparities have deep-rooted causes which no government would find it easy to remove, the backwardness and poverty of the southeast is another cause of Kurdish resentment, as per capita incomes in the region are put at 50 per cent or less of the national average.

The PKK receives external assistance from Syria, and has also been able to operate from Iraqi Kurdistan, but its main source of support is in Turkey itself. Abdullah Öcalan claims to have abandoned the idea of establishing an independent Kurdish state, aiming only for autonomy within Turkey. It is impossible to establish the exact extent of the PKK's popular support, but a survey of opinion among Kurds in the southeast and the big cities conducted in 1995 reported that only 13 per cent of respondents favoured an independent Kurdish state, with a large majority supporting autonomy or the reform of local administration. In response, the Çiller government committed itself to withdrawing the emergency regime in the southeast, which gives the police and army exceptional powers, and promised to give elected local authorities throughout Turkey more powers. However, by the summer of 1995 nothing had been done to achieve this. Constitutional autonomy, let alone independence, for the southeast is also firmly excluded from the agendas of all the main political parties.

The broader debate about human rights revolves almost entirely around the Kurdish question. Articles 141 and 142 of the Penal Code, which formerly banned the expression of Marxist opinions, were withdrawn in 1991. Consequently, virtually all points of view, except Kurdish separatism or ultra-Islamicism, now enjoy relatively free expression in Turkey. The constitutional amendments passed in July 1995 also lifted previous bans on links between the trades unions and political parties, and extended the right to union representation, though not the right to strike, to civil servants. Following the amendments, the main remaining restriction on the freedom of speech is contained in Article 8 of the 1991 'Law for the Struggle against Terrorism'. This outlaws statements deemed to endanger the territorial integrity of the state. Apart from this, the most frequent cause of complaint is the regular use of torture by the police on ordinary criminal suspects, as well as those charged with political crimes. Though successive governments have promised to end this abuse, they have failed to do so.

Constitutionally, Turkey is a secular state, and the laws and governmental system are exclusively based on western models. However, since the Özal era, the state's Directorate of Religious Affairs, which oversees all Sunni mosques and employs their Imams, has received an increasing share of the budget. Religious education, both in the normal state schools and in special schools of Imams and preachers, has also been expanded. At the same time, more radical Islamic currents have emerged. In the political arena, they are articulated by the Welfare Party (WP) led by Necmettin Erbakan. Without openly calling for the establishment of an Islamic state (which is still illegal), the WP demands the reassertion of Islamic morality and a 'just order' and strongly opposes Turkey's closer association with western Europe. It enjoys substantial support in the southeast, in small towns, throughout Anatolia and among the poor and disadvantaged in the big cities, who have lost faith in the mainstream secular parties. The steady reassertion of Sunni Muslim values by the state has also tended to alienate followers of the minority Alevi sect, resulting in serious disturbances in Alevi districts of Istanbul in March 1995.

The Welfare Party's success in the March 1994 local elections, in which it captured the mayoralities in Istanbul and Ankara, among many other cities, provoked speculation that it might be able to win national political power. However, its rise must be put in perspective. For most Turks, ethnic national identity still seems to be dominant, combined with an acceptance of Islam as a moral and spiritual belief system, rather than a political ideology. As a sign of this, a poll conducted among almost 16,000 citizens of Istanbul at the end of 1992 for *Milliyet* newspaper reported that nearly 70 per cent of the respondents defined themselves as Turks, 21 per cent as Muslim Turks, and only 4 per cent purely as Muslims (the remaining 5 per cent identified themselves as Kurds, or members of other minority ethnic groups). At 19 per cent, the WP's share of the total vote in the 1994 local elections was well short of the 35 per cent or so it would need to win an overall majority in parliament, and its popularity does not seem to have grown markedly since then. In the meantime, the fact that it has to deal with the day-to-day problems of running Istanbul and several other municipalities has forced it to accommodate itself to the secular political system.

THE ECONOMY: CHANGES, CHALLENGES AND PROSPECTS

Since the 1930s, as industry has expanded the economy has moved away from its traditional dependence on primary production. Although about 40 to 45 per cent of the workforce is still employed in agriculture, mainly on small peasant-owned farms, farming now accounts for only around 16 per cent of gross domestic product (GDP), compared with 34 per cent for industry (including construction) and 50 per cent for services. This pattern is repeated in foreign trade, in which industrial products (particularly textiles, clothing and steel) now account for 85 per cent of exports and agricultural products (mainly tobacco, fruit and nuts) for only 15 per cent. Nominal per capita gross national product (GNP) in 1995 stood at $2,158. At purchasing power parities, the Organisation for Economic Co-operation and Development estimates suggest that per capita GNP can be put at around $5,000 for 1995. Including 1994, when GDP at constant prices exceptionally fell by 5.4 per cent, annual real GDP growth averaged 4.1 per cent between 1983 and 1994.

This growth is reflected in social and cultural change, as the urban population now accounts for about 59 per cent of the total (compared with only 19 per cent in 1950) and literacy has reached about 75 to 80 per cent. Thanks to better education and family planning services, annual population growth rate has dropped from a high point of 2.8 per cent in 1955–60 to an estimated 1.6 per cent in 1995. On this basis, the population can be expected to reach about 67 million by the year 2000, when the next full census will be taken.

During the 1980s, Özal put the liberalisation and modernisation of the economy at the top of his agenda, and scored some important successes. Between 1983 and 1990 GNP grew by an average of 5.3 per cent per annum in real terms. Encouraged by a floating exchange rate and the withdrawal of other controls, exports increased from $2.9 billion in 1980 to $13.7 billion in 1991, while imports rose from $7.9 billion to $21.0 billion in the same period. On the debit side, the government failed to limit its own expenditure in line with resources. The consequent resort to deficit financing increased the money supply, so that annual average inflation ran at about 47 per cent between 1983 and 1991. In spite of his Thatcherite rhetoric, Özal also failed to divest the state of its huge industrial empire, most of which made large losses, and was thus responsible for an important part of the public sector deficit.

Although Demirel had attacked Özal's economic policies from the opposition benches, he and his successor Tansu Çiller essentially continued them after they gained power at the end of 1991. Initially, the economy continued on its inflationary growth path, with real GDP rising by 6.0 per cent in 1992 and 7.5 per cent in 1993. Wholesale price inflation continued at 62 per cent and 68 per cent respectively during each of the two years. During 1993, increased interest by overseas investors also pushed up the combined index of the Istanbul stock market from around 4,000 at the beginning of the year to over 20,000 by the end of December – a gain in dollar terms of over 200 per cent over the year. By the first quarter for 1994, however, the crisis point had arrived, as it became clear that the economy had developed an acute case of inflationary overheating. In 1993, exports had grown to $15.3 billion, but imports had surged to a record $29.4 billion. Invisible earnings, such as tourism and emigrants' remittances, failed to fill the gap, so that the current account balance of payments deficit reached almost $6.4 billion. The government's failure to get a grip on its own finances was also illustrated by the fact that the public sector borrowing requirement had risen from 7.8 per cent of GDP in 1987 to 12.2 per cent in 1993, and that Turkey's foreign debt (mostly incurred by the government and its agencies) had increased to $48.8 billion from $32.6 billion in 1987.

The inevitable crash began in January 1994 when two New York credit rating agencies reduced Turkey's rating to sub-investment grade. This touched off a precipitate depreciation of the Turkish lira, as people rushed to change cash and other assets into foreign exchange. On 6 April, the exchange rate reached TL39,933:$1, a nominal devaluation of 175 per cent since the beginning of the year. The Central Bank tried to arrest the slide through market interventions and rapid rises in interest rates, but this had little effect other than to reduce foreign exchange reserves, which fell from $6.3 billion at the end of 1993 to

$3.1 billion by 15 April 1994. The government failed to take effective action until 5 April, when it announced an emergency programme of tax increases and restrictions in government expenditure. In a bid to regain international confidence, it also sent a letter of intent to the International Monetary Fund (IMF) in which it undertook to adhere to tight budgetary targets for the rest of 1994 and for 1995, as well as eliminating the current account deficit and lowering the inflation rate. The IMF responded in July by granting Turkey an emergency stand-by credit worth $742 million over the following 14 months.

The effects of these measures – both positive and negative – had become clear by the middle of 1995. In the external accounts, the rapid devaluation in the first half of 1994 coupled with the restriction of internal demand had the expected effect of increasing exports and reducing imports, to $18.4 billion and $22.6 billion respectively. Earnings from tourism and other services ran at $11.7 billion and emigrants' remittances at $2.7 billion, so that even after allowing for outgoings on the services account (principally debt interest payments) Turkey had a surplus on current account of $2.6 billion. The Central Bank's gold and foreign currency reserves rose to $7.7 billion at the end of the year, and the exchange rate stabilised during the last two quarters, to stand at around TL38,000:$1 in December 1994. In these respects, the government had actually done better than the targets set by the IMF. However, it failed to curtail its expenditure to the degree pledged and the sharp increases in the prices of state-supplied goods and services pushed up the annual inflation rate to 125 per cent. Moreover, the sharp contraction of demand reduced GNP by 6 per cent, with worst effects on the real wages of industrial workers, particularly in the state sector. In effect, ordinary citizens had been forced to pay a heavy price for the government's failure to keep a grip on the economy in earlier years.

During the first half of 1995, it appeared that the economy was recovering from the crisis of the previous year and that, with a resurgence of demand and industrial output, real GNP growth could be restored to around 5 per cent per annum. Nonetheless, inflation was still expected to run at around 80 per cent per year in 1995, with the prospect of no more than a gradual fall in following years. The recovery of domestic demand was also leading to a renewed surge of imports, so that the current account surplus of 1994 could not be expected to recur. In the medium term, the projected customs union with the EU, assuming it were implemented, would bring increased external competition. However, it would also remove limitations on Turkey's exports to the EU (especially textiles) and should then aid the modernisation of industry by increasing the inflow of foreign investment. Since Turkey still has a wide resource endowment, a substantial domestic market and a growing and adaptable population, it can expect to return to steady growth, assuming that better economic management by the government can break the boom-and-bust cycle of earlier years.

FOREIGN POLICY TRENDS

Until the end of the Cold War, foreign policy was not a major subject of political debate in Turkey since (apart from periodic crises over Cyprus) there was a generally stable external environment and a wide national consensus on foreign policy issues. Turkey was relatively little affected by the Arab-Israeli dispute or other regional clashes. For the Turks, their position as neighbours of the USSR and Bulgaria meant that the global confrontation between the western powers and the USSR normally took clear primacy over regional conflicts – the exact opposite of the position of most Middle Eastern states. Only the extreme left seriously questioned Turkey's membership of NATO, or the main lines of government policy over Cyprus. There was broad public support for closer association with the European Community (subsequently the European Union), except among a minority of pan-Islamists and unreconstructed Marxists. In relations with other Middle Eastern countries, there was general support for the establishment of closer economic ties with the Arab world while avoiding any serious military or political commitments.

During the 1990s, these orientations have largely continued, but the collapse of the USSR has transformed the external parameters. During the earlier part of the post-Cold War period, it was frequently suggested that Turkey's international importance would decline, since its former value as the linch-pin of western security in the eastern Mediterranean had ceased to exist. Since then, however, it appears that its international significance has been re-shaped but not ended. In the post-Soviet era, new conflicts have emerged in the Balkans, Transcaucasia and central Asia alongside surviving ones in the Gulf. Turkey's geographical position, as well as its ties with the west, gives it an actual or potential role in all these regions, in which the western powers need to secure Turkey's co-operation.

In an uncertain world, Turkish policy has tended to be cautious. Immediately after the disintegration of the USSR, it was sometimes suggested that Turkey could emerge as a kind of regional hegemon in the ex-Soviet states on Russia's southern periphery, with whom it shared linguistic and religious links. Experiences since then have dampened much of this enthusiasm. On the one hand, the post-Soviet central Asian states have been anxious to establish their own separate identities and disinclined to accept some sort of Turkish hegemony. On the other hand, Russia's residual power in the region, especially in the military sphere, has been greater than many observers expected. Turkey's relations with Russia are not without their tensions, since Turkey opposes apparent attempts by Moscow to re-establish control over its ex-Soviet periphery. This is exemplified by current Turkish attempts, in the face of Russian opposition, to secure the construction of oil and gas pipelines from Azerbaijan and central Asia to the Mediterranean on Turkish rather than Russian territory. On the other hand, Turkey recognises that it cannot afford a head-on collision with Russia, given its size and economic potential. Russia now buys about four per cent of

Turkey's exports and provides about six per cent of its imports – in particular, natural gas, on which Istanbul and Ankara rely for heating. Nor can Turkey take the risk of direct military commitments in the former Soviet republics. Its own shortage of resources does not allow it to play a dominant economic role in the region, but Turkish firms have been able to fill in important interstices in the central Asian economies – in particular, in the fields of telecommunications and the textiles industry. Cultural and other links have also been extensively developed.

An apt example of the dilemmas faced by Turkish policy makers is the conflict between Armenia and Azerbaijan over the disputed enclave of Nagorno-Karabakh. Turkish public opinion strongly favours Azerbaijan, but the government has studiously avoided military commitments to the Azeris, and has tried to avoid alienating Armenia. Similarly, in the war in Bosnia-Herzegovina, Turkey has given strong diplomatic support to the Bosnian Muslims but limits its military role to participation in the UN protection force (UNPROFOR), in which it has a detachment of 1,500 troops. At the same time, it strongly supports US attempts to bring about a peace settlement in Bosnia and, if such a settlement is achieved, Turkey can be expected to play an important role in providing troops for an international peace-keeping force.

In the Middle East, the Gulf crisis of 1990–91 also upset previous foreign policy assumptions, mainly because its unpredictability made it hard to adhere to established positions. Turkey's main actions in the crisis were first to apply UN sanctions against Iraq, primarily by shutting the Kirkuk-Yumurtalik pipeline, secondly to reinforce its troops along its border with Iraq, thus tying down about nine Iraqi divisions, and thirdly to allow the US to use NATO airbases on Turkish soil to attack targets in northern Iraq. Immediately after the Gulf war, it agreed to allow US, British and French planes the use of íncirlik airbase, near Adana, as part of the Operation Provide Comfort, which enforces the northern Iraqi no-fly zone. But if these policies won Turgut Özal the gratitude of the western powers, they were not universally popular at home, mainly because most Turks did not want the country to be sucked into a war in any part of the Middle East.

The mandate for Provide Comfort has to be renewed by the Turkish parliament at six-month intervals. This has been achieved on the due dates, but not without fierce debate, since there is reluctance to give indirect support to the de facto independence of the Iraqi Kurds. Turkish forces have also repeatedly carried out military operations in northern Iraq to destroy alleged PKK bases. On occasions, the *peshmerga* militias commanded by Mas'ud Barzani have joined in these attacks on the PKK. However, the Turkish relationship with the Iraqi Kurds is delicate and often mutually suspicious. On the one hand, Turkey strongly opposes the territorial division of Iraq but realises that it must maintain contacts with the Iraqi Kurdish leaders and prevent them from acting against its interests. On the other hand, while Mas'ud Barzani and Jalal Talabani cannot entirely ignore the plight of the

Turkish Kurds they also recognise that they cannot afford to risk a direct or violent clash with Turkey since it provides their only secure route to the outside world. In the late summer of 1995, it also appeared that Barzani's Kurdistan Democratic Party was receiving some help from Turkey in his attempts to remove the PKK from northern Iraq. However, Turkey was anxious to avoid getting sucked into the armed struggle for power in Iraqi Kurdistan between Barzani and Talabani.

The longest-running problems in Turkey's foreign relations are its bilateral disputes with Greece and the associated conflict over Cyprus. On the first score, Turkey strongly opposes periodic threats by Athens to declare a 12-mile limit to its territorial waters in the Aegean (in place of the present six miles) since this would leave 70 per cent of the sea under potential Greek control. This issue sparks off periodic press wars and sharp diplomatic exchanges between the two countries. However, both sides have pulled back from the brink of war and seem likely to go on doing so. On the Cyprus question, Turkey has encouraged peace talks between the leaders of the two communities on the island. Almost certainly, Ankara would like the problem settled, not least because it is a constant irritant in its relations with the western powers. At the same time, no Turkish government can afford to put overt or excessive pressure on the Turkish Cypriots to reach a settlement, as this would provoke sharp protests from nationalist opinion at home. In the absence of a settlement, the mutual stand-off appears to be one which all the parties can live with, though it is unlikely to last indefinitely.

In spite of the end of the Cold War, Turkey has continued a close relationship with Washington, mainly because successive US administrations have recognised its importance as an ally in the Middle East. Relations with western Europe have been more troubled, principally because of greater European sensitivity on the Kurdish problem and on human rights, yet for obvious geographical reasons have more potential for development. Turkey became an Associate Member of what was then the European Economic Community in 1963 and still hopes eventually to acquire full membership of the EU. Given the huge budgetary costs of full membership to the rest of the EU, as well as political problems caused by the human rights and Cyprus issues, this ambition is not likely to be achieved in the near future. On the other hand, it is possible that if the EU is eventually reconstructed on a more flexible basis, so as to accommodate the former communist countries of eastern Europe as well as Turkey, then the economic obstacles to membership could be overcome. On this basis, assuming a favourable political climate, Turkey could become part of a re-shaped EU some time in the next century. In the meantime, the implementation of the customs union, provided it goes ahead, will be an important milestone in an important and developing relationship.

William Hale

16
YEMEN

HISTORICALLY, THE NAME 'YEMEN' refers to an area encompassing the provinces of Asir and Najran, in what is now Saudi Arabia, and the Republic of Yemen, formed in May 1990 after the unification of the Yemen Arab Republic (the YAR or North Yemen) and the People's Democratic Republic of Yemen (the PDRY or South Yemen). Although the notion of a unified Yemen has long commanded considerable support among Yemenis both north and south of the pre-1990 border, the quite separate political paths taken by the two entities over the last 150 years has meant that union has been fraught with difficulty, indeed at times has seemed impossible to sustain.

EARLY HISTORY

Yemen converted to Islam during the lifetime of the Prophet Muhammad, and Yemenis formed a large proportion of the armies which carried out the Islamic conquests. However, as the political centre of gravity of Islam moved away from the Arabian peninsula, Yemen declined. In 897 the northern tribes invited Yahya ibn al-Hussain, a descendant of the Prophet, to be their imam, thereby founding the Zaydi imamate, which was to last until its overthrow in 1962.

Zaydism is a branch of Shi'ism now more or less confined to the south-west of the Arabian peninsula and with little in common with the major other branches of Shi'ism. The Zaydi imam must be a descendant of the Prophet and be elected by the *ulama* (religious scholars). He must also be able to back up his claim by force. For most of the period between its foundation in 897 and the beginning of the 20th century the writ of the imamate remained tenuous and was largely confined to the northern mountains. In addition, given the elective nature of the office, it is not surprising that it passed through several different families over the centuries. In consequence, 'the Zaydi imamate' was a fluid entity at best, its domains and effectiveness alike changing frequently. The non-Zaydi parts of the country, which account for over half the population of the former North Yemen and the entire population of the former South Yemen, were, and still are, Sunni Muslim.

The Zaydi imamate survived many vicissitudes, including the conquest by the Ayyubids in 1173. This united the southern and western parts of the country, so that until the early 16th century a series of Sunni dynasties controlled the south and west while the Zaydis controlled the north. In 1536 the Ottomans established a foothold in Yemen, mainly in order to exclude the Portuguese from the Red Sea.

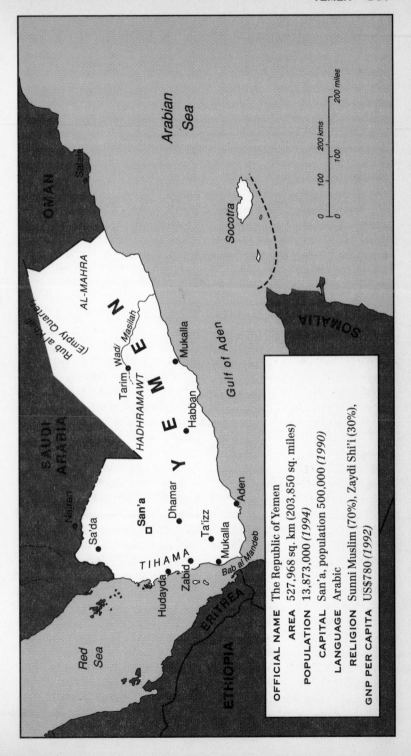

OFFICIAL NAME   The Republic of Yemen
AREA   527,968 sq. km (203,850 sq. miles)
POPULATION   13,873,000 (1994)
CAPITAL   San'a, population 500,000 (1990)
LANGUAGE   Arabic
RELIGION   Sunni Muslim (70%), Zaydi Shi'i (30%),
GNP PER CAPITA   US$780 (1992)

Although the term is clearly anachronistic, there was something of a 'national revival' in the early 17th century, in which the Imam Qasim al-Mansur Billah and his son managed to unite the tribes sufficiently to expel the Ottomans and extend their authority over substantial parts of the north and south. However, a long period of fragmentation and isolation followed in which the power of the imamate declined. In 1804, the Wahhabis, who had captured Mecca from the Ottomans in 1803, occupied the Tihama, the Red Sea Coast. In alliance with the Zaydi Imam al-Mahdi Abdullah (1816-35), a force despatched from Egypt by Muhammad Ali ejected the Wahhabis, but Muhammad Ali's own territorial ambitions were such that the imam did not regain control of the Tihama until the end of Muhammad Ali's reign.

YEMEN UNDER THE OTTOMANS AND THE BRITISH

By this time other factors were at work which were eventually to crystallise the division between North and South. In the first place, after a series of fruitless negotiations initiated in 1834 over the lease or purchase of Aden with the Sultan of Lahij, in 1839 Captain Haines of the Indian Navy took possession of the town in the name of the Government of India. The following year, under British and French pressure, Muhammad Ali withdrew from all the territories he had occupied, including Yemen. A few years later the Ottomans reoccupied Yemen, taking Hudayda on the Red Sea coast in 1849. Before this, Imam Muhammad Yahya had appealed unsuccessfully to Haines for a treaty of protection with Britain on the lines of those signed with the rulers of the Gulf states.

The Ottomans then tried to reassert their authority in both north-eastern and south-western Arabia. On the Gulf coast they occupied al-Hasa and in 1871 took San'a. The Ottomans were determined to incorporate the area as fully as possible into their reformed empire, and indeed Yemen 'elected' two delegates to the first Ottoman parliament in 1875. While the reforms remained largely theoretical as far as Yemen was concerned, schemes of agricultural improvement and land law reform were launched and the foundations of a public educational system laid. In addition, Ottoman commercial and penal law was introduced, as well as, at least in theory, the Ottoman civil code of 1876.

At the turn of the century the Imam Muhammad Hamid al-Din (1891-1904) denounced Turkish rule as unIslamic. This gained him a large measure of support, but the revolt which followed was put down severely by the Ottomans. His successor, Yahya (1904-48), also called for a 'national' rising, partly in protest against the Ottomans' willingness to participate with the British in the demarcation of a frontier between the British-controlled 'South' (i.e. Aden) and 'Ottoman Yemen', all of which Yahya considered potentially his own. The British, meanwhile, gradually extended their influence over the South by a series of exclusive treaties with tribal leaders. For their part, due to pressures elsewhere in the Ottoman empire, the Ottoman provincial authorities were obliged to reduce the garrison in Yemen, signing a treaty with Yahya in 1911 which left him in full control of the highlands. The Ottomans continued to rule the Tihama, where they remained until the collapse of their empire in 1918.

Yahya remained neutral in the First World War, resisting British attempts to court him and generally abiding by the terms of the 1911 treaty. Yahya also resented British support for the Sharif of Mecca and his family, and their pretensions to extend their authority over the rest of the Arab world. While Yahya remained impervious to British bland-ishments, the British paid subsidies to al-Idrisi, the ruler of Asir – the area to the immediate north-west of modern Yemen – to get him to sub-orn some of Yahya's tribal supporters, though with little result.

YEMEN BETWEEN 1918 AND 1962

After 1918 the division between the British-administered South, on the one hand, and the North, on the other, deepened. In addition the British occupied Hudayda in 1919, and on evacuating it in 1921 encouraged al-Idrisi of Asir to take it over. Whatever the merits of this policy, it should be remembered that the Tihama had not been controlled by the imamate for any substantial period since the mid-17th century. None the less, Britain's intention was of course to weaken Yahya, who also claimed sovereignty over some of the southern tribes, who in theory were bound to the British authorities in Aden by treaty but who in fact had transferred their allegiance to Yahya after the Ottomans' departure.

Tensions over the southern tribes continued until 1934, when Yahya signed the Treaty of San'a with Britain. This effectively acknowledged the boundaries drawn up by the British and the Ottomans earlier in the century, although it was agreed that no formal demarcation of the fron-tiers should take place. Yahya had also sought outside support against Britain with the conclusion of a treaty with Italy in 1926. In fact, the spectre of closer Italian involvement in Yemen and the Red Sea hung over Britain's relations with Yemen until the signature of the Anglo-Italian Agreement of April 1938. Under its terms both countries under-took to respect each other's interests in the region.

During the interwar period Yahya consolidated his power in the North, while the British extended theirs in the South. In 1930, Ibn Saud made the final enlargement of his kingdom by annexing Asir, two years later renaming the new state the kingdom of Saudi Arabia. In the spring of 1934 a war broke out between Saudi Arabia and Yemen in which the Saudis seemed poised to take over the Tihama. However, probably because Ibn Saud realised his forces would have difficulty penetrating beyond the coastal plain, by early June the two parties signed a treaty of friendship which recognised what is still the north-western border between them. In the South, Aden continued to grow in importance as a port and naval base. In 1937 Britain incorporated the Aden Protectorate into Aden Colony, and made the resulting entity a

Crown Colony. 'Aden' meant the port and its immediate hinterland while the Protectorate contained 24 small states extending from Bab al-Mandab on the Red Sea in the west to the Hadhramawt and Oman in the east.

Although Anglo-Yemeni relations were generally cordial after 1934, an important source of friction between Aden and San'a was the presence of a large number of exiles from the North in Aden. Both Yahya (who was assassinated in 1948) and his son and successor, Ahmad (1948-62), largely succeeded in isolating Yemen from the rest of the world. Few foreigners – and almost no other Arabs – were allowed in. There were no foreign embassies or newspapers and no modern schools. In addition, there were only two or three modern roads and no more than a handful of doctors.

In such circumstances, and with the economy of northern Yemen dependent on subsistence agriculture well into the 1970s, many Yemenis came to believe that the only solution was migration. By the 1940s about 750,000 of them, mostly from the southern highlands and the Tihama, had left. Much of what opposition there was to the imamate before 1962 (apart from more personal expressions of hostility on the part of individual tribal leaders) came from abroad, first from Aden, where the Free Yemeni Movement was established in 1944, later from Cairo. In Aden, by contrast, there was freedom of political association, a lively trade union movement, a relatively free press and the kind of educational and welfare services that could be expected in a success-ful and cosmopolitan colony.

In the course of his reign Yahya managed to extend his rule over most of 'North Yemen', including the Tihama, where his son Ahmad subjugated the Zaraniq tribe in 1928. However, Yahya aroused consid-erable and ultimately fatal opposition by insisting that Ahmad be recog-nised as his successor in his own lifetime. This led to his assassination in 1948 by backers of Abdullah al-Wazir, themselves supported by the Free Yemeni Movement, who considered al-Wazir's claims to the ima-mate at least as legitimate as Ahmad's. The shock of the assassination rallied the tribes around Ahmad, who quickly regained control and moved the capital to Ta'izz.

1962: THE END OF THE IMAMATE

Ahmad ruled until his death in 1962, and to some extent lessened the country's isolation. He accepted both Soviet and Chinese assistance, and, rather quaintly, joined the United Arab Republic of Egypt and Syria soon after its formation in 1958. Ahmad continued his father's hostility to the British in the South, where, although retreating from empire elsewhere, they appeared intent on digging themselves further in. The Federation of South Arabia was formed in February 1959, with a government consisting almost exclusively of leaders of the various tribal states, and in 1962 the Colony (with its much more politically sophisticated constituency) was forcibly united with the Federation.

The late 1950s and early 1960s were of course the heyday of Nasserist Arab nationalism, when there was much wild talk (and intense radio propaganda) of doing away with the governments of Arab kings, princes, sultans and imams. In this heady atmosphere, Ahmad's death in September 1962 was seized upon as the signal for a coup against his son and successor Muhammad al-Badr. This was carried out by a combination of Yemeni and Egyptian officers a week later. Since the imam's palace had been heavily bombarded, it was assumed that al-Badr had been killed, and the Yemen Arab Republic was declared under the presidency of Colonel Abdullah Sallal prompting a civil war between 'royalists' and 'republicans' which lasted until February 1970.

In essence, the 'republicans' were backed by Egypt, which despatched 50,000 troops, and the 'royalists' by Saudi Arabia. Again in broad terms, the Shafi'i areas and the three main cities (San'a, Ta'izz and Hudayda) were 'republican', though only in the sense that they opposed the return of the imam. In addition, Ahmad had managed to alienate a number of Zaydi tribal leaders during his reign, with the result that that many of them fought with the opposition to his son. Furthermore, the country's rudimentary administration meant that before 1962 there were substantial areas where the writ of 'the state' did not run at all, and that a tribe's adhesion to 'royalists' or 'republicans' was determined chiefly by considerations of practical advantage.

By 1967, it was clear to Nasser that he was making little headway in Yemen. He thus gratefully siezed the chance offered at the Khartoum summit of withdrawing his troops in exchange for Saudi financial assistance. For a while this made little difference, given the nature of the terrain and the kind of tribal warfare involved, and the war dragged on to 1970. At this point the republicans, now aided by the new regime in Aden, had managed to gain the upper hand, and had set up a three-man council of state, headed by Qadi Abd al-Rahman al-Iryani. Al-Iryani was a figure from a traditional background whom the Saudis felt able to accept, especially in view of the political complexion of the new government in Aden. At that point the Saudis stopped funding the royalists and the fighting ceased; the Yemen Arab Republic was recognised by Saudi Arabia and the United Kingdom. Al-Iryani set up a 'government of national reconciliation' which included figures from both sides.

INDEPENDENCE IN THE SOUTH, MILITARY RULE IN THE NORTH

In November 1967, Britain withdrew from Aden. The last few years of the British presence had been spent in attempting to prop up the tribal leaders of the Federation against the Aden-based National Liberation Front. In a further development, the nationalist movement was split between pro-Egyptian and pro-Soviet factions, in which the pro-Soviet faction, led by Qahtan al-Sha'abi, gained the upper hand. This resulted in the creation of an Eastern European style centralised state with a command economy dependent on the Soviet Union. Inevitably, it came into conflict with Saudi Arabia. In the North, al-Iryani's government was weakened partly by continued Saudi interference, partly by the incoherence of the state structure itself.

A period of relative stagnation came to an end in 1974 when an officer from a *qadi* background, Lt-Col. al-Ibrahim Hamdi, took power in a military coup. Al-Hamdi favoured a strong state, which was anathema to some of the northern chiefs who felt they would lose power. In a confusing succession of events, he was assassinated in October 1977, a fate also suffered by his successor, the chief of staff, Ahmad al-Ghashmi, nine months later. In June 1978 the present president, Ali Abdullah Salih, came to power. These political assassinations were connected with swings in policy in favour of greater independence from Saudi Arabia and for closer links with Aden, which since June 1969 had been run by Salim Rubay'i Ali and Abd al-Fattah Isma'il. The government was riven by ideological splits and increasingly inspired by socialism on the Chinese model. But with both states producing entirely dissimilar constitutions in 1970, unity remained as elusive as ever. The repression practised in the South caused the departure of large numbers of the population, mostly to the North, across the long, unguarded border. In June 1978 Salim Rubay'i Ali tried to make contact with al-Ghashmi, probably in an effort to entice him away from the Saudis, but the envoy he sent was carrying a briefcase with a bomb which killed the YAR president; by all accounts that was most unlikely to have been Ali's intention. When the news reached Aden, Ali's opponents had him executed.

Early in 1979 the South, now led by Ali Nasir Muhammad and Abd al-Fattah Isma'il, launched an attack on the North, whose army collapsed with alarming speed. In March the two states signed an agreement in principle to unite, and, perhaps as a condition, Abd al-Fattah Isma'il went quietly into exile in the Soviet Union, while Ali Nasir Muhammad became president. Over the next few years relations waxed and waned in proportion to Saudi policy, which was largely concerned to keep the two states apart.

Early in 1986 Ali Nasir Muhammad sought to rid himself of hostile elements in the politburo. A brief but bloody civil war followed at the end of which Ali Nasir Muhammad was obliged to flee, first to Ethiopia and then to San'a. The next four years were relatively peaceful for the South. The prime minister, Haydar Abu Bakr al-Attas, took over from Ali Nasir Muhammad and launched a period of reconciliation, both internally and with Saudi Arabia and Oman. Al-Attas had some success in attracting aid and investment from the Gulf States and Iraq. In addition, with the onset of *perestroika* he launched a wholesale reform programme, leading to multi-party local elections in 1988.

UNITY

At first Ali Abdullah Salih's position as president of the YAR was uncertain, especially during the PDRY's invasion in 1969. However, Salih gradually consolidated his power and managed, moreover, to maintain good relations with both the US and the USSR. In addition, the discovery of oil in 1984 provided a boost to an impoverished economy largely dependent on immigrant remittances from Saudi Arabia.

In July 1988 apparently free elections for a Consultative Council, in which over one million voted, were held. With Ali Abdullah Salih in power in the North and Haydar Abu Bakr al-Attas in the South, the impulses towards unity in both states were increased further. Proposals from the mid-1980s that the newly discovered oilfields be jointly exploited were followed by agreements that Aden be reopened as a free port and the electrical systems of the two states unified. By spring 1990, the movement towards unity seemed unstoppable. It duly materialised in May. Salih became president, al-Attas prime minister and Ali Salim al-Baydh vice-president.

The enthusiasm for unity was not matched by any very serious attempts to cope with the practical difficulties which would inevitably accompany it, however. Thus the North, where the Muslim Brethren had a substantial foothold, found the South insufficiently 'Islamic', while some old communists in the South found it hard to adjust to the more painful aspects of economic and political liberalisation. On the other hand, a number of new political parties were formed and a constitution put to a referendum in May 1991.

The first major test of the new state came with the invasion of Kuwait in August 1990, which coincided with Yemeni membership of the UN Security Council (and its chairmanship in December 1990). Principally because of its economic links with Iraq, Yemen refused to condem the Iraqi invasion. Saudia Arabia responded by immediately expelling 750,000 Yemeni workers with the loss of $2 billion in remittances a year while aid from the US and some of the Gulf States was suspended. This disastrous start was the prelude to a general breakdown in law and order in the latter part of 1991 and early 1992. There were political assassinations in the North and South alike and in March a major strike of 100,000 workers in Aden protesting at rises in the cost of living. In these disordered circumstances, the Muslim Brethren easily recruited followers from among those deported from Saudi Arabia.

Reconciliation with the Gulf States began slowly from 1992, though relations with the US and Europe improved more quickly. The EC in particular expressed approval at the strides apparently being taken towards democracy. In April 1993 the new state held its first general election. The General People's Congress (North) won 123 of the 300 seats; the Yemeni Socialist Party (South), 56 seats; and the Yemeni Islah Party (partly Muslim Brethren) 51. Independents took the remaining 47 seats. The leader of the Islah Party, Abdullah al-Ahmar, was elected speaker, and a government was formed with representatives of all three parties.

Nonetheless, by the summer of 1993 it was clear that a major crisis was close. The causes were not hard to identify. Where the South had a more or less efficient centralised state the North relied on immigrant remittances, foreign aid and a dynamic private sector, all of which had been adversely affected by the Gulf War. It was obliged to contend, too, with the perennial problem of anarchic tribes outside its control. Moreover the South resented having to put up with the status quo in the North. For their part political leaders in the North seized the chance to make quick profits in the South, adding to resentment of them there. Though something of an oversimplification, the general effect of unification was the de facto annexation of the South by the North

In mid-August the vice-president, Ali Salim al-Baydh, withdrew to Aden after a trip abroad and refused to return to San'a unless 18 demands were met, generally in the direction of more effective government and an end to external interference and tribal violence. It is important to understand that at this stage the armies of the two former entities had not been merged. By the autumn, political assassinations and lawlessness were rife; foreigners were kidnapped and tribesmen attacked oil installations.

The situation worsened dramatically in 1994. Against a background of rioting in San'a and Ta'izz over high prices and the devaluation of the riyal, troops from the North and the South alike massed on the former frontiers. Efforts at mediation by Jordan, Oman and other states proved fruitless, and by May the two former states were effectively at war. The Southern ministers were dismissed from the government. On May 21, al-Baydh declared the South the independent Democratic Republic of Yemen, which was immediately recognised by the United Arab Emirates and Saudi Arabia. On 7 July, after fierce fighting the North, having taken Aden and Mukalla, claimed victory. By the end of July the conflict ended, having cost nearly 1,000 lives and $3 billion worth of destruction. Al-Baydh took refuge in Oman.

The situation remained chaotic, especially after the dismantling of the Southern army, most of whose weapons fell into the hands of the Northern tribes. Tensions with Saudi Arabia continued, although the possibility of using al-Baydh as the head of an opposition in exile (which was probably envisaged in mid-1994) receded. The economy remained parlous, with oil exploration and production resumed only in the spring of 1995.

Thus Yemen remains unified, but by force rather than free choice. Many outside parties, notably Saudi Arabia, had a vested interest in the failure of the kind of unification originally envisaged, and moreover were fearful of such manifestations of participation as the 1993 elections. With only modest natural resources and an economy in chaos, the Northern-dominated state will presumably make its peace with Saudi Arabia and attempt to attract the foreign investment it needs. Stripped of any independent military power, the South will almost certainly be obliged to conform.

Peter Sluglett

17
OIL IN THE MIDDLE EAST

THE DEVELOPMENT OF THE Middle East's oil reserves since the 1940s and 1950s has brought great wealth to many countries in the region. Only Cyprus, Israel, Lebanon, Morocco, Jordan, the Sudan and Turkey have little or no crude oil production. However, all the Arab states are linked economically or politically through joint-venture investments in oil-related activities and through organisations such as the Arab League, the Gulf Co-operation Council (GCC), the Organisation of Arab Petroleum Exporting Countries (OAPEC) and the Organisation of Petroleum Exporting Countries (OPEC).

According to some estimates, the Middle East (excluding North Africa) holds 660 billion barrels of proven oil reserves, around 65 per cent of the total discovered in the world (1994 figures). Ninety-nine per cent of these reserves are located in the countries surrounding the Persian Gulf; the remaining one per cent is in Egypt. North African reserves were estimated at 36 billion barrels as end-1994. The industrialised world is consequently highly dependent for its oil supplies on these Persian Gulf states. Likewise, the Middle East's economies rely heavily on income derived from either crude oil and oil-derived product exports and from economic links with oil-rich countries.

Despite a high level of concern since the early 1970s over the political implications of Western dependence on oil from the Persian Gulf, petroleum liquids still accounted for around 46 per cent and 41 per cent of the primary energy needs of Western Europe and North America respectively in 1994. The political concerns of the West were demonstrated by the adoption of policies designed to safeguard supplies, such as the development of alternative energy sources and conservation and efficiency measures. At the same time, a growing awareness of the interdependence of the world's economies will help both oil consumers and producers to realise the merits of co-operation.

HISTORY
Exploration for oil in the Middle East began in the 19th century, with the first wells drilled in Iran in 1884 by Hots and Co. of Bushehr. However, it was not until the early years of the 20th century that oil was struck in commercial quantities. The search for oil in Iran was conducted by William Knox D'Arcy, who secured a concession from the Shah in May 1901. The concession included mineral exploitation rights

throughout Iran with the exception of five northern provinces awarded to the Russo-Persia Naphtha Company in 1896. The financial terms of the concession required the payment of £40,000 upon the establishment of a company to manage operations within the concession and 16 per cent of the future net profits of that company. On 26 May 1908, almost seven years to the day after the signing of the concession agreement, the Concession Syndicate Company, owned by the Burmah Oil Company, but with D'Arcy as director, struck oil at Masjid-i-Sulayman. In Egypt, the first commercial oil discovery, known as the Gemsa oilfield, was made by the Egyptian Oil Trust in March 1909.

1909 proved a significant year. In it, the first cargo of Middle Eastern oil, transported first by pipeline from the Masjid-i-Sulayman oilfield, was loaded at Abadan on the Shatt al-Arab waterway. However, the development of oil production and markets was slow and at the outbreak of the First World War Persia was producing only two million barrels annually, less than half a per cent of total world production. In the same year the Concession Syndicate Company was re-formed as the Anglo-Persian Oil Company, which later acquired and took on the name of a small distribution company in England, British Petroleum.

During the First World War production from the Masjid-i-Sulayman oilfield more than doubled, from 2.9 to 8.6 million barrels. This production was transported to the Abadan refinery, completed in 1912, which supplied the growing fuel-oil demand of the Royal Navy and also exported kerosene as heating oil.

The outbreak of the First World War had set back complex negotiations relating to oil exploitation rights in Iraq, then a part of the Ottoman Empire, between Turkey, Germany and Great Britain. The reconciliation of the three countries' interests through the formation of the jointly owned Turkish Petroleum Company (TPC) in 1912 was short lived. After the defeat of Germany and the Ottoman Empire, new players, namely France and the United States, expressed their wish to be included in any agreement authorising exploration in Iraq.

Negotiations over shares in TPC and its Iraqi concession were concluded in July 1928 with the signing of the Red Line Agreement between Royal/Dutch Shell, Anglo-Persian, Compagnie Française des Pétroles, Gulbenkian (who had founded the original TPC in 1912) and the Near East Development Company, a consortium of American oil companies. This famous agreement represented a truce between American and British interests. Within this 'red line' area, which included the Arabian Peninsula, Iraq, Lebanon, Palestine, Syria and Transjordan, no member of the TPC (now the IPC) could act without the other. This was to prove a great advantage for other oil companies operating within the area who were not constrained by this agreement, such as Standard Oil of California (Socal). The conclusion of negotiations had been hastened by the discovery of the huge Kirkuk oilfield in October 1927 and the desire on the part of all participants to realise the potential of this oil-bearing region.

The status of Iraq as an oil producer was greatly enhanced in the

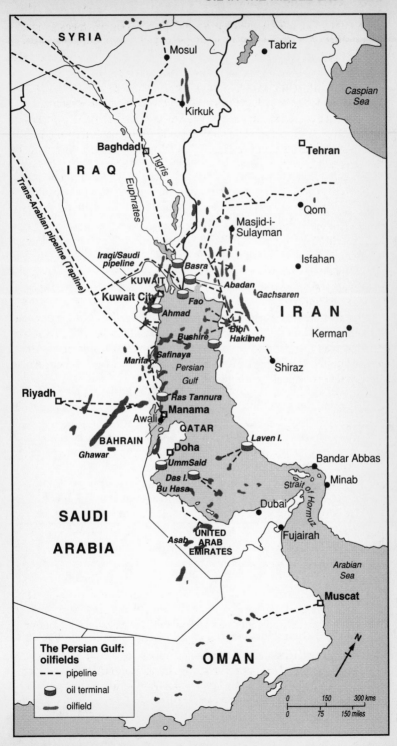

The Persian Gulf:
oilfields

‑ ‑ ‑   pipeline

◖   oil terminal

▬   oilfield

1930s by the Iraq Petroleum Company's construction of the 267-mile pipeline, with a capacity of around four million tons per year, linking the Kirkuk field to terminals at the ports of Haifa and Tripoli in Palestine and Lebanon respectively.

The shock discovery of the Awali oilfield in Bahrain in October 1931 by a newcomer to the Middle East, Socal (now Chevron), began a scramble on the part of the oil companies in the Persian Gulf to secure concessions over neighbouring states. In the 1930s the search spread to Bahrain, Kuwait, Qatar and Saudi Arabia. With the help of St John Philby, explorer and diplomat as well as friend of the Saudi king, Socal secured the mineral exploitation rights over the whole of Saudi Arabia on 29 May 1933. This concession has since proved the richest in the world. Its proven oil reserves were estimated at 261 billion barrels in 1994, 26 per cent of all known reserves.

The Second World War had an ambiguous effect on the pace of oil development in the Middle East. For countries with established oil production and export infrastructures, namely Bahrain, Egypt, Iran, Iraq and Saudi Arabia, the period was one of rapid expansion. However, 78 billion barrels of Kuwaiti oil reserves located in the late 1930s, out of a total 97 billion barrels, were left undeveloped for the duration.

POST-1945

The post-war period saw the meteoric rise of Saudi Arabia and Kuwait as oil producers. The development of Iran by Anglo-Persian and the development of Iraq by the IPC foundered in the 1950s as a result of political instability in those countries and with their respective neighbours. Meanwhile, the extraordinary efforts of two new companies, the Kuwait Oil Company, owned by Anglo-Iranian (formerly Anglo-Persian) and Gulf Oil, plus the Arabian American Oil Company (Aramco) owned by Socal, Socony-Vacuum Oil Company (now Mobil), Standard Oil of New Jersey (now Exxon) and Texaco, increased oil production in Kuwait and Saudi Arabia. It rose from nought and 58,000 barrels (respectively) per day in 1945 to 1.24 million and 1.62 million barrels per day in 1960. The 1950s was also the most significant decade for the Middle East – specifically the Gulf – in terms of oil exploration: 157 billion barrels of recoverable oil were discovered. 1951 saw the discovery of the two largest oilfields yet known, both Saudi Arabian: the Ghawar and the (offshore) Safinaya oilfields.

While the Kuwait Oil Company was primarily concerned with the infrastructure and output of oil in Kuwait, Aramco was beginning to show growing maturity towards the management of its oil operations and in consolidating its position in world oil markets. On 2 December 1950 the 1,070-mile pipeline linking the oilfields in eastern Saudi Arabia with the port of Sidon in Lebanon became fully operational. The pipeline reduced the distance between the oilfields on the Persian Gulf to the major centre of oil demand in Europe by some 3,500 miles. At the same time, diversification of outlets helped Gulf oil producers to avoid interruption to their oil exports from political turmoil near their borders or along established shipping routes. Aramco's management of its oil operations was furthered in the 1950s with oilfield programmes designed to optimise recovery through the use of water and gas injection. In addition, as well as expanding the crude capacity of the Ras Tannura refinery, built in 1945, Aramco began to add more complex processes to increase the quality and diversity of its oil product exports.

Middle East oil production and exports increased four-fold between 1960 and the early 1970s. At the same time, world demand for oil tripled. However, despite this apparent stability, the conditions for a revolution in the world oil market were being established. The growing confidence of the oil producers, underlined by their foundation of the Organisation of Petroleum Exporting Countries (OPEC) in 1960, was placing increasing stress on their relations with oil companies and the major oil-consuming countries.

By the late 1960s, the combination of government fiscal incentives and the desire on the part of oil companies to diversify their sources of oil income had led to a surge of exploration in the higher-cost oil provinces outside the OPEC region, of which the Middle East is the most important part. Before the first oil price shock in October 1973, production had begun in the large oil provinces of western Siberia, northeast China, offshore Malaysia and offshore Australia, while the development of the North Sea, Alaska and the Reforma province of Mexico was at an irreversible stage. Certain Middle East countries which had remained outside OPEC, such as Egypt and Oman, gained from its reorientation of investment, their combined oil production increasing from 61,000 barrels per day in 1960 (Omani production did not begin until 1967) to 730,000 barrels per day in 1970.

On its own, the increase in the supply of non-OPEC oil would not have altered the balance of power in the world oil market. However, the impact on world oil markets of the price shocks of 1973 and 1979–80 was sufficient both to reduce the growth of the industrialised world's demand for oil and to encourage the pace of oil development outside OPEC. The result was that, in order to maintain the high oil price introduced in 1973, OPEC was forced to take on the role of residual supplier and to cut oil production and exports. From its 1976 peak of around 21.6 million barrels per day, Persian Gulf oil production fell to around 10.2 million barrels per day in 1985.

During the 1970s and 1980s those Middle Eastern countries with large surpluses of oil production for export had two concerns. The first was how to invest their new-found wealth; the second, how to retain their market share without adversely affecting the oil price. Investment in oil-related industry was seen as a partial solution to both concerns.

Since 1970, therefore, oil investment in Middle Eastern countries has gradually been redirected from the upstream sector – namely, crude oil exploration, production and export capacity – to the downstream sector – namely, refining, petrochemical and energy-intensive industries.

OIL AND POLITICS IN THE MIDDLE EAST

From the perspective of the West the prime importance of the Middle East lies, simply, in its oil resources. All the political crises in the Middle East, namely the Iranian nationalisation of 1951, the Suez Crisis of 1956, the Arab-Israeli wars in 1967 and 1973, the Iranian revolution and subsequent Iran-Iraq War of 1979–88 and the invasion of Kuwait by Iraq in August 1990, have involved the interruption of, or threat to, oil supplies, often triggering intervention by Western powers.

The Middle Eastern countries have never been slow to realise the equation of oil and politics. The political history of oil in the Middle East can be divided into two periods. In the first, from 1932 to 1974, the governments of the oil-exporting countries vied with the oil companies for control over their natural resources. Having succeeded in gaining control over the crucial instruments of policy – production and price – the oil-exporting countries, alone or in concert, have sought a balance between economic and political objectives. For instance, an economic decision taken by one oil-exporter to raise oil production in order to maximise revenues may have the effect of lowering prices across the world markets. In turn, this may irreversibly lower the revenues for other oil exporters producing at the upper limit of their capacity. The initial economic decision must therefore take into account its associated effect on political relations in the region. A similar argument may be viewed in reverse in relation to the economic well-being of the oil-consuming countries.

1932 TO 1974

The history of nationalisation dates back to the 1930s. The first full-scale nationalisation of oil resources and operations was engineered by President Cardeñas of Mexico in 1938. However, even earlier, in 1932, Reza Shah of Iran, annulled the oil concession rights awarded to Anglo-Persian in 1901. Three over-lapping motives lay behind this appropriation and were to resurface time after time during the contest of political wills between government and company. The first related to the Shah's lack of control over oil production and pricing, and thus control over a major part of the country's revenues. This concern was prompted by the drastic fall in Iranian oil revenues in 1917. The second related to the contradiction between the fundamental principles of concessions and of national sovereignty. The third was the Shah's intention to use his sovereign power as a bargaining tool in his negotiations with the British government, who had purchased 51 per cent of Anglo-Persian in 1914. Nonetheless, having renegotiated the terms of the concession Reza Shah gave it back in 1933.

The assertion of oil producers' aspirations were fated to fail again as a result of the dismissal of Iranian Prime Minister Mosaddeq in August 1953. On 1 May 1951, Mosaddeq succeeded in forcing the new Shah, Mohammed Reza Pahlavi, to sign a law nationalising the country's oil resources. Mosaddeq's move followed the failure of Anglo-Iranian to agree satisfactory terms of renewal for the original oil concession granted in 1901 and revised in 1933. Mosaddeq was in a strong position. Aramco had recently agreed to an unprecedented increase in the Saudi government's take to 50 per cent of profits less the exploration, development and production costs. In addition, the outbreak of the Korean War had made the West more dependent on petroleum product supplies from the Middle East to fuel the military effort in the Far East. They were also keen to maintain good diplomatic relations with Iran to prevent the incursion of Soviet influence. However, Mosaddeq was no mere lone opportunist: he had tapped strong nationalist and anti-British sentiment in Iran and, even if he had wanted to, was constrained in his negotiations by these popular feelings. In the end, Mosaddeq failed because he had acted in isolation, without the co-operation of other oil-exporting countries. The embargo on Iranian oil engineered by the West was successful in harming the Iranian economy and turning public opinion against Mosaddeq.

THE ROLE OF OPEC

The lesson of Mosaddeq's attempt at nationalisation was not lost on other oil producers in the region. The third attempt by governments to wrest control over indigenous oil resources began with the formation of OPEC in Baghdad in 1960. All the elements evident in 1932 were again apparent. First, the initial catalyst for the meeting in Baghdad was the sudden 15 per cent fall in governments' oil revenues between 1959 and 1960. This was the result of the oil companies' unilateral decisions to cut posted prices. Secondly, Middle Eastern and, more especially Arab, oil exporters' national sentiments had grown hugely in confidence as a result of Nasser's successful moves against Britain and France in the Suez crisis of 1956. Thirdly, the move was an expression of the bargaining power of the founders of OPEC, namely Kuwait, Iran, Iraq, Saudi Arabia and Venezuela (Qatar joined in 1961). It had the effect of forcing the oil companies to raise posted prices and deterring them from future unilateral actions with regard to posted prices.

The founding statutes of OPEC were not so much revolutionary as 'a charter for change'. The objective of the organisation was price stabilisation, possibly through prorationing production, on behalf of all member states, meaning that individual member states were precluded from unilateral negotiations with the oil companies. The challenge to the oil companies that OPEC presented led inevitably to a deterioration of relations between the oil companies and the organisation during the 1960s. The slack oil market conditions of the 1960s led to resentment over the fall in oil prices (in real terms) and the suspicion of bias in the allocation of production increases between oil-exporting countries. Positive hostility to the West as a whole was furthered by the Six Day War in June 1967.

Following the war and Israel's crushing victory, in June 1967, OPEC issued the Declaratory Statement of Petroleum Policy in Member Countries. The statement called for member countries to develop their oil reserves directly and that only where state-owned technology was insufficient should overseas companies be allowed to share ownership of reserves. Further, it called for government participation in all current oil operations and direct control over the posted, or tax-reference, price.

The upturn in the oil market in the late 1960s and early 1970s enabled OPEC to realise its ambitions. The catalyst to that realisation was provided by the October War between Israel and the Arab world in 1973. At a meeting of the six OPEC Gulf producers – Iran, Iraq, Kuwait, Qatar, Saudi Arabia and the UAE – in Kuwait on 16 October 1973, it was resolved that OPEC should 'establish and announce the posted prices of crudes in the Gulf'. The following day nine Arab member states of the Organisation of Arab Petroleum Exporting Countries resolved to cut production by a minimum of five per cent. In just two days the Middle Eastern states had taken control of the two crucial instruments for their economic and political independence: the control of oil production and pricing.

1974 TO THE PRESENT

Four areas of political and strategic concern may be discerned in the formulation of oil exporters' production and pricing policies: regional stability; the Arabic-speaking world; the Third World; and the world economy. These represent different priorities for each according to political circumstance and the individual resource endowment of the oil exporter.

Between the advent of the first oil price shocks in October and December 1973 and December 1985, OPEC remained loyal to its first objective: price stabilisation at an agreed level. In the tight oil market conditions up to 1982 the OPEC countries were able to control price with only implicit reference to production prorationing through the use of Arabian Light as the 'marker' crude.

However, with the Persian Gulf states increasingly pursuing different political objectives, it was no surprise that this unanimity proved impossible to sustain. Both in December 1976, at the OPEC conference in Doha and, more significantly for the oil market, between 1979 and 1981 in the wake of the second oil price shock, a two-tier price system emerged. Saudi Arabia, concerned by the possible implications of a high oil price for the world economy and for future oil demand, exercised its sovereign right to sell its oil at a lower price. Saudi Arabia has always taken a longer-term view on the oil market because its revenue needs are low relative to its potential oil income. Other countries without surplus revenues or oil-producing capacity, such as Iran and Iraq, must face the more immediate problems of revenue maximisation.

The fall in world oil demand and the concurrent rise in non-OPEC production over the early 1980s made it impossible for OPEC to achieve its price objectives without a significant sacrifice of oil production. In 1982 it was agreed that this sacrifice should be shared on the basis of a production prorationing scheme. However, Saudi Arabia was to be excluded on the basis that it had to be free to adjust its output of Arabian Light, the marker crude, to fine-tune the impact on the price of production cuts.

In December 1985, after three years of accusation and counter-accusation relating to production quota violations, the fixed-price system was finally laid to rest by the decision 'to secure and defend for OPEC a fair share of the world oil market'. The result was the price collapse of 1986, when the price of a barrel of Brent fell from over $30 (in August 1985) to under $10 (in June 1986). The collapse meant that a new price objective had to be agreed by the Persian Gulf states. The probability of agreement was remote, however, with relations strained by increasing mutual suspicion over quota 'cheats' and by the continuing threat to regional stability posed by the Iran-Iraq War.

It was in reaction to the increasing political instability around the Gulf that Bahrain, Kuwait, Qatar, Oman, Saudi Arabia and the UAE formed the Gulf Co-operation Council (GCC) on 25 May 1981. A major concern during the 1980s was the threat of Iranian fundamentalism to the traditional regimes of the GCC States. The GCC States were concerned both militarily (in the case of Iraq's being defeated Iran would threaten their borders) and internally, as a result of Shi'i terrorist bombings and assassination attempts.

The adoption of the low oil price objective of $18 per barrel by the GCC States and Iraq, in spite of Iran's wishes, cannot be viewed in isolation from this political context. Whether intentional or not, the low oil prices of 1986–88 were instrumental in the economic attrition of Iran and, so, in ending the war. Iraq was able to support the low oil price objective without suffering a drastic fall in oil revenues due to the supply of 'war-relief' crude from the Neutral Zone.

The ending of the Iran-Iraq War led to further divisions in the price objectives of the Persian Gulf states, despite the continuing adoption of the $18 reference price. Iran still called for higher prices but was effectively marginalised. The UAE continued to refuse to support any increase in price until its long-term grievance against its allocated quota was settled within OPEC. The primary concern of Saudi Arabia and Qatar, meanwhile, continued to be the maintenance of regional stability. However, after 1988 Kuwait and Iraq began to adopt strongly opposing positions on the price issue. Iraq, increasingly confident that the military threat from Iran had been curtailed, no longer had any interest in a low oil price. Its inability to increase revenue through an increase in production left Iraq little option but to persuade its neighbours to reduce production in favour of a higher price. Kuwait, on the other hand, increasingly began to see its long-term interest in a fruitful economic relationship with the West as its overseas operations grew and its production capacity proved sufficient to satisfy revenue needs at a lower price.

The growing tension between Iraq and Kuwait over the oil price issue in the late 1980s climaxed in Iraq's invasion of Kuwait in August 1990 and the war of January 1991 which effectively reversed Iraq's territorial gains. The overwhelming legacy of a decade of war in the Persian Gulf was the destruction of all the visible gains that three countries, namely Iran, Iraq and Kuwait, had secured from the exploitation of their dwindling natural resources. Added to this, Saudi Arabia and Kuwait were faced with huge financial commitments both to pay for the cost of the Allied campaign and, in the case of Kuwait, the subsequent reconstruction. Iraq was left in dire economic straits and will face years of hardship after the lifting of sanctions because of debt and reparation payments.

The campaign to liberate Kuwait initially divided the Arab world. The involvement of foreign troops and their continued presence in Saudi Arabia and Kuwait reawakened deeply rooted Arab fears of the West. The shockwaves continued to be felt long after the withdrawal of Iraqi forces. Both the Kuwaiti and Saudi ruling elites have experienced increasingly vocal opposition from previously loyal sections of their societies, a trend which cannot be entirely disassociated from the loss of credibility the regimes suffered as a result of foreign military involvement in a dispute between Arab neighbours. As a result both ruling elites view their security as being increasingly dependent on the West rather than on the Arab world.

The devastation caused by this decade of war and the resultant loosening of political ties have had economic repercussions for all the Arab world. The growing financial commitments of Saudi Arabia and the costs of reconstruction imposed on Kuwait, Iran and Iraq have removed the ability of any one of these producers to make an altruistic sacrifice of oil revenues in the pursuit of the OPEC reference price of $21 per barrel set in July 1990 (admittedly under a great deal of duress from Iraq). Until the OPEC member states are able to rebuild the trust necessary to conduct an effective production prorationing scheme the achievement of any reference price will be beyond their control. The result of this fiscal tightening and continued political tension has been that the flow of remittances and aid from the oil-rich Gulf producers to other Arab states has dwindled.

The economic outlook does not seem bright. The population explosion is continuing and will generate heavier and heavier financial commitments on governments. Likewise the burden of reconstruction is likely to impinge on Kuwaiti, Iranian and Iraqi development plans for some time to come. To finance these plans Kuwait, Iran and Saudi Arabia intend to increase capacity substantially despite the current weakness of oil markets. Given the continued strength of non-OPEC production and the inevitable re-entry of Iraq to the international fold no improvement in the oil price seems possible without concerted action by OPEC members.

On the political front, the peace talks between Israel and the Palestinians and the peace treaty with Jordan may eventually yield a peace dividend and remove a source of disruption to oil supplies. But the successful completion of these talks and the establishment of a durable peace are not yet firm certainties.

OIL AND THE ECONOMIES OF THE MIDDLE EAST

Oil revenues and economic growth are fundamentally linked in the oil-exporting states of the Middle East. The investment of oil revenues has had a particular impact on their economies which distinguishes them from other Third World countries. First, the economic development plans of the oil states tend to concentrate on high-technology investment in the energy and energy-intensive industries. Secondly, surplus revenues tend to be ploughed back into investment in public services and infrastructure, which, given the cyclical nature of oil markets, generally results in 'bust and boom' construction cycles. Thirdly, the more traditional forms of economic activity, such as agriculture and handicrafts, tend to shrink as a result of labour migration to other sectors and to cities.

However, these broad trends cannot in themselves explain the different ways in which oil revenues have affected the economic structures, and determined the economic strategies, of the Middle East. To do this, a useful distinction can be made between the 'desert-oil' and 'oil-plus' economies of the region. These distinctions are made on the basis of population, land availability and non-oil investment opportunities.

'Desert-oil' describes those Middle East economies – Bahrain, Kuwait, Libya, Oman, Qatar, Saudi Arabia and the UAE – with slim or non-existent traditional resource bases, the result of little cultivable land and small indigenous populations. This category may be further divided between the larger countries with geographically disparate settlements – Libya, Oman and Saudi Arabia – and the remainder, which are essentially city-states.

'Oil-plus' economies – Algeria, Egypt, Iran, Iraq and Syria – have large populations with rich agricultural resources. They have diverse sources of income linked closely to the productivity of the indigenous population. This provides opportunities for investment in sustainable types of production rather than in sectors linked to finite energy resources. The 'plus', therefore, refers to the resources accruable to those economies with a diversified resource base.

The relative importance of oil to the Middle East's economies can be gauged in several ways. Here, three of many possible measures are employed to determine the similarities and differences in the impact of oil revenues on the structure of the economies. These are: the ratio of GDP per capita to oil revenue per capital; oil exports as a percentage of total exports; and the composition of non-oil GDP.

First, a high ratio of GDP per capita to oil revenue per capita implies either that the economy has successfully employed oil revenues to diversify its sources of income or that the economy had diverse sources of income before oil revenues became important. Of the Persian Gulf producers the three highest ratios are those of Saudi Arabia, Iraq and Bahrain, with 5:2, 4:9 and 4:5 respectively (1988 figures are the most recent available for all three countries, although the Saudi and Bahraini ratios have not changed greatly since). In the case of Saudi

Arabia, the ratio may be overstated as the enormous interest derived from accumulated oil revenues and the effect on non-oil income of oil revenue investment has not been included in the measure of annual oil income from exports. As an 'oil-plus' economy, Iraq's high ratio requires no explanation. However, Bahrain's high ratio accurately conveys the large investment that has been made, not only in energy and energy-intensive industries but in offshore banking and services.

The second measure – oil exports as a percentage of total exports – is used to determine the extent to which non-oil investments have led to the production of tradeable goods and services. With the exception of Bahrain and the UAE (for which the information available is insufficient to draw firm conclusions), the dependence of the Persian Gulf on oil to generate foreign currency earnings ranges from 88 per cent to 99 per cent (1988 figures). Despite the oil price shocks and subsequent increase in income over the 1970s and early 1980s, investment has failed to produce tangible results in the form of exports. Bahrain, with only 78 per cent dependence on oil exports in 1988, has fared slightly better but still has a long way to go.

Having established that the non-oil GDP sector has not generated exports it is illuminating to look at the composition of this sector and so to gauge the reasons for this. As expected, the percentage share of agriculture in the non-oil GDP of Middle East economies conforms to the logic of the initial economic category of each state. The 'oil-plus' economies have the greatest percentage share, the large 'desert-oil' economies the second largest, and the small 'desert-oil' economies the smallest (around two to three per cent). However, another distinction not apparent in these percentages stems from the different attitudes to agricultural investment. In the 'desert-oil' economies investment is made in capital-intensive agricultural programmes, such as the wheat programme in Saudi Arabia, to encourage exports. By contrast, in the 'oil-plus' economies, agricultural practices remain largely traditional.

The share of industry in non-oil GDP needs careful interpretation as the relative weight of industry is not indicative either of its absolute level or, more importantly, of the energy-related composition of that share. In fact, despite the small share of industry in Iraq, Oman and Saudi Arabia it is precisely these 'oil-plus' and large 'desert-oil' economies that have the greater diversity of non hydrocarbon-based industries – food processing, textiles, consumer durables, immediate goods, transport equipment, mechanical and electrical machinery and appliances.

An obvious common feature between all types of Middle East oil economies is the small share of agriculture and industry relative to the share of the 'tertiary' sector, which includes all commerce, infrastructure and services in non-oil GDP. Why?

From this view of the structure of the Middle East's economies it seems that government investment of oil revenues has not created a real and sustainable resource base. Two factors, both extraneous to oil, have worked against them. The first is the sparse real resource base throughout the region, especially in the desert-oil economies. However, even in the oil-plus economies, where there are relatively greater opportunities for investment, the large indigenous populations have reduced the impact of oil revenues on a per capita basis. The second factor, which is often overlooked, is that until 1973 most Middle East countries were still relatively poor. In spite of the fact that Iran produced ten times more oil than Egypt in the 1960s, Egypt nonetheless led Iran in terms of many development criteria. From this perspective, and given the huge land expanses and disparate nature of the population in some countries, even creating the infrastructure necessary to economic development so quickly can be viewed as a success. Furthermore, the nature of the oil revenues makes it difficult to redistribute them to the population in a way conducive to economic development. The income derived from oil is unrelated to the cost of its production and therefore accrues directly to government. This delinks the productive effort and generation of income in the economy and has significant economic and political ramifications.

In the desert-oil economies, for example, the high per capita revenue generated by oil exports has had a marked effect on the potential for economic development. Governments know that distributing oil wealth among the population tends inevitably to reduce economic incentives; oil wealth is not always conducive to economic effort. In the 'oil-plus' economies, with oil revenues per capita generally much smaller, economic incentives remain more potent. Equally, however, with less to go round, there is a natural tendency for these governments to distribute principally to reinforce their own power bases. The resulting inequalities tend almost inevitably to encourage social and political tensions. The Iranian revolution of 1979 is one such example.

The redistribution of oil revenues for the purposes of economic development must also be balanced against the public demand for quality services and security. The diversion of funds to public services is especially marked in the desert-oil economies, where the indigenous population has come to expect a high standard of living. More often than not, medical and education services, for example, are free, while the necessary staples of life, such as electricity, food, water and petrol, are subsidised. A parallel development in desert-oil economies is the encouragement of inefficient bureaucracies as a result of the need to reward political loyalty.

The ownership of such rich natural resources brings with it the need for security. This need is particularly marked in the Persian Gulf, which has been the focus of so many political crises. Sadly, the huge expenditures on defence and security services made by most oil-exporting countries in the Middle East are at once unavoidable and useless.

Robert Mabro

18
ISLAM

MUCH HAS BEEN WRITTEN about the phenomena associated with Islamic 'resurgence', 'revival', 'renewal,', 'reassertion' or 'fundamentalism' over the last 25 years. Yet reviewing this vast literature highlights a striking irony. Whereas until quite recently Islamic political movements were dismissed as mere relics of the past, today they are consistently stressed as the most likely way forward in a number of Muslim societies. Indeed, many commentators now seem to believe that no political or social force can prevent the seemingly inevitable triumph of Islam across the Middle East. It is a mark of the widespread acceptance of this looming 'Islamic triumphalism' that political groups of all colours – socialist, pan-Arabist or liberal – have taken to borrowing from Islamic manifestos, whether to stem challenges to them from Islamic opposition groups or to mount challenges of their own against ruling regimes.

But however general the success of Islamic movements in the Middle East, they are far from being a united force. Indeed, what divides them is in many ways as important as what unites them. Ideologies and strategies vary greatly, just as much as the kind and the range of the support they enjoy and the nature of their relations with states across the region. The Muslim Brethren in Jordan, for example, are considerably closer to the regime than are their Egyptian counterparts to that in Egypt. Any generalisations based on either case, let alone the more dramatic and turbulent circumstances in Algeria, about the nature and role of Islamic movements within the Arab world at large are likely to be flawed and misleading.

In fact there is considerable tension between and among Islamic movements over the most effective ways for the Islamic cause to be advanced – how to move from 'what is' to 'what ought to be'. Islam means different things to different people and the texts and legacies derived from Islamic history are subject to multiple and even contradictory interpretation. After all, both the conservative, dynastic and pro-Western Saudi regime, just as much as the populist, clerical and anti-Western Khomeinist regime in Iran, base their claims to legitimacy on Islamic grounds and make competing assertions to represent 'Islam in power'. Advocates of Islamic reform and revolution elsewhere illustrate the same point. Quite often, struggles within the same ideological family are sharper than those across ideological divides, the result chiefly of rival Islamic groups competing for the support of the same or similar constituencies. In the circumstances, it is hard not to see the ringing assertion that 'Islam is the solution' as little more than an emotional rallying cry.

Enough time has passed since the first Islamic revolution – that in Iran in 1979 – to make possible a reassessment of the notion of Islamic 'revolutionary contagion', the Islamic domino theory. Despite consistent assumptions in the immediate aftermath of the Iranian Revolution that any one of a number of Arab states would be the next to fall victim to a similar Islamic takeover – Egypt, Syria and Iraq chief among them – in fact only Sudan has remodelled itself in the direction of political Islam and then through a military coup rather than an Iranian-style popular uprising. Furthermore, Sudan is hardly able to present itself to other Muslims as an inspiring example of political pluralism, economic growth or social stability. At the same time, for all that Iran and Sudan may be the exceptions rather than the rule, it remains undeniable that the rise of populist Islam since the late 1970s has been dramatic and substantial. Whether promoting individual piety, attacking social injustice or attempting to remodel states according to an idealised image of the founding period of Islam, Islamic movements are in the ascendant across the region.

It is how Islamic movements can most effectively assume political power which has sparked the fiercest controversies, particularly since the Iranian Revolution, the seizure of the Ka'ba by the neo-Ikhwan of Saudi Arabia, the assassination of President Sadat by the Jihad in Egypt and the Hama uprising by the Muslim Brethren in Syria, all of which took place in the three years between 1979 and 1982. It may be significant that a similar and more recent surge of interest in the same phenomenon has taken place since 1992, sparked by the escalation of Islamic activism in Algeria, Egypt, Yemen, Jordan and the Gulf States.

Explanations for this new assertiveness have, perhaps inevitably, varied. None the less, all seem agreed that resurgent Islamic sociopolitical movements cannot be understood without taking into account the impact of the deep-rooted and protracted crises faced by regimes across the Middle East, crises which have arisen partly as the legitimacy of state systems have declined – in other words as authoritarianism and repression have replaced what in most cases was a fragile democracy at best. In such chaotic and disordered social settings, where disillusion and despair have become all too common, political Islamic movements have found a receptive base and an enthusiastic response to their political appeal and assertiveness. To put it another way, many of their successes stem directly from the failings of existing regimes. Such successes, however, may have their limits. It may be wise for those now stressing the inevitable triumph of Islam to consider the fate of secular nationalism in the 1950s. During that time it was every bit as widely and enthusiastically touted as the way forward for the Arab world as Islam is today.

ISLAM AND THE WIDER WORLD

The rise of Islam cannot be explained solely by reference to the domestic circumstances of individual countries in the Middle East. With the region as a whole the focus of protracted and intensive international scrutiny, above all Western scrutiny, it is clear that external influences, too, have played their part in the growth of Islam. An obvious, if crude, example is that to many Islamists the US-led UN coalition mounted to expel Saddam Hussein from Kuwait in 1990 was seen as yet another Western-inspired crusade to 'crush Muslims'. In much the same vein, a great deal of Islamic opposition to regimes across the region is based on the belief that their rulers have been puppets of the West 'nourished at the tables of Zionism and imperialism'. It is perhaps no surprise that resurgent Islamic movements have had most appeal in those countries which have been exposed to the greatest Western influences. Iran, Morocco, Tunisia, Algeria, Egypt and Jordan are all cases in point, all of them exhibiting the same symptoms of 'socio-cultural contamination'.

The international dimension has a potent economic side, too. Morocco, Tunisia, Algeria, Egypt, Jordan and Sudan have in common not only active Islamic movements, but high levels of indebtedness to the West. During the 1970s and 1980s, all experienced mass protests following the implementation of stringent economic measures imposed by the International Monetary Fund. Islamic movements have been quick to exploit the resentment created by the IMF both by denouncing those rulers who have bowed to IMF pressures as Muslims in name only and by providing rival social services, such as health care and education, in place of those cut back to implement the IMF plans. Such practical steps have in some cases gone far toward reinforcing the political credentials of Islam among the poor, especially in cities.

The Arab-Israeli conflict has been probably the single most significant international factor in the rise of Islam. Repeated and overwhelming Arab military defeats at the hands of the Israelis – in 1948, 1967 and 1973 – were a prime cause for the downturn in popularity and credibility of Islam's main political rivals: the secular nationalist and pan-Arab regimes. In 1967, for example, for all the rhetoric and bombast of Nasser and others, they proved themselves no more able to defeat the Israelis than their predecessors in 1948. Adding insult to injury, the defeat in 1967 was widely felt to be even more complete than that in 1948. It is scarcely an exaggeration to say that many Arabs were engulfed by bewildering and profound psychological pain in the face of so comprehensive a defeat and turned to religion for solace and comfort. Gradually a new generation emerged that was both better educated and more embittered than its predecessors. It too was unable to come to terms with the fact that so immature and small a state as Israel had been able to shatter three Arab 'Muslim' armies and it mounted stronger challenges to the regimes it held responsible – not for a setback, as the states themselves preferred to call it – but for a humiliating defeat. The temptation to attribute defeat to deviation from the path of

Allah in favour of non-traditional, Western-derived goals such as nationalism, socialism and the pan-Arab state was not resisted.

The role of oil in the Middle East has been of scarcely less importance in the growth of political Islam. Its impact has taken three forms. In the first place, the oil-rich states have taken advantage of the economic leverage available to them to remake, or at least to attempt to remake, the Muslim world in their own image. Regimes such as that in Saudi Arabia have never been slow to provide financial support to favoured Islamic groups in other Middle East states. Similarly, they have provided often substantial sums to governments of poorer Arab states on condition that, in return, they tolerate the activities of other favoured Islamic groups. Though true as far as it goes, this argument in fact both ignores to a degree the internal dynamics of poorer Arab and Muslim societies and overstates the influence of the regional infusion of oil money.

Perhaps more significant has been the labour migration that oil money has created. With such large numbers of Arabs working in oil-rich countries other than their own, they have been able to remit home significant sums. While much has gone to their families, much has also been sent to Islamic movements, who have used it to propagate their messages, provide a range of subsidised services, support the families of imprisoned members, establish economic and financial infrastructures and build a network of mosques (from which they habitually denounce governments, as well as recruit new members). In consequence, an unofficial financial network has evolved across the Middle East through Islamic movements linked at a variety of levels, thereby increasing their influence further.

Finally, the very uneven distribution of oil revenues in the Middle East has greatly increased social inequality and hence the social dislocation in which Islamic movements have been able to thrive. The widening gap between the haves and have-nots – particularly perhaps the conspicuous consumption of some elements in certain countries, against a background of widespread poverty, and their often enthusiastic adoption of Western ways – allied to the strong inflationary pressures generated by oil revenues have proved especially disruptive.

THE STRUGGLE FOR ISLAM'S SOUL

Islamic political literature reveals numerous ideological battles about the nature of Islamic political action, justification for revolution and the limits of obedience to Islam. Sharp debates have raged between the proponents of overtly political Islamic revolution, on the one hand, and the state-sponsored *ulama*, on the other. Where the former have tended to dismiss the latter as little better than parrots of the state and propagators of 'sultanic stipulations' issued by 'court clerics', the *ulama* have portrayed the militants as belonging to heretical cults addicted to violence for its own sake and led by amirs suffering from Mahdist delusions who know little about correct Islamic teachings. In attempts to contain militant Islamic movements, in a number of countries state-sponsored fatwas have been issued in which militancy has been deemed un-Islamic.

A further ideological rift is that between the Muslim Brethren and other more militant groupings, among them the Islamic Group, the Islamic Jihad, the Society of Muslims, the Muhammad Youth, the Soldiers of God, the Islamic Liberation Party and Those Who Have Been Saved From Hell. It is a split which goes back to the 1970s and the adoption by the Muslim Brethren of a generally more pragmatic attempt to reach an accommodation with their governments, to work with rather than against them. Militant Islamic activists responded with contempt, deriding any compromise with 'the infidel holders of power' as misguided at best, un-Islamic at worst. Their argument centred around the belief that Muslims everywhere were enduring a period of *jahiliyya*, the term used to describe the 'ignorance' of the time before Islam. This condition was defined by the Islamic martyr Sayyid Qutb, executed by Nasser in 1964, as one inevitably repeated whenever a Muslim society 'veers from the Islamic way whether in the past, the present or the future'. Islam can never by compromised as the Muslim Brethren proposed. Rather, it is an indivisible package whose immediate and complete implementation is a simple matter of necessity, obligation and doctrine. By giving comfort to the 'infidel state' and lending credence to Western notions of national sovereignty at the expense of divine sovereignty – the government of humans in place of the government of God – the Muslim Brethren were accused of betrayal. No Islamic law, they argued, could emerge from any attempt to implement anything less than Islamic law pure and unadulterated. In short, the militants maintained, the Muslim Brethren had failed to grasp what Qutb had made abundantly clear: un-Islamic institutions would not and could not produce Islamic solutions.

According to figures such as the leaders of Islamic Jihad secular national leaders would never respond to appeals, sermons, party activities, legal arguments or peaceful marches. For them, no movement calling itself Islamic should suggest piecemeal reforms that prolong the lifespan of the regime it must dismantle. Instead the state of *jahiliyya* has to be confronted and eradicated via insurrection. This approach has to be led by a 'Qur'anic generation of a new type', the select few who know what nobody else knows – and who moreover command the strategy and tactics necessary to attain it through a disciplined hierarchical organisation.

In response, the leaders of the Muslim Brethren emphasised not only that they had chosen the path of moderation as the most prudent course of action, but in doing so they were following the example of the Prophet. A series of articles by Mustafa Mashhur maintained that the Prophet did not start his struggle by using force to destroy the idols of the *jahiliyya*. Rather, he only began eight years after the migration to Medina, when the Islamic movement had accumulated sufficient power to conquer Mecca. In addition, he asserted, while it is an Islamic duty to attain power, this should not automatically be equated with violence. The first level of power is doctrinal, as manifested in the strength of faith and conviction. The second level is organisational power, as evidenced by group cohesion and effectiveness. Finally, there is material power, as reflected in military strength and physical preparedness. For Islamic groups to start by military confrontation is to adopt a course of action doomed to failure because it disregards 'the example of the Prophet'.

The leaders of the Muslim Brethren were also keen to stress that their course of action was modelled after Qutb's analysis, contrary to what some 'misguided enthusiasts' had claimed. In that sense they presented Qutb as the true source of 'Islamic reformism'. To illustrate the argument, they referred to a statement attributed to Qutb himself in which he made the point that many of the young Islamists in prison with him were not of the same age or the same educational level as himself. Some were workers, others students, and their aptitude for and understanding of Islam of them all naturally varied. Similarly, some were in prison only briefly and thus met Qutb for perhaps no more than an hour or two. As a result, their accounts of what Qutb taught varied, while some of it was distorted and incomplete. In other words, the point of departure for the Islamic movement is not the establishment of an Islamic system *per se*, so much as the planting and spreading of Islam's doctrine and moral education. Again, according to the Muslim Brethren, the wisdom of pursuing moderation can be further appreciated by considering the ruthless government campaigns against militant Islamic movements which governments were all too easily able to brand terrorist.

ISLAM AND THE STATE

Broadly speaking, opposition Islamic movements belong to two types: radical (militant) and legalist (political). Although the declared objective of each is the establishment of an Islamic state and society, they differ greatly over strategy and tactics. First are those groups identified with 'militant Islam'. They combine a strong emphasis on the necessity of ideological purity for Islamic activists with a keen sense of urgency deriving from what they consider to be conditions under which 'true Muslims have become a minute minority'. Against such a background, they feel an obligation to act as dedicated fighters against state systems they see as the embodiment of contemporary *jahiliyya*, to assassinate their leaders and attack their institutions. The militants' strategy has three principal objectives. First, they aim to shake the state's main foundation, its *hayba* (the people's sense of awe towards it) by demonstrating its inability even to protect its heavily guarded political leaders or its strategically located military installations. Second, they aim to force states to strike back indiscriminately, so that the resulting popular reaction reinforces resentment towards them. Third, both courses should in time generate a stream of martyrs who can be used to sustain Islamic fervour and to act as symbols of a struggle which must endure until the regime collapses.

Second, there are those groups associated with political Islam. They renounce both individual and collective violence as counter-productive, emphasising the logic of a gradualist Islamic programme, and reject the assumptions of urgency held by the militants. They focus on propagating *al-da'wa* (the call) and on 'purifying' individuals and societies alike against secularism, though this has not prevented their establishing secular institutions of their own – banks, investment companies, clinics, publishing houses, schools, day-care centres and the like. In providing such social services and building popular support, they particularly target the urban poor. They participate in the political process within the official parameters of permissible action while working to extract concessions from the state to allow them greater access to the masses and, through them, to power.

So far, the principal successes of the militant groups have been in attracting attention to themselves rather than in achieving anything that resembles their stated objectives. In fact, their significance has often been exaggerated. At times this has been done by state authorities themselves to justify the imposition or the extension of various restrictions on opposition political activities in general. That said, there have been exceptions to the rule, most notably the Iranian Revolution, though even there its success in seizing power was due less to a campaign of insurrection than to a massive popular upheaval. Afghanistan, where a coalition of Islamic movements was able to seize power after a protracted guerrilla war, is another case in point. On the other hand, their hold on power proved fairly short-lived. Having been propped up principally by the Soviet Union, the new Islamic regime in Kabul was unable to sustain itself once the Soviet Union cut its losses in Afghanistan and left the country. A further bitter civil war followed.

Elsewhere – Egypt, Syria, Jordan, Tunisia, Morocco and Algeria – the gap between the goals and the achievements of militant Islamic groups, never very narrow to begin with, has become progressively wider. The reasons are not hard to find. First, Islamic militants have become notoriously jealous and suspicious of rival militant groups, with the inevitable result that they are plagued by in-fighting. No group has ever been powerful enough to see off the others; nor has compromise with rival groups ever been likely. At the same time, Islamic militants of all hues have had to contend with the challenge posed by more moderate groupings. In rejecting the kind of informal state structures championed by the moderates, the militants have found it all the harder to assemble the necessary financial and organisational support to mount a serious bid for power. Third, their bitter denunciations of legitimate governments have guaranteed continued persecution. It is not merely the militants themselves who have suffered this kind of repression. Their families, indeed whole neighbourhoods, have been singled out for punishment. This not only undermines the militants' putative power bases still further, it also generates hostility towards them on the part of the very people they claim to champion. That governments are then able to paint the militants in the blackest of black colours, at home and abroad, serves only to set back their cause further. This is not to say that governments have been able to suppress the militants entirely, even if they have reduced their activities greatly. 'Physical liquidation' – in other words, assassinations – by the militants continue, as do other acts of violence. However the regimes targeted by the militants not only survive but have become more ruthless and systematic in their pursuit of the militants.

The Islamic moderates, by contrast, have enjoyed much greater success. They have gained significant levels of support in countries across the region and at all levels of society, from university professors to labour unions. Generally speaking, the more liberal the ruling regime, the greater the success of the moderates. This is not to suggest, however, that even the most liberal regimes enourage moderate Islamic movements because they believe in encouraging a range of political opinion for its own sake. Rather, their motives are entirely pragmatic and stem from the realisation that Islam is far too potent a force to be ignored and that it is vastly preferable to seek an accommodation with moderate Islamic groups in an attempt to gain wider popular support than to suppress them. At the same time, these regimes have made abundantly clear that there are strict limits to what they will tolerate. Were the moderates to go too far, 'vigorous repressive action' would be unleashed in an unambiguous demonstration that 'democracy' has 'sharp teeth'. Whatever the apparent success of the moderates, in other words the restrictions within which they are obliged to operate, the chances of even the most politically sophisticated Islamic group assuming power through the ballot box is scarcely greater than the likelihood of their militant counterparts seizing it through armed insurrection. However, it is important to stress that no single ruling regime in the Middle East other than those in Iran and Sudan has any intention of surrendering power to Islamic groups of any shade.

Ibrahim A. Karawan

BIBLIOGRAPHY

INTRODUCTION
A History of the Modern Middle East, William R. Cleveland (Westview Press, Boulder and Oxford, 1994)
A History of the Arab Peoples, Albert Hourani (Faber, London, 1991)
The Israel-Arab Reader, ed. Walter Laqueur (Penguin, Harmondsworth, 1995)
Islam and Revolution in the Middle East, Henry Munson (Yale University Press, New Haven, 1987)
State, Power and Politics in the Making of the Modern Middle East, Roger Owen (Routledge, London, 1992)
Islam in the World, Malise Ruthven (Penguin, Harmondsworth, 1984)
Democracy without Democrats? The Renewal of Politics in the Muslim World, ed. Ghassan Salamé (I. B. Tauris, London, 1994)
Palestine and the Arab-Israeli Conflict, Charles D. Smith (Macmillan, London, 1992, 2nd ed.)

Chapter 1: EGYPT
Sadat and After: Struggles for Egypt's Political Soul, Raymond W. Baker (I. B. Tauris, London, 1990)
The Return of Consciousness, Tawfiq Hakim (Macmillan, Basingstoke, 1985)
The Prophet and Pharoah, Gilles Kepel (Al-Saqi Books, London, 1985)
Milestones, Sayyid Qutb (American Trust Publications, Indianapolis, 1990)
In Search of Identity, Anwar Sadat (Collins, London, 1978)
Radical Islam, Emmanuel Sivan (Yale University Press, New Haven, 1990)
Mubarak's Egypt: Fragmentation of the Political Order, Robert Springborg (Westview Press, Boulder, 1989)
The History of Modern Egypt, Panayotis J. Vatikiotis (Weidenfeld and Nicolson, London, 1991, 4th ed.)
The Egypt of Nasser and Sadat, John Waterbury (Princeton University Press, Princeton, 1983)

Chapter 2: THE GULF STATES
Oil and Politics in the Gulf: Rulers and Merchants in Kuwait and Qatar, Jill Crystal (Cambridge University Press, Cambridge, 1995, 2nd ed.)
Oman in the Twentieth Century: Political Foundations of an Emerging State, J.E. Peterson (Croom Helm, London, 1978)
Oman: Politics and Development, Ian Skeet (Macmillan, Basingstoke, 1992)
Arabia's Frontiers: The Story of Britain's Boundary Drawing in the Desert, J.C. Wilkinson (I. B. Tauris, London, 1991)
The Origins of the United Arab Emirates: A Political and Social History of the Trucial States, Rosemarie S. Zahlan (Croom Helm, London, 1978)

Chapter 3: IRAN
Iran Between Two Revolutions, Ervand Abrahamian (Princeton University Press, Princeton, 1982)
Revolution and Economic Transition: The Iranian Experience, Hooshang Amirahmadi (SUNY Press, Albany, 1990)
The Turban for the Crown: The Islamic Revolution in Iran, Said A. Arjomand (Oxford University Press, Oxford, 1988)
The Political Economy of Modern Iran, Homa Katouzian (New York University Press, New York, 1981)

Iran After the Revolution, eds. Saeed Rahnema and Sohrab Behdad (I. B. Tauris, London, 1995)

Chapter 4: IRAQ
Culture, History and Ideology in the Formation of Ba'thist Iraq 1968-1989, Amatzia Baram (Macmillan, Basingstoke, 1991)
The Old Social Classes and the Revolutionary Movements of Iraq: A Study of Iraq's Old Landed Classes and its Communists, Ba'thists and Free Officers, Hanna Batatu, (Princeton University Press, Princeton, 1978)
Iraq Since 1958: From Revolution to Dictatorship, Marion Farouk-Sluglett and Peter Sluglett (I. B. Tauris, London, 1990)
The Republic of Fear: Saddam's Iraq, Samir al-Khalil (Hutchinson, London, 1990)
The Shi'is of Iraq, Yitzhak Nakash (Princeton University Press, Princeton, 1994)
Britain in Iraq 1914-1932, Peter Sluglett (Ithaca Press, London, 1976)

Chapter 5: ISRAEL
The Israeli Economy: Dreams and Realities, Yair Aharoni (Routledge, London, 1991)
Israelis; Founders and Sons, Amos Elon (Penguin, Harmondsworth, 1982)
The Israel Arab Reader, Walter Laqueur (Penguin, Harmondsworth, 1995)
No Trumpets, No Drums: A Two-State Settlement of the Israeli-Palestinian Conflict, Sari Nusseibeh and Mark Heller (I. B. Tauris, London, 1992)
In the land of Israel, Amos Oz (Chatto & Windus, London, 1983)
The origins of Zionism, David Vital (Oxford University Press, Oxford, 1980)

Chapter 6: JORDAN
Jordan: Crossroads of Middle Eastern Events, Peter Gubser (Westview, London, 1983)
Water and Power: The Politics of Scarce Resources in the Jordan River Basin (Cambridge University Press, Cambridge, 1993)
The Modern History of Jordan, Kamal Salibi (I. B. Tauris, London, 1993)
Collusion Across the Jordan: King Abdullah, the Zionists and the Partition of Palestine, Avi Shlaim (Oxford University Press, London and New York, 1988)
King Abdullah, Britain and the Making of Jordan, Mary C. Wilson (Cambridge University Press, Cambridge, 1987)

Chapter 7: THE KURDS
Aga, Shaikh and State; The Social and Political Structures of Kurdistan, Martin van Bruinessen (I. B. Tauris, London, 1992)
People Without a Country: The Kurds and Kurdistan, ed. Gérard Chaliand, trans. Michael Pallis (Zed Press, London, 1993)
The Kurds in Turkey: A Political Dilemma, Michael Gunter (Westview, Boulder, 1990)
Le Mouvement National Kurde, Chris Kutschéra (Flammarion, Paris, 1979)
The Kurds: A Nation Denied, David McDowell (I. B. Tauris, London, 1992)

Chapter 8: LEBANON
The Long Peace: Ottoman Lebanon 1861-1920, Engin Akarli (I. B. Tauris, London, 1993)
The Making of Modern Lebanon, Helena Cobban (Hutchinson, London, 1984)
Syria and Lebanon: A Political Essay, Albert Hourani (Oxford University Press, London, 1946)
Amal and the Shi'a: The Struggle for the Soul of Lebanon, Augustus Richard Norton (University of Texas Press, Austin, 1987)
A House of Many Mansions: The History of Lebanon Reconsidered, Kamal Salibi (I. B. Tauris, London, 1988)

Chapter 9: LIBYA

Libya, J. Wright (Benn, London, 1969)
Libya: A Modern History, J. Wright (Croom Helm, London, 1982)
Libya, Chad and the Central Sahara, J. Wright (Hurst, London, 1989)
The Green and the Black: Qadhafi's Politics in Africa, ed. R. Lemarchand
  (Indiana University Press, Indianapolis, 1988)
Qadhafi's World Design: Libyan Foreign Policy 1969-1987, R. B. St. John
  (Saqi Books, London)

Chapter 10: THE MAGHRIB

A History of the Maghrib in the Islamic Period, J. M. Abun-Nasr (Cambridge
  University Press, Cambridge, 1987)
The Islamic Movement in North Africa, F. Burgat and W. Dowell (University of
  Texas Press, Austin, 1993)
North Africa: Nation, State and Region, ed. E. G. H. Joffé (Routledge, London
  and New York, 1993)
*The Ambiguous Compromise, Language, Literature and National Identity in Algeria
  and Morocco*, J. Kaye and A. Zoubir (Routledge, London and New York, 1990)
L'état du Maghreb, eds. C. Lacoste and Y. Lacoste (Editions Le Fennec,
  Casablanca, 1991)

Chapter 11: THE PALESTINIANS

Palestinians: The Making of a People, Baruch Kimmerling and Joel S. Migdal
  (The Free Press, New York, 1993)
A History of the Israeli-Palestinian Conflict, Mark Tessler (Indiana University
  Press, Bloomington, 1994)
Palestine in Transformation, 1856-1882, 'Studies in Social, Economic and
  Political Development', Alexander Schölch (Institute for Palestine Studies,
  Washington D.C., 1993)
1948 and After: Israel and the Palestinians, Benny Morris (Oxford University
  Press, New York, 1990)
Occupier's Law: Israel and the West Bank, Raja Shehadeh (Institution for
  Palestine Studies, Washington D.C., 1988, 2nd ed.)

Chapter 12: SAUDI ARABIA

Arabian Oasis City: The Transformation of Unayzah, Altorki and Donald Cole
  (University of Texas Press, Austin, 1989)
Religion and State in the Kingdom of Saudi Arabia, Ayman Al Yassini (Westview
  Press, Boulder, 1985)
Oil Monarchies: Domestic and Security Challenges in the Arab Gulf States,
  F. Gregory Gause III (Council on Foreign Relations Press, New York, 1994)
The Merchants: The Big Business Families of Saudi Arabia and the Gulf States,
  Michael Field, (Overlook Press, New York, 1985)
Saudi Arabia: The Ceaseless Quest for Security, Nadav Safran (Harvard
  University Press, 1985)
Saudi Arabia in the Nineteenth Century, R. Bayley Winder, (St. Martin's Press,
  New York, 1965)

Chapter 13: SUDAN

A History of the Sudan, P. M. Holt and M. W. Daly (Longman, London, 1988, 4th ed.)
Sudan After Nimeiri, ed. Peter Woodward (Routledge, London, 1991)
Turabi's Revolution: Islam and Power in Sudan, Abdelwahab El-Affendi
  (Grey Seal, London, 1991)
Economy and Class in Sudan, eds. Norman O'Neill and Jay O'Brien
  (Avebury, Aldershot, 1988)
Sudan, ed. M. W. Daly (Clio Press, World Bibliographical Series No. 40, Oxford,
  1992, 2nd ed.)

Chapter 14: SYRIA

Syria and the French Mandate: The Politics of Arab Nationalism 1920-1945, Philip S. Khoury (I. B. Tauris, London and Princeton, 1987)

Ba'th v. Ba'th: The Conflict Between Syria and Iraq, 1968-1989, Eberhard Kienle (I. B. Tauris, London, 1990)

Fragments of Memory: A Story of a Syrian Family, Hanna Mina, trans. O. Kenny (University of Texas Press, Austin, 1993)

The Struggle for Syria: A Study of Post-War Arab Politics 1945-1958, Patrick Seale (I. B. Tauris, London, 1987, 2nd ed.)

Asad of Syria: The Struggle for the Middle East, Patrick Seale (I. B. Tauris, London, 1988)

The Struggle for Power in Syria: Sectarianism, Regionalism and Tribalism in Politics 1961-1980, Nikolaos Van Dam, N. (Croom Helm, London, 1981)

Chapter 15: TURKEY

Turkey: A Short History, R.H. Davison (Eothen Press, 1988)

The Emergence of Modern Turkey, Bernard Lewis (Oxford University Press, Oxford, 1961)

History of the Ottoman Empire and Modern Turkey (2 vols.), Stanford J. Shaw and Ezel Kural Shaw (Cambridge University Press, Cambridge, 1977)

Turkey: A Modern History, Eric J. Zürcher (I.B. Tauris, London, 1993)

CONTEMPORARY POLITICS AND SOCIETY

The Crisis of Turkish Democracy, C.H. Dodd, (Eothen Press, 1990, 2nd ed.)

Turkish Politics and the Military, William Hale (Routledge, London, 1994)

Political Parties and Democracy in Turkey, eds. Metin Heper and Jacob Landau (I.B. Tauris, London, 1991)

Islam in Modern Turkey, ed. Richard Tapper (I.B. Tauris, London, 1991)

INTERNATIONAL RELATIONS

Turkey's New Geopolitics from the Balkans to Western China, Graham E. Fuller and Ian O. Lesser, (Westview for Rand Corporation, Boulder, 1993)

Turkey: The Challenge of a New Role, Andrew Mango, (Praeger, New York, 1994)

Turkey and the Middle East, Philip Robins, (Pinter, for Royal Institute of International Affairs, 1991)

Turkey in Post-Soviet Central Asia, Gareth Winrow, (Royal Institute of International Affairs, 1995)

Chapter 16: YEMEN

Tribes, Government and History in Yemen, Paul Dresch (Oxford University Press, Oxford, 1989)

Arabia without Sultans, Fred Halliday (Penguin, Harmondsworth, 1975)

Revolution and Foreign Policy: The Case of South Yemen, Fred Halliday, 1967-1987 (Cambridge University Press, Cambridge, 1990)

Yemen: The Search for a Modern State, John E. Peterson (Croom Helm, London, 1981)

Contemporary Yemen: Politics and Historical Background, ed. B.R. Pridham (Croom Helm, London, 1984)

Economy, Society and Culture in Contemporary Yemen, ed. B.R. Pridham (Croom Helm, London, 1985)

Chapter 17: OIL IN THE MIDDLE EAST

Oil Companies and Governments, J.E. Hartshorne (Faber and Faber, London, 1962)

Political Dimensions of the Gulf Crisis, R. Mabro (Oxford Institute for Energy Studies (OIES), 1990)

OPEC and the Price of Oil, R. Mabro (OIES, Oxford, 1990)

Middle East Economic Survey, Middle East Petroleum and Economic

Publications, Cyprus (published weekly since 1957)
OPEC: Instrument of Change, I. Seymour (Macmillan, London, 1980)

Chapter 18: ISLAM
Monarchs, Mullahs and Marshals: Islamic Regimes?, Ibrahim Karawan
   (*The Annals*, AAPSS, 1992)
Arab Resources, ed. Ibrahim Ibrahim (Croom Helm, London, 1983)
The Passing of Traditional Societies, Daniel Lemer (The Free Press, New York,
   1958)
Islamic Fundamentalisms and the Gulf Crisis, ed. James Piscatori
   (The American Academy of Arts and Scientists, 1991)
The Arab Predicament, Fouad Ajami (Cambridge University Press, Cambridge,
   1981)
Voices of Resurgent Islam, ed. John Esposito (Oxford University Press, New York,
   1983)
Muslim Extremism in Egypt: The Prophet and the Pharoah, Gilles Kepel
   (University of California Press, Berkeley, 1985)
Radical Islam, Enunanuel Sivan (Yale University Press, 1985)
'The Relative Decline of the Center: Egypt as a Case Study', *Journal of Arab
   Affairs*, vol. 8 (1989): 29-32

INDEX